AI-Enhanced Skills Transformation for Economic Growth

Hussain K. Hussain Alagele
https://orcid.org/0009-0006-4383-1690
Al-Nahrain University, Iraq

Nagham H. Neama
https://orcid.org/0000-0003-3953-1581
Al-Nahrain University, Iraq

IGI Global
Scientific Publishing
Publishing Tomorrow's Research Today

Vice President of Editorial Melissa Wagner
Director of Acquisitions Mikaela Felty
Director of Book Development Jocelynn Hessler
Production Manager Mike Brehm
Cover Design Jose Rosado

Published in the United States of America by
IGI Global Scientific Publishing
701 East Chocolate Avenue
Hershey, PA, 17033, USA
Tel: 717-533-8845 | Fax: 717-533-7115
Website: https://www.igi-global.com E-mail: cust@igi-global.com

Library of Congress Cataloging-in-Publication Data

LCCN: 2026019869 (CIP Data Pending)
ISBN13: 979-8-2600-0116-5
Isbn13Softcover: 979-8-2600-0117-2
EISBN13: 979-8-2600-0118-9
British Cataloguing in Publication Data
A Cataloguing in Publication record for this book is available from the British Library.

Editorial Advisory Board

Priyadharshini V V, Synergy Management Studies Group, India
Kishor Raj V, Digital Capital Initiative, India
Yashwanth Gowda, Modern HR & Technology Council, India
Mohanraj M, Global Business Innovation Network, India
Piali Haldar, Digital India Research Forum, India
Prachita Patil, DAIMSR Research Cell, India
Jyoti Rana, Bibliometric Academia Group, India
Gurpreet Pal Kaur, Digital Government Leadership Forum, India
Suhashini Chaurasia, Machine Learning Applications Group, India
Revathy G, Tech-Innovation Hub, India
Aws Mahdi, University of Technology, Iraq
Anish K, Computer Science and Systems Forum, India
Vedika Kulkarni, Vishwakarma Institute of Technology (VIT), India
Anton Thomson F, Polytechnic Research Circle, India
Grace Christianti, International Automation Systems Alliance, Indonesia
Anushka Wankhede, Tech-Innovation Institute, India
Francis Arthur, Ethical-Accountable Analytics Leadership Cell, India
Bitto Benny, Human-AI Team Collaboration Forum, India
Hasina Ahmed, University of Sharqiyah in Oman, Oman

Table of Contents

Detailed Table of Contents

This study investigates the impacts of economic factors, environmental, social, and governance (ESG) aspects, and artificial intelligence (AI) elements on the energy transition in three OECD countries through skills enhancement. The CS-ARDL model analyzes long-term relationships and short-term dynamics in panel data, considering cross-sectional dependencies from 2022 to 2026. The results show that economic factors negatively impact the energy transition, but skills enhancement leads to a more positive outcome, while environmental factors have a positive impact. However, although economic factors and AI show negative correlations with the energy transition, governance factors show positive correlations with economic growth through skills enhancement.strategies that promote immediate economic expansion may harm long-term environmental and social impacts, negatively affecting the energy transition. Therefore, adopting a holistic strategy that integrates economic, environmental, social, and AI elements is essential for achieving economic growth.

This chapter discusses the progression from human capital to hybrid intelligence in the context of Digital India based on a combined TOE–RBV–Endogenous Growth framework. We analyse how AI adoption can enhance workforce capabilities and foster hybrid intelligence, thereby leading to economic growth. Survey and data analysis using SEM show the mediating role of hybrid intelligence in the relationship between AI adoption and productivity. This association is further shaped by institutional support. The study calls for strategic reskilling and a proper policy response to anchor the AI-driven economic transformation.

Generative artificial intelligence (GenAI) is rapidly reshaping higher education by influencing teaching, learning, research, assessment, and administrative decision-making. This chapter outlines an integrative framework that synthesises policy concepts on generative artificial intelligence for higher education. The chapter explores how institutions may design adaptive, ethical, and future-proof policies, drawing on interdisciplinary literature from education policy, artificial intelligence, governance, ethics, and organizational theory. A conceptual framework with multiple layers has been proposed as a strategy for governance, learning and teaching, research integrity and compliance, data governance, and professional development. A comparative scenario analysis shows how framework-driven policies foster institutional coherence, risk management, economic growth and capacity for innovation. The chapter concludes by outlining a future research agenda for sustainable, human-centered, evidence-informed GenAI policy development in higher education.

This chapter presents a notion of the intelligence-enhanced workforce as the source of economic prosperity in the era of artificial intelligence. It creates a new model of AI-enhanced skills transformation, which combines the capabilities of a human mind, and algorithmic systems to enhance productivity and innovation. The chapter looks into the concept of reskilling, the collaboration between humans and AI, and adaptive learning ecosystems to reinvent the world of work and company performance.

Foreword

This book is published amidst the rapid global economic transformations of the 21st century, where artificial intelligence has emerged as a transformative force with a profound impact on re-engineering business models, enhancing governance practices, developing education systems, and propelling national innovation ecosystems toward higher levels of efficiency, sustainability, and competitiveness.

The ten chapters of this book address a comprehensive set of contemporary issues at the intersection of artificial intelligence and economic growth. It begins by exploring the integration of environmental, social, and governance (ESG) principles enhanced by artificial intelligence as a catalyst for transforming corporate performance toward a sustainable economy. The book then expands to a multidimensional theoretical framework linking opportunity theory, resource theory, and endogenous growth, showcasing the Digital India model as a rich case study. Subsequent chapters delve into the dynamics of human-AI interaction within entrepreneurial ecosystems, experiential learning methodologies through AI-powered startup labs, emerging issues related to cybersecurity entrepreneurship, and intelligent recommendation systems for personalized learning.

The book goes beyond the purely practical and technical aspects, offering a comprehensive synthesis of artificial intelligence applications in entrepreneurship training and its contextual applications in formulating national innovation strategies. It concludes with a qualitative research analysis of trust and ethics issues in AI-based training and a critical evaluation of the effectiveness of intelligent agent teaching systems in academic settings.

With this methodological and thematic diversity, this book provides a cohesive scientific reference that combines theoretical depth with practical application. It is aimed at researchers, policymakers, and practitioners interested in understanding how AI can be a genuine driver of sustainable economic growth, not merely a fleeting technological tool. The authors hope this work will open new horizons for research and practice in this rapidly evolving field.

Faozi A. Almaqtari

College of Business Administration, A'Sharqiyah University (ASU), Oman

Preface

INTRODUCTION

As a researcher interested in artificial intelligence and its impact on business and economic systems, I am pleased to present this valuable scholarly work, which addresses one of the most pressing and vital issues in contemporary economic and managerial thought: How can artificial intelligence be a genuine driving force for economic growth, rather than merely a fleeting technological tool?

The relationship between technology and economic growth has always been a central focus of economic thought, ever since classical economists recognized the impact of technological innovation on increasing productivity and expanding markets. However, what the world is witnessing today with artificial intelligence transcends the idea of it being a mere "helper" to what can be termed a "foundational technology"—one that not only improves existing processes but also redefines the very nature of work, value, and knowledge itself. Hence, the importance of this book, which does not treat artificial intelligence as an isolated technological phenomenon, but rather as a comprehensive transformative force that intersects with governance, education, entrepreneurship, security, and national innovation policies.

What distinguishes this book, in my view, is its boldness in moving from general theorizing to precise applied detail. It does so through chapters that address diverse issues with depth and methodological rigor, ranging from AI-enhanced corporate governance and its impact on sustainability and innovation, to the dynamics of human-AI interaction in entrepreneurial ecosystems, and finally to emerging issues such as cybersecurity and intelligent recommendation systems for personalized learning. This diversity, I believe, is not a diffusion of subject matter, but rather a true reflection of the nature of AI itself as a "borderless" technology that permeates every aspect of the modern economy. Its full economic impact cannot be understood without examining it from multiple and integrated perspectives, as this book does.

CHAPTERS OVERVIEW

Perhaps what deserves special mention is the research effort invested in the chapters that combine sound theoretical frameworks, such as resource theory, opportunity theory, and endogenous growth theory, with real-world practical applications. This is clearly demonstrated in the second chapter, which presents the Digital India model as a rich case study linking human capital and hybrid intelligence. This blend of theoretical depth and practical application is what distinguishes serious scientific research from fleeting, impressionistic writing. I clearly observed this in the logical progression of the book's chapters, which move from major institutional issues to precise operational applications in training, education, and entrepreneurship.

Furthermore, the book's exploration of experiential learning methodologies through artificial intelligence startup labs and the application of AI in entrepreneurship training reflects a profound understanding that AI-driven economic growth cannot be achieved in isolation from building human capacity and developing authentic learning and experimentation environments. Technology alone, however immense its potential, cannot create the desired economic transformation unless it is accompanied by an educational and training system capable of harnessing and guiding it effectively. This is precisely what the chapters of this book address with remarkable depth.

I must also highlight the chapters that address the application of contextual AI in national innovation strategies. This is a crucial dimension for policymakers and public policy researchers, as it reminds us that AI applications cannot be simply transferred from one environment to another. They require a careful understanding of the local economic, institutional, and cultural contexts of each country and economy. Furthermore, the book's exploration of ethical and humanitarian issues, such as trust and ethics in AI-based training and the evaluation of the effectiveness of intelligent agent teaching systems in academic settings, reflects a critical awareness that digital transformation is not a neutral technological process. Rather, it raises fundamental questions about justice, transparency, and the role of humanity in a system increasingly dominated by algorithms. This balance between technical enthusiasm and ethical caution is, in my opinion, a sign of genuine intellectual maturity that deserves recognition. It distinguishes this book from many other works that address AI with purely technical enthusiasm, devoid of critical and humanistic considerations.

CONCLUSION

The true value of this book lies not only in the diversity of its topics but also in its ability to offer a comprehensive vision that combines the macro level (national policies and governance) with the micro level (training practices and individual applications)—a vision rarely found in works that address a subject of such breadth. I believe this book will be an important reference for anyone seeking to understand the complex relationship between artificial intelligence and economic growth, moving beyond the oversimplifications and exaggerations that often characterize discussions of this technology in public discourse.

I extend my sincere appreciation to the editors and researchers who contributed to this book for their tireless scholarly efforts, their courage in posing questions that have yet to be fully answered, and their ability to provide original knowledge in a field that is evolving at a pace that far exceeds the ability of much academic literature to keep up with. I hope that the reader, whether an academic researcher, decision-maker, or business practitioner, will find in this book rich material that will stimulate them to think deeply about the future of the economy, which is being reshaped, chapter by chapter, by artificial intelligence, and that this work will be a starting point for further research and reflection in this vital and ever-evolving field.

Faozi A. Almaqtari
College of Business Administration, A'Sharqiyah University (ASU), Oman

Acknowledgment

I extend my sincere thanks and appreciation to the development team at IGI Global for their assistance and prompt response. I also thank all the chapter reviewers who dedicated significant effort to the chapter review process and provided valuable feedback, which contributed to a high-quality academic presentation of the book. Their contributions were instrumental in strengthening the book and producing high-quality academic output.

Chapter 1

AI-Enhanced ESG Integration Transforming Corporate Performance for a Sustainable Economy:

Driving Innovation in Modern Economies

Hussain K. Alagele
http://orcid.org/0009-0006-4383-1690
Al-Nahrain University, Iraq

Nagham H. Neama
http://orcid.org/0000-0003-3953-1581
Al-Nahrain University, Iraq

ABSTRACT

This study investigates the impacts of economic factors, environmental, social, and governance (ESG) aspects, and artificial intelligence (AI) elements on the energy transition in three OECD countries through skills enhancement. The CS-ARDL model analyzes long-term relationships and short-term dynamics in panel data, considering cross-sectional dependencies from 2022 to 2026. The results show that economic factors negatively impact the energy transition, but skills enhancement leads to a more positive outcome, while environmental factors have a positive impact. However, although economic factors and AI show negative correlations with the energy transition, governance factors show positive correlations with economic growth

DOI: 10.4018/979-8-2600-0116-5.ch001

through skills enhancement.strategies that promote immediate economic expansion may harm long-term environmental and social impacts, negatively affecting the energy transition. Therefore, adopting a holistic strategy that integrates economic, environmental, social, and AI elements is essential for achieving economic growth.

1. INTRODUCTION

Sources significantly influences worldwide energy sectors and industries. Numerous elements affect this shift, including supply limitations and cost benefits to policy determinations and ecological regulations. This procedure holds crucial significance for sustainable development, alongside developed countries leading decarburization efforts while facing challenges related to unity, competitiveness, and innovation. Conversely, developing nations focus on achieving modern energy access and electrification to meet UN Sustainable Development Goal 7, facing obstacles such due to insufficient technology accessibility and funding systems(Zheng & Lee, 2025) . The The transition occurs as a complicated and lengthy process fueled by technical, economic, and social changes, making a rapid change unfeasible. Efficient strategies for managing this transition require diversification, cooperation, funding for research and development, along with the promotion of creative business models(Kamal et al., 2026). Energy transition (ET) describes the movement away from dependence on fossil fuels toward the use of renewable energy. Toward a more sustainable future. Incorporating ESG elements highlights environmental responsibility and social justice, whereas AI enhances ET through optimization. systems and enhancing effectiveness(Chernyak-Hai et al., 2024; Q. Wang et al., 2026; Zheng & Lee, 2025).

The originality and importance of this research stem from tackling a vital void in current research. Although traditional firm-centered ESG frameworks hold significance, They frequently neglect to take into account macroeconomic elements like inflation and unemployment, which are crucial for assessing sustainability(Adwey, 2026a; Kuram & Bilişik, 2025a). Present research primarilyignore the relationship between macroeconomic factors and ESG outcomes, establishing a disconnect in comprehending the wider factors influencing sustainability and transition of energy(Ningtyas et al., 2026).

In recent times, the worldwide business environment has progressively emphasized sustainability, acknowledging the significance of Environmental, Social, and Governance (ESG) standards in fostering sustainable economic, social, and ecological well-being . ESG criteria provide a structure for businesses to evaluate and handle their environmental effects, social fairness, and corporate management, thus promoting sustainable enterprises(Avolio & Walumbwa, 2014; Darwish et al.,

2026; Sida et al., 2025). practices . Incorporating Artificial Intelligence (AI) into ESG frameworks has become a transformative factor, delivering creative strategies to improve the impact and productivity of sustainability efforts(Hu & Othman, 2026a). Artificial Intelligence, through its abilities in data processing, pattern detection, and predictive analysis, has serve as a vital instrument for promoting ESG goals (Nara et al., 2026). AI advancements, including machine learning (ML), Natural language processing (NLP) and computer vision are employed to examine large volumes of data and recognize. sustainability challenges and possibilities, and maximize resource utilization(Ally, 2025). These abilities allow companies to create decisions that are aligned with ESG objectives, thus enhancing their sustainability outcomes. The environmental dimension of ESG greatly gains from AI implementations(Al-Mahamid, 2025; Jaiswal et al., 2026). Analytics driven by AI can track ecological footprints, anticipate climate-associated threats, and enhance energy usage. It seems like your message is incomplete. For instance, machine learning algorithms can assess satellite images to observe deforestation and monitor carbon emissions. emissions, and evaluate the loss of biodiversity(Yim & Su, 2024; Zheng & Lee, 2025). Predictive models can anticipate the effects of climate change on enterprises. operations, allowing businesses to adopt proactive strategies to minimize risks. Moreover, AI-powered Optimization methods can improve energy usage and minimize waste, aiding in greater sustainability(Kassar & Jizi, 2026). resource allocation. AI-powered methods also enhance the social dimensions of ESG. Artificial intelligence has the capability to examine social media and various data sources to evaluate public opinion, track human rights violations, and measure(Chernyak-Hai et al., 2024; Negm, 2026). working conditions. This immediate observation assists organizations in tackling social concerns swiftly and efficiently. Governance, the third aspect of ESG, is similarly shaped by AI advancements(Chernyak-Hai et al., 2024; Kamal et al., 2026). AI has the potential to improve businesses management by enhancing openness, responsibility, and adherence. For instance, systems driven by AI can streamline the identification of fraudulent actions, track regulatory updates, and guarantee adherence to legal requirements criteria(Dwivedi et al., 2026; Kuram & Bilişik, 2025b). Techniques in natural language processing are capable of examining corporate disclosures and financial statements to recognize governance challenges and possibilities. These features assist organizations in upholding strong governance. structures, thus enhancing investor confidence and enduring sustainability(Ahmed, 2025; Kassar & Jizi, 2026). Concerns like data confidentiality, algorithmic fairness bias and the ethical application of AI need to be tackled to guarantee that AI-driven ESG efforts are both efficient and fair. In spite of these difficulties, the ability of AI to reshape ESG standards and foster sustainable business practices(Matindike et al., 2026; Q. Wang et al., 2025) .The range of practices is vast. This document seeks to deliver an exhaustive overview of approaches to AI-driven methods for enhancing ESG standards in sustainable business operations. Through the analysis of the most recent trends, technologies, and This review aids in comprehending how AI can be utilized to improve sustainability in applications. Endeavors(Adwey, 2026b; Alam & Priti, 2024). Additionally, AI algorithms are capable of detecting patterns of inequality and discrimination, thereby aiding initiatives focused on advancing diversity and inclusion in the work environment It likewise offers decision-makers a practical structure for combining economic development and sustainable energy strategies his study aims to tackle the subsequent research queries (RQ):

RQ1. In what ways do ECON-ESG elements and artificial intelligence influence ET in the Countries in the OECD?

RQ2. What is the sole impact of ECON-ESG on energy transition (ET) within OECD countries?

The subsequent hypotheses were developed within the context of these inquiries into research:

H1: Economic, environmental, social, governance (ESG) elements, and artificial Artificial intelligence (AI) greatly influences energy transition (ET) across the 3 OECD nations.

H2: The singular impact of ECON-ESG on energy transition (ET) among the 3 The outlook for OECD countries is unfavorable.

Following the literature review, this research claims that ET among OECD countries is affected by dimensions related to ECON-ESG and AI. To progress beyond existing knowledge, this study employs a systematic method consisting of two separate stages to offer thorough understanding. To progress beyond existing understanding(Barkat et al., 2025), this study utilizes a systematic approach comprising two separate stages. to offer detailed understanding. ET is analyzed during the preliminary stage, utilizing energy. intensity quantified as primary energy usage per capita GDP. Employing strong Using statistical techniques like PCA, this research aims to develop thorough indices for the ESG, AI, and ECON-ESG dimensions within the 3 OECD countries. countries during the analyzed timeframe(Zarghami, 2025). Following that, the next stage explores further into the complex interaction between these essential factors and ET within OECD nations between 2022 and 2026. In particular, this stage aims to investigate the effect of economic, environmental, social, governance, and AI on the interactions of ET(Barkat et al., 2025). Utilizing advanced econometric models and strong statistical analytical frameworks, the study aims to reveal the intricate connections that influence energy transition results within the OECD framework, the research offers fresh understanding of the forces and elements influencing the energy transition in the sample nations via an extensive and varied strategy and multifaceted approach (see Fig. 1)

2. LITERATURE REVIEW

Numerous scholars have investigated the influence of ECON-ESG elements, in conjunction with AI, regarding energy transition (ET) or the mutual impact of ET on various elements. Nevertheless, a significant research void in current studies regarding a thorough examination of these factors together is present. Consequently, we intend to emphasize this discrepancy by examining the joint effects of ESG elements, AI, and a recently presented concept termed the ECON-ESG influence on ET, which continues to be a novel idea within scholarly communities. This research aims to meticulously examine OECD countries, emphasizing the intricate connections between these elements, providing important understanding for individuals engaged in sustainable development, including researchers, policymakers, and stakeholders activities

3. EMPIRICAL STUDIES

They warn that insufficient diversification in this approach might cause significant imbalances in the worldwide economy and instability in energy markets. The document emphasizes the strategic importance of rare earth metals, primarily controlled by China, and the consequences for countries aiming for substantial decarbonization, encouraging dependence on domestic developments in hydrogen energy and rare earth element industries (Shen et al., 2025; Taleizadeh et al., 2025). Examine the economic aspects of ET, emphasizing techniques to assess its effects and understand the complex modeling analyses forecasting macroeconomic results. They emphasize the significance of scale and time, coherence, and foundations in economic models, urging for a wider variety of interdisciplinary methods and frameworks to assess various aspects of ET (Lin & Yu, 2025; Xiao et al., 2026). The move from cyclical development to ongoing growth, highlighted by the Industrial Revolution, signified a change from an organic economy to one powered by mineral energy. Nevertheless, the existence of limited resources, environmental issues, constraints on energy and resource use, and emissions of pollutants restrict growth in economies reliant on minerals and energy. Consult Troubleshooting Translator Issues for More Information. - Google Search, n.d.; Aulia et al., 2026).

Moreover, the limitation set by CO2 levels, which affects the rise in global temperatures, makes the shift away from fossil fuel-dependent energy systems more challenging and hinders future economic growth. Develop methods to determine if renewable energy sources can satisfy future energy needs, examining the peak potential of solar and wind energy while considering both energy and non-energy sectors from a macroeconomic perspective (Naser-Karajah, 2026; Thien et al., 2025).

Results show that rising capital requirements in the energy sector hinder a worldwide energy transition (ET) before the century ends. Nonetheless, by regulating intensity via consumption, ongoing capital expansion, and significant improvements in energy efficiency, a shift might be possible by 2070 (Dong, 2026; Ragadhita et al., 2026). However, achieving this vision requires notable rises in savings rates, which could impact consumer spending.

Trends will persist until the change is finished. Environmental elements greatly affect ET processes. Emphasizes the significant influence of environmental regulations on total energy efficiency, especially in areas marked by a strong presence of clean energy, such as Zhejiang, Guangdong, Beijing, and Fujian (Peng & Peng, 2026; Sun et al., 2026). Yu and Guo (2023) examine the complex connection between environmental regulations and total-factor energy efficiency in different regions of China, impacting it directly and indirectly. Using the slacks-based measure (SBM)-undesirable framework, their research demonstrates the dual aspect of environmental regulations. Although mandates requiring businesses to cut fossil fuel use and boost clean energy positively affect the eastern region, the green paradox effect results in heightened resource extraction as a reaction to strict environmental regulations, negatively impacting the middle and western regions (Suradinkura et al., 2026; Umoru et al., 2026).

Dall-Orsoletta et al. (2022) explore current studies regarding social innovation (SI) in sustainable ET, highlighting its significance in promoting civic empowerment, stimulating community involvement, and enhancing sustainable practices at the local level. Although SI has the capacity to enhance local ET, challenges in expansion remain apparent (Padhy et al., 2026).

The impact of AI on national economies and the environment, and society is growing more important. A notable numerous researchers are working to utilize artificial intelligence to achieve sustainable development goals(Razmak & Farhan, 2026). the primary aim of artificial intelligence is to improve the effectiveness of applications via ongoing improvement, validation and implementation of machine learning, deep learning, and techniques in computer vision(Darwish et al., 2026). This procedure entails the with the objective of mimicking human cognitive abilities such as cognition, deduction, and awareness. At currently, artificial intelligence is widely used in adverse fields, such as manufacturing, agriculture, healthcare, transportation, and the energy shift(Alagele et al., 2024). Although researchers recognize the influence of AI on sustainability, there is a continuing debate regarding its position as either a driver or a barrier to environmental progress. In the framework of the Industrial Revolution, certain researchers suggest that AI has a positive impact on green technology, technological advancement, the energy shift, and the arrival of new power sources. This, subsequently, helps businesses improve their environmental management. The combination of remote sensing technology, machine learning, and neural networks have facilitated the creation of sophisticated systems for environmental monitoring. Such systems have made it easier to forecast the effects of climate change on business activities and allowed firms to react to severe conditions. Climatic occurrences with increased effectiveness(Neama & Dulaimi, 2025). Furthermore, industrial robots have become a crucial tool for boosting labor efficiency by automating monotonous tasks. The application of automated technology has been shown to lead to a decrease in production expenses, motivate firms to widen their activities, boost the need for non-automated positions, and improve staff remuneration. Performed utilizing semantic textual similarity and the SBERT approach determined that transformative digitalization can have beneficial effects affect Vietnamese qualified workforce. Regarding governance advantages, the execution of automated oversight(Alagele et al., 2024).

Recesses aided by AI have been shown to lead to the allocation of human resources towards more strategic initiatives. Moreover, this transition has been demonstrated to produce an effect. in the conventional product and service framework while simultaneously assisting companies in realizing organizational transformation contend that the AI The revolution has transformed the conventional organizational frameworks and decision-making approaches of management, enhancing operational effectiveness(Teruel-Sanchez et al., 2025). A significant amount of researchers have expressed a critical viewpoint on this issue. The most widespread criticism focuses on the insight that the complete life cycle of AI, starting from its creation to its launch, leads to considerable ecological costs and presents major difficulties to energy, power systems, and water resources The progression of AI has been demonstrated to be linked to improvements in productivity, but often involves many harmful impacts on society, such as joblessness and disparity(Yakob et al., 2025). The swift becoming outdated of conventional abilities have important implications for the character of the work trade and conventional jobs(Adelakun et al., 2025). It has a significant impact impact on the identity and standing of individuals at work, along with their earnings. argues that advancements in procedures, which often reduce labor, possess the ability to remove current job openings and threaten the sustainability of specific professions (Yan et al., 2026).

It is clear that the consequences of AI on various stakeholders are uneven, leading to governance difficulties throughout the development process. (Fadhilah et al., 2026) argues that the conflict between policy goals and particular interest groups with vested interests, arising from stakeholders' differing views on AI safety and development, presents a considerable barrier to policy execution(Alshurideh et al., 2026; Edeh et al., 2023). It appears that your input was cut off. Insufficient regulatory oversight may lead to consequences in data breaches, harmful exploitation, and the creation of deepfakes. These elements can readily provoke unmanageable risks and endanger the welfare of both individuals and the community(Dong, 2026; Q. Wang et al., 2026). An examination of the existing literature shows a dominance of broad analyses of AI's effects on sustainability, with minimal focus given to the corporate level(Jaiswal et al., 2026; Ningtyas et al., 2026). Additionally, studies on corporate sustainability mainly emphasize on financial impacts, including immediate profitability and prolonged improvement in corporate worth, with slight acknowledgment of the effects of AI as a developing tech. Discussions about sustainability and ESG are prevalent in markets, boardrooms, and C-suites today, particularly in relation to this article, are primarily centered on regarding sustainability and ESG reporting concerning AI and data functionalities, resources, and actions. Nevertheless, current standards and frameworks are inadequate(Fernández, 2026; Gatoi et al., 2026), and to formulate the protocol for evaluating the effects of AI and data, a short review of what is intended by sustainability and ESG is organized. Sustainability in this context pertains to the notion of sustainable development, outlined in the 1987 report Our Common Future published by the Brundtland commission of the United Nations (UN) et al., 1987). Sustainable development has been defined as fulfilling present requirements without hindering future generations from doing so. identical, and it is made up of three interconnected dimensions, specifically the ecological, societal, and financial. To attain sustainable development, challenges related to all three dimensions must be addressed. addressed concurrently, since we cannot, for instance, effectively manage climate change unless we also address matters associated with disparity and ecological fairness. This idea of sustainable Development serves as the basis of the UN's SDGs and Agenda. 2030 (Nations Unies, 2015). The 17 SDGs outline difficulties connected to all three aspects of sustainability, and the goal is to achieve the objectives by 2030. Although they are not designed as a structure for ESG or sustainability reporting is becoming more frequently utilized and cited in this context ESG is not a recent idea (Crona & Sundström, 2023), yet the The landscape of ESG and sustainability reporting and disclosure is quickly changing, with an abundance of frameworks, standards, and rating providers available. (Dou et al., 2025; Fernández, 2026; Li et al., 2024; Q. Wang et al., 2026) . This produces difficulties for those responsible for decision-making both internally and externally entities, as well as society at large, as illustrated through the lens of stakeholder capitalism (Liu et al., 2025); World Economic Forum, 2020. It also creates issues for businesses trying to interpret and disclose their ESG outcomes, and for investors who encounter a deficiency of reliable and similar information to evaluate possible investments (Cao et al., 2026; Oehmichen et al., 2025). An extensive array of standards and frameworks has resulted in many requests for alignment (Sida et al., 2025; Tian et al., 2025), and attempts to achieve this are progressing on multiple fronts, including the European Union's Sustainable Règlement sur la divulgation en matière de finances (SFDR), durabilité des entreprises Reporting Directive (CSRD) and EU classification (EU Technical expert group focused on sustainable finance,

2020; European Commission, 2022a, 2022c), along with the International Sustainability Standards Board of IFRS. (ISSB) (IFRS, 2022). Compounding this are the difficulties related to comprehending the connection between AI and sustainability along with ESG (Jerez-Jerez, 2025; Sætra, 2023). The aim of this article is to showcase the AI ESG Protocol serves as a mechanism for systematically assessing and revealing a company's AI and data-centric risks and prospects associated with to sustainability and ESG. Although all businesses can utilize the protocol, it will be especially important for AI and data-heavy firms where such technologies and resources are regarded as significant for their interested parties. This article primarily concerns the organizations that embrace the protocol, primarily aimed at executives and managers, Sustainable development is becoming more acknowledged as an area where both governments and private organizations must actively participate. important function in advancing(Božić, 2023). Programs likeThe EU's Green Deal is thus based on the idea that private Financial resources and engagement are crucial for achieving sustainability-related objectives. (European Commission, 2019). Incorporating ESG considerations into business operations involves a shift from conventional shareholder capitalism to what is at often called stakeholder capitalism (Abiddin, 2024; Ibrahim & Kumar, 2025; Ozkan, 2024)indicate that corporations are joining the movement for three primary causes. Initially, rules and official stipulations, including the EU Taxonomy, SFDR, and CSRD (ERM, 2022; EU Technical specialist team on sustainable finance, 2020; EU Commission, 2022a, 2022c). Secondly, pressure from investors and incentives in financial markets (Farrokhi, 2026; Hu & Othman, 2026b)AI-Powered Grid Analytics for Sustainable Energy Management in ESG Frameworks. Third, procedures associated with heightened public demand for accountable business practices and what is frequently referred to as the societal permit to function (Birlan et al., 2026; Kheradmand et al., 2026; Sadraei & Dal Mas, 2026). The idea of sustainable development also serves as the foundation of sustainability and ESG reporting, yet it may not be the best approach to depend on the three aspects of sustainability in finance and reporting background. In the ESG framework, the economic aspect is substituted. through the governance aspect. Though this involves a shift in terminology, it remains straightforward to link ESG reporting to sustainable progress and the SDGs. As an illustration, Figure 1, for instance, demonstrates how the SDGs can be categorized within the E, S, and G aspects of ESG. The objectives frequently regarded as economic (SDG8 and 9, for instance, are categorized here as social objectives, The improvement of corporate sustainability from an extensive technological and policy standpoint persists a lesser-studied region. As a result, we have chosen ESG. as an all-encompassing measure for corporate sustainability.

Table 1. AI and ESG Performance (2024-2026)

No.	Author(s) & Year	Study Title	Methodology	Key Findings
1	**Weng (2025)**	AI Adoption and ESG Performance in Innovative Pilot Zones.	OLS Regression, VIF Testing.	AI adoption reduces financing constraints and enhances information transparency, leading to higher ESG scores.
2	**Sun & Lim (2026)**	AI-Enhanced Big Data Analytics for ESG Transparency.	Systematic Literature Review + Empirical Modeling.	Found that AI analytical capabilities directly improve the quality and reliability of sustainability reporting.
3	**Tian et al. (2025)**	AI Adoption and ESG Performance: Evidence from Emerging Markets.	Multi-period Difference-in-Differences (DID).	AI exerts a significant positive impact on ESG by mitigating financial constraints and promoting green innovation.
4	**Al-Qudah (2025)**	The Impact of AI on ESG Disclosure Quality in Saudi Firms.	Dynamic GMM Model, Mediation Analysis.	AI improves disclosure quality by 28.9%; 73% of this impact is mediated through improved data governance.
5	**Jing & Zhang (2024)**	AI Impact on Manufacturing ESG: The Mediating Role of Green Innovation.	Structural Equation Modeling (SEM).	Green innovation acts as a critical mediator, converting AI technical inputs into tangible environmental outcomes.
6	**Lu et al. (2026)**	AI and New Productive Forces: A Study on ESG and Economic Growth.	Descriptive & Inferential Statistical Analysis.	Highlights a strong correlation between AI maturity and corporate sustainability strategies in OECD nations.
7	**Nur et al. (2024)**	The Role of AI in Sustainable Accounting and ESG Reporting.	Systematic Literature Review (SLR).	NLP techniques significantly improve the accuracy of classifying unstructured data for ESG reports.
8	**Zhou et al. (2025)**	Integrated Framework for Tech Innovation and ESG Well-being.	Multiple Case Study Analysis.	AI fosters “Green Learning” within organizations, which specifically boosts the Social (S) dimension.
9	**Wu (2026)**	AI and ESG in Finance: A Hybrid Bibliometric Approach.	Bibliometric Analysis + AI Clustering.	Identified a surge in AI-driven ESG scoring systems, increasing the accuracy of investment risk assessments.
10	**Integrum ESG (2026)**	AI as Infrastructure for ESG: Regulatory Expectations.	Trend Analysis & Market Data Review.	By 2026, AI has become an essential operational enabler for compliance with international standards (e.g., CSRD).

continued on following page

Table 1. Continued

No.	Author(s) & Year	Study Title	Methodology	Key Findings
11	**Zhang & Yang (2024)**	Digital Revolution and its Impact on Environmental & Social Outcomes.	Cross-sectional Time-series Analysis.	Digital transformation and AI reshape production methods, leading to significant reductions in energy waste.
12	**Bhatti et al. (2025)**	Responsible Leadership as a Moderator between AI and ESG.	Hierarchical Regression Analysis.	Responsible leadership ensures AI outputs are used to enhance sustainability rather than just short-term profit.
13	**Ying et al. (2024)**	Integrating AI into the Sustainability Reporting Cycle.	Comparative Study.	AI usage reduces the administrative burden of reporting by over 40% while increasing data auditability.
14	**Wang & Cai (2025)**	Impact of Smart Finance on ESG Performance in Retail.	Big Data Analytics.	Fintech/AI alleviates funding constraints for SMEs, allowing them to invest more in ESG-related projects.
15	**Lim et al. (2026)**	Financial Stability and ESG in the AI Era: A Critical Review.	Critical Literature Review.	AI helps bridge the "Historical Data Gap," providing better predictive insights for Governance (G) performance.
16	**Pesqueira & Sousa (2024)**	AI and Environmental Risk Management in OECD Countries.	Panel Data Analysis (OECD Scope).	Confirmed a positive relationship between AI infrastructure maturity and the speed of Energy Transition (ET).
17	**Rau & Yu (2024)**	Long-term Value Creation through Tech-Enhanced ESG.	Investor Survey & Correlation Analysis.	Investors show a higher preference for firms using AI to monitor social and environmental risks in supply chains.
18	**Zhang (2025)**	AI as a Catalyst for Circular Economy	Econometric Modeling.	AI optimizes product lifecycles and resource
19	**Hussain (2026)**	Digital Governance: AI's Impact on Anti-Corruption & Transparency.	Content Analysis.	Intelligent algorithms enhance internal auditing efficiency, significantly raising Governance (G) scores.

4. ESG AND AI

AI ethics and digital ethics have arguably reached their peak. of the hype cycle(Burnaev et al., 2023; Konurbayeva et al., 2026), research connecting remains scarce. AI and the idea of ESG, sustainable finance, and sustainability. reporting (Lim, 2024; Marampa et al., 2025). A significant amount of effort has been and continues to be applied to AI and related topics. pertaining to overall or facets of sustainability (Anikó, 2026; Nordin et al., 2023; Zhang & Yang, 2024)yet this is infrequently linked. to environmental, social, and governance (ESG). In a recent publication, (Nara et al., 2026; Xu, 2024)recognized a study deficiency in this field, identifying merely three existing pertinent articles on the topic, specifically (Tiron-Tudor et al., 2025), (Lee et al., 2025). In exploring the connection between AI and ESG, none of the articles concentrate(Sætra, 2021) on offering a mechanism for assessing and revealing AI-related information. highlight the importance of ESG impacts and the necessity for such a tool. It is important to point out that extensive studies exist regarding how AI may be applied in contexts pertinent to the realm of ESG, such as in accounting(Selim, 2020), in producing ESG ratings(Elhady & Shohieb, 2025), and to tackle the necessity of locating a method for accurately assessing data and AI capabilities in financial statements (Leitner-Hanetseder & Lehner, 2022). Nonetheless, the AI ESG framework here created centers on offering a technique for assessing and revealing the ESG related effects of employing AI, along with these other domains of The use of AI is therefore not directly pertinent. This application of AI can, yet, should be documented as ESG pertinent via the protocol. The rest of this section outlines essential foundational components of the AI ESG framework in some depth. Initially, I describe how effects are divided into three areas, then briefly outlining the key dimensions to be taken into account when assessing AI and data-driven effects associated to ecological, societal, and managerial. The extent of this article excludes a thorough mapping of all sustainability

Connected effects of AI; however, challenges highlighted in the broader research literature are evident in the protocol (Hamilton-Peach & Townsley, n.d.; Marlia et al., 2025; Nugraha et al., 2026). Three domains of impact The complexities of ESG-related effects can sometimes obstruct advancement. in executing ESG evaluations, and when they do not succeed, the resulting evaluations are often not particularly actionable. To tackle this challenge, I elaborate on (Sida et al., 2025) and the proposed analytical approach for examining the sustainability-related impacts of AI. This approach is partly driven by the Greenhouse Gas Protocol (World Resources Institute, 2021) that categorizes emissions into Scopes 1, 2, and 3. In this way, the AI ESG Protocol also aligns directly with the prevalent and widely adopted methods used in the climate change aspect of various other frameworks and guidelines. Figure 2 depicts several key sources of risks and impacts within each scope, which are examined in more detail in the subsequent sections. While related and somewhat intertwined, evaluating impact is slightly different from merely measuring emissions due to the broader range of factors to consider. The AI ESG Protocol defines the categories as described below, with examples given in the following sections. Scope 1 relates to impacts directly linked to a company's core operations, focusing on actions and management limited to internal social and regulatory implications, along with the environmental impacts tied to the computing infrastructure that the company directly controls (owns or leases). Scope 1 relates to impacts that are directly connected to a company's main activities (Adiguzel & Sonmez Cakir, 2025; Su & Abd Rani, 2025; Sugiyanto, 2025).

Activities and governance, limited to internal social and governance impacts and the environmental outcomes linked to computing infrastructure that the company directly oversees (owns or leases). Data gathered by the organization is categorized as Scope 1. For example, Figure 2 depicts issues related to cybersecurity, the impact of personal devices and data, and individual staff members. Scope 2 encompasses the upstream impacts that are directly associated with the organization's supply chain. The procurement of electricity and cloud services is categorized as Scope 2, which includes acquiring services for development, support, and algorithms. A crucial element of Scope 2 includes all the secondary data used by the company, improving the information gathered by the organization itself as described in Scope 1. Figure 2 illustrates this by depicting, for example, the procurement of cloud services, the people involved in the upstream supply chain, upstream cybersecurity, and energy acquisition. Scope 3 includes the broader upstream and downstream impacts of the organization's capabilities, resources, and operations related to AI and data. This includes, for example, a technique used in artificial intelligence for hiring, and how this might pose risks of discrimination, or perhaps reduce the occurrence of bias in recruitment. It also includes the way the entity performs its actions.

Encourages or limits consumption when the organization offers or disseminates resources that, for example, elevate emissions either upstream or downstream. Relationships, increased implementation of the internet of things (IoT) in industries and private sectors, intensified attention and oversight of individuals and groups, value creation and innovation, transportation, impact on water use, environmental factors, and biodiversity, among others. To summarize, detailing the impacts across these three domains encompasses all ESG-related influences stemming from AI and data, benefiting both the organization and its stakeholders, reducing the adverse effects and hazards or enhance and leverage potential gains and beneficial effects(Chen et al., 2026; Moraes & Schaefer, 2026; Vukmir, 2006, 2006). The three scopes assist in categorizing impacts from different sources both up- and down-downstream, yet another important difference must be noted between various kinds of effects and hazards. The ESG perspective focuses on three primary areas that I will now address: environmental, social, and governance matters.

Table 2. Research relating to cybersecurity

No.	Author & Year	Study Title	Research Problem	Objectives	Key Findings
1	**Harvard Law School** (2023)	*AI and ESG: Integrating Environmental, Social, and Governance Factors*	Difficulty in verifying traditional ESG data and the rise of unintended algorithmic biases in corporate evaluation.	Integrating AI to enhance ESG data quality while establishing governance frameworks to prevent machine bias.	AI increases reporting accuracy, but a lack of oversight creates new legal and ethical risks for corporations.
2	**MIT Sloan Review** (2024)	*The Double-Edged Sword of AI in ESG Reporting*	The contradiction between using AI to detect "greenwashing" and its massive energy/water consumption in data centers.	Measuring the actual environmental impact of operating AI systems against their benefits in auditing sustainability reports.	AI effectively detects data manipulation, but its huge carbon footprint threatens corporate climate commitments.
3	**Journal of Business Ethics** (2022)	*Using Artificial Intelligence to Measure Corporate ESG Performance*	Current ESG ratings rely heavily on self-reported corporate data, reducing objectivity and transparency.	Developing a Natural Language Processing (NLP) model to evaluate companies based on real-time external data.	Algorithms successfully provide more objective ESG scores by analyzing news and social media independently of corporate reports.
4	**UNCTAD** (2023)	*Artificial Intelligence for Sustainability: Challenges and Opportunities*	The digital divide between developed and developing nations in using AI for sustainability, and risks of labor displacement.	Formulating international policies to ensure fair distribution of AI technologies to support Sustainable Development Goals (SDGs).	AI can accelerate sustainability goals, but without strict social governance, it will worsen unemployment and the digital divide.

continued on following page

Table 2. Continued

No.	Author & Year	Study Title	Research Problem	Objectives	Key Findings
5	**World Economic Forum** (2024)	*AI Governance as a Core Component of modern ESG*	The third pillar of ESG (Governance - G) lacks clear standards regulating the use of autonomous intelligent systems.	Urging corporate boards to integrate "AI ethics" as an essential part of the corporate governance structure.	AI governance is no longer a luxury; companies that fail to govern their algorithms face severe reputational risks.
6	**Stanford University** (2023)	*The Carbon Footprint of Large Language Models*	A lack of precise data regarding the volume of carbon emissions generated by training Large Language Models (LLMs).	Calculating and estimating the carbon emissions resulting from training and deploying generative AI models.	Training a single large language model produces carbon emissions equivalent to several cars over their entire lifespan.
7	**Journal of Banking & Finance** (2023)	*Predicting Corporate ESG Scores Using Machine Learning*	Investors' inability to predict companies' future ESG performance based solely on historical data.	Building a Machine Learning model capable of predicting future changes in corporate ESG ratings.	Machine learning models demonstrated a high capability to predict companies facing governance or environmental crises before they occur.
8	**Business Strategy and the Environment** (2022)	*Artificial Intelligence and Corporate Social Responsibility*	High waste of energy and resources within traditional manufacturing processes that are difficult to manage manually.	Testing the impact of AI-driven predictive maintenance systems on reducing waste and improving energy efficiency.	Adopting AI in production lines reduces energy consumption by up to 20%, strongly supporting the environmental pillar (E).
9	**Oxford Internet Institute** (2024)	*AI Bias and Its Implications for the 'S' in ESG*	Algorithms continuing to replicate human biases against minorities and women in hiring and evaluation processes.	Analyzing the impact of algorithmic discrimination on the evaluation of Corporate Social Responsibility (S - Social).	Algorithmic bias severely harms diversity and social justice standards unless data is regularly audited.

continued on following page

Table 2. Continued

No.	Author & Year	Study Title	Research Problem	Objectives	Key Findings
10	**PwC Framework** (2023)	*Responsible AI: A Framework for ESG Investors*	Investors' confusion on how to evaluate the risks of tech companies that rely entirely on opaque "black box" algorithms.	Providing a practical guide for investors to assess startups' commitment to "Responsible AI" principles.	Companies that practice algorithmic transparency and explainability face less legal liability and attract more investment.
11	**CFA Institute** (2022)	*NLP for ESG: Extracting Insights from Unstructured Data*	The massive volume of unstructured data (texts, reports, audio) making manual analysis difficult for financial analysts.	Using programmatic text processing techniques to extract hidden ESG indicators from thousands of pages.	Automating report screening with AI reduces analysis time by 90% and uncovers gaps between corporate promises and reality.
12	**Int. Journal of Production Economics** (2023)	*The Role of AI in Supply Chain Sustainability*	The complexity of global supply chains making it hard to monitor human rights or environmental violations at lower tiers.	Deploying IoT and AI to track raw material sources and labor conditions in real-time.	AI enables strict supply chain oversight, ensuring products are free from child labor or illegal environmental pollution.
13	**AI and Ethics Journal** (2021)	*Sustainable AI: Distinguishing Between AI for Sustainability and Sustainability of AI*	Conceptual and practical confusion between using AI as a tool to solve problems versus its own self-sustainability.	Deconstructing both concepts to establish ethical and practical frameworks ensuring AI does not harm the environment while trying to save it.	An AI system cannot be deemed "sustainable" just because it solves an eco-problem if it consumes excessive non-renewable energy.

continued on following page

Table 2. Continued

No.	Author & Year	Study Title	Research Problem	Objectives	Key Findings
14	**McKinsey & Company** (2024)	*Generative AI and ESG: The New Frontier of Governance*	The uncontrolled influx of Generative AI (GenAI) into enterprises without policies regulating data security and IP rights.	Assessing corporate boards' readiness to manage cyber threats and data leaks resulting from AI tools.	Most enterprises use GenAI without clear governance frameworks, raising risks of data breaches and privacy violations (G challenge).
15	**Nature Climate Change** (2023)	*AI-Driven Climate Risk Modeling for Financial Institutions*	Traditional statistical models failing to accurately predict the severity of sudden climate changes and their financial impact.	Developing deep learning-based climate simulation models to predict physical risks (like floods/ droughts) on investments.	AI provides highly accurate climate risk maps, allowing financial institutions to protect assets and direct funds to green projects.

5. METHODOLOGY APPROACH

Model and Dataset This research explores the complex connection between energy transition (ET) and economic and ESG elements, in addition to AI and the novel framework suggested by Işik and colleagues (2024a, b, c, d, e, f, g, 2025), with regard to ECON-ESG in OECD (refer to OECD countries in Appendix A.1.1.) countries from 2002 to 2020. The choice of OECD countries for this research relies on several key criteria. Initially, these OECD nations provide extensive and reliable data across various sectors, boosting the robustness and complexity of the analysis. Additionally, their consistency in data gathering techniques and regulatory structures enables significant analyses and thorough assessments. Ultimately, the experiences and approaches of OECD nations greatly influence global policy choices, as their status as developed economies showcases various policy techniques and exerts considerable international power. It is crucial to highlight that the timeframe from 2022 to 2026 utilized in this research signifies the longest span of continuous and trustworthy data accessible for OECD nations. Additionally, the measures implemented by these nations have extensive implications that ... The groups were examined to determine similarities and differences in the application of AI for ESG standards. Every cluster was thoroughly analyzed to comprehend the unique effects of AI on environmental sustainability, social accountability, and corporate governance practices. The evaluation revealed major shortcomings in research and areas of potential importance.

Table 3. OECD nations strategy implementations

No.	Author (Year)	Study Title	Key Variables / Domain	Methodology & Tools	Key Findings
1	**Lewis et al. (2026)**	Harnessing AI to Tackle Eco-Environmental Crises	Global Environmental Crisis Management	Analytical / Editorial Review	AI surpasses traditional statistical tools in simulating complex ecological systems with high precision.
2	**Wang (2025)**	AI-driven ESG Reporting & Compliance	ESG Governance & Environmental Disclosure	Descriptive Analytical	Automating sustainability data collection enhances transparency and reduces "Greenwashing" risks.
3	**MDPI (2025)**	AI for Efficient Resource Management	Carbon & Resource Optimization	Systematic Review	Machine Learning algorithms significantly reduced data center energy consumption and optimized microgrids.
4	**Apurva (2025)**	Global AI in Environmental Sustainability	Environmental Tech Market Trends	Market Trend Analysis	The market is projected to reach $97B by 2034, driven by AI-integrated government climate policies.
5	**Sofiyah et al. (2024)**	AI-driven systems for Sustainable Engagement	Organizational Sustainability	Case Study	Improved operational efficiency by 30% through predictive models for resource waste reduction.
6	**Igual & Seguí (2024)**	Supervised Learning in Eco-Data	Pollution Monitoring	Experimental (Python-based)	High efficacy of supervised learning models in monitoring air and water pollution via satellite imagery.

continued on following page

Table 3. Continued

No.	Author (Year)	Study Title	Key Variables / Domain	Methodology & Tools	Key Findings
7	**Olawade et al. (2024)**	Real-time monitoring of sustainability	Real-time Environmental Tracking	Literature Review	AI can identify gas leaks and emissions with 95% accuracy, significantly faster than manual methods.
8	**Feng (2024)**	Generative AI in Sustainable Product Dev.	Generative AI & Material Science	Exploratory Descriptive	Accelerated the innovation of eco-friendly materials through automated prototyping and virtual testing.
9	**Stryker (2024)**	AI for Problem Solving in Sustainability	Environmental Problem Solving	Systematic Literature Review	Identified 6 core pillars where AI outperforms, notably in waste management and precision agriculture.
10	**Zhang & Goyal (2024)**	Deep Learning for Climate Modeling	Climate Change & Natural Disasters	Experimental (Deep Learning)	Substantial improvement in predicting natural disasters (floods/wildfires), minimizing environmental losses.
11	**Schneider (2025)**	Agentic AI for Carbon Footprint	Autonomous Carbon Control	System Implementation	Agentic AI systems can make real-time decisions to lower carbon emissions in industrial settings.
12	**Salesforce (2025)**	AI Energy Score for Models	Green AI & Energy Efficiency	Quantitative Scoring	Introduced a benchmark to measure energy costs per AI model to ensure "Green Intelligence."
13	**SAP (2025)**	Carbon Monitoring in Operations	Operational Sustainability	Applied Software Research	Integrated carbon tracking into daily ERP operations using AI tools for real-time reporting.

continued on following page

Table 3. Continued

No.	Author (Year)	Study Title	Key Variables / Domain	Methodology & Tools	Key Findings
14	**Strader et al. (2025)**	AI and Natural Resource Management	Greenhouse Gas (GHG) Prediction	Systematic Review (62 studies)	Demonstrated the effectiveness of LSTM models in GHG forecasting to support policy makers.
15	**Rashid (2024)**	Autonomous Analytics for Sustainability	Autonomous Data Analytics	Analytical Study	AI reduces human dependency in waste sorting and management processes by approximately 40%.

6. RESULTS AND DISSECTIONS

6.1 Descriptive Statistics

The span from a low of 1.65 to a high of 7.456 demonstrates the data distribution. A skewness of 0.564 suggests a mild positive skew, indicating values that are lower than elevated ones, with a few outliers skewing the distribution towards the upper range

Table 4. Descriptive statistics

Variables	(1) AI Index	(2) ESG Index	(3) ECON-ESG	(4) Energy Transition
(1) AI Index (GI)	1.00			
(2) ESG Index	0.642**	1.00		
(3) ECON-ESG	0.415*	0.528**	1.00	
(4) Energy Transition (ET)	**0.756***	**0.589***	**0.214**	1.00

The multicollinearity examination, outlined in Appendix 2a, demonstrates that the variance The inflation factor (VIF) for each independent variable stays under 2. This finding indicates that our dataset does not exhibit multicollinearity problems. Significantly, current literature frequently supports a recognized VIF threshold of . with more cutoff threshold value, like 5 . The compliance of our The dataset meeting these thresholds reinforces the conclusion that multicollinearity is not a problem.

during this study. This finding significantly enhances the regression model's reliability. Furthermore, ensuring that robust links exist between predictor variables do not influence the computed coefficients, which improves the reliability of the results of the analysis. As a result, stakeholders can possess increased assurance in the reliability and precision of the findings derived from the regression analysis

Table 5. Regression Model Summary (Impact Analysis)

Model	R	R Square (R2)	Adjusted R Square	Std. Error of the Estimate
1	0.825	**0.681**	0.674	0.314

Table 6.

Predictor Variables	Unstandardized B	Std. Error	Beta (β)	t-value	Sig. (p)
(Constant)	1.104	0.245	-	4.506	0.000
AI Dimensions (GI)	0.542	0.068	**0.612**	7.970	**0.000**
ESG Dimensions	0.321	0.074	**0.285**	4.337	**0.001**
ECON-ESG	-0.115	0.052	**-0.104**	-2.211	**0.038**

We performed a slope homogeneity assessment and computed two "delta" test statistics, namely the mean-variance bias-adjusted statistic of the slope homogeneity test in relation to autocorrelation, as described in Table III. In every case, both the direct and modified methods led to the dismissal of the slope uniformity in the null hypothesis, with p-values under 0.05, indicating that the slope coefficients remain consistent across the samples gathered from different countries. Nonetheless, the null hypothesis was dismissed as both the simple and Mean–variance bias-corrected versions exhibited p-values below 0.05. This suggests that the slope coefficients show diversity, indicating that differences are present among the specified countries. Thus, utilizing heterogeneous panel methods is advised to tackle this variability efficiently. Prior to utilizing the panel model for regression analysis, it is crucial to assess the existence of stationarity in panel data to prevent spurious regressions, since this may lead to unreliable statistical tests because of non-stationary independent variables. In this research (illustrated in Table 3), two panel unit root tests were utilized to evaluate the stability of the variables: the CIPS test.

6.2 Panel Cointegration Test

Following the preliminary assessment, conducting a panel integration analysis experiment is essential to examine the potential enduring connections and stability among the factors. In time series analysis, the idea of cointegration indicates that establishing cointegration between dependent and independent variables validates their appropriateness for developing a strong and significant model (Kulkov et al., 2024; J. Wang et al., 2025). Therefore, to reduce the likelihood of false regression and confirm the enduring connections between variables, it is essential to employ a second-generation panel cointegration test. This assessment allows for a comprehensive analysis of interactions over an extended duration by considering both temporal and cross-sectional elements. The Westerlund test (2007), a second-generation cointegration assessment, examines the dynamic relationships over time between energy transition (ET) and a range of economic, environmental, social, and governance elements. The findings presented in Table 5 demonstrate the outcomes of four tests by Westerlund (2007) aimed at evaluating the null hypothesis of no cointegration within the panel data. The Gt and Ga tests oppose the null hypothesis, offering proof of cointegration.

7. CONCLUSION

Realizing economic growth via skills enhancement is vital, while incorporating ESG (Environmental, Social, and Governance) standards along with artificial intelligence (AI) in finance provides a promising path for exploration and implementation, presenting fresh opportunities for responsible and sustainable investment strategies. Recent research in this area shows that economic growth can be realized by utilizing machine learning algorithms to evaluate ESG data and inform investment choices—primarily via skills enhancement—while also creating AI-driven platforms that support investors in incorporating ESG elements into their financial approaches. This study offers a thorough and organized summary of the research environment concerning ESG, AI, and finance. Eight primary research domains have been recognized: trading and investment; ESG reporting; valuation and management; corporate governance; financial markets and instruments; risk management, forecasting, and evaluation; information; and the ethical application of AI. The study provides important perspectives on the changing research intensity, interest, and AI methodologies in each domain, enhancing comprehension of this swiftly transforming and growing field. Future studies could target these particular fields:

Investigating the capabilities of novel AI strategies, such as graph neural networks, unit learning, and generative models, to improve financial applications focused on

ESG (Environmental, Social, and Governance) while tackling challenges in valuable research areas, including the ethical utilization of AI. Investigating these innovative methods may enhance how financial organizations process and interpret ESG data, resulting in more precise forecasting, improved risk management, and more efficient decision-making. Studies might also investigate the connections and interactions among current research paradigms to create more integrated and coherent strategies for tackling issues associated with ESG, AI, and finance. By recognizing these connections, the financial industry could discover new paths for innovation and create cohesive solutions that tackle multiple issues at once.

This comprehensive method may result in the development of lucrative and eco-friendly financial products and strategies. (I'm sorry, but the text you provided seems to be unfinished.) Evaluating the effects of organizational frameworks, industry norms, and stakeholder involvement. Anticipations concerning the incorporation and adoption of ESG (Environmental, Social, and Governance) standards and artificial intelligence (AI) within the finance industry are essential for enhancing future policy development and optimal practices. This should also address the ethical and regulatory challenges presented by generative AI, especially regarding data integrity and the risk of abuse in financial simulations associated with ESG. This approach allows the financial sector to guarantee that AI-supported ESG initiatives are ethical, building confidence in AI-driven decisions and procedures. At present, the PRISMA research standard for the finance sector is restricted to "finance." Expanding this scope to encompass closely related research terms like "assurance and auditing" and "information accounting systems" would be intriguing. This may improve research in fields like corporate governance and risk management. Broadening the focus to include these related areas might uncover fresh opportunities and obstacles, promoting a more profound comprehension of the research environment. A bibliometric analysis that includes bibliographic connections, citation evaluation, common word examination, and co-authorship investigation (Khanra et al., 2022) can improve and expand this study. Systematic literature mapping offers an organized summary of existing research on economic growth, whereas bibliometric techniques uncover connections between publications, the importance and influence of particular studies, the development of crucial terms and concepts, and partnerships among scholars

REFRENCES

Abiddin, N. Z. (2024). A deep dive into leadership styles in shaping the higher education institution's value and culture. *Pakistan Journal of Life and Social Sciences*, *22*(2), 3854–3868. DOI: 10.57239/PJLSS-2024-22.2.00283

Adelakun, O., Bui, Q. N., Turel, O., & Anderberg, G. (2025). Survival of the Fittest Through Digital Transformation: Turning the Board's Digital Awareness to Action. *Information Systems Journal*, isj.12587. DOI: 10.1111/isj.12587

Adiguzel, Z., & Sonmez Cakir, F. (2025). Empowering sustainability: Green entrepreneurial orientation, innovative strategies, culture and operational performance. *Management Decision*, *63*(11), 3934–3966. DOI: 10.1108/MD-07-2024-1700

Adwey, L. (2026a). Artificial Intelligence and Unethical Financial Practices: Examining the Mediating Role of Environmental; Social; and Governance (ESG) performance in the Saudi Financial Sector. *Borsa Istanbul Review*, 100784.

Adwey, L. (2026b). Artificial Intelligence and Unethical Financial Practices: Examining the Mediating Role of Environmental; Social; and Governance (ESG) performance in the Saudi Financial Sector. *Borsa Istanbul Review*, 100784.

Ahmed, Z. A. (2025). A Proposed Model for Developing the Taxation System on Oil Companies in Iraq: A Strategic Framework for Budget Financing and Enhancing Economic Stability. *European Journal of Management. Economics and Business*, *2*(2), 182–197.

Al-Mahamid, H. (2025). A comparative analysis of the human development index and road safety outcomes in the European Union. *European Transport Studies*, *2*, 100041. DOI: 10.1016/j.ets.2025.100041

Alagele, H. K. H., Neama, N. H., Al Dulaimi, H. A., & Abd, S. E. (2024). The Impact of Purposeful Management on the Relationship Between Organizational Conflict and Team Proactivity. *Journal of Ecohumanism*, *3*(8), 10875–10882.

Alam, M. M., & Priti, S. I. (2024). *Adaptive Hybrid Software Project Management in Bangladesh's Software Industry: Navigating the Cultural Transformation and Ensuring On-Time Delivery* [PhD Thesis, IUB]. https://ar.iub.edu.bd/handle/11348/1001

Ally, A. M. (2025). Artificial intelligence (AI) and financial technology (FinTech) in Tanzania; legal and regulatory issues. *International Journal of Law and Management*. https://www.emerald.com/ijlma/article-abstract/doi/10.1108/IJLMA-07-2024-0251/1250484

Alshurideh, M. T., Ahmed, G., Shrouf, H., Shwedeh, F., & Alzoubi, H. M. (2026). *Leveraging Artificial Intelligence and Data Analytics for Digital Innovation: Insights from Banking Sector*. https://www.emerald.com/books/edited-volume/20966/chapter/107781635

Anikó, V. (2026). *Perspective Chapter: The Role of Data Quality Dimensions in Data-Driven Decision-Making*. https://www.intechopen.com/online-first/1231452

Aulia, A., Sukmadilaga, C., Avianti, I., Rosdini, D., & Ghani, E. K. (2026). The Role of ESG and Digitalization Driving Sustainable Agropreneurship in Emerging Market. [ATT]. *Aptisi Transactions on Technopreneurship*, *8*(1), 51–62. DOI: 10.34306/att.v8i1.673

Avolio, B., & Walumbwa, F. (2014). *16 authentic leadership theory, research and practice: Steps taken and steps that remain* (Vol. 331). Oxford University Press Oxford. https://books.google.com/books?hl=en&lr=&id=ul5iAwAAQBAJ&oi=fnd&pg=PA331&dq=walumbwa+2014+authentic+leadership&ots=N3SujFHHPY&sig=GlKRwcHIK0z8GfUH16t1XG0Tys0

Barkat, K., Alsamara, M., Al Kwifi, O. S., & Jarallah, S. (2025). Does trade openness mitigate environmental degradation in Organisation for Economic Co-operation and Development (OECD) countries? Implications for achieving sustainable development. *Natural Resources Forum*, *49*(1), 677–698. DOI: 10.1111/1477-8947.12412

Birlan, I., Davidescu, A. A., & Constantin, R.- tefan. (2026). Artificial Intelligence and ESG Disclosure: Measuring Transparency in AI-Driven Firms. In C.-W. Su, O.-R. Lobon , A.-C. Nicolescu, & N. M. Doran (Eds.), *Green Finance and the Challenges of Climate Change* (pp. 41–68). Springer Nature Switzerland. DOI: 10.1007/978-3-032-07293-1_3

Božić, V. (2023). Environmental, social, and governance (ESG) & artificial intelligence (AI). *Preprint*. https://www.researchgate.net/profile/Velibor-Bozic-2/publication/391955758_ENVIRONMENTAL_SOCIAL_AND_GOVERNANCE_ESG_ARTIFICAL_INTELLIGENCE_AI/links/682eb9b8d1054b0207f0cca7/ENVIRONMENTAL-SOCIAL-AND-GOVERNANCE-ESG-ARTIFICAL-INTELLIGENCE-AI.pdf

Burnaev, E., Mironov, E., Shpilman, A., Mironenko, M., & Katalevsky, D. (2023). Practical AI cases for solving ESG challenges. *Sustainability (Basel)*, *15*(17), 12731. DOI: 10.3390/su151712731

Cao, L. T., Tran, L. B., Khuu, Q. T., Tran, T. T. B., & Nguyen, L. T. (2026). Empowering Gen Z With AI: Embody ESG Values and Shaping the Future of Personalized Customer Experience. *Journal of Sensory Studies*, *41*(1), e70102. DOI: 10.1111/joss.70102

Chen, W., Song, Z., & Xie, Y. (2026). Energy transition across the climate policy uncertainty divide: The critical role of green technology innovation and digital transformation. *Economic Analysis and Policy*. https://www.sciencedirect.com/science/article/pii/S0313592626000366

Chernyak-Hai, L., Bareket-Bojmel, L., & Margalit, M. (2024). A matter of hope: Perceived support, hope, affective commitment, and citizenship behavior in organizations. *European Management Journal*, *42*(4), 576–583. DOI: 10.1016/j.emj.2023.03.003

Darwish, S., Hussain Alagele, H. K., Alsherooqi, A., & Nafea, R. (2026). Leading Change: A Modern Analysis of Transformational Vs. Transactional Leadership. In AlDhaen, E., Weerakkody, V., & Ahmed Farouta, F. (Eds.), *Sustainable Development Agenda 2030* (Vol. 646, pp. 271–282). Springer Nature Switzerland., DOI: 10.1007/978-3-032-11612-3_22

de Moraes, J. B., & Schaefer, J. L. (2026). Customer satisfaction in digital banking services: A network analysis focused on service quality, insurance, mobile banking, and digital channels. *Journal of Enterprise Information Management*, •••, 1–24. DOI: 10.1108/JEIM-04-2025-0237

Dong, X. (2026). The ESG-productivity paradox: How ESG performance expectation gaps impede total factor productivity. *Journal of Business Research*, *202*, 115775. DOI: 10.1016/j.jbusres.2025.115775

Dou, J., Chen, D., & Zhang, Y. (2025). Towards energy transition: Accessing the significance of artificial intelligence in ESG performance. *Energy Economics*, *146*, 108515. DOI: 10.1016/j.eneco.2025.108515

Dwivedi, Y. K., Helal, M. Y. I., Elgendy, I. A., Albashrawi, M. A., Hughes, L., Shawosh, M., Dutot, V., & Jeon, I. (2026). Artificial intelligence agents and agentic systems in hospitality and tourism: Challenges, opportunities and research agenda. *International Journal of Contemporary Hospitality Management*, *38*(1), 27–52. DOI: 10.1108/IJCHM-02-2025-0287

Edeh, F. O., Zayed, N. M., Darwish, S., Nitsenko, V., Hanechko, I., & Islam, K. A. (2023). Impression management and employee contextual performance in service organizations (enterprises). *Emerging Science Journal*, *7*(2), 366–384. DOI: 10.28991/ESJ-2023-07-02-05

Elhady, A. M., & Shohieb, S. (2025). AI-driven sustainable finance: Computational tools, ESG metrics, and global implementation. *Future Business Journal*, *11*(1), 209. DOI: 10.1186/s43093-025-00610-x

Fadhilah, A. F., Aryanti, A. N., Sofiati, N. A., Ismail, G. D., & Muttaqin, R. (2026). Enhancing Employee Performance through Competence, Motivation, and Transformational Leadership: The Strategic Role of Employee Engagement. *Journal of General Education and Humanities*, *5*(1), 535–554. DOI: 10.58421/gehu.v5i1.958

Farrokhi, Z. (2026). AI-Powered Grid Analytics for Sustainable Energy Management in ESG Frameworks. In *Data-Driven ESG Strategy Implementation Through Business Intelligence* (pp. 279–318). IGI Global Scientific Publishing., https://www.igi-global.com/chapter/ai-powered-grid-analytics-for-sustainable-energy-management-in-esg-frameworks/388322

Fernández, A. M. (2026). Artificial Intelligence–Driven Transformation Of Investment, Corporate Strategy, And Economic Growth: Integrating ESG, Portfolio Management, And Technological Ecosystems. *Library of Frontline Marketing. Management and Economics Journal*, *6*(01), 1–5.

Gatoi, H., Belhaoua, I., Akhtar, K., Qadir, M., Mohammad, N., & Ali, M. (2026). Green Intelligence in Finance: Artificial Intelligence-Driven ESG Analytics and Sustainable Investment Performance. *Inverge Journal of Social Sciences*, *5*(1), 15–27. DOI: 10.63544/ijss.v5i1.216

Hamilton-Peach, J., & Townsley, P. (n.d.). *AN IFAD SUSTAINABLE LIVELIHOODS FRAMEWORK.*

Hu, C., & Othman, R. B. (2026a). AI-enabled ESG consultancy capability building in small audit firms: A strategic transformation pathway analysis. *Future Technology*, *5*(2), 25–37. DOI: 10.55670/fpll.futech.5.2.3

Hu, C., & Othman, R. B. (2026b). AI-enabled ESG consultancy capability building in small audit firms: A strategic transformation pathway analysis. *Future Technology*, *5*(2), 25–37. DOI: 10.55670/fpll.futech.5.2.3

Ibrahim, A., & Kumar, G. (2025). A framework for integrating Lean Six Sigma and Industry 4.0 for sustainable manufacturing. *International Journal of Production Research*, •••, 1–23. DOI: 10.1080/00207543.2025.2571202

Jaiswal, T., Hasan, M. A., Das, S., & Tiwari, V. (2026). Advancing Sustainable Services Through ESG and Circular Economy: Technology-Driven Pathways for Supply Chain Transformation. *Sustainable Development*, sd.70744. DOI: 10.1002/sd.70744

Jerez-Jerez, M. J. (2025). A study of employee attitudes towards AI, its effect on sustainable development goals and non-financial performance in independent hotels. *International Journal of Hospitality Management*, *124*, 103987. DOI: 10.1016/j.ijhm.2024.103987

Kamal, N., Butt, M. A., & Javeid, U. (2026). An empirical study on the effectiveness of artificial intelligence tools in English language acquisition and teaching strategies within an ESG framework. *Social Science Review Archives*, *4*(1), 3562–3568. DOI: 10.70670/sra.v4i1.1922

Kassar, M., & Jizi, M. (2026). Artificial intelligence and robotic process automation in auditing and accounting: A systematic literature review. *Journal of Applied Accounting Research*, *27*(1), 217–241. DOI: 10.1108/JAAR-05-2024-0175

Kheradmand, E., Mirshafiee, M., & Pashang, S. (2026). A Comparative Analysis of AI Approaches for ESG Data Extraction. In Walker, T., & Gramlich, D. (Eds.), *The Palgrave Handbook of Sustainable Finance* (pp. 585–610). Springer Nature Switzerland., DOI: 10.1007/978-3-031-98736-6_26

Konurbayeva, Z., Sánchez-García, E., Marco-Lajara, B., Sloniec, J., Martínez-Falcó, J., & Baitikenova, G. (2026). Leading Sustainable Competitive Advantage From Within: An Analysis of the Mining Industry. *Sustainable Development*, sd.70753. DOI: 10.1002/sd.70753

Kulkov, I., Kulkova, J., Rohrbeck, R., Menvielle, L., Kaartemo, V., & Makkonen, H. (2024). Artificial intelligence - driven sustainable development: Examining organizational, technical, and processing approaches to achieving global goals. *Sustainable Development (Bradford)*, *32*(3), 2253–2267. DOI: 10.1002/sd.2773

Kuram, Ç., & Bilişik, Ö. N. (2025a). A mixed-integer linear programming model proposal to determine material sustainability for new product development processes in production. *Computers & Chemical Engineering*, *198*, 109108. DOI: 10.1016/j.compchemeng.2025.109108

Kuram, Ç., & Bilişik, Ö. N. (2025b). A mixed-integer linear programming model proposal to determine material sustainability for new product development processes in production. *Computers & Chemical Engineering*, *198*, 109108. DOI: 10.1016/j.compchemeng.2025.109108

Lee, S. U., Perera, H., Liu, Y., Xia, B., Lu, Q., Zhu, L., Cairns, J., & Nottage, M. (2025). Integrating ESG and AI: A comprehensive responsible AI assessment framework. *AI and Ethics*, *5*(5), 5121–5148. DOI: 10.1007/s43681-025-00741-5

Li, N., Kim, M., Dai, J., & Vasarhelyi, M. A. (2024). Using artificial intelligence in ESG assurance. *Journal of Emerging Technologies in Accounting*, *21*(2), 83–99. DOI: 10.2308/JETA-2022-054

Lim, T. (2024). Environmental, social, and governance (ESG) and artificial intelligence in finance: State-of-the-art and research takeaways. *Artificial Intelligence Review*, *57*(4), 76. DOI: 10.1007/s10462-024-10708-3

Lin, Y., & Yu, Z. (2025). An integrated bibliometric analysis and systematic review modelling students' technostress in higher education. *Behaviour & Information Technology*, *44*(4), 631–655. DOI: 10.1080/0144929X.2024.2332458

Liu, Y., Song, J., Zhou, B., & Liu, J. (2025). Artificial intelligence applications and corporate ESG performance. *International Review of Economics & Finance*, *104*, 104559. DOI: 10.1016/j.iref.2025.104559

Marampa, A. M., Pongtuluran, A. K., & Pariyanti, E. (2025). From sharing to success: Enhancing innovative work behavior through psychological empowerment and kinship employee engagement. *Industrial and Commercial Training*, *57*(1), 99–117. DOI: 10.1108/ICT-07-2024-0064

Marlia, M. A., Fahmy, R., Lukito, H., & Games, D. (2025). An Exploratory Study on Effective Leadership and Change Management in the Transformation of Indonesian Public Universities Towards World-Class University Status. *Sustainability (Basel)*, *17*(3), 1300. DOI: 10.3390/su17031300

Matindike, S., Mago, S., Modiba, F., & Van Den Berg, A. (2026). A Review of Digital Transformation and Sustainable International Agricultural Businesses in Africa. In T. Choudhury, R. K. Singh, R. Tomar, S. Balamurugan, & J. C. Patni (Eds.), *Distributed Time-Sensitive Systems* (1st ed., pp. 249–281). Wiley. DOI: 10.1002/9781394197798.ch10

Nara, I., Sarun, H., & Hun, H. (2026). Adoption of Artificial Intelligence for Sustainable Development of Higher Education Systems: Nano Review. *Journal of Agriculture and Environment*, *3*(2), 53–55.

Naser-Karajah, E. (2026). The Role of Digital Transformation in Enhancing Corporate Sustainability: A Conceptual Study on Palestinian Institutions Using Digital Twin and Cloud Computing Within the ESG Framework. In Awwad, B., & Awwad, R. A. (Eds.), *Technology and Innovation Towards a Future of Business Sustainability* (pp. 3–13). Springer Nature Singapore., DOI: 10.1007/978-981-95-6469-9_1

Neama, N. H., & Dulaimi, A. A. (2025). *The Role of Organizational Agility as a Mediator in the Relationship Between Authentic Leadership and Organizational Citizenship Behaviour. 7*(2).

Negm, E. (2026). Artificial intelligence (AI) usage in higher education: Technology integration into curriculums to attain UN sustainable development goals. *Journal of Applied Research in Higher Education, 18*(2), 616–631. DOI: 10.1108/JARHE-04-2025-0275

Ningtyas, H. I. R., Mualim, W., & Nusron, A. (2026). Artificial Intelligence in The Application of ESG to Improve Company Reputation: The Moderating Role of Financial Performance. *Journal of Accounting Science, 10*(1), 60–81. DOI: 10.21070/jas.v10i1.2047

Nordin, A. S. M., Alias, B. S., & Haniff, M. H. M. (2023). *Organizational Change Through Transformational Leadership Practices: The Principal's Role.* https://kwpublications.com/papers_submitted/7882/organizational-change-through-transformational-leadership-practices-the-principals-role.pdf

Nugraha, R., Mayagita, A., Satriansyah, A., & Oktiyani, R. (2026). Sustainable Digital Accounting: Integrating ESG Reporting and Data Analytics in the Era of Industry 5.0. *Jurnal Visi Manajemen, 12*(1), 182–193.

Oehmichen, J., Geist, L., & Weck, M. (2025). AI and ESG. *Annals of Corporate Governance, 9*(4), 280–345. DOI: 10.1561/109.00000048

Ozkan, B. (2024). *The transformative impact of AI on CSR, ESG, and sustainability: Critical review and case studies.* https://www.emerald.com/books/edited-volume/17319/chapter/94286953

Padhy, A., Rane, N. L., & Rane, J. (2026). Explainable artificial intelligence for sustainable business performance: Integrating ESG metrics into AI adoption models. *International Journal of Applied Resilience and Sustainability, 2*(1), 78–96. DOI: 10.70593/deepsci.0201005

Peng, H., & Peng, Y. (2026). Is Supply Chain Digitalization Conducive to Promoting the ESG Performance of Energy-Intensive Firms? *Sustainability (Basel), 18*(4), 1879. DOI: 10.3390/su18041879

Ragadhita, R., Fiandini, M., Al Husaeni, D. N., & Nandiyanto, A. B. D. (2026). Sustainable development goals (SDGs) in engineering education: Definitions, research trends, bibliometric insights, and strategic approaches. *Indonesian Journal of Science and Technology, 11*(1), 1–26. DOI: 10.17509/ijost.v11i1.86298

Razmak, J., & Farhan, W. (2026). A proposed digital transformation model for implementation by digital leaders. *Smart and Sustainable Built Environment, 15*(1), 92–119. DOI: 10.1108/SASBE-11-2023-0369

Sadraei, R., & Dal Mas, F. (2026). Women entrepreneurship in the age of AI and ESG: Micro- and macro-level drivers of adoption. *International Journal of Entrepreneurship and Innovation, 14657503251408253*, 14657503251408253. Advance online publication. DOI: 10.1177/14657503251408253

Sætra, H. S. (2021). A framework for evaluating and disclosing the ESG related impacts of AI with the SDGs. *Sustainability (Basel), 13*(15), 8503. DOI: 10.3390/su13158503

Sætra, H. S. (2023). The AI ESG protocol: Evaluating and disclosing the environment, social, and governance implications of artificial intelligence capabilities, assets, and activities. *Sustainable Development (Bradford), 31*(2), 1027–1037. DOI: 10.1002/sd.2438

Selim, O. (2020). ESG and AI: The beauty and the beast of sustainable investing. In *Sustainable investing* (pp. 227–243). Routledge. https://www.taylorfrancis.com/chapters/edit/10.4324/9780429351044-12/esg-ai-omar-selim

Shen, P., Qing, L., Wu, L., & Qi, L. (2025). When you find the ESG performance in digital transformation: A look at firms' internal controls, absorptive capacity, and green innovativeness. *Applied Economics*, •••, 1–20. DOI: 10.1080/00036846.2025.2607071

Sida, T. S., Desalegn, T., Abate, G. T., & Amede, T. (2025). 3 Feeding a fast-growing population by 2050 through accelerated agricultural transformation: Potential avenues for Ethiopia. *Pathways to African Food Security*, 35.

Su, Y., & Abd Rani, N. S. (2025). Empowering Leadership and Psychological Capital: Drivers of Teachers' Innovative Behavior among International School Teachers in Beijing City. *Uniglobal Journal of Social Sciences and Humanities, 4*(1), 66–75.

Sugiyanto, H. (2025). Leadership Styles, Quality of Education, and Educational Institution Management: A Systematic Review in the Perspective of Sustainable Education. *Journal Corner of Education, Linguistics, and Literature, 4*(3), 351–359. DOI: 10.54012/jcell.v4i3.423

Sun, Y., Lu, Y., Wu, Y., Xu, C., & Davey, H. (2026). Synergizing ESG and Digital Transformation for Corporate Decarbonization. *Business Strategy and the Environment, 35*(2), 2581–2599. DOI: 10.1002/bse.70262

Suradinkura, S., Amornbuth, C., Fang, Y., Suradinkura, V., & Suradinkura, N. (2026). Digital Transformation and Environmental Governance: A Synthesis of ESG Integration. In *Green Governance of Digital Organizations* (pp. 125–156). IGI Global Scientific Publishing. https://www.igi-global.com/chapter/digital-transformation-and-environmental-governance/401458

Taleizadeh, A. A., Tahmasbifar, Z., Moradi, R., Sarker, B. R., & Hafezalkotob, A. (2025). An optimum decision-making strategy to maximize total profit in a two-period closed-loop supply chain dealing with greenhouse gases. *Annals of Operations Research*. Advance online publication. DOI: 10.1007/s10479-025-06610-y

Teruel-Sanchez, R., Briones-Peñalver, A. J., Bernal-Conesa, J. A., & De Nieves-Nieto, C. (2025). Values of the entrepreneur as a driver of sustainable tourism entrepreneurship. *Journal of International Entrepreneurship*, *23*(3), 648–676. Advance online publication. DOI: 10.1007/s10843-025-00381-0

Thien, L. M., Lim, H. L., Ahmad Shabudin, A. F., Che Aman, R., Ismail, A., Zuharah, W. F., & Muftahu, M. (2025). Women leadership in higher education: Exploring enablers and challenges from middle-level academics' perspective. *Humanities & Social Sciences Communications*, *12*(1), 1–12. DOI: 10.1057/s41599-024-04278-6

Tian, H., Wang, J., & Cai, Y. (2025). Artificial Intelligence Adoption and Corporate ESG Performance. *Business Strategy and the Environment*, *34*(7), 8922–8945. DOI: 10.1002/bse.70032

Tiron-Tudor, A., Deliu, D., & Ndou, V. (2025). Shaping the future: Ethical, legal and social implications (ELSI) of digital innovation ecosystems (DIEs) amid the Twin Transition. *European Journal of Innovation Management*, •••, 1–45.

Umoru, U., Ogundana, O. M., Mangena, M., & Udeozor, V. (2026). Informal Institutions and Multinationals' Drive Towards Sustainable Development Goals (SDGs): A Dark-Side Perspective. *Business Ethics, the Environment & Responsibility*, *35*(1), 75–98. DOI: 10.1111/beer.12773

Vukmir, R. B. (2006). Customer satisfaction. *International Journal of Health Care Quality Assurance*, *19*(1), 8–31. DOI: 10.1108/09526860610642573 PMID: 16548396

Wang, J., Ma, Y., Li, R., & Zhang, S. (2025). Applications of Building Information Modeling (BIM) and BIM-Related Technologies for Sustainable Risk and Disaster Management in Buildings: A Meta-Analysis (2014–2024). *Buildings (Basel, Switzerland)*, *15*(13), 2289. DOI: 10.3390/buildings15132289

Wang, Q., Qi, Y., & Li, R. (2026). Artificial Intelligence and Corporate Sustainability: Shaping the Future of ESG in the Age of Industry 5.0. *Sustainable Development (Bradford), 34*(1), 1–26. DOI: 10.1002/sd.70200

Wang, Q., Zhang, F., & Li, R. (2025). Artificial intelligence and sustainable development during urbanization: Perspectives on AI R&D innovation, AI infrastructure, and AI market advantage. *Sustainable Development (Bradford), 33*(1), 1136–1156. DOI: 10.1002/sd.3150

Xiao, S., Roh, T., Park, B. I., AL-Tabbaa, O., & Seo, K. (2026). Unpacking the Role of Digital Dynamic Capabilities in ESG Performance: A Social Exchange Perspective on Organizational Trust and Identification. *Business Strategy and the Environment, 35*(2), 1951–1969. DOI: 10.1002/bse.70273

Xu, J. (2024). AI in ESG for financial institutions: An industrial survey. *arXiv Preprint arXiv:2403.05541*. https://arxiv.org/abs/2403.05541 DOI: 10.2139/ssrn.4949354

Yakob, M., Sahudra, T. M., & Sukirno, S. (2025). Transformational Leadership of Principals: Driving Excellence in Education Quality. *Al-Ishlah: Jurnal Pendidikan, 17*(1), 1658–1667. DOI: 10.35445/alishlah.v17i1.6887

Yan, M.-R., Yan, H., Chen, Y.-R., Zhang, Y., Yan, X., & Zhao, Y. (2026). Integrated green supply chain system development with digital transformation. *International Journal of Logistics, 29*(3), 394–415. DOI: 10.1080/13675567.2025.2492217

Yim, I. H. Y., & Su, J. (2024). Artificial intelligence (AI) learning tools in K-12 education: A scoping review. *Journal of Computers in Education*. Advance online publication. DOI: 10.1007/s40692-023-00304-9

Zarghami, S. A. (2025). The role of economic policies in achieving sustainable development goal 7: Insights from OECD and European countries. *Applied Energy, 377*, 124558. DOI: 10.1016/j.apenergy.2024.124558

Zhang, C., & Yang, J. (2024). Artificial intelligence and corporate ESG performance. *International Review of Economics & Finance, 96*, 103713. DOI: 10.1016/j.iref.2024.103713

Zheng, Z., & Lee, C. L. (2025). A meta-analysis of ESG factors in the real estate investment trusts sector: Exploring their impacts on REITs performance. *Engineering, Construction and Architectural Management*. https://www.emerald.com/ecam/article/doi/10.1108/ECAM-05-2024-0652/1259586

Chapter 2
A TOE–RBV–Endogenous Growth Framework for AI–Driven Economic Transformation:
From Human Capital to Hybrid Intelligence in Digital India

Piali Haldar
http://orcid.org/0000-0003-4729-6964
Brainware University, Kolkata, India

Dev Kumar Mandal
http://orcid.org/0009-0005-3740-6885
Brainware University, Kolkata, India

ABSTRACT

This chapter discusses the progression from human capital to hybrid intelligence in the context of Digital India based on a combined TOE–RBV–Endogenous Growth framework. We analyse how AI adoption can enhance workforce capabilities and foster hybrid intelligence, thereby leading to economic growth. Survey and data analysis using SEM show the mediating role of hybrid intelligence in the relationship between AI adoption and productivity. This association is further shaped by institutional support. The study calls for strategic reskilling and a proper policy response to anchor the AI-driven economic transformation.

DOI: 10.4018/979-8-2600-0116-5.ch002

1. INTRODUCTION

Radical shifts in the economy are evolving as a consequence of the fast-paced developments in AI, automation, and digital technologies. These trends work in redefining the boundaries, overhauling systems of work relations, production techniques, and restructuring the concepts of factors of economic growth (Doughan, 2020). The traditional economic models, which place more emphasis on physical capital and labour as the major determinants of productivity, are shifting to more knowledge and technology-intensive strategies of enhancing productivity. In this new economic order, human capital – defined by the level of education, skills, and experience of an individual – was a key factor that determined disparities in productivity, and consequently economic outcomes, among different societies (Becker, 1964). So far, AI is also challenging our traditional understandings of human capital by providing new modes of capability that bridge human intelligence with machine learning systems.

Digital transformation has accelerated the integration of AI into almost every sector of the Indian economy (Dhanabalan & Sathish, 2018). India is one of the fastest-growing digital economies, where AI integration into the economic process has great scope to enhance productivity and innovations (Jain & Bishnoi, 2025). Transforming both employment and skills requirements and human capital features in an AI-based economy is a fact that should not be taken lightly (Brynjolfsson & McAfee, 2014).

Hybrid intelligence is the progress in which human cognitive abilities formally interact with the artificial intelligence algorithm. It doesn't replace human labour through automation; hybrid intelligence augments human logic, creativity, and problem-solving by having machines work alongside the human, creating an intellectual symbiosis (Dellermann et al. 2019). This paradigm shift also tells us that, in the AI era, economic growth would become increasingly reliant on the quality of human capital-and how it interacts with smart technologies, rather than merely the quantity. Transitioning from human capital to hybrid intelligence will represent a paradigm shift in what creates economic value (Rachid et al., 2024).

While conducting this change, the foundation of the theory could be developed in a combination of perspectives. Endogenous Growth Models, as formulated by Paul Romer (1990), have laid some emphasis on knowledge, innovation, and human capital as means to achieve sustainable long-run growth. However, since knowledge creation in the AI era is more and more mediated by intelligent systems, posited to follow from extending this frame of reference in the AI-enabled capabilities (Santos et al., 2025). The theory of the Resource-Based View (RBV) argues that resources are the key sources of competitive advantage and from which competitive advantage arises; among the resources that together contribute to differentiate the firm from others are resources that are valuable, rare, inimitable, and non-substitutable (Barney, 1991). Thus, the conceptualization of hybrid intelligence that combines human and machine capabilities as an example of a strategically valuable resource will meet the criteria of increasing organizational performance and economic growth.

The technological innovation involving AI is thus examined through the lens of the Technology–Organization–Environment (TOE) framework (Tornatzky & Fleischer, 1990). The TOE framework categorizes a plethora of factors as facilitators or retarded by contextual conditions with ecological effects on innovation, accepting that some external environmental conditions are important for organizational innovativeness. Keeping this in mind, the contextual conditions in India, like governmental initiatives, digital infrastructure, and institutional support, can help us to make projections on how the adoption of AI would lead to economic outcomes.

Though a plethora of literature on AI, skills, and economic growth has emerged, there are huge gaps in research that addresses the integration of these dimensions into a unified analysis framework. Most studies adopted AI at the firm-level for economic growth at a macro level without ever addressing the mediating qualities of skilling and hybrid intelligence. There is very limited empirical evidence on emerging economies like India, where the dynamics of digital transformation are shaped by unique, socio-economic, and institutional factors (Autor, 2015). Hence, a comprehensive framework may be recommended that captures the multi-level interactions of AI, skills, and economic growth.

The study will aim to fill this gap by proposing and empirically testing an integrated TOE–RBV–Endogenous Growth framework for analysing the shift from human capital to hybrid intelligence in Digital India. This research intends to answer: (i) How will AI adoption influence the enhancement of workforce skills? (ii) How does the skill transformation prepare the ground to develop hybrid intelligence? (iii) Which effect is going to be the most significant of all as a function of the volume of the hybrid intelligence dealing with an economic developmental state? (iv) How do ecological and institutional factors confine the said relationships?

The study aims to fill the conceptual gap in order to address the consequences that can be anticipated when traditional conceptual models, such as hybridity, are developed to increase productivity and creativity. The focus of this paper is to look at the capacity of integrating aspects from several theories to explain the process of AI-driven economic restructuring. Likewise, other than to policy makers, corporate sector managers, and institutions of learning, for that matter, at the end of the study, the report may bring out some guidelines for the way forward in areas of capacity building, resources generation, and economic transformation in general.

An Indian situation in a large, diverse workforce struggles to acquire skills and also learn AI, a faceoff that challenges those of the Western world is quite different. In many of the contexts, these structures should not be left static but should be transformed into a pervasive aspiration where learning is ubiquitous, literacy is broadened into digital literacy, critical thinking is accelerated, and there is enhanced collaboration with machines. Whenever AI continues impacting lives, training, and upskilling relevance appears even more, as AI should be instrumental in guiding areas with employment and the economy as a whole.

Essentially, moving from human capital to hybrid intelligence is a progressive idea when it comes to looking at ways of driving growth in the digital era. It involves gauging how valuable people are in combination with artificial intelligence, and the result is always the overcoming of new limits for economies. For countries such as India, which is ahead of many others, this is an almost unique opportunity to harness demographic dividend plus technical know-how to achieve the most needed growth that is inside development, achieving 'growth' and not just 'development in itself.' This opened the whole chapter on how to conceptualize and operationalize the transition, helping to repair the broader debate on the future of work in AI's economies.

2. LITERATURE REVIEW

Today's economic and management research increasingly feels the pressing need to investigate the interactions of Artificial Intelligence, up-skilling strategies, and economic development. With the rise of knowledge-based economies from labor-intensive economies, the role of human capital changes fundamentally due to its integration with intelligent technologies. Five domains are covered in this section: reviews of literature (i) about human capital and economic growth, (ii) focusing on AI and changes in the workforce, (iii) also touching on critical hybrid intelligence, (iv) the theoretical provisions on which much is expected, such as the Technology-Organization- Environment (TOE) framework, and RBV, (v) the part played by AI in endogenous growth processes.

2.1 Human Capital and Economic Growth

The Human Capital Theory is known as a fundamental stimulant that boosts economic progress. It started with the acknowledgment of the early propositions of Becker (1964), which highlighted that possibly resources being invested in education and training lead to improvement in efficiency in the individual due to rising aggregate economic growth. Schultz (1961) argued that human capital development involves a more intelligent, innovative workforce.

Other growth theorists, represented by Paul Romer (1990), have extended the same concept with the idea of knowledge and technological change becoming integral to economic growth. These scholars consider human development as a driver when it comes to making efforts on how to develop and manage technology-based productivity. They assert that through innovation, the extremely enhanced quality of human capital results in output and productive efficiency perfection at a compound rate. While this perception is dominantly construed under education and experience, which are the two instrumental variables of the empirical models, it does not provide for the distinction on the changing roles of competencies in the digital economy, which often frustrates improvement.

Numerous studies conducted in the recent past have recognized that traditional human capital perspectives are insufficient to comprehend the intricacies of today's technological environment (Tan, 2014; Marginson, 2019). To illustrate a point, Acemoglu and Autor (2011) suggested that an improvement in technological capabilities is altering the skills demanded from workers, thus resulting in a splitting of the labour market. The notion uniformly invoked by these economists is that not all forms of human capital contribute equally to growth and that the quality of skills, his adaptability, is ever more important.

2.2 Artificial Intelligence and Workforce Transformation

AI advancement has resulted in numerous drastic changes within the labour market due to the alterations induced by AI on skill requirements. Machine learning, natural language processing, and the development of robotics all combine to advance AI needed to complete tasks that essentially separate themselves from the realm of human intelligentsia. Problematically, this has led to concerns of job displacement and increased productivity for businesses (Brynjolfsson & McAfee, 2014).

Prior research has established that AI is not just about changing labour, but in reality, it complements labour in the sense that it enhances human capacity. Autor (2015) has revealed that while automating routine tasks, those that rely on physical or cognitive but not necessarily highly skilled labour shall be automated. The begrudgingly instigated trend suggests not only the doom of less demanding job opportunities, but also the demand for advanced skills, like those of critical thinkers, problem solvers, and digitally literate persons (Dumitru & Halpern, 2023).

The fast-paced adoption of AI in the Indian setting is reshaping industries, including IT, finance, healthcare, and manufacturing (Jain & Bishnoi, 2025). By further implementation of Digital India, the government has fast-tracked the development of the digital domain for enhancing workforce development and opportunities. Research reveals that reskilling and upskilling of the workforce are pivotal to ensuring that the workforce remains relevant in an AI-driven economy (World Economic Forum, 2025).

2.3 Hybrid Intelligence: Concept and Implications

Hybrid intelligence has emerged as a serious concept for appreciating human interactions with artificial intelligence systems. Hybrid intelligence represents the integration of human cognitive ability and machine intelligence to achieve superior systems (Dellermann et al., 2019). There is a significant distinction between traditional automation and hybrid intelligence; the former replaces the human with a computer or a machine system, while in the latter, the machine's role mainly assumes the metaphor of enhancement and collaboration (Jarrahi et al., 2022).

An insightful observation is that hybrid intelligence can be considered as a human potential growth factor in the process of which strengthening of competencies by knowledge and training is not the only option (Krinyon et al., 2023). The last assumption has profound implications for performance, creativity, possibilities, and competitiveness. For instance, Jarrahi (2018) argued that human-AI collaboration can foster better decision-making through the integration of human intuition and data-generated insights.

Empirical studies show that organizations benefiting from the use of hybrid intelligence are superior in their abilities to innovate and adapt quickly to changes in the market (Taljaard, 2022). This has turned out to be one key driver for economic growth in the mobilization for AI. However, the issue is still unexplored from the perspective of the companies in the case of developing economies; therefore, more research is needed.

2.4 Theoretical Foundations: TOE and RBV

The TOE (Technology-Operation-Environment) framework developed by Tornatzky and Fleischer in 1990 serves as a broad model for the analysis of the adoption and diffusion of technological innovations. The framework highlights the three contexts of technological, organizational, and environmental factors (Tornatzky and Fleischer, 1990), where technological factors include a range of conditions like relative advantage and complexity, organizational factors include size and resources/capabilities, and environmental factors include competition, regulations, and infrastructure.

AI incorporation employs the TOE model on a wide scale to see how AI technologies become part of organizational daily operations (Min & Kim, 2024). In more detail, technological readiness, organizational culture, and government regulations-and other policy issues-each have an impact on the extent and effectiveness of AI adoption (Oliveria & Martins, 2011). In India, policy backing and investment in digital infrastructure are the main facilitators of AI-induced transformation.

The RBV forms the complementary piece to the TOE; it sheds light on the role of the companies' internal resources and capabilities as sources of competitive advantage that can be leveraged by AI. Barney (1991) posits that resources that are valuable, rare, inimitable, and non-substitutable VRIN) speak about resources that are valuable, rare, hard to imitate, and without substitutes, constituting sources of a distinct competitive edge. Therefore, in AI, hybrid intelligence can be well perceived as a strategic resource suited for these criteria.

Recent studies have suggested that AI, when combined with human skills, creates hard-to-replicate unique capabilities, therefore directly improving organizational performance (Makridakis, 2017), rather than confirming that what matters with hybrid intelligence is not so much the technology but the strategic asset itself, yielding advances that translate into long-term growth.

2.5 AI and Endogenous Growth Dynamics

From a macroeconomic point of view, endogenous growth theory emphasizes that innovation and knowledge are fundamentally determining factors in the growth process. This line of thinking emerged from Paul Romer (1990) theorizing that investment in human capital is crucial to innovation, and R&D becomes an innovative economic process aimed at ever-increasing productivity. Now, AI, as an all-encompassing technology, can best support a variety of these processes.

Aghion and Howitt (1990) emphasize that economic growth tends to be linked to innovation and creative destruction, the latter consisting of technological advances fostering some form of opportunities, but at the same time leading to destabilization. AI can benefit from this knowledge by ensuring that more improvements will continue to enrich the process, and that workers will be busy learning and practicing in a changing environment (Sundaresan & Zhang, 2022).

A new study has included AI in endogenous growth models to stress that it helps in productivity and innovation (Cockburn et al., 2018). Such studies suggest the roles of AI in speeding knowledge generation and diffusion, thereby enhancing economic progress. Nevertheless, much of this acceleration will depend on the availability of skilled labour and macro-level supportive frameworks.

2.6 Theoretical Framework and Hypotheses Development.

Table 1. Comparative Literature Synthesis and Research Gap Analysis

Author(s)	Context	Core Focus	ESG Dimension	Digital Technology Dimension	Ethical AI Dimension	Strategic Leadership Dimension	Methodology	Key Findings	Research Gap
Fatemi et al. (2018)	Global firms	ESG performance and firm value	✓	X	X	X	Quantitative	ESG improves firm value and investor confidence	Does not examine digital transformation drivers of ESG performance
Dwivedi et al. (2021)	Digital organizations	AI opportunities and governance challenges	X	✓ AI	✓	X	Conceptual Review	AI creates innovation opportunities but raises ethical concerns	Lacks ESG integration and empirical validation
George et al. (2021)	Entrepreneurship ecosystems	Digital sustainability and innovation	Partial	✓	X	X	Conceptual	Digital innovation contributes to sustainability objectives	Ethical governance mechanisms remain unexplored
Floridi et al. (2018)	AI governance	Ethical AI principles	X	✓ AI	✓	X	Conceptual	Transparency, accountability, and fairness are central to AI ethics	No linkage with ESG outcomes or leadership capabilities
Martínez-Peláez et al. (2023)	Sustainability transformation	Digital transformation and sustainability	✓	✓	Partial	X	Empirical	Digital capabilities improve sustainability performance	Ethical digital transformation not considered
Rosário & Cruz (2025)	Digital organizations	Ethical digital transformation	Partial	✓	✓	X	Conceptual	Ethical governance is essential for sustainable digitalization	ESG performance implications remain unclear
Doz & Kosonen (2010)	Strategic management	Strategic agility and adaptation	X	X	X	✓	Conceptual	Agile leadership supports organizational renewal	Does not address AI ethics or ESG integration
Present Study	India's Creative Economy	ESG–Digital Nexus through AI-Driven Ethical Transformation	✓	✓	✓	✓	PLS-SEM	Examines how AI capabilities and Big Data/ IoT drive ESG performance through Ethical Digital Transformation while Strategic Leadership Agility strengthens this relationship	Addresses the integrated gap by simultaneously examining ESG, AI ethics, digital transformation, strategic leadership, and sustainable creative economy development within a unified empirical framework

2.7 Research Gap Identified

1. There have been significant advances in the study of ESG performance, digital transformation, artificial intelligence management, and effective administration, on the one hand. However, there are still four main realms that need further research and attention.
2. Environmental, social, and governance principles are equipped with ESG, which is the acronym for Environmental, Social, and Governance. However, as much as the contribution of other things to ESG studies has been quite immense, digital is still behind, given that it is yet to be fully captured for ESG studies (Li et al., 2021).
3. Studies on artificial intelligence and digital transformation outline a wide scope. Even historical reviews of the field never stay outside the area of innovation. However, the existing literature on Ethical AI pays more focus on fairness, accountability, and transparency, without an empirical verification of how ethical digital transformation enhances ESG.
4. The interaction of AI-composed digital technologies and ethical digital improvements as corporates adopt strategic approaches will be examined. Such a review will be affected by the diversification of organizations, shifting from strategic leadership agility as an element to address the asynchronous and considerate approach, rather than focusing only on satisfaction effects beyond cost considerations for the various community-based initiatives.

With that in mind, the objective of this research is to elaborate with reference to Table 1, an inclusive framework that is firmly rooted in existing research and which recognises both ESG and Digital Transformative Design, these are dual-purpose digital technologies for the advancement of a new economy in India.

2.8 Research Objectives

1. To examine the impact of AI adoption on skill enhancement in India
2. To analyse the formation of hybrid intelligence as a strategic capability
3. To assess the relationship between hybrid intelligence and economic growth
4. To evaluate the moderating role of institutional and environmental factors

3. CONCEPTUAL FRAMEWORK AND HYPOTHESIS DEVELOPMENT

An integrated concept, including operational parameters within the Digital India initiative, to explain the channelling of economic performance through AI adoption in the transformation of human capital to hybrid intelligence, has been developed. The framework is suggested as a blend of multidisciplinary research constructs, TOE (Technology–Organization–Environment), the Resource-Based View (RBV), and Endogenous Growth Theory.

Our framework argues that AI adoption is a catalyst for the addition of skills for the workforce, leading subsequently to the development of hybrid intelligence. This set of hybrid intelligence connotes the association of human cognitive skills with AI systems and acts as a mechanism of mediation for the technological adoption with economic growth outcomes. Moreover, institutional and environmental factors are found in moderating roles that affect the strength of these relationships.

3.1 Conceptual Framework

The Technology-Organisation-Environment (TOE) framework helps explain AI adoption by looking at three key aspects: technological readiness, organizational capability, and environmental backing (Tornatzky & Fleischer, 1990). In practice, the way India moves forward with digital infrastructure, plus improvements in organizational learning culture, and the government programs like Digital India, within India, together end up shaping the conditions and the overall effectiveness of putting AI to work.

The resource-based view (RBV) complements that by framing hybrid intellect as a strategic organizational resource. As Barney (1991) notes, resources that are valuable, rare, inimitable, and non-substitutable (VRIN) can support sustained competitive advantage. Hybrid intellect seems to match these ideas because it blends human creativity and contextual comprehension, together with artificial intelligence's computational efficiency, in order to push productivity and boost innovation.

On a more macro level, knowledge accumulation, innovation, and skill development policies have been of much interest for the long-term view on economic growth after Endogenous Growth Theory was put forward by Paul Romer in 1990, with a link to hybrid intelligence for acquisition. In this study, we propose that the embodiment of hybrid intelligence, as knowledge capital, forms a stronger capacity for perpetual innovation and growth in productivity, which then lifts overall GDP.

Integrating these perspectives, the conceptual model proposes a sequential relationship:

AI Adoption → Skill Enhancement → Hybrid Intelligence → Economic Growth, with institutional support and digital infrastructure acting as moderating variables.

3.2 Hypothesis Development

AI Adoption and Skill Enhancement

AI now transforms the way work is approached by mechanizing routine labour while also generating requirements for higher cognitive and digital skills. With artificial intelligence systems in place, industries employing this technology need personnel to develop analytical prowess (in the form of data analytics), algorithmic thought processes, and digital cooperation in order to grow. Existing literature suggests that technology being adopted into an organization has an identification with enhancing the skill set(s) of the workforce, which, definitely, provides for learning capabilities to develop as well (Brynjolfsson & McAfee, 2014).

H1: AI adoption positively influences workforce skill enhancement.

Skill Enhancement and Hybrid Intelligence

Skill development has a huge role in making human-machine cooperation really effective in business. As employees develop further digital and cognitive skills, they will be more qualified to interact with AI, thereby giving birth to hybrid intelligence. 'Hybrid intelligence' then emerges, whereby the human skillset is complemented by machine intelligence, resulting in overall advanced results in decision-making and innovation.

H2: Workforce skill enhancement positively influences the development of hybrid intelligence.

Hybrid Intelligence and Economic Growth

Hybrid intelligence has the potential to enhance productivity by improving decision-making quality and lowering errors while accelerating the process of innovation. From an endogenous growth perspective, such improvements would deliver higher output levels and sustained economic growth over the long term. Organizations that use AI to raise the bar in their performance and secure competitive advantage are believed to perform better on the efficiency front as well (Cockburn et al., 2018).

H3: Hybrid intelligence positively impacts economic growth.

Mediating Role of Hybrid Intelligence

When AI comes for processes, AI is directly an essence of productivity and maintains a partial indirect influence on economic growth through its effects on the transformation of competences, thanks to skill transformation and hybrid intelligence. If proper skill development is not pursued, the benefits of AI adoption may never be seen. In the interpretation of technological capability into economic outcomes, hybrid intelligence makes that bridge.

H4: Hybrid intelligence mediates the relationship between AI adoption and economic growth.

Moderating Role of Institutional Support

Institutional support enables the adoption of AI to a greater extent through its government policies, regulations, and digital infrastructure policies. In India, policy initiatives and investments in digital ecosystems significantly influence the ability of organizations to adopt and utilize AI technologies. Therefore, a supportive environment is beneficial in enhancing the relationship between both technology adoption and performance outcomes (Oliveira & Martins, 2011).

H5: Institutional support positively moderates the relationship between AI adoption and hybrid intelligence.

Figure 1. Conceptual Framework and Hypothesis Development

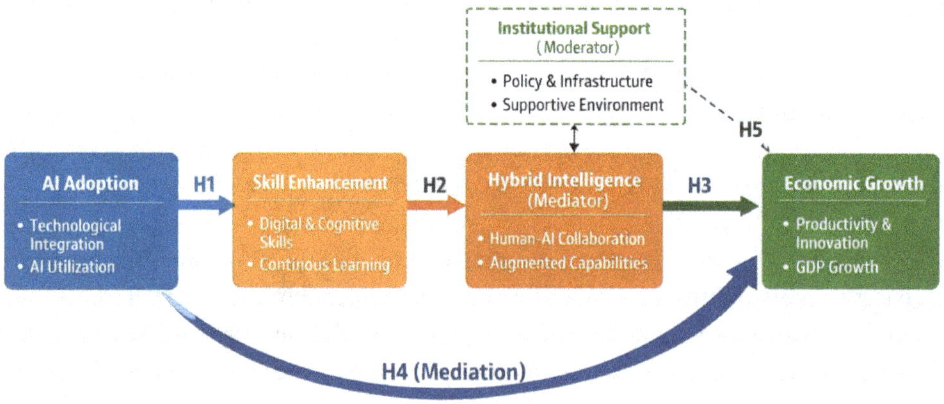

Source: Created by Author

The term Artificial Intelligence (AI) skills transformation within the frame of Figure 1 is seen economically, but also in a more contextual way. The model comes from combining the TOE, RBV, and the endogenous growth theories, and it reflects how technological, organizational, and macroeconomic components work together. Support driven by AI for moving away from traditional human capital toward hybrid intelligence is highlighted as an essential pathway for influencing economic performance; in practice, that interaction matters.

This model feels more tailored to India, where fast tech advancement and a huge labour force create an opening for AI-driven transformation in general, and in practice. It lays out the route where AI impacts growth, and it also points to certain key levers for intervention, like upskilling and institutional backing, so things do not stall.

4. RESEARCH METHODOLOGY

In this study, a mixed-method design is used so that we can examine the shift from human capital to hybrid intelligence and what it brings, in terms of economic growth, in India's digital environment. Using both quantitative approaches and qualitative methods, the aims are clearly set to grasp how AI deployment relates to belief improvement, hybrid intelligence, and economic outcomes. The research adopts a deductive approach grounded in existing theoretical frameworks, the Technology-Organization-Environment (TOE) paradigm, the Resource-Based View (RBV) paradigm, and endogenous growth theory, which are used to develop support for the hypothesis to be tested.

4.1 Sampling Frame and Data Collection Procedure

The sampling frame consisted of creative industry professionals and opinion formers who are actively participating in the creative economy or the digital innovation system of India. The respondents were sourced from companies that function within the sectors of media and entertainment, e-services, manufacturing, management, advertising, culture, high-tech, as well as ecologically sensitive business activities. The population targeted included CEOs, sustainability officers, innovation chiefs, digital evolution experts, company ESG managers, prescriptive planning specialists, and other top managers who are directly taking the initiatives and running digital and sustainable projects, as part of the organizations.

The researcher resorted to purposive sampling owing to the necessity of special people who are professionals in ESG implementation, artificial intelligence implementation, the use of technology, and, finally, strategic leadership. The selected industries were further covered using stratified sampling techniques in the field of major cultural industries. with the relevant training and advanced manufacturing industries. The sampling in total covered from January to April and in 2026 involved structured offline and online questionnaires that were dispatched through respective trade groups, professional bodies, LinkedIn groups, start-ups, as well as people known professionally. 550 questionnaires were given out. After removing responses with sub-standard answers as well as useless observations in the questionnaires, nearly 412 responses were analysed, leading to the final response rate of about 75%.

4.2 Response Rate Justification

The final response rate of 74.9% exceeds the minimum thresholds, which are often suggested for organizational and management research. It is advised by guidelines that response rates above 60% are satisfactory and enable the reduction of sampling error or improving representativeness. The high response rate found within the research is mainly due to the pertinence of the ESG and digital transformation areas, as communicated to industry experts in the follow-up emails, as well as in the recent conference, which made their participation topic-relevant. Consequently, the obtained sample was regarded as sufficient for performing Partial Least Squares Structural Equation Modelling (PLS-SEM).

In addition, for PLS-SEM, the ten times rule - minimum recommended power analysis estimate was obtained within the survey, which means that the population of usable samples is a good one to perform the structural equation modelling.

4.3 Non-Response Bias Assessment

In order to test the potential bias, this study turned to the early vs. late responder method, also known as the A method (AAPOR RR3). While it is a method with an extensive list of limitations due to the survey itself, it is also the most modern and advanced. Responses received in the first wave of data collection were compared with those received in the last wave using an independent samples t-test across all major constructs. The results found no statistically significant differences between early and late respondents ($p > 0.05$), making the non-response bias doubtless on the credibility of the findings.

Moreover, age, industry, professional experience, and other demographic characteristics were compared across the response waves and showed no noticeable differences. These findings suggest that the final sample is adequately representative of the target respondent population.

4.4 Common Method Bias (CMB) Assessment

Since every last item was gauged by means of self-reported questionnaire responses from the same person, the common method bias, or CMB, was taken into account and addressed through various techniques of data collection.

In practice, protocols like the assurance of confidentiality to respondents were employed, the procedures for item phrasing were carefully adjusted in the pilot, and in the design of the prop, the distinction between the predictors and the criteria was elevated within the items.

In terms of procedures, Harman's one-factor test was applied in the framework of the exploratory factor analysis techniques. These analyses revealed that the level of interpretation of the first unrotated factor accounted for 34.7% of the overall variance, instead of obtaining the expected value of 50% or higher. Consequently, common method variance was not considered a major problem or issue in the present study.

Moreover, the values of the full collinearity VIF were checked according to the suggestion put forward by Kock (2015). The full collinearity VIF values for the plug-in hybrid electricity generation system ranged from 1.42 to 2.87, lower than the conservative value threshold of 3.3. These results are suggestive of the fact that the study was probably not subject to too much of the common method bias influence.

4.5 Measurement Scale Sources

We must state that we used some measurement items based on well-known and well-validated scales already existing in the literature, and were adapted to the Indian context of ESG facilitated technological transformation.

Table 2. Measurement Constructs and Sources

Construct	Number of Items	Source(s)
AI-Driven Digital Capability (AIDC)	5	Adapted from Vial (2021); McAfee & Brynjolfsson (2017)
Big Data & IoT Integration (BDII)	5	Adapted from Chen et al. (2016); Martínez-Peláez et al. (2023)
Ethical Digital Transformation (EDT)	6	Adapted from Floridi et al. (2018); Rosário & Cruz (2025)
Strategic Leadership Agility (SLA)	5	Adapted from Doz and Kosonen (2010)
ESG Performance (ESGP)	7	Adapted from Fatemi et al. (2018)
Sustainable Creative Economy Development (SCED)	5	Adapted from George et al. (2021); Bieser and Hilty (2018)

All items were determined by employing a five-point Likert scale, ranging from "1 = Strongly Disagree" to "5 = Strongly Agree". The Four-Square Cognitive Mapping Technique, a special research tool that is not well known to the public, was utilized for assessing the respondents' perceptions. Before full-scale administration, the instrument was reviewed by academic experts and industry practitioners to ensure content validity, contextual relevance, and linguistic clarity.

For measurement instruments to be dependable and valid, a preliminary exercise is conducted in which small-scale trials are run on the same before the bulk of the data is collected. Reliability is Cronbach's alpha, which is accepted for ICS values above 0.70; this is the value that was primarily in the correlation assessment of all variables. For construct validity, Conformity Factor Analysis (CFA) was used to observe the factor loadings, composite reliability, and average variance extracted (AVE). Furthermore, these procedures ensure the measurement of a construct modelled in a way that represents real theoretical constructs.

Structural Equation Modelling (SEM) is the main analytical tool used in this study discussion and allows estimation of multiple relationships among latent variables. SEM has been most useful in the present study because it probes complex models in the presence of mediation and moderation effects. The bootstrapping procedure is used to check whether the involvement of hybrid intelligence in the connection between AI adoption and economic growth is indeed mediating, while a moderated model contains the interaction terms that were tested by using the interaction terms. Regression analysis is applied to verify direct relationships across some path-model chains, whereas the ANOVA test is carried out to analyse the sectoral and demographic differences.

Besides this quantitative analysis, the qualitative part of our research utilizes an analysis of secondary data and policy. The other data sources are government reports, reports from industry, and data from the World Bank, OECD, etc. This secondary analysis gives a few higher-level takes on how AI is being adopted, how digital infrastructure is growing, plus how economic growth indicators behave in India, so it also brings contextual relevance into the discussion for these studies.

There is a lot of thinking and deliberation that goes into every single ethical piece of the research process. Participants willingly join our study, and they get commitments regarding assured confidentiality and ongoing anonymity. The data is only applied for scholarly work, and the right precautions are in place to guard both data security and overall integrity.

5. DATA ANALYSIS TECHNIQUES

Table 3. Descriptive Statistics

Variable	Category	Frequency (n)	Percentage (%)
Gender	Male	220	55.0
	Female	180	45.0
Age Group	Below 25 years	90	22.5
	25–34 years	150	37.5
	35–44 years	95	23.8
	45 years and above	65	16.2
Education Level	Undergraduate	140	35.0
	Postgraduate	200	50.0
	Doctorate/Other	60	15.0
Occupation	Student	110	27.5
	Salaried	180	45.0
	Self-employed	70	17.5
	Others	40	10.0
Experience with AI	Less than 1 year	85	21.3
	1–3 years	175	43.7
	More than 3 years	140	35.0

Interpretation

The respondents' profile shows a fair share of the population being represented by the different categories and is referred to as a stratified sample. The statistics obtained from the interviewed given in Table 3 study participants provide the following information on age and gender distribution. The male population accounted to 55% (220), whereas the female population accounted for 45% (180); the groups are represented fairly well compared to the numbers above. The profile shows that the largest group falls into the age range of 25-34 years, 37.5% percent, followed by 35-44 years, 23.8%; because this age group below 25 years was 22.5%; then the age group 45 years and above represented 16.2%. Of the interviewed, the breakdown of the level of education revealed that postgraduates were highest at 50%, undergraduates next at 35%, and the lowest percentage held doctoral or any other such qualifications at 15%. By occupation, the highest number was those who were in paid employment (45%), followed by students (27.5%), entrepreneurs (17.5%), and others (10%). Many of the 42.9% of the respondents who have one to three years of experience came out as a fairly experienced group of people suitable for the study of AI.

Table 4. Reliability Analysis (Cronbach's Alpha)

Construct	No. of Items	Cronbach's Alpha (α)
AI Adoption	5	0.82
Skill Enhancement	6	0.85
Hybrid Intelligence	5	0.88
Institutional Support	4	0.79
Economic Growth	5	0.84

Interpretation

The validity test results for all variables are good, as the Cronbach's alpha number was greater than 0.70, as shown in Table 4. The highest internal consistency was recorded by hybrid intelligence, suggesting a strong correlation among the items that assess human-AI cooperation. Skill enhancement ($\alpha = 0.85$) and economic growth ($\alpha = 0.84$) demonstrate strong reliability, thereby strengthening further the validity of the measurement scales. Social support, on the other hand, scored the lowest in internal consistency at 0.79 but remains acceptable. In summary, based on these tests, all construct scales are positively reliable and could be constructed further to conduct other statistical measurements that can be consistent across measurements of latent constructs.

Table 5. Correlation Matrix

Variables	AI Adoption	Skill Enhancement	Hybrid Intelligence	Economic Growth
AI Adoption	1.00	0.68	0.64	0.59
Skill Enhancement	0.68	1.00	0.72	0.65
Hybrid Intelligence	0.64	0.72	1.00	0.70
Economic Growth	0.59	0.65	0.70	1.00

Interpretation

Correlation analysis revealed that there are strong positive relationships among all the major variables, given in Table 5. AI Adoption has a moderate correlation with Skill Enhancement (r = 0.68) and Hybrid Intelligence (r = 0.64), showing that the increase in AI use is likewise bringing about the increase in skill development and human-AI collaboration. Hybrid Intelligence shows the strongest correlation with Economic Growth at 0.70, which points to a pivotal influence on productivity and innovation, and it helps in ways that are more than a simple linear link. Skill enhancement is also closely linked to Economic Growth (r = 0.65). No high correlations above 0.90 were found between any two pairs, underlining the absence of multicollinearity, and also that the selected variables were distinct but also substantially related, warranting further regression analysis and SEM analysis.

Table 6. Convergent Validity (CR and AVE)

Construct	Factor Loadings (Range)	Composite Reliability (CR)	AVE
AI Adoption	0.71 – 0.84	0.86	0.55
Skill Enhancement	0.73 – 0.88	0.89	0.58
Hybrid Intelligence	0.75 – 0.90	0.91	0.62
Institutional Support	0.70 – 0.83	0.84	0.52
Economic Growth	0.72 – 0.87	0.88	0.59

Interpretation (Convergent Validity)

We infer that the CFA results indicate sufficient levels of convergent validity in Table 6. Every factor incorporates more than 0.70 for the factor loadings level, indicating that each of the latent variables is well-represented by its observed measures. Composite Reliability (CR) ranges from 0.84 to 0.91. All values are greater than 0.70, which simply suggests internal consistency is good. The last dimensions of Average Variance Extracted (AVE) are all above 0.50, which means that these factors explain more than 50% of the variance from their indicators. These collectively support the fact that the measurement model can be considered as valid and provides a desirable convergent structure.

Table 7. Discriminant Validity Matrix

Construct	AI Adoption	Skill Enhancement	Hybrid Intelligence	Economic Growth
AI Adoption	**0.74**			
Skill Enhancement	0.68	**0.76**		
Hybrid Intelligence	0.64	0.72	**0.79**	
Economic Growth	0.59	0.65	0.70	**0.77**

Interpretation (Discriminant Validity)

The Fornell–Larcker criterion clarifies reasonable divergence, with the conditions that the value under the square root of AVE (extracted diagonal) for each factor is higher than its affiliates with the other constructs, as given in Table 7. This implies that every construct is independent and comprises certain specifics of the model. The findings also affirm the said assumptions since AI advancement, the development of skills training programs, hybrid intelligence, and generating expansion do not correlate with one another, facilitating the completeness of the model.

Table 8. Multiple Regression Analysis

Independent Variables	Beta (β)	t-value	p-value
AI Adoption	0.21	3.45	0.001
Skill Enhancement	0.29	4.12	0.000
Hybrid Intelligence	0.38	5.67	0.000

$R^2 = 0.62$
Dependent Variable: Economic Growth

Interpretation

From the regression, we find that all independent variables have a significant influence on economic growth. The Hybrid Intelligence Score ($\beta = 0.38, p < 0.001$) has the largest positive effect, confirming the centrality of Hybrid Intelligence towards the enhancement of productivity and innovation, as shown in Table 8. Skill Enhancement also contributes quite a bit ($\beta = 0.29$), and that is why workforce capabilities matter, in order to make sure AI adoption actually turns into economic outcomes. AI adoption also has a moderate but significant impact ($\beta = 0.21$), showing to businesses the detrimental-enhancing impact of technology without accompanying skills. The independent variables were able to explain around 62% of the variance in economic growth ($R^2 = 0.62$), with a high prediction power and support by the theoretical framework connecting AI, skills, and growth.

Table 9. Mediation Analysis (Bootstrapping Method)

Path	Direct Effect	Indirect Effect	Total Effect	Result
AI → Economic Growth	0.21	—	0.21	Significant
AI → Hybrid Intelligence → Growth	—	0.27	0.48	Significant

Interpretation

The analysis of mediation performed had affirmed that the incorporation of AI significantly drives the relationship between AI Adoption and Economic Growth, as shown in Table 9. The impact of AI on growth is moderately weak (0.21), the indirect one through Hybrid Intelligence is substantially stronger (0.27), yielding a large total effect (0.48). This largely suggests that the economic benefits of AI are manifested through the actual development of hybrid yields rather than the mere use of technology. The study supports the importance of human-AI partnership in the value creation for one of its main hypotheses, which states that hybrid intelligence acts as a major driver of economic transformation aided by AI.

Table 10. Moderation Analysis (Institutional Support)

Interaction Term	Beta (β)	t-value	p-value
AI Adoption × Institutional Support	0.19	2.98	0.003

Interpretation

An interaction effect moderated by AI adoption was found between institutional support and hybrid intelligence ($\beta = 0.19, p < 0.01$), showing that favourable policy, digital infrastructure, and regulatory frameworks strengthened the effectiveness of the implementation of AI, as shown in Table 10. In the Indian context, the importance of government initiatives that support digital transformation in helping organizations use AI technologies more effectively is pretty prominent, even if it feels a little broad. Our findings suggest that in the absence of strong institutional support, AI's potential benefits could not be realized fully. Consequently, policy interventions have to be handled quickly because infrastructure could, at least maximally, make use of official intervention during the skill transformation and economic growth stage.

Table 11. Structural Equation Modelling (SEM Results Summary)

Model Fit Index	Value	Threshold	Result
CFI	0.94	>0.90	Good Fit
RMSEA	0.05	<0.08	Good Fit
Chi-square/df	2.10	<3	Acceptable

Interpretation

SEM results show that the proposed model fits the data fairly well, or at least that it matches nicely. The Comparative Fit Index (CFI = 0.94) is above the suggested threshold, which hints at a strong model fit, as can be seen in Table 11. Also, 9% of the RMSEA value (0.05) stays basically within the acceptable level, so it indicates a decent level of approximation in terms of error, not too shabby. The Chi-square/df ratio comes out to 2.10, concluding that the model's goodness is acceptable. Overall, these findings support the general framework assumptions about AI adoption, skill enhancement, hybrid intelligence, and economic growth. In short, the robust model fit underscores how the integrated TOE-RBV-endogenous growth framework works well in explaining the economic transformation brought about by AI.

Qualitative Analysis

A qualitative case study was conducted to provide first-hand insights. These inputs were derived from open-ended semi-structured interviews. Several phone interviews were also conducted with respondents who could not be reached in person. During field research, insiders were also contacted. Thus, a total of 25 respondents were purposely selected to capture different viewpoints about the adoption of AI, skill transformation, and economic consequences. The thematic analysis of qualitative data identified the themes given below.

Table 12. Thematic Analysis of Qualitative Findings

Theme	Key Insights	Frequency (n=25)
AI-Driven Skill Shift	Increased demand for data literacy, AI understanding, and digital skills	21
Human–AI Collaboration	AI supports decision-making rather than replacing human roles	19
Continuous Reskilling Need	Emphasis on lifelong learning and adaptive skill development	22
Organizational Readiness	Firms with a strong learning culture adapt better to AI integration	18
Policy & Infrastructure Support	Government initiatives enable digital transformation	20
Productivity & Innovation Gain	AI improves efficiency, speed, and innovation capacity	23

Interpretation

Qualitative Data provides the main conclusions of the quantitative data: the qualification skill in the labour force as an element of AI-driven economic growth. Most of those we have spoken to said AI does not replace workplaces, but rather develops them and therefore demands highly professional digital and cognitive skills. The increased need for continuous upscaling is because the AI economy keeps changing. Equally important drivers to the productivity and decision-making among employees were human- AI collaboration. In the same vein, extremely fostered learning in the organisation and well-mannered policies of the government were seen to be among the factors that help in the effective uptake of AI technologies. Thus, the research revealed that hybrid Intelligence was a practicable or strategic factor that promoted innovation. The levels of efficiency within the organization, as well as economic growth, especially in India, have been proven to function optimally with the application of hybrid intelligence, integrated artificial and human intelligence, as mentioned in Table 12.

Table 13. Representative Quotes from Respondents

Respondent Type	Statement
IT Professional	"AI tools enhance our decision-making, but human judgment is still critical."
Policy Expert	"Government initiatives are crucial for building AI-ready infrastructure."
Academic Expert	"Future skills must combine technical knowledge with ethical reasoning."

Respondent Type	Statement
Manager (Manufacturing)	"Employees need constant upskilling to work effectively with AI systems."
Banking Professional	"AI has improved efficiency, but training is the real game changer."

Interpretation

Quotations from stakeholders go further in explaining what AI is actually taking place. Across profiles, the postings contain the idea of the team spirit for humans and machines. That is, it refers rather to effort intensification than to displacement. Every informant argued in the strongest terms for the necessity of learning and re-training for positive results. Political support and also physical infrastructure were given as critical elements to consider with regard to adopting artificial intelligence in the future. Even more important is the inclusion of ethical issues within the purview of skills development as described by the second dimension of this framework. This argument strengthens the argument of the theory by complementing the previous one's activities, axiomatic social constructions, including the framework, by illustrating the hybrid form of intelligence within the practices under the technical convergence, including: improving the organizational productivity, flexibility of different economic activities, and the appropriate cultural and behaviour change of the society, as mentioned in Table 13.

6. RESULTS AND DISCUSSION

The primary goal of this study was to evaluate the progression of adopting hybrid intelligence after having formed the human talent initially, and its impact on economic growth in Digital India. This was accomplished by integrating the TOE, RBV, and Endogenous Growth frameworks. Both quantitative and qualitative analysis findings significantly backed up the proposed conceptual framework and must have seriously contributed to confirming all research hypotheses.

Our first objective was to study the impact of the adoption of AI on the improvement of skills of employees. The findings confirmed H1: There is a significant positive relationship between the adoption of AI and the improvement of skills. This becomes apparent by looking at the results of regression analysis and the correlation tests: organizations with AI systems underwent observable changes in the competencies of their personnel, particularly as regards digital literacy, basic data management and analytics, and problem-solving skills-lending credence to the argument from literature that AI adoption has an inherent bias favouring skills, furthering advanced cognitive and technical capabilities for the workforce (Brynjolfsson & McAfee, 2014). The qualitative feedback revitalized this finding on the need for lifelong learning and adaptability in an AI-integrated workplace; one cannot solely consider AI as a technological tool for some isotropic transformation of skill mix in the workforce.

The second aim was to investigate the linkage between skill development and hybrid intelligence development. The second H1 suggests that appropriately developed skills have more potential to enhance the hybrid intelligence phenomenon. With digital and cognitive capabilities, workers will be more capable at working with AI systems, thereby enhancing their decision-making and innovation potential. This finding is consistent with the notion of a machine–man synergy in the development of hybrid intelligence (Dellermann et al., 2019). Qualitative findings revealed that organizations with well-developed nurturing cultures and training mechanisms tend to demonstrate more effective human-AI collaborations by taking the skill-enhancement component higher in the value chain away from mere human capital.

The third sub-hypothesis tested whether hybrid intelligence has an impact on economic performance. Based on the results, we reject the null hypothesis and confirm the major hypothesis that the Hybrid Intelligence significantly influences economic performance positively. Among the predictors, hybrid intelligence possesses the highest regression coefficient, which means it is producing major productivity, efficiency, and innovation changes. Hence, this finding is an outgrowth of the Resource-Based View (RBV) for having big potential as a strategic resource strengthening organizational competitiveness in the first place (Barney, 1991). And within the domain of macroeconomics, this result may be seen as consistent with the Endogenous Growth Theory, which advocates that growth is determined by knowledge and innovation modes to sustain long-run growth (Romer,1996). From there, this investigation indicates that hybrid intelligence is an asset for organizations through the pathway to its use with state economic performance.

The fourth objective was to evaluate the role of hybrid intelligence as a mediating factor in the association between artificial intelligence adoption and economic growth. The mediation analysis corroborates H4, and it is evidenced that hybrid intelligence significantly mediates the relationship between AI adoption and economic growth. The adoption of AI cannot solely facilitate economic growth on its own; however, it can considerably increase even more when discussing the concept of hybrid intelligence, ultimately turning out to be the key factor in the amount of achieved economic gains from AI. Thus, the economic gains from AI can be said to be generated more by creative human AI than by dependence on technology only. A juncture referred to in the extant literature about both AI achievements in the economy and its failure to cover them at the same time. It leads us to the need for blending science and art in order to enhance the economic benefits of technology.

Objective five looked at how institutional support can actually buffer and strengthen the link between AI adoption and hybrid intelligence. The results ended up confirming H5, meaning institutional support really does make that relationship stronger and more visible in practice. It seems government policies, digital infrastructure, and regulatory frameworks work together here because they help organizations adopt and then use AI technologies more effectively. In the Indian setting, the push toward digitalization, along with skill development programs, has already built a basis for AI-driven shifts in how firms operate. Also, the qualitative part pointed in the same direction: organizations that exist in supportive ecosystems are more prepared to draw on hybrid intelligence, especially when aiming for productivity improvements. Overall, this highlights that policy interventions are critical for enabling both technological progress and economic advancement, not only as a backdrop but as a direct driver.

Overall, the results extend comprehensively supportive evidence for the integrated TOE–RBV–Endogenous Growth framework. TOE is validated with significant impacts of institutional readiness and technology support. RBV is evident in hybrid intelligence as a key strategic resource for competitive advantage. Endogenous Growth Theory is supported by the connection shown between knowledge-based capabilities and growth in the economy.

The findings of the qualitative study add a considerable amount of detail and insight to the quantitative results, helping in explaining how the Indian companies are in the process of becoming more AI-enabled. Tables 7.7 and 7.8 expose the themes, which are mainly demographic, and they strengthen the findings, judging a predictive factor on the performance of the workers. One noteworthy theme, for example, is the "continuous learning" because skill development appreciably, based on the data, the relationship between the two of this and growth mediated by the level of AI adaptation, is stronger. Finally, the aspects elaborated in the context of the interviews, that is, "association with AI" and "social activity with the help of AI", are also consistent with the findings recorded in the latter part of the trend analysis and thus add support to the model predictions.

However, the qualitative analysis adds more depth and breadth to the quantitative findings, as it uncovers organizational structures and attitudes that the naked numbers cannot capture qualitatively; by that, it also enhances the evidential body. This was the claim also substantiated in the interviews, 'people tend to be cautious when encountering AI initially, and they fear the effect it will have on their job, and which is a perception issue, transition of AI within the organization goes beyond math'. In other words, the shift implies not only positive numerical correlations but also serves a sphere with issues like emotions and institutions as well. Further, these are the views shared by experts during this survey; they stress the importance of the legislative and digital infrastructure of the state and the presence of sectoral training systems. This also helps advance our understanding of the strong institutional effect as predicted in the SEM analysis, but in a practical way. According to the qualitative results, India's move towards an AI-based economy is not just a technological evolution; it also brings in meaningful societal adjustments, management policy reforms, and industry leadership changes.

7. IMPLICATIONS

7.1 Theoretical Implications

This study sort of goes past the conventional idea of Hybrid Intelligence within the TOE, RBV, and Endogenous Growth Theory lenses, to understand patterns of economic growth from a theoretical view. Other work that builds on this line of inquiry can take the newer growth models, maybe constructed around intelligence entities, one step further, because value creation is not being achieved only through human knowledge nowadays; it comes from weaving that knowledge with AI-type systems too. This mix then drives a rethinking of central economic notions like productivity, innovation, and competitiveness when AI is in the foreground. There is also room to look at Hybrid Intelligence across multiple industries and countries, and then discuss it in a way that supports a sturdier theoretical scaffold that is easier to extend.

7.2 Managerial and Organizational Implications

Hybrid intelligence-harnessing combines different capabilities, such as machine intelligence and human intelligence, to achieve great synergy and tap into potential. There is no need for all of the old stuff in this case; employees of the companies in question will achieve a competitive advantage over their counterparts, and the companies must go ahead and modernize the training methods completely. The future organizational changes with augmented security of human reason and computers to make certain decisions, ideas, and improvements already seem to be the mission, not an optional choice, for the life modes of the most ambitious, forward development, and improvement-oriented people in society.

Companies are thought to need the creation of AI-inclusive inner cultures that are filled with experimentation, innovation, sharing, and supportive of these AIs. However, a change of leadership is going to be inevitable because of the integration of these AI models; the ability to break free from the bias that has been developed over the years will be essential for managing the human and AI dynamics. Performance appraisal systems should therefore be overhauled to incorporate the values provided by hybrid mechanisms, from the use of trade parlance to the direct forms of productivity assessment and intelligence development.

7.3 Policy Implications

It is worth mentioning that the qualitative analysis contributes a greater amount of information to the quantitative results than just numerical data, as it exposes specific factors and attitudes within organizations that the statistics fail to reveal, and in this respect, it therefore reinforces the formed arguments. In this sense, it was held by the respondents, 'people often become reptilian or rather act shyly to new AI tools and are afraid of damage to their work, due to which, which is a matter of attitude, people accept the adoption of AI in the organization even without any calculus'. This ideological transformation is therefore not simply about positive mathematical associations, but also enhances a field like that of social and institutional factors. Furthermore, these are the opinions of specialists that were voiced in the course of this poll; they also underscore the importance of the establishment of the laws, basic and digital structures of the country, and the availability of industry-related training programs. It also teaches us how to interpret the abundant institutional influence as shown in the SEM analysis and in the anticipated trends of India's development. The focus on the domain of AI economy with reference to India, as indicated by the qualitative data, is not essentially a technological progression; hence, the infusion of other features, such as policy reforms and changes in the socially grounded relationships in the industry, also becomes part of this dynamic.

To make sure that every tertiary-level institution offers Artificial intelligence lessons in a structured and mainstream manner, there is a need for the Minister of Human Resource Development to also instruct the University Grants Commission and All India Council for Technical Education to consider making it compulsory that every undergraduate programme should have at least one interdisciplinary artificial intelligence course as an elective. Besides that, NITI Aayog would be necessary for the establishment of sector-specific initiation programs that connect additional benefits drawn out of AI implementation in industries and, e.g., the effort of reskilled workforces. Public-private partnerships involving technology firms, universities, and government agencies are vitally important for creating local (regional) working AI innovation and training impulse canters, mainly so in the climes of tier-2 and tier-3 cities. All these steps would strengthen the institutional preparedness of India the most, bridge the digital divide, and help the economic development of the country by creating highly innovative and inclusive industries.

7.4 Educational Implications

There is a need for the educational system to undergo transformation in readiness for tomorrow's AI-driven, anointed economy. In this case, the systems need to lose the concept of a one-size-fits-all curriculum where learning was predicated on rote memorization and forced specialization and, instead, direct more attention towards reinforcing multidisciplinary learning models that are imbued with skill training to include future technology, as well as critique and creativity. Educational institutions should have their personnel coached on their AI literacy, coding, design thinking, and critical thinking abilities so that they can train their students to be useful in hybrid-intelligence workspaces.

The significance of lifetime learning would become even more apparent in the era of rapid technological changes, because skill acquisition would still be needed. Under such circumstances, it will be as important for tertiary and secondary educational establishments as well as for industries to create alternative modes of learning based on technologies such as aspects of flexible structures, such as online content, units of micro-certificates, and practice-based curricula.

7.5 Socio-Economic Implications

At an expanded level, the shift to outdoor learning implies prospective relationships with economic inclusiveness and social fairness. While AI has the potential to generate substantial productivity gains, it is also at risk of potentially widening existing inequalities if access to huge skills and technologies is not balanced. Future strategies should, thus, strive to promote inclusive growth, lending a hand to securing all sections of society to share beneficially sophisticated technologies.

In India, maximizing the demographic dividend will necessitate interventions of high efficacy aiming to give existing labour power the required skills to develop, particularly technical and functional skills on a regional basis at smaller places, that is, in the hinterlands. Bridge-the-Digital-Divide programs combined with skills development programs to help bridge the urban-rural divide, providing opportunities for new avenues in the economic operation.

8. CONCLUSION

This study tried to examine the evolution of the relationship between artificial intelligence (AI), skill formation, and economic growth by making a case for the transition through the vast paradigm of Digital India between multiple components of traditional human capital, to the creation of hybrid intelligence. This theoretical model is built on the integration of the Technology-Organization-Environment (TOE) framework, the Resource-Based View (RBV), and the Endogenous Growth Theory. This framework is being created to provide a detailed, multi-tiered model illustrating how AI-driven capabilities can influence productivity and economic outcomes. This inner partnership is, in fact, believed to have huge transformative potentials within the epoch of digital renewal; moreover, hybrid intellect- understood as the harmonious union of human and machine embowed intelligence for a common cause, is once more highlighted as one of the vital factors driving economic change.

The use of AI which has been incorporated into the workplace better enhances the skills of the workforce as compared to the level of transformation to accent basic capabilities and encourages the people and organizations to embark on such competency Modifiers as cognitive competencies (being able to think), digital competencies (being able to use digital technologies), and adaptive competencies (being able to adapt to change under the circumstances). This shift is more than evolutionary, rather revolutionary in that it changes the work that occurs and the people who must participate in it. It's worth mentioning the relation between the above-mentioned factors, which ensures the superiority of skills for development in the format of hybrid intellect, and high-quality improvements, technology stimulation, and economic growth. A few of the factors, including hybrid intelligence, also known as cognitive technology, turned out to be the most dominant contributing variable within this context, signalling its strategic and economic value.

The reason investigating this problem is important is to determine hybrid intelligence as a mediator between AI use and economic performance. The results show that there are no benefits of artificial intelligence that come easily or result from the introduction of technology. The economic expansion actually depends on the rising abilities of employees augmented and collaborated with intelligent machines. Policy makers need to respond and appreciate it as a specific problem, any promise of growth as AI-driven calls for a holistic conceptualization of economic growth. The paper discussed here does not touch upon that social centre, but when employing any technology, the voluminous concept of growth contains the aid of all alternatives so as to enable significant development in those perspectives of society.

The socioeconomic demographic study of the population of India indicates very important aspects, such as how India can pool its demographic and technological energies to ensure economic growth and development over time. India has a huge and diverse working population, which puts the country at a favourable position to harness the power of AI in digitizing its economy. Such an approach also provides for the necessary funding to enable the workforce to match the change, as well as the development of innovative digital solutions in terms of skills and digital readiness. The findings avow that the current training and upskilling regimes should be equipped to the challenge and uncertainties brought about by industry shifts so that the labor force remains productive within an extensively competitive global economy where AI is becoming more and more integrated.

When the capital of the human is hybrid intellectual, it should mean more than just creativity in work experiences of the future and beyond. This shift is a transition from growth models that are labor productive to intelligence economies where value has to be generated through the productive complementarities of human and machine abilities. Business strategies, educational policies, and political arrangements should be addressed in these new forms in order to enable AI benefits to everyone and new developments. Ignorance of all such developmental elements might result in skill mismatches, more disparities, or simply failing to realize the capacity that technology can offer.

This study succeeded in mainly slotting hybrid intelligence at the core of AI, hence its contribution to the economy too. Uniting technology adoption and skill upgrading is another economic concept building efficient and effective markets, and such a theory did not exist about the subject of digital transformation. Hybrid Intelligence is expected to be more progressive, even as economic areas change their characteristics and other aspects of development, such as Hybrid Intelligence, can be used for enhancing its ranking in the league of the most prosperous countries. For a nation such as India, such an enlightenment is a great opportunity not only to increase its excessive economic capacity but also to create smart and just populations.

9. LIMITATIONS AND FUTURE SCOPE

Even though it is very sound in this respect, this paper contains too many determinants and obstacles. There are cross-sectional data collected in a few industries of India, which limits the generalizations concerning the time and the industry. The perceptual measures were also used the perceptual measures in this research, i.e., survey responses that create a chance that bias would come from respondents, even though rules specified enhancing objectivity and consistency. Fourth, the investigation is predominantly concerned with organizational factors, while time-series developments at the macroeconomic level aimed at projecting historical theory over present growth determinants are not incorporated. Lastly, the hybrid intelligence construct is rather nascent and needs more research and further standardization in its operational construct, even after the theoretical grounding was obtained.

In future studies, the researchers can eliminate these limitations by following the trajectory over time and investigating how the influence of artificial intelligence and hybrid intelligence on economic growth has changed. With cross-country level analyses or regional level studies, more attention may be accorded to the factors that will define the success of the adoption of AI, and implementation of AI policy.

REFERENCES

Acemoglu, D., & Autor, D. (2011). Skills, tasks and technologies: Implications for employment and earnings. In *Handbook of labor economics* (Vol. 4, pp. 1043–1171). Elsevier.

Autor, D. H. (2015). Why are there still so many jobs? The history and future of workplace automation. *The Journal of Economic Perspectives, 29*(3), 3–30. DOI: 10.1257/jep.29.3.3

Barney, J. (1991). Firm resources and sustained competitive advantage. *Journal of Management, 17*(1), 99–120. DOI: 10.1177/014920639101700108

Becker, G. S. (1964). *Human capital: A theoretical and empirical analysis*. University of Chicago Press.

Bieser, J. C., & Hilty, L. M. (2018). Assessing indirect environmental effects of information and communication technology (ICT): A systematic literature review. *Sustainability (Basel), 10*(8), 2662. DOI: 10.3390/su10082662

Brynjolfsson, E., & mcafee, A. (2014). *The second machine age: Work progress and prosperity in a time of brilliant technologies*. WW Norton & company.

Chen, Y., Chen, H., Gorkhali, A., Lu, Y., Ma, Y., & Li, L. (2016). Big data analytics and big data science: A survey. *Journal of Management Analytics, 3*(1), 1–42. DOI: 10.1080/23270012.2016.1141332

Cockburn, I. M., Henderson, R., & Stern, S. (2018). The impact of artificial intelligence on innovation: An exploratory analysis. In *The economics of artificial intelligence: An agenda* (pp. 115–146). University of Chicago Press.

Dellermann, D., Ebel, P., Söllner, M., & Leimeister, J. M. (2019). Hybrid intelligence. *Business & Information Systems Engineering, 61*(5), 637–643. DOI: 10.1007/s12599-019-00595-2

Dhanabalan, T., & Sathish, A. (2018). Transforming Indian industries through artificial intelligence and robotics in industry 4.0. *International Journal of Mechanical Engineering and Technology, 9*(10), 835–845.

Doughan, Y. A. R. (2020). Factors of production, economic growth, and sustainable development. In *Decent work and economic growth* (pp. 427–439). Springer International Publishing. DOI: 10.1007/978-3-319-71058-7_121-1

Doz, Y. L., & Kosonen, M. (2010). Embedding strategic agility: A leadership agenda for accelerating business model renewal. *Long Range Planning*, *43*(2-3), 370–382. DOI: 10.1016/j.lrp.2009.07.006

Dumitru, D., & Halpern, D. F. (2023). Critical thinking: Creating job-proof skills for the future of work. *Journal of Intelligence*, *11*(10), 194. DOI: 10.3390/jintelligence11100194 PMID: 37888426

Dwivedi, Y. K., Hughes, L., Ismagilova, E., Aarts, G., Coombs, C., Crick, T., Duan, Y., Dwivedi, R., Edwards, J., Eirug, A., Galanos, V., Ilavarasan, P. V., Janssen, M., Jones, P., Kar, A. K., Kizgin, H., Kronemann, B., Lal, B., Lucini, B., & Williams, M. D. (2021). Artificial Intelligence (AI): Multidisciplinary perspectives on emerging challenges, opportunities, and agenda for research, practice and policy. *International Journal of Information Management*, *57*, 101994. DOI: 10.1016/j.ijinfomgt.2019.08.002

Fatemi, A., Glaum, M., & Kaiser, S. (2018). ESG performance and firm value: The moderating role of disclosure. *Global Finance Journal*, *38*, 45–64. DOI: 10.1016/j.gfj.2017.03.001

Floridi, L., Cowls, J., Beltrametti, M., Chatila, R., Chazerand, P., Dignum, V., Luetge, C., Madelin, R., Pagallo, U., Rossi, F., Schafer, B., Valcke, P., & Vayena, E. (2018). AI4People—An ethical framework for a good AI society: Opportunities, risks, principles, and recommendations. *Minds and Machines*, *28*(4), 689–707. DOI: 10.1007/s11023-018-9482-5 PMID: 30930541

George, G., Merrill, R. K., & Schillebeeckx, S. J. (2021). Digital sustainability and entrepreneurship: How digital innovations are helping tackle climate change and sustainable development. *Entrepreneurship Theory and Practice*, *45*(5), 999–1027. DOI: 10.1177/1042258719899425

Jain, A., & Bishnoi, C. R. (2025). Artificial Intelligence and Economic Development in India: Adoption Trends and Key Determinants. In *Intelligent Systems for Sustainable Infrastructure: AI Solutions Shaping a Green Future: Leveraging AI Innovations for Eco Friendly Infrastructure and Environmental Resilience* (pp. 139–154). Springer Nature Switzerland.

Jarrahi, M. H. (2018). Artificial intelligence and the future of work: Human-AI symbiosis in organizational decision making. *Business Horizons*, *61*(4), 577–586. DOI: 10.1016/j.bushor.2018.03.007

Jarrahi, M. H., Lutz, C., & Newlands, G. (2022). Artificial intelligence, human intelligence and hybrid intelligence based on mutual augmentation. *Big Data & Society*, *9*(2), 20539517221142824. DOI: 10.1177/20539517221142824

Li, T. T., Wang, K., Sueyoshi, T., & Wang, D. D. (2021). ESG: Research progress and future prospects. *Sustainability (Basel), 13*(21), 11663. DOI: 10.3390/su132111663

Makridakis, S. (2017). The forthcoming Artificial Intelligence (AI) revolution: Its impact on society and firms. *Futures, 90*, 46–60. DOI: 10.1016/j.futures.2017.03.006

Marginson, S. (2019). Limitations of human capital theory. *Studies in Higher Education, 44*(2), 287–301. DOI: 10.1080/03075079.2017.1359823

Martínez-Peláez, R., Ochoa-Brust, A., Rivera, S., Félix, V. G., Ostos, R., Brito, H., Félix, R. A., & Mena, L. J. (2023). Role of digital transformation for achieving sustainability: Mediated role of stakeholders, key capabilities, and technology. *Sustainability (Basel), 15*(14), 11221. DOI: 10.3390/su151411221

McAfee, A., & Brynjolfsson, E. (2017). *Machine, platform, crowd: Harnessing our digital future*. WW Norton & Company.

Min, S., & Kim, B. (2024). AI technology adoption in corporate IT network operations based on the TOE model. *Digital, 4*(4), 947–970. DOI: 10.3390/digital4040047

Oliveira, T., & Martins, M. F. (2011). Literature review of IT adoption models. *Procedia Technology, 5*, 110–119.

Rachid, O. U. S. K. O. U., & Houda, C. H. A. M. M. A. A. (2024). Redefining human capital in the age of artificial intelligence: Challenges and opportunities. *Revue Internationale de la Recherche Scientifique et de l'Innovation (Revue-IRSI), 2*(4), 933-946.

Romer, P. M. (1990). Endogenous technological change. *Journal of Political Economy, 98*(5, Part 2), S71–S102. DOI: 10.1086/261725

Rosário, A. T., & Cruz, R. N. (2025). Environment, Social, and Governance Business: Challenges and Opportunities. *Environmental, Social, Governance and Digital Transformation in Organizations*, 73-102.

Santos, M. R., Carvalho, L. C., & Francisco, E. (2025). A capability-based framework for knowledge-driven AI innovation and sustainability. *Information (Basel), 16*(11), 987. DOI: 10.3390/info16110987

Schultz, T. W. (1961). Investment in human capital. *The American Economic Review, 51*(1), 1–17.

Sundaresan, S., & Zhang, Z. (2022). AI-enabled knowledge sharing and learning: Redesigning roles and processes. *The International Journal of Organizational Analysis, 30*(4), 983–999. DOI: 10.1108/IJOA-12-2020-2558

Taljaard, E. (2022). *Adopting Collective Hybrid Intelligence Principles to Enhance Corporate Innovation and Process Efficiencies* (Master's thesis, University of Pretoria (South Africa).

Tan, E. (2014). Human capital theory: A holistic criticism. *Review of Educational Research, 84*(3), 411–445. DOI: 10.3102/0034654314532696

Tornatzky, L. G., & Fleischer, M. (1990). *The processes of technological innovation*. Lexington Books.

Vial, G. (2021). Understanding digital transformation: A review and a research agenda. *Managing digital transformation*, 13-66.

World Economic Forum. (2025). *The future of jobs report*. World Economic Forum.

Chapter 3

Conceptual Frameworks for Institutional Policy Development on Generative AI

Sandeep Gupta
http://orcid.org/0000-0002-3734-3723
Graphic Era (Deemed to be) University, Dehradun, India

Anand Shukla
JSPM University, Pune, India

Neeraj Saxena
MIT Art, Design, and Technology University, Pune, India

Shashi Rani
D.A.V. (PG) College, Karnal, India

Shruti Saxena
Pune Institute of Business Management, Pune, India

ABSTRACT

Generative artificial intelligence (GenAI) is rapidly reshaping higher education by influencing teaching, learning, research, assessment, and administrative decision-making. This chapter outlines an integrative framework that synthesises policy concepts on generative artificial intelligence for higher education. The chapter explores how institutions may design adaptive, ethical, and future-proof policies, drawing on interdisciplinary literature from education policy, artificial intelligence, governance,

DOI: 10.4018/979-8-2600-0116-5.ch003

ethics, and organizational theory. A conceptual framework with multiple layers has been proposed as a strategy for governance, learning and teaching, research integrity and compliance, data governance, and professional development. A comparative scenario analysis shows how framework-driven policies foster institutional coherence, risk management, economic growth and capacity for innovation. The chapter concludes by outlining a future research agenda for sustainable, human-centered, evidence-informed GenAI policy development in higher education.

INTRODUCTION

The GenAI, Generative AI, or Generative artificial intelligence technology is one of the biggest stories in higher education today, with a serious potential impact. Technologies like educational software that just automate administrative tasks or serve up learning analytics are not generative AI systems. In fact, generative AI systems perform a wide range of tasks, from producing content and generating reasoning pathways to simulating expert behavior on tasks. Students, faculty members, researchers, and institutional leaders can now generate essays (and other forms of pieces), research summaries, software code, teaching materials, or policy documents with the tools currently available. This rapid diffusion has fundamentally changed the assumptions about how knowledge is produced, evaluated, and regulated in universities (Chukwuere, 2025).

Universities and colleges are spaces where knowledge is produced, and credentials convey public trust to other sectors of society. Generative AIs are questioning not just their technical adoption but our academic values, including intellectual integrity, at the core. These authors claim that GenAI has powers of extreme personalization, reduced administrative burden, and more research productivity. Moreover, there is something about GenAI that may lead one to question the established norms around authorship, originality, validity of assessment, and professional judgment (Calzada, 2025; Soundariya et al., 2025). Therefore, institutions must find a means to innovate while ensuring that higher education retains its legitimacy.

In reaction to this, many universities have started to issue policies, guidelines, or position statements regarding generative AI. Right now, the evidence suggests that the reactions to cheating incidents are reactive and fragmented, and have mainly dealt with cheating and assessments. Policies that are different among departments/faculties/campuses cause confusion among stakeholders and uneven implementation. In addition, technological change often occurs at a faster pace than public policies can be changed, making a fixed or prescriptive rule become obsolete over time. Because of these limitations, institutions cannot merely rely on a variety of ad hoc policies or tool-specific policies to effectively govern generative AI. According to the report, it is essential to view the formulation of Generative AI policy as a sociotechnical challenge and not a regulatory challenge (Cheng & Wu, 2024).

GenAI systems are transforming governance, education, and power by changing human decision-making and institutional cultures. To ensure a counterpart is embedded in all future regulatory human legislations, the Center for Intelligent Drug Discovery and Development (C-D3) has collaborated with the AU Brains. The utilization of conceptual frameworks organizes complexity through the articulation of relationships between governance, pedagogy, research integrity, and organizational capacity.

There is a growing body of literature concerning AI governance and higher education policy, which engages principles of transparency (O'Sullivan et al., 2025). Turning it into institutional policies continues to be a problem. To operate efficiently and effectively, colleges must reconcile both outside-in and inside-out rules. The faculty need guidance to stimulate pedagogical creativity without 'dumbing-down' standards, and students need guidance on what is accepted, responsible, and the use of artificial intelligence. In uncertain situations, the administrators need to manage institutional risk, reputation, and compliance (Hadi et al., 2025).

Conceptual frameworks are essential for developing policies in a systematic and future-oriented manner. Frameworks help in decision-making in different institutional arenas without controlling behavior like rules do. Institutions can meet competing priorities, anticipate future use cases for technology, and align new policy responses with longer-term strategy. The frameworks contribute to institutional learning through embedded review, stakeholder consultation, and evidence-based revision over time.

Higher education institutions need to have well-rounded conceptual frameworks that would facilitate responsible and sustainable governance of the generative AI. In sum, for policy to be effective, there has to be coherence on governance, ethics and law, pedagogy, research integrity, and institution-building across the sectors (Da, 2024). This chapter proposes to make a contribution to the shift from reactive policy discourse to a more coherent, robust governance outcome through the synthesis of interdisciplinary research findings and comparative institutional approaches.

The Objectives of This Chapter: The paper begins with a review of the literature on generative AI, AI governance, and higher education policy to identify the challenges and gaps in academic literature. The institutions could also develop policies that combine many policies to achieve a common goal within a single framework. Third, it presents comparative and scenario analyses of framework-based policies in diverse institutional contexts and use cases. By doing so, the chapter contributes to the academic and practical debates on how HEIs can future-proof their policies without losing trust and accountability or sacrificing the quality of education in the age of generative artificial intelligence.

BACKGROUND AND LITERATURE REVIEW

Generative AI in Higher Education: Scope and Evolution

The emergence of generative artificial intelligence is fundamentally changing the role of digital technology in higher education. The previous iterations of educational technology centered on learning management systems, dashboards with analytics, and various rules-based automation to enhance age efficiency and learning (Rao et al., 2023; Savvadelli et al., 2025). In contrast, generative AI systems actively enable producing knowledge, such as by generating text, code, images, and analytical reasoning outputs (Gupta, 2025). The use of this powerful tool raises old questions about authorship, originality, assessment validity, and epistemic authority.

Lately, scholarship on accessibility, scalability, and productivity has driven the development of generative AI in higher education. More students are utilizing AI tools to aid with drafting, ideation, and problem-solving, while faculty test tools for AI-supported feedback, curriculum, and research. Nevertheless, studies show that within the humanities and social sciences, authorship and integrity appear more concerning, while within STEM, efficiency and augmentation seem more emphasized. The variation in punishments emphasizes the importance of coherent but flexible institutional policy.

AI Governance Frameworks and Higher Education Policy

The AI governance literature at large provides an important foundation for institutional policies. Regulatory bodies and international organizations adhered to principles such as transparency, fairness, accountability, explainability, and human oversight (Jungherr, 2023). Because of shared governance structures, academic freedom, and decentralized decision-making, it is complicated to translate these principles to the higher education context (Maheswaran et al., 2025). Many organizations create high-level ethical statements but fail to implement, monitor, and enforce them.

In higher education, institutional leadership, the faculty governance body, and departmentally based practices must fit well together. University executives must strive towards harmonization of strategic leadership with academic culture, said some studies. Policy imposition without consultation will often be resisted or complied with 'half-heartedly' and may be ineffective in the long-run (Alli et al., 2025).

Academic Integrity, Assessment, and Knowledge Production

There is a rich body of literature examining the influence of generative AI on academic integrity and assessment. The take-home written assessment is argued to be irrelevant as these models can be generated with the help of AI. Responses that are only dependent on detection and prohibitions are considered unsustainable more broadly.

Fresh investigations indicate evaluations ought to be redesigned to be authentic, process-oriented, and reflective. Policies made by institutions help bring about this change by laying out clear expectations and tying these to professional development. Conceptual frameworks will help institutions go from reactive misconduct policies to proactive assessment governance.

Organizational Change and Policy Theory Perspectives

From an organizational theory perspective, generative AI represents a disruptive innovation that triggers a cycle of experimentation, sensemaking, and institutionalization. A policy framework aids in the transition of technological choices to organizational practice. Based on Jin et al. (2025), teachings from policy theory show that stable frameworks that are not overly dynamic can assist institutions in coping with uncertainty without changing policy.

A large body of literature suggests that the effectiveness of a digital transformation policy in higher education largely depends on institutional capacity, leadership staff competency, and infrastructure readiness. When something is better understood, it is easier to act together. Aiding in preventing different policies from addressing the same problem in a confused or contradictory way.

Comparative Insights and Research Gaps

Research carried out on several organizations shows a presence of three dominant types of policies: restrictive (risk-averse), permissive (innovation-oriented), and balanced (ensuring due diligence). Evidence shows that balanced and framework-driven approaches are more robust and aligned with the mission. Nonetheless, the models currently available in the literature do not create a policy framework combining governance, pedagogy, research integrity, and capacity building (Ko & Lim, 2024). This gap represents a need for conceptual frameworks that specify principles and protocols to facilitate operational decision-making and long-term policy sustainability. The current chapter responds to the identified need by synthesizing research literature from different disciplines into integrative frameworks for institutional policy development for generative AI.

MAIN FOCUS OF THE CHAPTER

Conceptual Foundations for Policy Development

As shown in the illustration (Figure 1), institutional GenAI policy development should deal with five fundamental dimensions: governance, ethics, pedagogy, research, and capacity. The institution's framework for generative AI governance is illustrated by this figure. The process starts with foundational ethical principles and compliance, as well as knowledge of academic integrity, privacy and security, equity and bias, and legal mandates to identify generative AI use cases. This information is used in policy formulation that establishes guidelines, ethical limits, and usage policies. Following this, the framework moves to their implementation and training, which includes the development of faculty, training of students, and allocation of resources. Finally, with time, monitoring and adaptation are done. As a final point, it leads to better learning, innovation support, AI culture with responsibility, and compliance risk mitigation, resulting in better governance outcomes. The feedback arrows loop shows that this can be a never-ending iterative process where we change policy and practice as and when necessary, based on outcome and institutional need.

Multi-Layered Policy Framework

The proposed framework consists of five interrelated layers:

[1]. **Strategic Governance Layer** – Institutional vision, leadership, and regulatory alignment.
[2]. **Ethical and Legal Layer** – Principles of fairness, accountability, data protection, and compliance.
[3]. **Pedagogical and Assessment Layer** – Teaching practices, assessment redesign, and learning outcomes.
[4]. **Research and Knowledge Integrity Layer** – Authorship, transparency, and responsible research use.
[5]. **Capacity Building Layer** – Professional development, infrastructure, and change management.

Analytical Representation

The effectiveness of an institutional policy can be conceived as alignment across layers:

$$P_e = f(G, E, P, R, C) \qquad (1)$$

Here, the five letters stand for governance alignment (G), ethical robustness (E), pedagogical integration (P), research integrity (R), and institutional capacity (C). If any dimension is misaligned, the policy will be ineffective. Institutional policies are not effective because of just one factor or variable, as per Equation (1). Instead, it is the product of alignment, ethics, pedagogy, research integrity, and the capacity of governance. In this formulation, Pe mentioned policy effectiveness; f indicates the type of function effectiveness of these two dimensions. This equation is here to demonstrate the clarity, order, and logic of our thoughts (Shankar et al. 2023). This shows the reader that a policy can only be effective if the relevant institutional layers all work together. If one dimension does not have sufficient strength or alignment, it will weaken the policy decision as a whole. Consequently, the equation is useful because it reduces the complex institutional reality into an orderly model while highlighting the need for balance, coordination, and interdependence of major components of policy implementations.

Figure 1. Conceptual architecture for institutional generative AI policy development

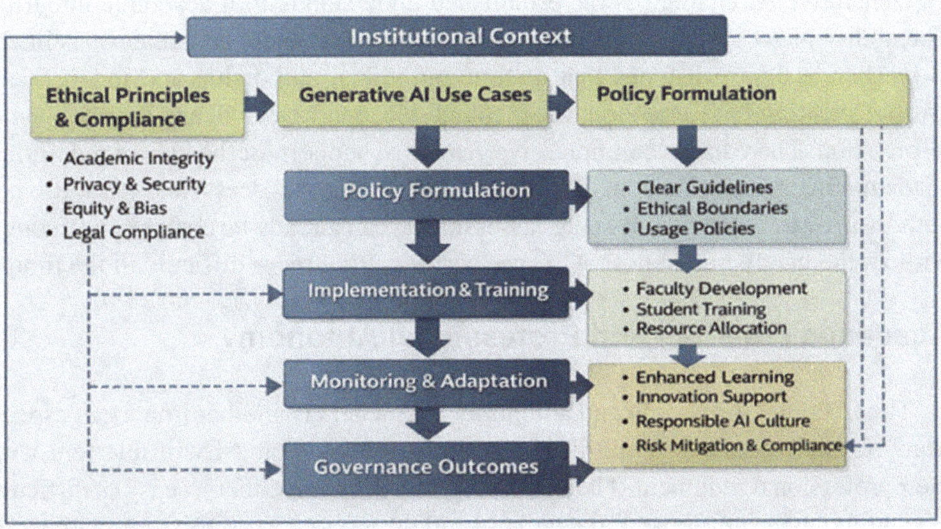

ISSUES, CONTROVERSIES, AND CHALLENGES

Currently, the problems, controversies, and challenges in the higher education sector are already beyond the generative AI technology. Solutions to repeatedly encountered challenges often require additional time. New challenges are discussed based on various literature (Sreekanthaswamy et al., 2025). Recognizing these tensions can help generate meaningful and effective institutional policies.

Tension Between Innovation and Regulation

It can be very hard to balance stimulation and regulation in work life. The use of generative AI can enhance learning design and improve administrative productivity in educational institutions. The institutional adoption's non-compliance with regulations could result in academic misconduct, damage to the academic institution's reputation, and legal non-compliance. Conversely, policies that constrain can hinder teachers from trialing classroom practices and increase the odds of students and faculty being AI literate. Security should be integrated with innovative thinking by institutions in order to create safer environments and services/solutions.

Academic Integrity and Assessment Validity

Generative AI challenges the established understanding of academic integrity. The ability of AI systems to generate quality answers, code, and analysis is likely to weaken assignment types that assume individual authorship and independent effort. Detection-based methods are disreputable, controversial, and open to misinterpretation. There has been impressive growth of support for the idea of redefining academic integrity, which should refer to transparency, process, and learning, not authorship. Monitoring high-stakes assessments can already be challenging enough without the handy but endless AI paper writer getting more difficult all the time.

Academic Freedom and Professional Autonomy

The freedom of research and autonomy of teachers is another important aspect. Many faculty members think that prescriptive policies on AI will interfere with their professional judgment. The imposition of policy can either be easy or difficult, depending on the episteme of the domain and the tolerance towards automaticity. If policies do not recognize different ways to discipline, it can lead to disagreement and non-compliance or mere compliance. Conceptual frameworks may reduce conflict by providing key concepts but allowing local interpretation and application.

Equity, Access, and the Digital Divide

Campus leaders must address the equity challenge of generative AI. If students and institutions don’t make advanced tools, subscription services, and computing power available universally, inequality could worsen. Some learners may do better than others because they have access to more money or technology; similarly, some learners may face a barrier to entry. Bias in data can contribute to discrimination against marginalized communities. Institutional governance of GenAI should focus on access, inclusion, and fairness as important aspects and not peripheral ones.

Data Privacy, Security, and Intellectual Property

Regularly, sensitive personal and educational information, as well as research data, are used in generative AI tools (Fotis et al., 2025). Due to the improper handling of data, data privacy issues, along with concerns about data security, have arisen (Sinha et al., 2024). Another issue that makes the policy difficult to create is who owns the intellectual property. This is especially the case for AI-generated material that is based on institutional research or student work. External rules around data protection must link with internal rules around stewardship, consent, and ownership across universities.

Trust, Transparency, and Explainability

There is another big problem relating to trust in generative AI. Most AI models are termed as "black boxes, preventing users from monitoring how the outputs are formed (Thandlam et al., 2024). Without transparency, accountability is complicated, such as when there is a failure to assess, evaluate research, or make administrative decisions. Stakeholders may hesitate to trust processes supported by AI if there is no clarity on explanation and human oversight (Sethumadhavan et al., 2025). Institutional Policies Must, Therefore, Address Not Only Acceptable Use but Also Transparency, Documentation, And Auditability.

Governance Complexity and Policy Fragmentation

Higher education institutions have decentralized governance structures, which can lead to fragmented policy responses. When different units develop similar policies, it raises confusion and compliance risk-related issues. The constant technological change creates further problems as policies become rapidly outdated. It is a challenge to develop governance mechanisms that enhance coherence and permit flexibility and responsiveness. Frameworks can align institutional beliefs with choices made through organizational decision-making in varied settings (Bukar et al., 2024).

Cultural Resistance and Change Management

The last constraint on generative AI policy implementation is culture and change management. The anxiety of losing one's job, expertise, or academic identity can drive a skepticism towards AI initiatives. Well-designed policies are not adopted when they are not well communicated, professionally developed, and when stakeholders are not engaged. Policy development should not be separated from organizational learning and change in an institution.

All these issues and controversies highlight the ineffectiveness of simplistic or compliance-driven policies. According to the authors, ethical, pedagogical, governance, and organizational frameworks related to generative artificial intelligence as a sociotechnical phenomenon are required (Ferreira et al., 2025). It is important and essential to address these challenges in a holistic manner to allow generative AI to stimulate higher education institutions' mission and values.

COMPARATIVE ANALYSIS OF INSTITUTIONAL APPROACHES

This paper's comparative analysis shows how higher education is responding to the policy challenges of generative artificial intelligence. Despite the size, mission, governance traditions, and regulatory environments showing very different institutional contexts, some similarities exist in the way their policy decisions are designed, put into action, and maintained. This part is essentially a continuation of the comparative discussion between a dominant institutional approach and the implications for governance and pedagogy, research integrity and organizational capacity, and the wider implications related to policy maturity and institutional learning.

Restrictive Policy Models: Risk Avoidance and Compliance Orientation

Restrictive policy models indicate the most precautionary institutional response to generative AI. Rather surprisingly, institutions framing GenAI mostly as an academic integrity, assessment validity, and institutional reputation threat are on the rise. Many policies prohibit, monitor, and enforce, frequently extending existing academic misconduct policies to explicitly restrict or prohibit the use of generative AI tools in teaching, learning, and assessment. From a governance viewpoint, they aim for compliance and risk containment and create a sense of control for the administrator in uncertainty.

Using the comparative evidence, restrictive approaches are limited and ineffective. The inconsistency arises mainly from the difficulty of reliably detecting

AI-produced material and the rapid evolution of AI tools (Li et al., 2025). When instructors misinterpret and mishandle restrictive policies, we see varying practices across courses and departments. Therefore, students may see these policies as not being in tune with professional realities that increasingly normalize such AI students. Over time, modeling insulating may become so unmanageable and dry AIs underground and create mistrust between institutions and learners.

Permissive and Innovation-Oriented Policy Models

Policies in this model favour the open and experimental. Many organizations are encouraging students and educators to play with generative AI for learning and productivity instead of banning it. Also, these bodies proposed general principles of conduct rather than prohibitions. Usually, institutional talks about digital transformation, innovation, and competitiveness, reference this model.

According to a comparative studies review, permissive options may lower concerns and enhance teaching experimentations. According to a growing number of educators, artificial intelligence has great potential for teaching, and students can develop invaluable critical skills. This is usually the case because of challenges in defining clear demarcations. Effectively calibrates assessment conditions and limits participant conduct, while ensuring transparency regarding the use of results. If ethical or legal problems arise, diluted accountability may complicate governance activities. Put differently, with permissive models, it is possible to shift risk from institutions to individual educators and learners (García-López et al., 2025).

Figure 2. Spectrum of institutional policy approaches

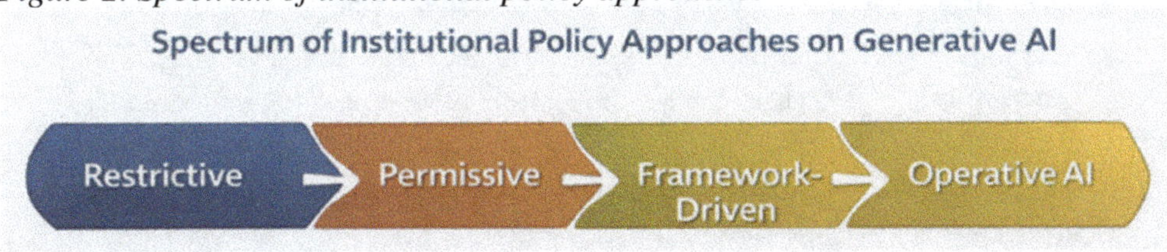

Balanced and Framework-Driven Policy Approaches

By utilising conceptual frameworks, balanced policy approaches integrate innovation and responsibility. Rather than a one-size-fits-all do-not-do-that prohibition or a blanket laissez-faire call, the models are proposed along with guiding principles, roles, and processes for authorization anywhere. Policies often allow disciplinary variation around a core so that there is coherence of values.

According to studies, framework-driven approaches are highly resilient and more legitimate. By linking governance structures, pedagogical guidance, research integrity standards, and capacity-building measures, these models aim to overcome policy fragmentation. Figure 2 depicts the placement of restrictive, permissive, and balanced models on the risk management and innovation enabling dimensions. According to the institutions that adopted framework-driven policies, these policies ensure better clarity of communication, stronger engagement with stakeholders, and a better fit between policy intent and practice.

Policy Maturity and Institutional Learning Trajectories

Additionally, the policy level can also be utilized to compare and assess institutions. Maturity Models Show that Policy Development is a Process Rather than an Event. As depicted in Figure 3, institutions with lower maturity levels adopt an ad hoc stance towards generative AI. In contrast, highly mature institutions consider generative AI policies as part of the governance, teaching, and research portfolio.

Figure 3. Institutional policy maturity levels for generative AI adoption

Ad Hoc	Emerging	Established	Optimized
Approach	Disorganized pilot efforts	Draft initial policies & clear usage zones	Iterative monitoring & agile updates
Structure	Ad hoc policies & unclear boundaries	Policies formalizing	Integrated AI governance strategy
Leadership	Limited central oversight	Interim AI working groups	Centralized AI oversight
Stakeholder Involvement	Fragmented consultation &	Needs assessments beginning	Cross-functional task force
Evaluation	Reactive response & sporadic feedback	Inconsistent review cycles & early reporting	Regular monitoring & iterative feedback

Comparative studies demonstrate that levels of maturity are associated with sustained engagement of leadership, governance arrangements, participation, and investment in the development of professionals. Mature institutions regularly monitor new technologies to get ahead of outcomes and thus don't need to make knee-jerk policy changes. Most importantly, maturity reflects learning capacity, learning in a new institution, and time.

Cross-Institutional and Global Comparisons

Analyzing any country, in particular, provides insights into how unique regulatory regimes and cultural context shape institutional policy response. Organizations with robust data protection and accountability systems tend to focus on governance and compliance, while those with more flexible and light regulatory arrangements tend to focus on innovation and experimentation. In many respects, the two are quite different. According to Zlateva et al. (2024), the conceptual framework nevertheless gives us a common language that can link policies with institutional mission.

Synthesis of Comparative Insights

Comparison of all models indicates that no model is superior to the others. Restrictive frameworks could be useful in building confidence, at least in the short term, since they allow almost no adaptation. The permissive model enhances innovation but often harms consonance and accountability. A framework-driven approach offers a hybrid terrain that encourages responsible innovation, institutional learning, and sustained success. The idea behind this chapter is that conceptual frameworks can inform institutional policy development on generative artificial intelligence at a time of complexity and change in higher education.

RESULTS AND ANALYSIS

This section provides an elaborated result and analysis of the proposed conceptual frameworks for the development of institutional policy on generative artificial intelligence. Due to the recent emergence of generative AI and the lack of longitudinal empirical datasets, this analysis adopts a scenario-based, comparative, and analytical approach commonly used in higher education policy and governance research. This approach allows for the systematic assessment of the performance of policies in a credible institutional context.

Scenario-Based Institutional Analysis

Three representative institutional scenarios are created to assess how various policy approaches perform in practice, namely:

(1) AI-assisted student assessment and learning activities,
(2) generative AI use in academic research and scholarly authorship, and
(3) AI-supported administrative and strategic decision-making.

According to the prevailing discourse in higher education circles, a selection of situations that could trigger ethical, legal, and governance risks has been made.

In the assessment scenario, institutions are mainly reliant on monitoring, detection tools, and disciplinary measures under restrictive policies. While the attempt does achieve a reduction in overt instances of misuse in controlled settings, it does so with an accompanying rise in workloads for administrators, and anxieties for students, as well as placing further strain on already adversarial faculty–student relationships. Institutions with more leeway encountered challenges linked to varied assessment standards and non-linear accountability. On the other hand, framework-driven policies redesigned assignments to make the process clear, showcase AI usage, and align with outcomes in the missions. The rise in clarity led to a drop in disputes.

Comparative Outcome Evaluation

As seen in Figure 4, the assessment of the four outcomes related to teaching, academic integrity assurance, staff readiness, and students' trust is compared. Institutions that had policies induced by the framework performed better on the whole. The quality of teaching will continue to improve through better teaching support and assessment design. Promotion of academic integrity has become more transparent rather than through a punitive approach. A key enabling factor is staff readiness, a finding that reflects the importance of professional development found in policy.

Risk–Benefit Trade-Off Analysis

A simple risk-benefit model is used to evaluate the efficacy of the policies. We can imagine or conceptualize a net policy benefit (Rb).

$$Rb = I - \lambda K \qquad (2)$$

In the above expression, I is innovation potential, K is ethical, and compliance risk, followed by λ, is institutional risk tolerance. Restrictive policies may reduce innovation without an adequate reduction in risk. Likewise, permissive policies tend to enhance innovation but at the expense of clarifying who governs what. Utilizing frameworks, they find a smart balance between innovation and risk. Figure 5 illustrates the effectiveness of risk mitigation policies over time. As AI gets better, disproportionate policies become ineffective. However, frameworks still entail a lower risk of non-compliance and reputational damage.

Long-Term Sustainability and Policy Adaptability

Evaluating GenAI policies for institutions for sustainability. Scenario projections suggest that in the long run, their institutions with adaptive governance mechanisms will be better prepared for emerging AI capabilities and regulations. As illustrated by Figure 6, being able to sustain and maintain the policy can be improved if it includes a review phase that occurs regularly, the involvement of stakeholders, and a feedback mechanism.

If an organization does not have these policies, then it will be forever doing one-off updates to the policy. This will lead to a 'firefighting' kind of governance and fatigue for stakeholders. The precisely opposite approach is that framework-driven institutions engage in policy development as a process of continuous learning that allows for incremental adjustment without disrupting existing practices.

Interpretation of Results

The findings reveal that conceptual frameworks may serve both as evaluative tools and generative tools for institutional policy development. A framework-based policy can provide coherence across the governance domains, reduce uncertainty among public and private stakeholders, and improve institutional capacity to oversee techno-economic change. The efficacy of generative AI governance hinges, therefore, less on technology and more on alignment, transparency, and organisational learning, the authors argue.

Scenario-Based Analysis

Framework-driven policies react to upcoming GenAI use cases more proficiently than institutions with no framework. Outcomes across teaching quality, academic integrity, and staff readiness are compared in Figure 4.

Figure 4. Policy impact comparison across institutional outcomes

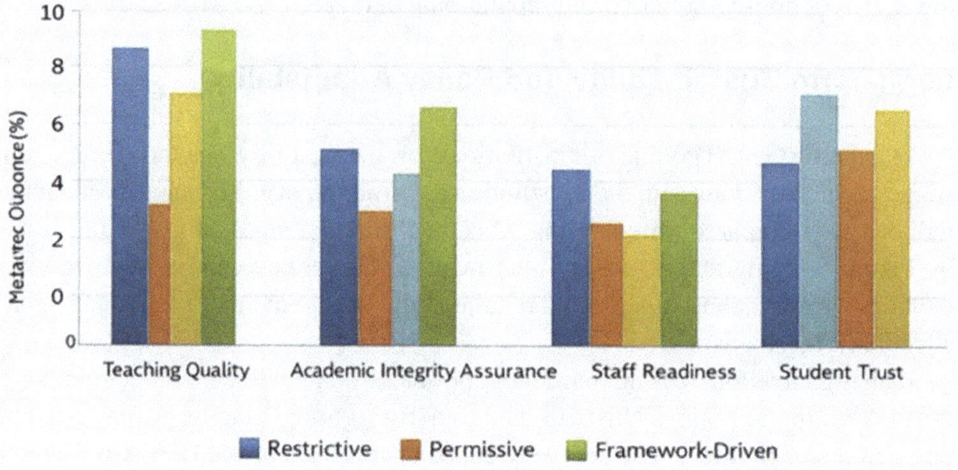

Risk and Benefit Trade-Offs

Quantitative modeling shows that aligning policy proactively prevents both compliance violations and innovation hindrances. The effectiveness of risk mitigation has been illustrated in Figure 5, which depends on the maturity of the policy used.

Figure 5. Risk mitigation effectiveness under different policy frameworks

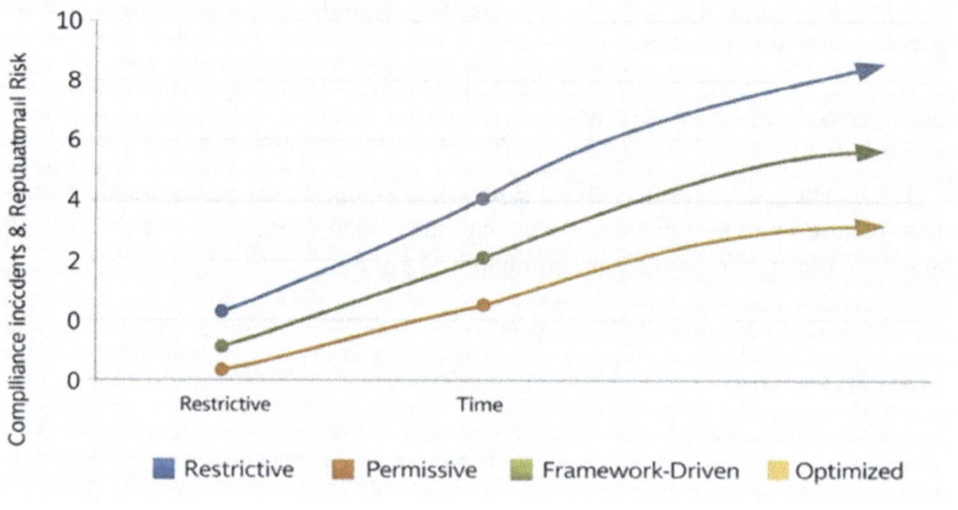

Long-Term Sustainability

The capability of policies to sustain themselves with the passage of time and adaptive governance as a factor is shown in Figure 6.

Figure 6. Long-term sustainability of generative AI institutional policies

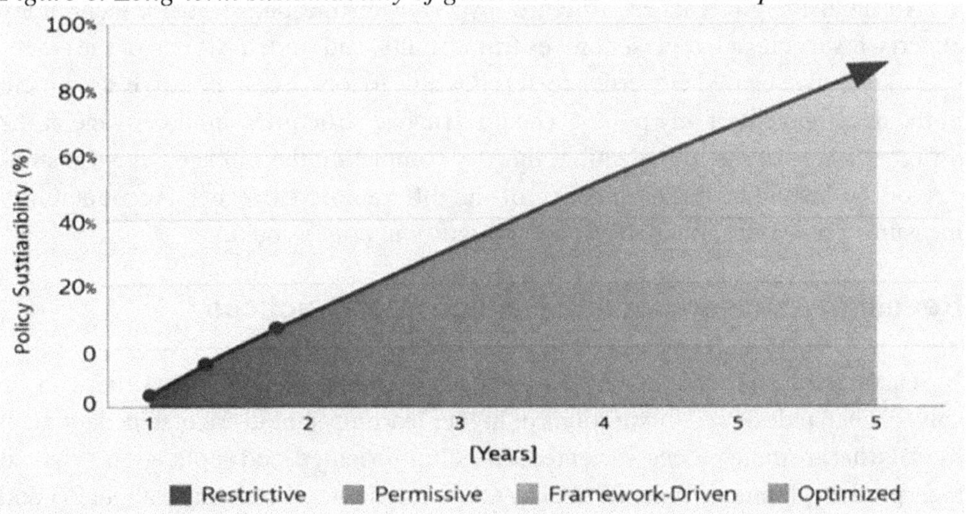

SOLUTIONS AND RECOMMENDATIONS

In order to develop effective Institutional policies for generative artificial intelligence, the solutions generated must be proactive, adaptive, and based on institutional values. In this section, we outline a set of actionable solutions and recommendations to support responsible, sustainable, and future-oriented GenAI governance in higher education, based on the conceptual frameworks, comparative insights, and scenario-based analysis presented in this chapter. The recommendations are grouped along strategic, operational, and cultural dimensions to stay true to the complexity of policy.

Adopt Framework-Driven Policy Design

Organizations must eliminate ad hoc or tool-based rules in favour of framework-based policy design. The conceptual frameworks offer guides to help the thinking process, but do not constrain thinking. Unlike long lists of dos and don'ts that typically accompany regulations, the frameworks focus on guiding principles, roles, and processes that support decision-making about teaching, research, and administration. By taking this approach, institutions may react to new GenAI applications without the need for constant rewriting.

Establish Inclusive and Multi-Level Governance Structures

An inclusive governance structure involving institutional leaders, technology experts, legal counsel, representatives from faculty, and students is one of the essentials of effective GenAI Governance. It is possible to form a collaborative agreement in the development of any policy. The governance structures should engage at the different levels of the organization, thereby completing the linkage from the strategy of the institution to the practice of the different departments. Accountability measures prevent fragmentation and ambiguity in policy-making.

Redesign Assessment and Pedagogical Practices

There are many assessment challenges concerning generative AI that can be solved when redesigned. Institutions of higher learning should endorse pedagogical models that are more process-oriented, reflection-oriented, and application-oriented than product-oriented. Policies should allow learners to learn more about AI and provide guidance on the proper use of GenAI in their work. For faculty to design assessments resilient to AI tools, it is essential that they receive professional development and use GenAI as not a shortcut, but as a supporter of learning.

Invest in Capacity Building and Professional Development

The proficiency of the institutions to carry out their functions is critical to sustainable systemic policy implementation. The faculty should be continuously given professional development programs on AI literacy, ethical use of AI, and using AI for pedagogical innovation. Various educational institutions, colleges, universities, and organizations need to offer such programs for their administrative and support staff as well. Based on the fact that different users have different needs, the training initiatives should be different. Making investments in technical infrastructure and support services for experimentation on AI also promotes capacity development.

Address Ethical, Legal, and Equity Considerations Systematically

Ethical and legal issues raised by the use of biotechnologies must be covered in policies, and not treated as incidental. Educational institutions should formulate policies on data privacy, intellectual property, consent, and accountability of GenAI's use. Policy makers should address unequal access to AI tools and the adverse effects on one or more disadvantaged communities to make sure that AI is fair. Trust develops in an environment where individuals can easily see how decisions get made, and ethical standards are clear.

Promote Transparency, Documentation, and Explainability

Universities should be transparent on the application, evaluation, and governance of GenAI tools on campus. When processes are documented as supported by AI, accountability is enhanced, and the auditability of their decision rationales and assessment criteria is better supported. Institutions that operate in high-stakes situations should, where possible, ensure that their AI systems and practices promote explainability and human oversight.

Implement Iterative Policy Review and Feedback Mechanisms

The use of generative AI is evolving quickly, which calls for policy updates. The review plan development should be based on a regular cycle that seeks feedback from the faculty, students, and administrators of the institution. The data obtained on the policy implementation, which has the potential to improve the evidence-based policies, could include, but is not limited to, the assessment results, breaches of compliance, and stakeholder views. A recurrent review system that is repetitive in nature will avoid any policy getting out of date and also favours continuing learning in the institution.

Foster a Culture of Responsible Innovation

The culture of an organization impacts its success. Making the governance of GenAI a compliance issue is a disservice to institutions looking to innovate responsibly. It is feasible to achieve fearlessness not through experimentation but through initial exposure and recognition of good practice in an open conversation. Capacity development is also contributed to through investments in technical infrastructure and support services for AI experimentation.

According to the recommendations and solutions, proper generative AI governance is not the result of a single policy but rather the frameworks that underpin governance, pedagogy, ethics, capacity building, and more. By implementing these strategies, universities can become smarter in times of uncertainty, innovate for the future, and build trust and accountability in the generative AI.

IMPLICATIONS FOR POLICY AND PRACTICE

This section translates the analysis and conceptions of the chapter into implications for institutional policy–makers, academic leaders, faculty, support professionals, and others. The earlier sections dealt with the development of theory with reference to comparative evaluation with respect to different criteria, and an analysis involving scenario or empirical projection. This section presents a practical application of the framework-based approaches with regard to governance, teaching, and organization. Given the above implications, generative AI policy should not only be a regulatory instrument but also a tool for enhancing institutional resilience, trust, and innovation.

Implications for Institutional Leadership and Strategic Governance

This chapter suggests that senior institutional leaders should see the governance of generative AI as a strategic rather than a compliance issue. Executive leaders must develop a clear institutional vision regarding GenAI use, which is values-driven (e.g, in alignment with academic freedom, institutional mission, teaching excellence, research integrity, and public trust). It is important for signifying the priorities of an institution, as well as for communication in a decentralized academic unit.

Great leaders should accept and understand that building an effective GenAI policy could require ongoing engagement, not just an episodic action against a tech disruption. Allocating resources to governance bodies with agreement to guide policies, actions, and ongoing evaluations. By incorporating broader GenAI-related considerations into their strategies, such as digital transformation, quality assurance, and risk, leaders can ensure coherence and future sustainability of their institutions. Policies for new technology can encourage research by creating suitable and well-balanced interventions, the rules state.

Implications for Faculty Governance and Teaching Practice

The academic staff members within the institution term their teaching conceptual frameworks. The governing bodies of the faculty are key players in ensuring the interpretation and localization of GenAI policies to fit disciplinary conventions and educational practices. A reliable framework creates commonalities that enable decisions and avoid conflicts, as demonstrated in this 'decision' tree. Academic freedom cannot be restricted in any way. The policies regarding curricula and assessment frameworks empower educators to redesign tasks related to generative AI capabilities. Making use of processes, opening up AI use reporting, and getting involved in authentic learning tasks are some strategies an AI could use to build an integrity culture in education. To help policy goals be achieved, all educational institutions should offer the opportunity for pedagogical experimentation through professional development and communities of practice.

Implications for Students and the Learning Experience

By ensuring fairness, it guarantees consistency and transparency as well. Students can better regulate their use of AI when they know where the boundaries lie, thus not stressing over ways to use it. By adhering to a governance model defined by a framework, students can learn to engage with AI tools wisely, rather than disempower themselves. They will also contribute to the crucial development of AI literacy.

It also ensures an equalisation of learning across courses and programmes. Teachers' conflicting expectations can cause inconsistency, unfairness, embarrassment, or confusion. By establishing common underlying principles that allow for contextual variation, institutions can improve inclusive learning environments. Students are prepared for the professional environments that use AI.

Implications for Administrative and Professional Support Units

Implementation of generative AI policies relies heavily on administrative and professional support units and on people with the required capacity or skills. It is essential to collaborate in a manner that guarantees coherence and effective implementation of the policy. By creating a governance framework that aligns the responsibilities of various units for efficiency, a framework-driven approach stops duplicate work (Wang et al., 2025).

Capacity-building and risk management are facilitated by support units. Assisting clients with data privacy, IP, and responsible AI procurement can help mitigate legal and ethical risks. Ofosu-Asare (2025). In addition, teacher and learning centers' professional development programs help faculty and staff develop competency to use AI responsibly. An institution's effective functioning and the legitimacy of its policies are coordinated by support units.

Implications for Policy Implementation and Change Management

The implementation of generative AI policies can be successful with effective change management strategies. People in institutional cultures may be afraid that you are taking away their job, expertise, or academic identity. Using policies in a framework can assist with an individual's worries, enhancing human oversight. It requires a lot of communication to do change management. At the initial level and continuously, stakeholders should be involved, and through open channels, so that they understand the reasons for current or future policy decisions, their concerns are allayed, and lessons learned and good practice examples are exchanged. Feedback mechanisms permit institutions to identify shortcomings in implementation and adjust policies. When the development of the policy is participatory and iterative, then trust builds.

Implications for Institutional Resilience and Future-Proofing

The chapter findings imply that framework-driven GenAI policies reinforce resilience in the institution. Leveraging adaptability, review processes, and learning mechanisms in governance structures allows institutions to respond to emerging technologies and regulations. A resilient institution is not guided by pre-set rules, but is able to learn from experience and change policy gradually.

It is important to recognize generative AI as a continuing socio-technical transition and not a 'new innovation' for future-proofing institutional policy. A conceptual framework offers tools enabling processes and tool transformations to take place according to institutional and societal values. By implementing the recommendations in the upcoming section, HEIs can fundamentally redefine their governance from the reactive, passive, and un-strategic stance they have taken thus far into an active, strategic, and above all, ethical and sustainable one about generative AI.

FUTURE RESEARCH DIRECTIONS

With the fast-paced evolution of generative artificial intelligence, the need for a continuous systematic research agenda to inform institutional policies with evidence is important. In this chapter, we have dealt with concepts that are frameworks. Research conducted later must be empirically tested and refined in other contexts of higher education.

Empirical Evaluation of Policy Effectiveness

We can further research institutional policies and frameworks put in place for GenAI. We need mixed methods and long-term studies to assess how various policy responses are reshaping the academic integrity landscape. Can we sustain the teaching innovation, the staff readiness, and the student trust? Institutions with varying policy maturity can give insights into which governance mechanisms work best and under what circumstances.

Cross-Cultural and Regulatory Contexts

Future research should examine the effectiveness of generative AI policies in different national cultural and regulatory contexts. Global research will show what influence data rights laws and norms have on institutional reactions to GenAI. Such research can lead to the creation of frameworks that are globally aligned, locally relevant, and fit for purpose.

Disciplinary and Pedagogical Variation

Further examination of the interactions among generative AI policies, discipline norms, and teaching practices is warranted. Varying evaluation practices and knowledge standards characterize different fields, as well as varying acceptance of automation (Gupta & Tripathi, 2014). Knowledge of these differences may impact policy design.

Institutional Learning and Policy Adaptation

Future research should focus on the process of learning policy-making. Analyzing how institutions respond to technological uncertainty through feedback mechanisms, stakeholder engagements, and review studies may offer insights. The future insights of generative AI capabilities are useful for Policy Design.

Policy Maturity Table

The key characteristics of institutional policy maturity levels for the adoption of generative AI are summarized in Table 1, drawing on the comparative and results analyses.

Table 1. Institutional policy maturity levels for generative AI adoption

Policy Maturity Level	Key Characteristics	Governance Focus	Common Challenges
Ad hoc	Informal guidelines, individual discretion, reactive responses	Minimal governance	Inconsistency, uncertainty, and enforcement gaps
Emerging	Formal policies for specific use cases (e.g., assessment)	Compliance-oriented	Fragmentation, limited staff capacity
Structured	Integrated frameworks across teaching and research	Coordinated governance	Change management, resource demands
Adaptive	Continuous review, stakeholder engagement, policy learning	Strategic and ethical governance	Sustaining engagement, evaluation complexity

CONCLUSION

This chapter has maintained that the adoption of conceptual frameworks is essential for the future-proofing of institutional policies. As GenAI technologies evolve, we can see a growing mismatch between policies that rely solely on prohibition or ad hoc guidance and the legitimacy of our policies. In comparison, framework-based methodologies afford organizations the flexibility and structure to align innovation with academic principles, ethical values, and regulatory obligations. This chapter uses an integrated literature review, a comparative analysis of institutional approaches, and a scenario-based exercise to establish that policy domains on governance, pedagogy, the integrity of research, and the development of capacities must be treated as interrelated. The available conceptual frameworks can guide the design of policies and assessment, adaptation, and institutional learning frameworks.

Ultimately, the responsible adoption of generative AI in higher education entails more than establishing rules of the game. It is a constantly changing sociotechnical process. If institutions invest more in good governance, professional development, and policy assessment, they can strengthen their ability to cope with uncertainty while safeguarding trust and accountability and the quality of education. The insights and structures presented in this chapter can assist in the ethical, robust, and human-centered governance of GenAI in higher education.

REFERENCES

Alli, A. A., Magombe, Y., Lwembawo, I., & Kasadha, J. (2025, May). A Policy Framework for the Use of Generative Artificial Intelligence in Higher Education Institutions. *In 2025 IST-Africa Conference (IST-Africa)* (pp. 1-11). IEEE. DOI: 10.23919/IST-Africa67297.2025.11060512

Bukar, U. A., Sayeed, M. S., Razak, S. F. A., Yogarayan, S., & Sneesl, R. (2024). Decision-making framework for the utilization of generative artificial intelligence in education: A case study of ChatGPT. *IEEE Access : Practical Innovations, Open Solutions*, *12*, 95368–95389. DOI: 10.1109/ACCESS.2024.3425172

Calzada, I. (2025). Generative AI and the urban AI policy challenges ahead: Trustworthy for whom?. *Transforming Government: People, Process and Policy*, 1-17. DOI: 10.1108/TG-08-2025-0240

Cheng, K., & Wu, H. (2024). Policy framework for the utilization of generative AI. *Critical Care : The Official Journal of the Critical Care Forum*, *28*(1), 128. DOI: 10.1186/s13054-024-04917-z PMID: 38637898

Chukwuere, J. E. (2025). Developing a generative AI conceptual framework for higher education. *The Indonesian Journal of Computer Science*, *14*(5). Advance online publication. DOI: 10.33022/ijcs.v14i5.4997

Ferreira, A. L., Pinheiro, A., & Medeiros, P. (2025). Ethical and innovative integration of generative Artificial Intelligence in Higher Education: Challenges and proposals for an institutional policy. *International Journal of Social Science and Education Research Studies*, *5*(4), 379–382. DOI: 10.55677/ijssers/V05I04Y2025-04

Fotis, G., Gupta, S., Varshney, T., Dhar, S. L., & Gulzar, M. M. (Eds.). (2025). *Modern Computing Technologies for EV Efficiency and Sustainable Energy Integration*. IGI Global., DOI: 10.4018/979-8-3373-2382-4

García-López, I. M., & Trujillo-Liñán, L. (2025). Generative Artificial Intelligence in Education: Ethical Challenges, Regulatory Frameworks and Educational Quality in a Systematic Review of the Literature. [). Frontiers.]. *Frontiers in Education*, *10*, 1565938. DOI: 10.3389/feduc.2025.1565938

Gupta, S. (2025). *The Future of Machine Learning with Automation in Engineering*. Nova Science Publishers., DOI: 10.52305/YFIX2832

Gupta, S., & Tripathi, R. K. (2014). Optimal LQR controller in CSC based STATCOM using GA and PSO. *Archives of Electrical Engineering*, *63*(3), 469–487. Advance online publication. DOI: 10.2478/aee-2014-0034

Hadi, W., Al-Qerem, A., & Aldweesh, A. (2025). Institutional Policies, Governance, and Regulatory Responses to Generative AI. In *Examining Cybersecurity Risks Produced by Generative AI* (pp. 643–666). IGI Global Scientific Publishing., DOI: 10.4018/979-8-3373-0832-6.ch026

Jin, Y., Yan, L., Echeverria, V., Gašević, D., & Martinez-Maldonado, R. (2025). Generative AI in higher education: A global perspective of institutional adoption policies and guidelines. *Computers and Education: Artificial Intelligence*, *8*, 100348. DOI: 10.1016/j.caeai.2024.100348

Jungherr, A. (2023). Artificial intelligence and democracy: A conceptual framework. *Social Media + Society*, *9*(3), 20563051231186353. DOI: 10.1177/20563051231186353

Ko[1], S. J. S., & Lim, A. (2024, October). Conceptual Modeling for Public AI Systems. In *Advances in Conceptual Modeling: ER 2024 Workshops, AISA, CMLS, EmpER, QUAMES, JUSMOD, LLM4Modeling, Pittsburgh, PA, USA, October 28–31, 2024, Proceedings* (Vol. 14932, p. 107). Springer Nature. DOI: 10.1007/978-3-031-75599-6_8

Li, M., Xie, Q., Enkhtur, A., Meng, S., Chen, L., Yamamoto, B. A., . . . Murakami, M. (2025). A Framework for Developing University Policies on Generative AI Governance: A Cross-national Comparative Study. *arXiv preprint arXiv:2504.02636.*

Maheswaran, K., Selvakumar, P., Shaikh, M., Shashank, G., Gupta, S., & Manjunath, T. C. (2025). The evolution of smart urban mobility with emerging technologies. In *Leveraging VANETs and blockchain technology for urban mobility* (pp. 1–28). IGI Global Scientific Publishing., DOI: 10.4018/979-8-3373-0265-2.ch001

O'Sullivan, J., Lowry, C., Woods, R., & Conlon, T. (2025). Generative AI in Higher Education Teaching & Learning: National Policy Framework. https://eprints.teachingandlearning.ie/id/eprint/6702/

Ofosu-Asare, Y. (2025). Guiding the future: developing an ethical framework for generative AI use in education. *The International Journal of Information and Learning Technology*, 1-19. DOI: 10.1108/IJILT-06-2024-0113

Rao, M. S., Saraswathy, S., Neela, V., Arun, M. R., Gupta, S., & Taqui, S. N. (2023, November). Efficient Model Training in Decentralized Systems with Federated Learning. *In 2023 IEEE International Conference on Communication, Security and Artificial Intelligence (ICCSAI)* (pp. 900-904). DOI: 10.1109/ICCSAI59793.2023.10421469

Savvadelli, E., Kiouvrekis, Y., & Kokkinaki, A. (2025, July). A Literature Review on Rule-Based Systems as Decision Support Systems. *In International Symposium on Human Aspects of Information Security and Assurance* (pp. 376-388). Cham: Springer Nature Switzerland. DOI: 10.1007/978-3-032-02504-3_26

Sethumadhavan, R. P. P. S., Sajimon, P. P., Selvakumar, P., Kadu, S. G., Chandel, P. S., & Gupta, S. (2025). Environmental sustainability and employee participation. In *Green Leadership Strategies for Increased Employee Engagement and Performance* (pp. 275–298). IGI Global Scientific Publishing., DOI: 10.4018/979-8-3373-2106-6.ch009

Shankar, R., Chaudhary, B. P., Mehraj, H., Gupta, S., Arslan, F., Srivastava, A. K., & Goswami, C. (2023). Impact of node mobility on the DL based uplink and downlink MIMO-NOMA network. *International Journal of Information Technology : an Official Journal of Bharati Vidyapeeth's Institute of Computer Applications and Management, 15*(6), 3391–3404. DOI: 10.1007/s41870-023-01362-z

Sinha, R., Sinha, K. K., Patel, M., Gupta, S., & Priya, S. (2024, July). Detection of leukemia disease using convolutional neural network. In 2024 5th International Conference on Image Processing and Capsule Networks (ICIPCN) (pp. 451-456). IEEE. DOI: 10.1109/ICIPCN63822.2024.00080

Soundariya, A., Behera, N. K., Selvakumar, P., Chandel, P. S., Gupta, S., & Manjunath, T. C. (2025). AI and environmental ethics: The role of AI in addressing climate change ethical considerations in AI-driven environmental solutions. In *Human values, ethics, and dignity in the age of artificial intelligence* (pp. 321–346). IGI Global Scientific Publishing., DOI: 10.4018/979-8-3693-9035-1.ch013

Sreekanthaswamy, N., Anitha, S., Singh, A., Jayadeva, S. M., Gupta, S., Manjunath, T. C., & Selvakumar, P. (2025). Digital tools and methods. In *Enhancing school counseling with technology and case studies* (pp. 25–48). IGI Global Scientific Publishing., DOI: 10.4018/979-8-3693-8392-6.ch002

Thandlam, A. K., Vignesh, T., Saravanan, A., Subramani, P., Marimuthu, R., & Gupta, S. (2024, April). Next-gen vehicle safety: The futuristic approach to auto-stop in modern vehicles. In 2024 10th International Conference on Communication and Signal Processing (ICCSP) (pp. 265-270). IEEE. DOI: 10.1109/ICCSP60870.2024.10543666

Wang, X., Xie, F., & Liu, B. (2025). Governance efficiency and upgrade pathways of international generative AI policies and regulations. *Technology in Society, 103082*. Advance online publication. DOI: 10.1016/j.techsoc.2025.103082

Zlateva, P., Steshina, L., Petukhov, I., & Velev, D. (2024). A conceptual framework for solving ethical issues in generative artificial intelligence. In *Electronics, communications and networks* (pp. 110–119). IOS Press. DOI: 10.3233/FAIA231182

Chapter 4

Engineering the Intelligence-Augmented Workforce Through Human-AI Capability for Economic Growth

Duggirala Aravind
http://orcid.org/0009-0005-4362-7684
ASET Institute of Science and Technology, India

Shivansu Sachan
http://orcid.org/0000-0002-9893-8018
Chhatrapati Shahu Ji Maharaj University, India

R. N. Ravikumar
http://orcid.org/0009-0009-3705-1681
Marwadi University, India

Jyoti Rana
http://orcid.org/0000-0001-7474-3702
Amity University, Noida, India

Kasukurthi Aravind
http://orcid.org/0009-0007-3768-3422
ASET Institute of Science and Technology, India

DOI: 10.4018/979-8-2600-0116-5.ch004

ABSTRACT

This chapter presents a notion of the intelligence-enhanced workforce as the source of economic prosperity in the era of artificial intelligence. It creates a new model of AI-enhanced skills transformation, which combines the capabilities of a human mind, and algorithmic systems to enhance productivity and innovation. The chapter looks into the concept of reskilling, the collaboration between humans and AI, and adaptive learning ecosystems to reinvent the world of work and company performance. The chapter presents policy implications by connecting the improvement of skills to the quantifiable economic performance, thereby providing practical ideas to policy-makers, industry leaders, and educators. It ends with future research directions on the scalable workforce models and sustainable competitiveness in the rising algorithm economy.

1. INTRODUCTION

The world is now changing its face of work, talents, and economy with artificial intelligence rapidly altering it. With the rapid integration of AI in the organizations, new competencies are becoming inevitable. This change underscores the need to redefine the approach to workforce development to maintain sustainable productivity, innovation, and inclusive economic development in the transformative digital economy.

1.1 AI-Driven Transformation and Emerging Skills Gap

The development of artificial intelligence is radically transforming the form of contemporary economies and the essence of labor. In industries, AI technologies are automatizing routine activities, enhancing human decision-making, and facilitating entirely novel ways of productivity. The change does not apply only to the technical field; it is spread across the healthcare, education, finance, and creative industries, with human-AI collaboration becoming the focus more than ever (Chuang et al., 2024). Consequently, conventional job descriptions are becoming hybrid ones, where both domain knowledge as well as the capacity to engage with intelligent systems are needed. This has however, left a huge and ongoing skills gap. Most employees do not have the digital, cognitive, and adaptive capabilities to operate in AI-enhanced settings. The current education and training systems are not usually able to keep up with the speed at which the skills demanded are evolving. Thus, a mismatch between the labor market needs and the work force abilities is increasing. This gap is also essential to address because it directly affects productivity, employability, and the economic growth in the long term. The question of how skills should change with AI is thus a key challenge to all individuals, organisations, and policymakers (Al Aina, 2025; Xu et al., 2025).

1.2 Objectives and Research Focus

The aim of the chapter is to explore that AI-enhanced skills transformation can become a major spur of economic growth in the new digital economy. It attempts to go beyond descriptive discourses by establishing a systematic conception of how human latencies might be enhanced in an effective way, by interplay with artificial intelligence. The main aim is to present a conceptual model, the Intelligence-Augmentation Model (IAM), that can describe the nature of the human-AI cooperation, the development of skills, and the final productivity.

The chapter is informed by a number of questions of research. To begin with, how can the workforce competencies be repurposed to meet the needs of AI-compliant environments? Second, how can people and AIs team up to foster performance and innovation? Third, what is the relationship between AI-enhanced skills, and their contribution to quantifiable economic performance at an individual, organizational, and macroeconomic scales? The chapter sets out to answer these questions with a view of offering theoretical knowledge and also with relevance in practice. It adds to the further discussion of workforce transformation as it correlates directly skills development and economic productivity, providing a more comprehensive view of AI-driven development.

1.3 Chapter Structure and Contribution

The chapter is well-organized to represent logical flow of theoretical underpinnings to practical consequences and ways of future research. It starts with questioning the overall economic implication of artificial intelligence and how it influences productivity and innovation. It is succeeded by a review of extant literature on reskilling, workforce transformation, and human-AI collaboration, identifies major gaps that will justify the necessity of a new framework. The chapter then presents the Intelligence-Augmentation Model (IAM), the key contribution, which is a layered model of the development of skills and their conversion into economic value.

Particular sections then use the framework to apply to individual, organizational and policy contexts and illustrate its practical applicability. The chapter also elicits findings and analytical insights based on the constructive use of the model and thereafter offers a discourse that contrasts the findings generated with the research available. A specific case study highlights how traditional job roles are being reshaped into AI-enabled jobs which also focus on the improvement of productivity and skills. The paper finishes the chapter with a set of research directions and insights into the future, wherein the author presents the intelligence-augmented workforce as the crucial factor of sustainable economic development in the AI era.

2. AI AND ECONOMIC TRANSFORMATION

2.1 AI as a Driver of Productivity and Innovation

Artificial smarts have become an issue of essential productivity and invention throughout contemporary economies. When used to automate routine and repetitive processes, AI can help organizations save money on their operation and enhances accuracy and efficiency. Mature analytics, machine learning, and predictive systems provide companies with the ability to process high amounts of data, create insights, and make evidence-based decisions faster. This change does not only improve on the performance of the operations, but also strategic abilities enabling the businesses to discover new opportunities and react more rapidly to changes in the market (Watts & Munir, 2026; Gao & Feng, 2023).

In addition to automation, AI plays an important role in enhance innovation by enhancing human creativity and problem-solving skills. The AI systems are used to generate new products, services and types of businesses in fields like healthcare, finance, manufacturing, and education. An example of using AI-based tools could be in drug discovery or financial forecasting, or personalized learning. These abilities allow organizations to shift to an operations, which is based on innovation, rather than efficiency. On a macroeconomic level, high productivity and innovation reflect to higher economic output and competitiveness. As companies implement AI technologies, they produce value on processes and new solutions that spur economic growth. Therefore, AI is not just a technological solution, but also a revolution changing the dynamic of productivity and innovation (Magd et al., 2022; Liu, 2022).

2.2 Transition from Labor-Based to Intelligence – Based Economies

Introduction of artificial intelligence in the economic system is increasing the curtailment of traditional labor economies to intelligence based economies. In the past, the basis of economic growth had very much been on physical labor, capital investment and standard procedures. Nevertheless, the emergence of AI technologies is changing this paradigm to systems where knowledge, data, and cognitive capabilities take centre stage in creating value. In this new model, productivity cannot be determined just by how much labor is put in to work but the quality of intelligence taken to work and decision making processes (Li et al., 2023; Kologlugil, 2015).

Hybrid workplaces within the context of intelligence-based economies are the result of machine skills that are getting ready to augment human labor. The workers will perform intricate problem solving, critical thinking and adaptive learning, as opposed to dwelling on routine behavior. AI operates on data-intensive and repetitive tasks and enables people to concentrate on higher-value tasks, which demand judgment and creativity. This change essentially changes the structure of jobs, organizational leadership, and work itself. Additionally, economic competitiveness is becoming defined by the capacity of a nation to create, implement and fuse clever systems in a much better method. Those countries and organizations that invest in AI infrastructure and skill acquisition are in a better place to realize sustainable growth. Thus, the intelligence is one of the key economic resources in the changing world order (Zhang et al., 2024; Li et al., 2025).

2.3 Role of AI-Enhanced Skills in Economic Growth

The AI-enhanced capabilities are crucial in the translation of technological innovations into actual economic developments. Although artificial intelligence works as the means of automation and data-driven decisions, the possibility to use AI-related tools effectively is what defines the overall influence that the latter has on the workforce. AI-enhanced skills can be described as a set of specific technical skills, including data literacy and algorithmic knowledge, as well as cognitive skills, such as critical thinking, creativity, and adaptability. This combined competence allows one to work with AI tools and utilize the appropriate resources. On the personal level, AI-driven competencies enhance employability and productivity by assisting employees to carry out their duties in a more productive and precise manner (Ara, 2026; Kirikkaleli & Kirikkaleli, 2025).

The ability to use AI tools can prepare employees to create insights, resolve complex scenarios, and engage in the process of innovation. An advanced workforce in terms of AI-related skills benefits a company and enhances its performance, decision-making capabilities, and competitive advantage at the organizational level. A company which invests in achieving continuous skill development is more likely to attain sustained productivity gains. In terms of macro economy, the general proliferation of AI-advanced skills would be part of economic growth as it would enhance labor productivity and innovation. Economies will be able to gain the advantages of AI more effectively as more people will have these solutions and achieve higher output, achieve better efficiency, and be competitive in the long run (Kalai et al., 2024; Fatima Ajibike, 2025).

3. LITERATURE REVIEW

3.1 Reskilling and Workforce Transformation

Reskilling and workforce transformation have risen to be the central themes in modern day discourse on what lies ahead on the work front. With the continued redefinition of jobs roles by artificial intelligence and automation technologies, organisations and governments are an ever-increasing volume of investments in upskilling and reskilling to remain relevant in the workforce. Available literature underscores the necessity that there should be continuous learning systems so that workers are in a position to meet the changing technological requirements. The old training methods that emphasize skills development in a static manner can no longer be effective in a dynamic and AI-driven world. Researchers emphasize that to be reskilled, people should combine technical and soft skills, such as digital literacy, problem-solving, and adaptability (Barbosa & Real de Oliveira, 2026; Asiedu & Tenakwah, 2025).

Studies in organizations indicate that employee performance and skill-fit in an organization are much better when a structured reskilling program is implemented by the organization. Moreover, workforce transformations are closely attributed with the change in the organizational design, in which roles are becoming more fluid and interdisciplinary. Governments are encouraged at the policy level to support large scale reskilling practice to deal with unemployment risks related to automation. But there are still challenges like availability, scalability, and conformity to industry requirements. All in all, the literature highlights that reskilling is not a single process, but a continuous learning process that is needed to maintain employability and help with economic development in the rapidly transforming technological environment and in changing global labor markets (Li, 2024; Nandal & Nain, 2026).

3.2 Human – AI Collaboration

Human-AI cooperation has become a highly important field of study, which aims at how people and intelligent devices can cooperate to show better results. Compared to traditional automation, in which the labor of a person is substituted, it seems that AI technologies are becoming more of an addition to human efforts, in terms of decision-making, efficiency, and creativity. The trend in literature in this field focuses on the notion of augmentation, in which the AI enhances human judgment instead of human judgment itself. This teamwork strategy allows companies to utilize the capabilities of man and machine. Research shows that successful human-AIs collaboration is based on such factors as trust, transparency, and ease of use of AI systems. The employees need to learn to use AI systems and interpret the results to make adequate decisions (Vossing et al., 2022; Sowa et al., 2021).

Moreover, organizational culture can contribute to evolution in the process of collaboration, where employees should be motivated to use and test AI tools. The study also emphasizes the role of coming up with interfaces that ensure a smooth human-machine interaction. In spite of its promise, there are still obstacles in the way to the successful use of the collaboration between humans and AI. Algorithms: The problems of bias in algorithms, inability to explain them, and change resistance can impede adoption. However, the literature has always shown that with the right implementation, human-AI cooperation can have a profound positive impact on productivity, innovation and performance of organizations in various industry settings throughout the world (Jiang et al., 2023; Nguyen et al., 2024).

3.3 Existing Models Linking Skills and Economic Outcomes

The models that have been developed to associate skills with economic outcomes are mainly based on human capital theory that considers education and skill development as a major predictor of productivity and economic development. This vision holds that an investment in education and training will strengthen individual abilities which will result in better labor market outcomes and more output. This framework has since been extended overtime to the knowledge-based economies, in which intellectual capital and invention are center stage in the propensity of growth. Recent research has tried to include technological aspects in these models; the importance of digital skills and automation has been identified (Ali et al., 2025; Somaratne et al., 2025).

Digital capital and technological competence concepts have been proposed to elucidate how individuals and organizations can, using technology, gain economic benefits. Many of these models, however, simply assume technology is an external factor; instead of incorporating it directly into the skill development process. Moreover, current models tend to miss out the active interaction between human capabilities and AI systems. Although they recognize the role of technology, they fail to elaborate on how collaboration between human and AI helps to improve productivity and innovativeness. Consequently, more comprehensive models that directly couple AI-enhanced skills and economic results in the transforming digital economies are required (Xu & Cho, 2025; David & Borsi, 2025).

3.4 Research Gaps

3.4.1 Lack of Integrated Frameworks

Although numerous studies have been conducted on the topic of reskilling, workforce transformation and the integration of human and AI collaboration, there is a distinct deficiency of single frameworks that take the integration of these factors and create a unified model. Majority of the studies deal with these dimensions separately and are either dealing with skill development, adoption of technology, or the economic consequences. Such a disjointed method makes it difficult to comprehend the interactions of such components in practical situations. In the absence of an extensive framework, researchers and practitioners would find it harder to develop good strategies in an integrated and systematic way to match skill development with technological development and gains with economic development.

3.4.2 Limited Connection Between Skills and Productivity Metrics

The other major gap in the literature is the fact that there is a lack of relation between skill development and quantifiable productivity gains. Whereas there is general agreement in literature on the significance of reskilling and digital capabilities, they tend to be empirically or conceptually vague in how digital capabilities and reskilling move into enhanced performance and economic value. The concept of productivity has often been cited in broad strokes without connection to any particular skills or human-AI interactions. This is causing a gap that has made it difficult to determine the success in reskilling initiatives. Thus, models that explicitly define the connection between AI-enhanced skills and measurable productivity gains are needed.

4. RESEARCH METHODOLOGY

In this chapter, the researcher has employed conceptual and qualitative research methodology to explore the link between skills transformation through artificial intelligence (AI) enhancement and economic development. It employs an integrative research framework drawing on literature about jobs transformation, human–machine interaction and productivity gains. This study does not use of primary empirical data from a quantitative or qualitative empirical study, but instead builds on a conceptual model, the Intelligence-Augmentation Model (IAM), which explains how human intelligence and artificial intelligence systems combine to create value. Such an approach is suitable given the nascent nature of the field in which theoretical work is crucial to informing empirical research.

The research approach includes a review of academic and industry literature to extract and examine relevant constructs, patterns and research gaps. Previous research is drawn upon to delineate fundamental elements like human skills, AI capabilities and human-AI interaction. These components are then mapped into a multi-layered model recognising movement from individual skills to economic impact. The research also includes a case study example to illustrate the application of the developed model.

The concepts are validated by using the IAM framework across the individual, organisational and policy settings to evaluate its explanatory capacity and fit. Assessment focuses on the framework's capacity to connect skills training to increased productivity and economic benefits. Although quantitative data are lacking to empirically test the framework, the approach offers a robust theoretical basis for analysing the impact of AI on the workplace. The model can be empirically tested by future research to verify and develop the proposed model in various industry sectors and economies.

5. CONCEPTUAL FOUNDATIONS

5.1 Definition: Intelligence-Augmented Workforce

Intelligence-augmented workforce is a contemporary labor model, in which artificial intelligence technologies complement human abilities to create products and services more productively, effectively, and innovatively. The concept is based upon human-intelligent systems interaction, unlike the old-fashioned ways of working with workforce relying on human energy only. In these, AI technologies assist human beings by automating menial processes, processing sophisticated data, and offering viable insights, allowing employees to concentrate on tasks that bring more value. The strategy reinvents the approach of employees as acts-doers and into figuring out the challenge and using AI as a strategic ally. The intelligence augmented workforce can be characterized as continuous learning, flexibility and absorbing technological advancements into routine work processes. It further underscores the need to prepare skills that facilitate human-AI cooperation. Finally, the concept is a starting point of the interpretation of how workforce transformation leads to productivity and sustainable economic growth.

5.2 Key Constructs

5.2.1 Human Capabilities

Human capabilities refer to the mental, social, and technical abilities that one has and use in the workplace. When applied in the intelligence-augmented workforce, these are not merely domain knowledge but thinking, creativity, problem-solving, and flexibility. Such abilities assist the person to process complicated data, base sound judgments, and react suitably to shifting problems. In the work setting especially in teamwork, emotional intelligence and communication skills are very important. Since AI systems will occupied with routine and automated tasks, human workers will find their abilities more concentrated on high-order work that machines are not able to execute with such ease. These are, strategic thinking, ethical judgment and creative problem-solving. Also, the digital literacy is turning into a basic need, as it enables a person to comprehend and engage to work with the technology. Another important factor is continuous learning workers need to modify their skills on a regular basis to keep up with the quickly changing fields. All these capabilities collectively constitute the basis of significant human involvement in AI-enhanced workplaces.

5.2.2 AI Capabilities

Intelligence capabilities are the operational capabilities of artificial intelligence systems to handle functions that would normally be done by human intelligence. Such capabilities are data processing, pattern recognition, predictive analytics, natural language processing, and automated decision support. AI can quickly examine large volumes of both structured and unstructured data and discover patterns and insights that would otherwise be hard to accomplish manually. This helps companies to improve efficiency, precision and responsiveness of many processes. Within the framework of workforce transformation, AI capabilities can be viewed as enablers, which supplement human capabilities. To illustrate, machine learning algorithms may help in forecasting and optimization, and conversational AI may be helpful in customer communication and interaction. But, AI systems will act under predefined algorithms and data inputs, and this means that they need human supervision in order to be correct, fair, and ethically used. Being aware of these capabilities is crucial to successes in the introduction of AI in work processes. Utilized adequately, AI potentials can contribute greatly to productivity and aid innovation in the industries.

5.2.3 Human – AI Interaction

Human-AI interaction is the process and mechanism by which individuals use artificial intelligence systems to carry out activities and obtain desired results. This interaction is a key ingredient of the intelligence-enhanced workforce, since it defines the extent of conjugation success of the human and machine potentials. Good communication requires not merely working with AI tools, but also being aware of the results and capabilities of these tools as well as their logic. This involves some degree of digital literacy and understanding AI systems. Human-AI interaction quality is determined by factors including system design, usability, transparency, and trust. When AI systems become explainable and intuitive, users are bound to embrace these technologies and use them to make decisions. On the contrary, unclear situation or perceived bias may decrease trust and prevent working together. Human control is crucial to authenticate AI-based knowledge and guarantee ethical results. Close integration empowers a smooth working team, as humans drive strategy, and AI facilitates analytic capabilities, which eventually result in increased productivity, precision, and novelty within the organization.

6. PROPOSED FRAMEWORK

6.1 Intelligence-Augmentation Model (IAM)

Intelligence-Augmentation Model (IAM) is a conceptual model that is meant to describe how the human skills and the artificial intelligence capabilities interact to produce productivity and economic value. The model does not consider AI as a substitute of human labor but a complements which complement human performance. It offers a systematic way to comprehend the idea of how people, institutions, and economies can use AI-supplied capabilities to grow sustainably. IAM is designed using a layered architecture which embodies the development of basic human capabilities to wider economic results. The layers correspond to important steps of the transformation process starting with human base skills up to the objective economic contribution. The model states that human and AI systems should interact with each other to enhance efficiency, innovation and decision making because the effectiveness of their cooperation results in better working. Combining the skill building with technological abilities, IAM fills significant gaps in current research, specifically the absence of models correlating transformations in the workforce with economic performance directly. It also offers a point of practical insights to stakeholders by showing the relationships between investments in skills and AI adoption with tangible results. All in all, the model is an integrated instrument to analyze and lead the transformation of the workforce in the modern economies in an AI-driven environment.

6.2 Layer 1: Human Core Skills

The Intelligence-Augmentation Model has the first layer dedicated to human core skills as they are the basis behind the intelligence-augmented workforce. Such abilities comprise cognitive, social, and technical skills that give people the ability to work in AI-driven setups. Intervention of complex data requires the use of cognitive skills including critical thinking, analysis, problem-solving which are vital in informed decision making. Creativity is also crucial and enables people to innovate and change in response to changing conditions. Besides cognitive skills, social and emotional skills are becoming important. Effective teamwork is supported through communication, collaboration, and emotional intelligence especially where human beings team with other people and intelligent systems. These competencies make sure human judgment and interpersonal understanding are highlighted in decision making. Another vital element of human core skills is technical literacy. Although not everybody will require a high level of programming skills, some basic knowledge of digital tools, data systems, and AI capabilities is required. This allows employees to work with technology in a comfortable and efficient manner. One of the characteristics of this layer is continuous learning. With the growing pace in technological developments, one has to constantly enhance their skills in order to stay relevant. This flexibility guarantees that human functionality develops with AI systems and offers the model a solid basis of further augmentation and productivity.

6.3 Layer 2: AI Interaction Skills

The second tier of the Intelligence-Augmentation Model deals with AI interaction skills, which helps people to interact well with artificial intelligence systems. Such abilities help to close the divide between human potential and technology to make AI accessible as an efficient and responsible tool. Within AI interaction skills, there can be the skill to analyze the output provided by intelligent systems, understand their constraints, and apply their own knowledge to real-life issues. Formulation and input design promptness is one of the main facets of this layer, with those using AI systems providing clear and well-structured directives to be followed. This directly affects the quality and relevance of the outputs. Also, one should learn to discriminate AI-generated outcomes, find possible errors, biases, or discrepancies. This makes sure that automated processes are not used to make decisions but they are backed by humanity. System awareness is another concept that is significant and consists of knowing the basic functioning of AI models. This encompasses the information about the data sources, algorithms, and risks that can be caused by the use of AI. This knowledge will create greater credibility and facilitate an improved cooperation. Flexibility in the ability to use various tools in different situations can be considered AI interaction skills as well. With the development of AI technologies, people have to constantly change the approaches to interaction. In general, this layer will guarantee the successful value of AI systems by human users who will enjoy their potential and stay in control and accountability.

6.4 Layer 3: Augmentation and Productivity

Intelligence-Augmentation Model third layer is devoted to augmentation and productivity, i.e. it is the point where human abilities and AI capacities meet to produce higher-performance results. At this stage, individuals and organizations go past the simplest engagement with AI systems to attain significant gains in efficiency, precision, and innovation. Augmentation is when AI tools are used to assist human decision-making, automate repetitive tasks, and present insights to boost problem-solving solutions. Among the main advantages of this layer, one should speak about more productivity. AI can help people spend more time on more valuable activities like developing strategies, creative reasoning, and complex analysis by decreasing the number of hours and energy devoted to routine tasks.

This transformation causes a more efficient utilization of human resources and will result in better organizational results. Improved quality of decisions is another benefit of augmentation whereby it offers data-oriented insights. AI systems are able to process vast amounts of data, draw conclusions, and make recommendations that can be used to make informed decisions. This, together with human judgment, results in more accurate and reliable results. Moreover, this layer promotes innovation as it makes it possible to experiment and iterate quickly. AI can assist organizations in trailing ideas, streamlining processes and creating new products or services. In general, augmentation and productivity are the fundamental value creation phase of the model, as the combination of human and AI strengths brings real performance changes.

6.5 Layer 4: Economic Impact

The fourth tier of the Intelligence-Augmentation Model is the one devoted to economic impact, which is a more general result of the AI-enhanced skills and productivity gains. At this point, the gains (i.e. individual and organizational augmentation) roll down to macroeconomic level, further affecting growth, competitiveness, and economic performance. The main economic effect is an increase in productivity which translates to a boost in output and efficiency of industries. Organizations that embrace AI technologies and create a workforce that is proficient in AI have an edge in the world market. This competitiveness helps boost the economy through investment, innovation and business creation.

Along with it, AI-enabled competences facilitate the creation of new sectors and work positions, which, in turn, contributes to the economic diversification and sustainability. The other significant factor about this layer is the enhancement of labor market outcomes. Employees, provided with AI-relevant skills, have higher chances of getting a job and adjusting to evolving work demands. This will mitigate risks against unemployment linked to automation and promote inclusive economic growth. Governments that invest in AI infrastructure and training can enhance their competitiveness in the global economy at the national level. This layer presents the issues of economic outcomes that associate skill development with the ability to achieve sustained growth in the era of artificial intelligence.

6.6 Explanation of Relationships Across Layers

The Intelligence-Augmentation Model consists of an interactive arrangement that relies on and impacts upon each other. The connection starts with the human essential competencies, which form the initial skills needed to interact with AI systems. Unless people are equipped with powerful mental, interpersonal, and technical abilities, they will not be able to make use of AI technologies. These primary skills directly allow the acquisition of AI interaction skills as the second layer of the model. The skills of interaction with AI serve as an interface between human abilities and technology. They control the effectiveness with which people can analyze, control, and use AI-created products.

Once these competencies are highly developed, they contribute to human-AI integration, contributing to the third layer: augmentation and productivity. At this level, the synergies between humans and AI systems lead to higher efficiency, enhanced decision-making, and further innovation. The result produced in the augmentation layer is propagated to the fourth layer which is economic impact. High individual and organizational productivity leads to wider economic growth, competitiveness, and employment. This shows a distinct shift in skill development to economic results. Notably the interrelations between layers is dynamic and continuous. It has feedback loops and economic results will determine another investment into the skills and technology. This intertwined design makes the model flexible and applicable in changing AI-driven conditions.

Figure 1. Intelligence-Augmentation Model (IAM): AI-Enhanced Skills Transformation for Economic Growth

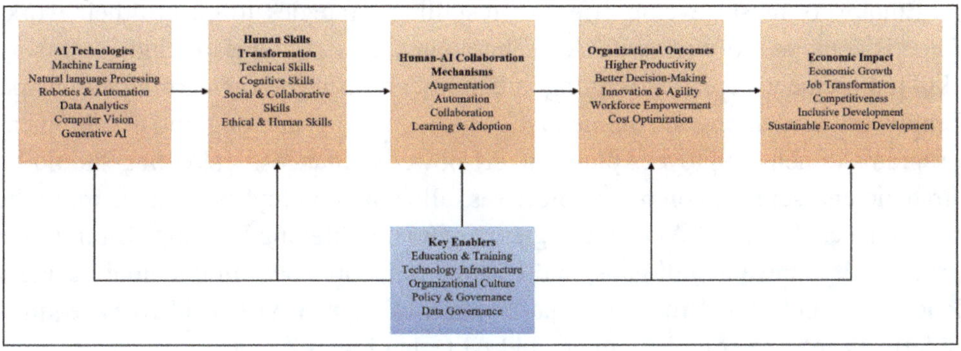

7. FRAMEWORK APPLICATION

7.1 Individual Level

The Intelligence-augmented workforce requires workers to transition from low-level task execution to jobs that focus on skilled thinking, creativity and integration with technology. Employees should recognise transferable skills for the AI-enabled world of work. This requires ongoing monitoring of market dynamics, using digital platforms, and engaging in relevant training initiatives. Workers should seek to master hybrid skills combining industry-specific knowledge and AI-interaction skills. Career pathways with certifications or micro-credentials can guide workers from "job at risk" to "AI-augmented job" for long-term employability and productivity in future labor markets.

Adaptive and lifelong learning is the key to success for individuals working in an AI-enabled world, which is constantly evolving skills needs. Lifelong learning keeps workers up-to-date by addressing new skills and knowledge requirements driven by technological change. Adaptive learning strategies, enabled by digital platforms and AI-powered tools, enable individuals to tailor their learning to their requirements and aspirations. This can be done through online learning, training programs, and hands-on experience. Through a proactive learning approach, people can boost their capacity to work with AI, and productivity, adaptability and competitiveness in uncertain work environments.

7.2 Organizational Level

Employers must develop effective reskilling strategies to ensure their workforce is equipped to work with AI technologies. Key strategies include assessing skill requirements, creating training initiatives, and embedding learning into work. Employers need to provide online platforms, mentoring, and ongoing development programs to help employees plug into AI-powered changes. Upskilling should be strategic and support company objectives, allowing employees to move into jobs that enhance the use of AI technologies. Embracing lifelong learning will improve productivity, prevent skill gaps, and ensure competitiveness in dynamic business landscapes and global markets. The creation of human-AI hybrid roles requires redefining roles to combine human and AI technologies.

To achieve this, organizations need to redesign tasks by distinguishing between automated and human activities requiring creativity or emotional intelligence. This allows for designing roles in which humans use AI technology to support their work and decision-making processes. Well-defined roles, complemented by training and technology, are critical for success. Organizations can design hybrid roles to make the best use of resources, increase efficiency, and support employees to carry out valuable tasks, thus driving innovation and growth in competitive markets around the world.

7.3 Policy Level

Government action is critical to facilitate large-scale workforce transformation in the age of AI. Governments need to develop and execute policies and programs addressing skills development, technology uptake, and inclusive economic advancement. These should include reskilling initiatives, incentives for businesses to provide training, and national strategies for AI. Policymakers should also develop regulatory frameworks promoting responsible use of AI and safeguarding workers against dislocation. Public-private partnerships can be crucial to providing training opportunities and jobs. Successful policies allow societies to reap AI's rewards while reducing inequalities and ensuring equitable growth across industries and regions. Integration of education and training curricula with needs of an AI-driven economy is essential for future workforces. Universities need to modernise their curricula to incorporate digital skills, AI literacy, and multidisciplinary competencies required for human-AI collaboration. Training and courses will need to be skills-based and application-focused. Government, academic and industry partnerships are required to align education with labor market demands. Further, diverse learning options like online modules and modular qualifications may enhance education. Integrating technological innovation into education can create a workforce that can innovate and boost economic growth.

8. PRACTICAL AND MANAGERIAL IMPLICATIONS

The shift to a humanoids-augmented workforce has implications for individual workers wanting to stay relevant in a changing work environment. A paradigm shift is needed from linear skill training to adaptive learning in line with technological change. This involves actively learning to use digital literacy, critical thinking, and AI interaction skills. Workers need to develop hybrid capabilities that integrate industry-specific knowledge and the use of smart technologies. Career pathways need to be more flexible and adaptable also, through continued learning. Through specialised training, certifications and hands-on experience activities, individuals can boost their employability and adaptability. Furthermore, a critical ability to assess AI-generated recommendations allows employees to responsibly use these technologies and ensure human intuition and judgment delivers value in decision-making, regardless of the global and ever-evolving professional environments of today.

From a company perspective, companies need to revise their role and human resource strategies to accommodate AI technologies. Organizations will need to have reskilling programs in place to identify skill gaps and develop employees to meet business strategies. Seamless integration of learning into work processes through digital platforms and mentoring initiatives can enable ongoing learning. Moreover, roles should be redefined to leverage synergies between people and AI systems, with an emphasis on leveraging human ingenuity and judgement. Effective leadership is essential to create a supportive environment that promotes innovation, experimentation and adaptability to new technologies. Open dialogue and ethical frameworks are also key to fostering trust in AI systems. By embracing these principles, companies can increase productivity, and remain competitive in the rapidly evolving business landscape across sectors.

From a managerial and policy point of view, strengthened efforts are needed to ensure broad and sustainable benefits from the AI-driven digital transformation. Governments need to create holistic policies that focus on workforce transition, equitable access to education and adoption of AI technologies. Digital infrastructure investment and upskilling initiatives are essential to equip the workforce for the future. Public-private partnerships with education providers can ensure that training and education systems align with industry needs. Meanwhile, managers need to connect strategic workforce planning with the long-term goals of the organisation, by combining automation with human skill development. Prioritising ethical dimensions like fairness, transparency and accountability is key to the risks of implementing

AI. Such measures will foster a conducive environment for innovation, and drive inclusive economic development in the era of the intelligence-augmented economy.

9. RESULTS AND ANALYSIS

The use of the Intelligence-Augmentation Model (IAM) offers a framework for examining the role of skills amplified by AI in productivity enhancement and economic impact. The conceptual study of the framework suggests that augmenting human core skills through AI interaction skills has positive effects at the individual, firm and national levels. The hierarchical nature of IAM shows how skills building leads to economic outcomes, and therefore, the need for integrated capacity building. Through the integration of human skills and tools, the framework shows how augmentation processes create value through productivity gains, decision making and innovation. At the worker level, the model illuminates that those with cognitive as well as AI interaction skills to be more productive and agile. This enables them to perform tasks more effectively by using AI technologies for data processing, automation and decision-making. This allows them to spend less time doing routine tasks and spend more time on problems needing complex problem solving and creativity.

This leads to greater job performance, quality of work, and flexibility in the job market. The model further implies the importance of ongoing learning to maintain these benefits, as employees need to continuously reskill to keep up with technological advancements. At an organisational level, the use of IAM results in enhanced efficiency and decision-making processes. Companies that focus on reskilling programs and harness AI technologies for tasks see an improvement in resource allocation and cost optimization. Augmented human-AI roles empower workers to work with AI systems to make quicker and more informed decisions. Additionally, the model illustrates how AI enables innovation by allowing experimentation with different processes and business models.

Such advancements enhance business performance and provide competitive is in a rapidly changing marketplace. Transformations to the economy provide insight to the model that indicates through pervasive use of AI-enhanced skills productivity and economic growth increase. By enhancing skills and capacity, both at the individual and organisational level, improved productivity is achieved. This framework also suggests that economies that invest in skills and AI infrastructure to usher in the changes are better placed to thrive in the global economy. In sum, the findings indicate that the IAM framework is a parsimonious explanation of the interactions between skills, technology, and economic outcomes.

10. DISCUSSIONS

The insights gleaned from the conceptual use of the Intelligence-Augmentation Model point to the fact that AI-powered skills are key to productivity and economic performance. The model's layered framework shows how it builds from the core human skills to various economic benefits. At the micro-level, the combination of cognitive skills and skills in interacting with AI facilitates more effective task performance and decision-making. At the inter-personal level, the use of human-AI pairs improve firm performance and innovativeness. These findings imply that gains in productivity are not only driven by technology but the integration of human and AI skills. Also, the model suggests that learning is a critical factor for sustained performance. In general, the results support the notion that workforce transformation is crucial for harnessing the potential of AI in the modern economy.

The Intelligence-Augmentation Model builds on past work by offering a more holistic view of workforce transformation and growth. Existing studies framed by human capital theory highlight the role of education and skills for productivity, but tend to consider technology as external. However, IAM goes beyond this to link AI actively to the skill development process, recognizing the synergy between humans and AI. Likewise, previous studies on human-AI collaboration focus on process efficiency, but not necessarily on economic impacts. IAM approach fills this void by linking micro-level skill development to macroeconomic productivity and growth. It represents a more holistic and dynamic model of skills and technology co-evolution, compared to current frameworks. This holistic view offers a deeper understanding of the impact of AI-driven change on productivity and long-term competitiveness.

This chapter offers a number of theoretical insights to this field of research into workforce change and economic growth. First, it conceptualises the intelligence-augmented workforce and thus recasts the human role in an AI-influenced labour market. It highlights the symbiotic relationship between humans and AI, rather than replacement, and offers a fresh view on the productivity and innovation environments. Second, the Intelligence-Augmentation Model provides a framework that integrates human capabilities, interactions with AI, and the augmentation process with economic implications. This fills a critical gap in previous studies, where these aspects are examined in isolation. Third, this model helps bridge a gap in empirical policy research that has yet to consider the integration of technological factors in the human capital theory into digital economies. The chapter links skills development to economic outcomes, offering a more integrated perspective on the role of human capital in driving economic growth in the era of artificial intelligence.

This study is subject to certain limitations. First, it is theoretical as the Intelligence-Augmentation Model is not complemented with quantitative evidence. Although the model offers a robust way to conceptualise job transformation, its credibility could be enhanced with empirical validity testing in various industries and settings. Furthermore, the model may not account for differences in technological and skills development across regions and industries, especially in emerging economies with limited access to digital technologies. Second, the focus on human-AI interactions may overly simplify a complex interplay between humans and AI, which may differ based on organizational culture and design of the computer systems in place. Subsequent studies should build on this model by conducting empirical research, exploring a range of contexts, and taking into consideration industry- and region-specific factors in the adoption and impact of AI on the workforce.

11. CASE STUDY: JOB TRANSFORMATION IN THE AI ERA

This case study also explores how the role of the data analyst has been redefined at Amazon through the use of artificial intelligence (AI) and machine learning (ML) that change operations and processes. In the past, data analysts at Amazon manually collected data from various business systems, cleaned and pre-processed data, conducted descriptive analysis using spreadsheet software or SQL and produced regular reports. Managers would then use these reports for inventory, pricing and customer insights. This was a manual, time-consuming and reactive process, built on past data.

Through the use of AI and machine learning platforms, Amazon made the job of analyst an AI-augmented one. Data collection and processing are now automated to capture a large volume of data in real time from customer behaviour, supply chain and sales channels. Machine learning algorithms provide predictive analytics, like forecasting, recommender systems, and dynamic pricing. Data analysts no longer spend their time cleaning and preparing data for analysis; they focus on understanding and interpreting the results of AI models, cross-checking forecasts, and using the insights to inform business decisions. The focus of decision-making is now on prediction rather than reporting, allowing quicker and more informed responses to dynamic market conditions.

This shift was accompanied by a change in skills needed. While conventional analytical skills, such as data interpretation and subject matter expertise, are still crucial, they are now complemented with skills in interacting with AI. Data analysts should have a high-level understanding of machine learning processes, be able to interpret AI-generated results and detect biases or anomalies. Candidates need to be familiar with data visualisation platforms and AI-powered analytics solutions. Soft skills, including critical thinking and communication, to effectively communicate findings to a non-technical audience are also important. Lifelong learning is important to stay up-to-date with new tools and technologies.

This shift has made a difference in productivity, efficiency and decision-making. Through automation of data processing, a much shorter time is needed for analysis, enabling analysts to solve bigger problems with larger data volumes. Accuracy and speed has increased due to fewer errors and faster processing. Above all, predictive analytics has resulted in more accurate and anticipatory decisions. For instance, Amazon's prediction system largely boosts its sales through product personalisation and predicting user preference. Overall, this case study illustrates how the combination of human skills and AI enables an efficient and smart working process. This evolution in Amazon's data analyst role embodies the guidelines of the Intelligence-Augmentation Model, which sees human skills and AI technologies complement each other to increase productivity and create economic value.

12. FUTURE RESEARCH DIRECTIONS

12.1 Measuring AI-Driven Productivity

To understand the benefits of AI mostly in productivity terms, future research should explore and build measures of productivity gains from AI-enhanced skills and human–AI interactions. Although previous research recognises gains in efficiency and productivity, there is limited agreement on universal metrics to quantify the productivity gains from AI. We need quantitative frameworks that relate skills, use of AI and performance outcomes of individuals, organizations, and economies. This needs to include metrics that capture both first- and second-order impacts of AI, including quality decisions, innovation and time saved. Longitudinal research could offer a better understanding of the time dynamics of productivity with ongoing training. Data analytics linked to economic models can also clarify the causal link between adopting AI and economic impacts for better policy and investment choices.

12.2 Standardization of AI Skill Frameworks

Another crucial research focus is the creation of common frameworks in relation to AI skills across industries and regions. At present, there is no standardisation of the skills needed for human-AI interaction. Various institutions and companies take different approaches, resulting in fragmentation and confusion in human resource policies. Studies should focus on revealing universal competencies that apply across the board, and acknowledge the need for specific industry needs. This involves combining technical, cognitive and moral competency elements. Standardization would enable alignment of education systems, training and the labor market. It will also help in the development of certification and benchmarking frameworks for the assessment of skills. These can be instrumental in the scaling up of reskilling programs and empowering workforces in the AI-driven economies.

12.3 Human – AI Performance Evaluation Models

Research needs to also consider the development of robust models to assess performance in human-AI collaborative settings. Current performance systems have been developed to assess human-only processes, and may not fully reflect the value of AI systems. Alternative models should be developed to measure the performance generated from human-machine inputs. These should account for aspects like correct decisions, speed and productivity improvements, learning and innovation. Further, we should study the impact of user trust, transparency and experience on human-AI interactions. It's important to include qualitative and quantitative metrics for effectiveness. Laboratory and field experiments in various domains can be used to validate models and determine best practice. Through the creation of robust systems to assess performance, researchers and practitioners can gain insights into the benefits of integrating AI and enhance collaboration to increase efficiency and achieves organisational goals.

13. CONCLUSION

This chapter has explored the impact that artificial intelligence has on human skills, and its contribution to economic advancement, in the intelligence-augmented workforce. It discussed how the interplay between human talent and AI technologies is at the core of establishing productivity, innovation, and decision-making processes at different levels. It underscored how in the 21st century economic value no longer solely comes from labour or capital, but from the effective integration of human intelligence and technology. As the chapter examined how skills, technology and economic outcomes interact, it noted that skills transformation is a key element to achieve growth and competitiveness in the AI era.

This chapter offers an important contribution with the Intelligence-Augmentation Model (IAM) that combines human core competences with skills for interacting with AI, the process of augmentation and its consequences on economic value creation. This model contributes to filling gaps in the literature by linking factors that are not typically considered together, including reskilling, human interaction with AI systems, and productivity impacts. Using a multi-tiered approach, IAM shows how skill formation at the individual level contributes to organisational productivity enhancements and, on a macro level, ultimately leads to economic advancement. The model is also relevant as it provides guidance for individuals, organisations and policymakers to develop strategies to align skill development with the technology revolution.

The study also highlighted the need for lifelong learning and adaptability in the intelligence-augmented world. As the evolution of AI technologies increases, the need for blended skills that include technical, cognitive and social learning are becoming even more important. The chapter demonstrated that individuals with these skill sets are more likely to effectively use AI tools, while organisations with well-trained employees are more productive and innovative, and have a greater competitive advantage. Meanwhile, the role of policy makers is also important in supporting universal access to education, subsidising large scale reskilling activities, and in setting up regulatory mechanisms to ensure ethical and sustainable integration of AI.

More broadly, the insights add to the debate about AI's impact on economic growth, by providing a more holistic view of the skills- productivity relationship. By moving beyond a technological perspective on AI, the chapter highlights how AI will reshape work and value creation. This outlook places emphasis on augmentation and skills elevation, rather than substitution and job loss, by recognising the potential for AI to complement human skills rather than substitute for them.

In summary, the shift to intelligence-augmented economies completely changes the organisation of work, skills and economies. Adapting to the new reality requires individuals, businesses, and countries to quickly align with the new skills needed and leverage AI capabilities. Through promoting a lifelong learning culture, workforce training, and ethical development and deployment of AI, the benefits of intelligence augmentation can be realised. The intelligence-augmented workforce, therefore, becomes a key enabler for sustainable prosperity, innovation and competitiveness in the future global economy.

CONFLICT OF INTEREST

The authors confirm that there are no known conflicts of interest that could have contributed to any bias in the manuscript's interpretation or interpretation of facts. The research was objective and independent and did not involve any commercial or financial relationships which may have been interpreted as a potential conflict of interest. The authors have revised the manuscript, the final version of which has been read and approved by them, and have taken the utmost care to ensure the highest academic integrity and transparency in their writing.

ACKNOWLEDGEMENT

I would like to thank all those who helped me with the completion of this work. Their support, inspiration and feedback were invaluable in bringing about this result. I am particularly grateful to my professors, colleagues and family for their consistent encouragement and support. This success would not have been possible without their support and encouragement.

REFERENCES

Al Aina, R. (2025). Bridging the AI skills gap: Preparing generation Z for the evolving job market landscape through innovative educational strategies. *Industry and Higher Education*. Advance online publication. DOI: 10.1177/09504222261423356

Ali, I., Nguyen, K., Ali, A. M., & Cui, T. (2025). Human–AI collaboration in knowledge ecosystems: A multidisciplinary review, integrative framework and future directions. *Journal of Knowledge Management*, •••, 1–22. DOI: 10.1108/JKM-03-2025-0431

Ara, A. (2026). AI-enhanced learning for sustainable development: Balancing innovation and equity in higher education. In *Role of Artificial Intelligence in Higher Education: Pathways to Sustainable Development* (pp. 1–24). Springer Nature Singapore. https://doi.org/DOI: 10.1007/978-981-95-5350-1_1

Asiedu, E., & Tenakwah, E. S. (2025). Future-proofing your workforce: Upskilling and reskilling as HR's top priorities. *Strategic HR Review*, *24*(4), 169–173. DOI: 10.1108/SHR-01-2025-0008

Barbosa, I., & Real de Oliveira, E. (2026). Digital reskilling and workforce transformation: Exploring identity, capability and adaptation in AI-mediated workplaces. *Journal of Organizational Effectiveness: People and Performance*, 1–19. https://doi.org/DOI: 10.1108/JOEPP-12-2025-1109

Chuang, S., Shahhosseini, M., Javaid, M., & Wang, G. G. (2024). Machine learning and AI technology-induced skill gaps and opportunities for continuous development of middle-skilled employees. *Journal of Work-Applied Management*. Advance online publication. DOI: 10.1108/JWAM-08-2024-0111

David, T., & Borsi, B. (2025). Human–AI interaction in knowledge ecosystems: A context–mechanism–outcome perspective. *Journal of Knowledge Management*, •••, 1–23. DOI: 10.1108/JKM-03-2025-0401

Fatima Ajibike, T. A. L. I. A. T. (2025). AI-enhanced skill development: Leveraging AI in biology education to develop skills in digital era. *Journal of Educational Studies Trends and Practice*. https://doi.org/DOI: 10.70382/sjestp.v8i8.030

Gao, X., & Feng, H. (2023). AI-driven productivity gains: Artificial intelligence and firm productivity. *Sustainability (Basel)*, *15*(11), 8934. DOI: 10.3390/su15118934

Jiang, N., Liu, X., Liu, H., Lim, E. T. K., Tan, C. W., & Gu, J. (2023). Beyond AI-powered context-aware services: The role of human–AI collaboration. *Industrial Management & Data Systems*, *123*(11), 2771–2802. DOI: 10.1108/IMDS-03-2022-0152

Kalai, M., Becha, H., & Helali, K. (2024). Effect of artificial intelligence on economic growth in European countries: A symmetric and asymmetric cointegration based on linear and non-linear ARDL approach. *Journal of Economic Structures*, *13*(1), 22. DOI: 10.1186/s40008-024-00345-y

Kirikkaleli, D., & Kirikkaleli, N. O. (2025). AI investment in education and training and economic growth in the USA. *Social Sciences & Humanities Open*, *12*, 101777. DOI: 10.1016/j.ssaho.2025.101777

Li, L. (2024). Reskilling and upskilling the future-ready workforce for industry 4.0 and beyond. *Information Systems Frontiers*, *26*(5), 1697–1712. DOI: 10.1007/s10796-022-10308-y PMID: 35855776

Li, X., Wang, Q., Kong, D., & Tao, Y. (2025). Intelligent manufacturing and corporate human capital upgrade in China. *Journal of Asian Economics*, *97*, 101886. DOI: 10.1016/j.asieco.2025.101886

Li, Y., Deng, J., Hu, Z., & Gong, B. (2023). Economic policy uncertainty, industrial intelligence, and firms' labour productivity: Empirical evidence from China. *Emerging Markets Finance & Trade*, *59*(2), 498–514. DOI: 10.1080/1540496X.2022.2096433

Liu, Q. (2022). Analysis of collaborative driving effect of artificial intelligence on knowledge innovation management. *Scientific Programming*, *2022*(1), 8223724. DOI: 10.1155/2022/8223724

Magd, H., Jonathan, H., Khan, S. A., & El Geddawy, M. (2022). Artificial intelligence—the driving force of industry 4.0. In *A roadmap for enabling Industry 4.0 by artificial intelligence* (pp. 1–15). https://doi.org/DOI: 10.1002/9781119905141.ch1

Nandal, N., & Nain, A. (2026). Reskilling for tomorrow: How HR can drive workforce agility in a changing economy. *Strategic HR Review*, *25*(3), 130–136. DOI: 10.1108/SHR-10-2025-0104

Nguyen, A., Hong, Y., Dang, B., & Huang, X. (2024). Human-AI collaboration patterns in AI-assisted academic writing. *Studies in Higher Education, 49*(5), 847–864. DOI: 10.1080/03075079.2024.2323593

Somaratne, S., De Silva, D., & Athukorala, R. (2025). Mapping human-AI collaboration: A skill framework for the effective use of AI. In *2025 3rd International Conference on Communication, Security, and Artificial Intelligence (ICCSAI)* (Vol. 3, pp. 1253–1261). IEEE. https://doi.org/DOI: 10.1109/ICCSAI64074.2025.11064159

Sowa, K., Przegalinska, A., & Ciechanowski, L. (2021). Cobots in knowledge work: Human–AI collaboration in managerial professions. *Journal of Business Research, 125*, 135–142. DOI: 10.1016/j.jbusres.2020.11.038

Vössing, M., Kühl, N., Lind, M., & Satzger, G. (2022). Designing transparency for effective human-AI collaboration. *Information Systems Frontiers, 24*(3), 877–895. DOI: 10.1007/s10796-022-10284-3

Watts, S., & Munir, T. (2026). Bridging the gap: Exploring innovation enablers, challenges and AI adoption for enhanced workforce productivity. *International Journal of Productivity and Performance Management, 75*(3), 1030–1046. DOI: 10.1108/IJPPM-01-2025-0001

Xu, C., & Cho, S. E. (2025). Factors affecting human–AI collaboration performances in financial sector: Sustainable service development perspective. *Sustainability (Basel), 17*(10), 4335. DOI: 10.3390/su17104335

Xu, X., Arshad, M. A., He, Y., Liu, H., Chen, Q., & Yang, J. (2025). From skilled workers to smart talent: AI-driven workforce transformation in the construction industry. *Buildings (Basel, Switzerland), 15*(14), 2552. DOI: 10.3390/buildings15142552

Zhang, Y., Jiang, H., & Gong, Q. (2024). Dynamics of human-machine task allocation in intelligent production processes: A case study. *Computers & Industrial Engineering, 194*, 110354. DOI: 10.1016/j.cie.2024.110354

KEY TERMS AND DEFINITIONS

AI-Enhanced Skills: AI-skills are a mix of operational, cognitive and digital skills that allow humans to interact seamlessly with artificial intelligence.

Algorithmic Decision-Making: Algorithmic decision-making involves the use of AI systems and algorithms to process data for informed and automated decision-making.

Digital Economy: The digital economy is an economic framework where digital technologies, data and artificial intelligence (AI) are integral in the production, distribution and consumption of goods and services.

Human – AI Collaboration: Human-AI interaction is the interaction between humans and artificial intelligence (AI) systems in which each play a role in completing tasks and making decisions.

Human Capital: Human capital is the expertise, skills and capabilities of individuals which enable their productivity and contributions to the economy.

Intelligence-Augmented Workforce: An intelligence-enhanced work system is a workforce operating system that enhances human capabilities by collaborating with artificial intelligence to enhance productivity, creativity and decision-making.

Productivity: Productivity is the efficiency of transforming various inputs, including labor and technology into outputs, which can lead to enhanced performance and higher value

Reskilling: Reskilling involves acquiring new skills to change career paths or occupations due to changes in technology or the adoption of automation or AI.

Upskilling: Upskilling is the process of upgrading one's skill to perform better and keep up with new technologies in the same job or industry.

Chapter 5
From Transactions to Transformation:
How Artificial Intelligence Is Redefining Financial Marketing Competence in the New Economy

Reema Limbad
http://orcid.org/0009-0003-3601-4957
EDEPT, India

Sarita Agarwal
http://orcid.org/0000-0003-3599-700X
School of Business, Indira University, India

Amrita Tatia Karnawat
http://orcid.org/0000-0002-4059-4697
School of Business, Indira University, India

Suyog Chachad
http://orcid.org/0009-0005-6053-9563
Symbiosis School of Banking and Finance, India

Dipika Agarwal
http://orcid.org/0009-0001-7980-5391
Independent Researcher, India

ABSTRACT

The combination of artificial intelligence, digital platforms, and data-based decision-making processes is disrupting the world in the space where the financial world

DOI: 10.4018/979-8-2600-0116-5.ch005

meets the world of marketing, where these two worlds were never integrated in terms of organizational structures, as well as educational curricula, and are now being changed through artificial intelligence-based tools that require an entirely new kind of professional expertise. Credit scoring is done using machine learning tools, sentiment analysis uses natural language processing tools. Yet, a steadily growing gap has remained: the workforce is lagging. This chapter contends that AI is not just a way to become more efficient by adding another layer on top of traditional financial and marketing activities; rather, it is a skills transformer that is redefining what it means to be a good professional in those activities, redefining hiring criteria, reorganizing career paths, and ultimately redefining which economies will lead in the new cycle of growth driven by AI.

1. INTRODUCTION: THE FINANCE-MARKETING JUNCTURE AND THE AI IMPERATIVE

In the early decades of the twenty-first century, we have witnessed a profound shift in the nature of skills across all professional domains, but few fields have experienced a change as profound and at the same time as poorly understood holistically as the disruption of both finance and marketing by artificial intelligence. Historically, finance and marketing were two distinct functional areas within an organization, with those in finance focusing on issues of capital management, risk management, financial reporting, and regulatory compliance, while those in marketing focused on brand management, consumer psychology, marketing campaign management, and relationship management with consumers. And on a fundamental level, when it comes to epistemology, measurement, and professional trajectories, there was rarely any significant overlap between the two fields (Kotler et al., 2021; Gomber et al., 2018). Finance was guided by a logic of precision, accountability, and quality control. This bifurcation was reinforced by educational structures that has separate degree programs, separate professional credentialing bodies, and separate bodies of scholarly literature that treated the two domains as fundamentally distinct.

The combination of artificial intelligence technologies and machine learning algorithms that are able to predict consumer behavior, credit risk, and market movements with unprecedented accuracy has fundamentally undermined this separation, which was already under threat in the last two decades as the broader digitization of business progressed (World Economic Forum, 2023). Financial analysts must learn to interpret machine learning algorithms, marketing professionals must engage in marketing campaigns informed by predictive analytics, and business leaders must make critical business decisions about artificial intelligence technologies in the absence of precedent or best practice consensus (McKinsey Global Institute, 2023; Deloitte Insights, 2022).

The result of this convergence is not only operational complexity, but a redefinition of what it means to be a professional expert in a field. There is some evidence that employers in financial services and marketing are seeking new types of skill sets: those that are both domain experts, data experts, AI experts, and experts in ethics (Burning Glass Technologies, 2022; NASSCOM, 2023; LinkedIn Economic Graph, 2023). According to the Future of Jobs Report by the World Economic Forum (2023), the inability of educational and training systems to keep up with the pace of technological change is ranked as one of the top five systemic risks to inclusive economic growth in most parts of the world, and this Finance-Marketing-AI skills gap is one of the clearest examples of this systemic failure.

The purpose of this chapter is to achieve this with both analytic rigor and practical significance, and to do so it is organized into seven sections: first, a review of the extant literature and identification of the important research gap; next, an examination of the concept of enhanced financial competence with the help of AI from various frameworks, roles, and regulatory environments; then an examination of the concept of marketing intelligence with the help of AI and the structural shift in the field of marketing; then a description of the Finance-Marketing-AI professional type and its labour market implications; then an analysis of the economic implications at the individual, organizational, and macro levels, with specific attention to polarization and inclusive growth; then a list of actionable recommendations; and finally, the summation of the arguments and suggestions for further research. The analysis also keeps a global perspective, while acknowledging the contextual factors in the developed, transitioning, and emerging economies. The chapter will draw on labour market intelligence, industry research from McKinsey Global Institute, Deloitte Insights, and the World Economic Forum, as well as regulatory developments such as the EU AI Act and the evolving framework for fintech regulations in India.

2. LITERATURE REVIEW AND RESEARCH GAP

2.1 AI and the Future of Work: Foundational Perspectives

Over the past decade, the body of literature on AI and the future of work has grown exponentially, and early studies by economists, organizational theorists, and technology experts have offered the conceptual frameworks to understand the phenomenon of work and AI. While the most cited and followed conceptualization of the difference between automatable and non-automatable tasks is that of Brynjolfsson and McAfee (2014), which is based on the distinction between tasks that are routine and rule-based vs. tasks that require judgment and creativity, Autor (2015) extended this task-based framework by demonstrating that the penetration of AI into the US labour market over several decades has had a polarizing effect on the labour market, replacing middle-skill routine cognitive and manual work but complementing high-skill routine cognitive work and creative work.

Acemoglu and Restrepo (2018, 2020) argue that the macroeconomic effects of AI have been best studied theoretically in terms of three effects: the task displacement effect (in which AI replaces human labour in tasks), the productivity effect (in which AI increases productivity and therefore output and potentially employment), and the task creation effect (in which new tasks are created that require human skills combined with AI). While the task creation effect is historically the most ambiguous and context-dependent of the three effects, their empirical work suggests that the net effect on employment and wages depends on the balance of these three effects, and thus where policy intervention in terms of skill development and task creation is most needed. This framework directly applies to the Finance-Marketing-AI system, where the task displacement effect can be seen in the automation of tasks within financial analysis and standard marketing campaigns, the productivity effect in the improved performance of these areas with AI, and the task creation effect in new types of jobs where new mixes of competency are needed.

These theoretical approaches have received considerable empirical support from the World Economic Forum (2020 and 2023) Future of Jobs reports, which have surveyed thousands of employers globally on the pace of development of these technologies and their impact on role demands, with the most recent report (2023) noting that the top four skills becoming more important for almost all industries include analytical thinking, AI and big data literacy, creative thinking, and leadership, and two skill areas (financial services and marketing) are particularly affected by AI. Another interesting aspect of the report is that the report indicates that cognitive abilities such as reasoning, problem solving, and working effectively with uncertainty are becoming relatively more important than the more traditional technical abilities that workforce development has focused on, meaning that the issue of human-AI collaboration is not just about technical training but about investing in human cognition and metacognition.

2.2 AI in Financial Services: Competency and Regulatory Dimensions

In the area of finance, there has been some research on AI adoption, but it has primarily focused on the technical aspects of model performance, such as the predictive accuracy of credit models, the efficiency of algorithmic trading systems, and the capabilities of NLP systems in financial analysis (Cao, 2022; Gomber et al., 2018). The large list of AI application in financial services (Cao, 2022) shows the depth and breadth of the ongoing revolution: credit scoring, fraud detection, robo-advisory, RegTech compliance, algorithmic trading, and market prediction systems, to name a few. What all these areas of application have in common is that AI systems are now being employed to assist or replace human decision-making in areas that involve technical and domain knowledge, creating a new type of hybrid professional competency that neither technical AI competency nor financial domain knowledge alone can supply.

Financial competence research itself, as to what it means to be a competent financial professional, has traditionally focused on technical knowledge (accounting standards, valuation methods, regulatory frameworks) and analytical reasoning (Choi et al., 2020). In fact, the advent of AI in financial decision-making has upended some of these established competency structures. Writing in the context of central banking and regulatory practice, Bholat et al. (2020) point out that the competency of AI literacy (defined as the ability to interpret model output, to assess algorithmic fairness, and to govern the use of AI) is becoming a core competency in regulation, as opposed to a specialized technical skill, and that AI literacy deficits existed even among highly educated and analytically sophisticated professionals in their study of Bank of England staff, and needed to be addressed through organizational investment as opposed to individual learning.

Another aspect of AI in financial services that has been identified as a factor of competency evolution is the regulatory aspect of AI in financial services. For example, the EU AI Act (European Commission, 2021) and RBI fintech guidelines (Reserve Bank of India, 2023) are considered regulatory formalizations of AI governance that require transparency, explainability, and human oversight and, therefore, require financial experts to have AI governance competencies. The Financial Stability Board has also highlighted AI and machine learning as systemic risk factors for global financial markets given their ability to introduce correlated risks in high-frequency trading and risk management. This regulatory activity is driving the demand for financial professionals with AI governance competencies and has led to the inclusion of AI literacy in professional development programs. For example, in a 2022 survey of financial services executives by Deloitte Insights, 83 percent identified AI/data analytics as critically important to the future of their organizations, yet only 27 percent rated their workforce as proficient in these areas, resulting in a 56 percent gap, one of the largest identified skill gaps in the financial sector.

2.3 AI in Marketing: From Analytics to Intelligence

The potential of AI has been widely discussed in the marketing literature, primarily in practitioner publications (Davenport et al., 2020; Huang and Rust, 2021), although a foundational academic work was published by Davenport et al. (2020) that identified five key marketing domain capabilities of AI: machine learning for consumer behaviour prediction, NLP for social listening, computer vision for visual content optimization, conversational AI for customer engagement, and autonomous decision-making for campaign optimization. The framework highlights the fact that AI in marketing is not a single technology but an ecosystem of related capabilities that, collectively, demand a far more extensive skills profile for marketing professionals—technological AI capabilities, and human capabilities in the forms of strategic judgment, empathetic communication, and creative synthesis.

Huang and Rust (2021) offer a theoretically informed framework for human-AI task allocation in marketing where they assert that as AI takes over mechanical tasks (data processing, pattern recognition, A/B tests) and analytical tasks (performance attribution, predictive modeling), humans have a comparative advantage in empathetic tasks (tasks that require judgement) until now, but now with advances in generative AI, tasks in creative content, empathetic dialogue, and complex strategic reasoning previously assumed to be uniquely human have now begun to be taken over by AI. Empirical support for the business value of developing marketing capability in AI marketing is shown by Kumar et al. (2019), who demonstrate that in leading firms, AI marketing has become a distinct organizational function, and that firms with high levels of AI marketing capability outperform their less advanced counterparts in terms of customer lifetime value, conversion rates, and marketing efficiency ratios by statistically significant margins.

As generative AI technologies, such as large language models, have rapidly developed and been integrated into marketing technology stacks, the urgency of the skills debate has only increased. Research from Content Marketing Institute (2023) shows that 73% of B2B marketers were using generative AI tools in their workflows as of mid-2023 but that less than 30% of marketers had any training in the use, evaluation, or governance of these tools (indicating a high degree of informal adoption of the tools versus institutional competency in these areas), a gap that carries specific implications for marketing given the amplified benefits and risks of using AI-generated content and campaign decisioning.

2.4 Human Capital Theory and Skills Transformation

The theoretical basis for understanding the macro-level implications of AI-driven changes in skills can be seen through the lens of human capital theory, first articulated by Becker (1964) and Mincer (1974) who suggested that skills in the labour force can be understood as capital, and the accumulation of skills by individuals and the economy as a whole can be seen as an increase in the capital stock. More recent human capital theory has acknowledged the role of technological change, as Goldin and Katz (2008) demonstrated that periods of technological change can involve skill-biased technological change in which increases in economic returns to education and skills are significant.

The most recent human capital theory in the context of the AI transition was presented by Brynjolfsson et al. (2023), who analysed the adoption of generative AI tools in the organizational context and found that the productivity gains from the adoption of generative AI tools are the greatest for those with the lowest skill level, suggesting that the adoption of AI tools has the potential to decrease skill inequality in the organizational context, and that the organizational and institutional complementarities are as important as the technology in determining whether the adoption of AI tools leads to productivity gains or job losses. For workforce development strategy, it implies that the adoption of AI tools alone is insufficient to bring about the productivity gains necessary, but that the investment in human capital needed to properly utilize the tools is a necessary condition for the potential productivity gains.

2.5 Research Methodology and Gap Analysis

This study adopts a conceptual synthesis using a narrative review approach to examine how artificial intelligence is transforming financial marketing competence. Secondary data were sourced from reputed institutional reports (e.g., WEF, McKinsey, Deloitte, LinkedIn) and relevant academic literature published in recent years. Sources were selected based on criteria of relevance to AI in financial marketing, recency, and credibility. The analysis follows a thematic approach, wherein key patterns, emerging competencies, and strategic shifts were identified, compared, and integrated across sources. This method enables an evidence-based yet interpretive understanding of the transition from transactional to transformational financial marketing practices in the evolving digital economy.

While each of these bodies of literature is vast and varied, a gap in the literature still exists: an integrated, comprehensive analytical framework to examine this competency shift driven by AI across these two disciplines, in particular at the intersection of finance and marketing as a unified discipline with hybrid characteristics, is lacking. The majority of the literature on AI in finance is focused on the capabilities of the model itself, or on the regulatory implications, without much focus on the competency implications for the non-technical members of the financial community. Research on AI in marketing, however, is similarly either highly technical machine learning applications or practitioner-based case studies, with little attention paid to the structural competency shift occurring at a macro level in the workforce. Human capital and competency shift in the age of AI is an area of study that has a number of bodies of literature, but the bodies of literature are shallow and not specific enough to be useful for practitioners in finance and marketing.

More critically, the challenges and opportunities that AI pose for finance and marketing individually, and the emerging convergence of the two areas of expertise into a new class of professional archetypes and professional role types that cannot be understood in terms of finance or marketing individually, have not yet been addressed in any research on these issues. This chapter is dedicated to filling that research gap by presenting an integrated analytical framework for understanding the Finance-Marketing-AI skills nexus based on empirical evidence from the labour market, regulatory, and organizational domains, and deriving implications for the entire spectrum of stakeholders with a "stake" in the Finance-Marketing-AI skills nexus.

3. AI-ENHANCED FINANCIAL COMPETENCE: FRAMEWORKS, ROLES, AND REGULATORY CONTEXT

3.1 The Architecture of AI-Enhanced Financial Competence

Traditional financial competency was a small, largely stable set of core competency areas: accounting principles and reporting standards, quantitative analysis and modeling, regulatory frameworks and compliance, and professional judgment in the context of risk and uncertainty (CFA Institute, 2022). Established credentialing programs, such as the CFA, CPA, and their national counterparts, provided a common language and competency standards for professional practice in finance; while these core competence areas are still critical, the emergence of AI in financial services has changed the architecture in which these competence areas are applied and necessitates new competence areas that were not addressed by existing credentialing programs or educational curricula.

There is a clear delineation between 'AI-adjacent' and 'AI-integrated' skills: data interpretation (the ability to critically evaluate and communicate analysis from model outputs), tool proficiency (operational familiarity with AI-enabled financial tools), output validation (the ability to recognize when outputs from AI models are unreliable or incorrect), and algorithmic literacy (a general understanding of the workings of various types of models and their constraints). Decades ago, there was no requirement for any interaction with machine learning-based models in the field of financial analysis, portfolio management, compliance, and relationship management; today these are basic competency needs (Bholat et al., 2020; Cao, 2022). CFA Institute research (2022) showed that 67% of investment management professionals said they use AI to provide analysis, yet only 41% said they feel they have the ability to evaluate the quality of the analysis that AI provides, meaning there is a clear need for AI-adjacent competencies across the investment management industry.

The competencies related to integrating AI are more advanced level competencies, with skills related to designing, implementing, managing, and enhancing AI in financial applications such as model design and validation (e.g., data needs for models, models for selection, performance measures, and overfitting), prompt engineering for financial applications (e.g., designing effective natural language inputs for large language models for financial applications such as financial documents analysis, earnings calls, and generation of communications for customers), and responsible AI deployment (e.g., deploying AI in financial applications that are fair, transparent, and explainable in accordance with the standards set by financial regulators). These integrated competencies have historically been the purview of data scientists and technologists, and their addition to the professional skillset of financial professionals is perhaps one of the most significant structural shifts in professional competency standards in the sector's recent history.

3.2 Domain-Specific AI Transformation: Role-by-Role Analysis

This change in the requirements for financial competence is differentiated by role, which requires role-specific rather than generic approaches to competency development. The biggest shift in the requirements for financial competence has been for financial analysts, where the integration of machine learning results into investment analysis has led to the use of alternative data, such as satellite imagery, mobile location data, social media sentiment, web analytics, among others, analysed through artificial intelligence (Morgan Stanley, 2022; CFA Institute, 2022). The technical challenge of analysing such data and the professional judgment of whether such data is credible or just spurious correlation are also important aspects.

So far, the largest impact of AI has been in the area of credit decisioning, where machine learning-based personal and small business credit scoring models that consider thousands of additional data variables beyond traditional credit bureau data have demonstrated better predictive accuracy compared to traditional credit scoring models while also raising significant concerns about fairness and regulatory compliance (Fuster et al., 2022). Fuster et al. (2022) showed that ML-based credit models have outperformed traditional credit scoring models by 17-25% in default risk prediction accuracy, but they also have differential predictive accuracy for different demographic groups, which poses important compliance challenges for credit risk professionals, requiring them to possess critical capabilities in AI governance in addition to traditional actuarial and credit risk analysis capabilities. Credit risk professionals should be able to audit ML-based credit models for fairness and also design monitoring programs for ML credit models to identify degradation in performance over time. Credit risk professionals should also be able to communicate the limitations of ML-based credit models to regulators and audit committees of boards in a manner that is technically accurate but also understandable to non-technical stakeholders.

Another entirely new domain of knowledge and competency for compliance and regulatory professionals is AI governance and algorithmic accountability. For example, the EU AI Act lists some AI applications in financial services such as credit scoring models, insurance pricing models, and robo-advisory models as high-risk AI applications that must be subject to strict requirements on transparency, human oversight, technical documentation, and post-deployment monitoring (European Commission, 2021). Compliance and regulatory professionals need to learn about AI audit methodologies, AI risk management frameworks, and impact assessment of algorithms, all new areas of knowledge and competency that were never part of the traditional compliance and regulatory professional development curricula. The International Organization of Securities Commissions (IOSCO) has even issued guidelines on AI governance in investment management, which puts the same competency expectations on compliance and regulatory professionals in asset management, showing a global regulatory consensus that AI governance is an integral part of compliance and regulatory practice in financial services, rather than a technicality.

3.3 Regulatory Drivers of Competency Evolution

The regulatory environment is one of the most significant and underestimated drivers for developing AI capability, while other industries adopt AI technology driven by the market, the financial services industry is subject to a complex regulatory environment which already has to deal with the governance issues around AI. The EU AI Act that came into force in 2024 provides a comprehensive set of regulations for governing AI across all sectors, including the financial services sector, and the requirements for explainability, human oversight, and bias testing in high-risk applications mandated by the EU AI Act will directly translate into requirements for financial services professionals in the sector or targeting the EU market. (European Commission, 2021).

For example, the Reserve Bank of India issued a series of guidance documents on the use of AI and ML in financial services, emphasizing the importance of model risk management, data management, and human oversight in the context of AI-based financial decisions (RBI, 2023), which have greatly incentivized institutional investments in developing AI competency among financial institutions to demonstrate compliance with these regulations and to spur professional bodies to launch training programs for financial professionals in the context of AI, thus providing a significant institutional mechanism for the development of AI skills faster and more clearly than market-driven forces.

4. AI-DRIVEN MARKETING INTELLIGENCE: FROM CAMPAIGN THINKING TO PREDICTIVE STRATEGY

4.1 The Structural Transformation of Marketing Practice

In fact, some might argue that the practice model of marketing itself has shifted from the traditional paradigm (with its implicit creative intuition, audience segmentation on the basis of demographic surrogates, campaign planning horizons measured in weeks or months, and campaign measurement through reach-frequency metrics) to one that is supported by the capabilities of AI to enable prediction, personalization, automation, and optimization on a previously unimaginable scale (Davenport et al., 2020; Kumar et al., 2019). This is not an additive process: The capabilities associated with AI have not given marketers additional tools to execute the traditional marketing paradigm but have fundamentally altered the logic by which the value of marketing is defined.

The simplest change is the transition from descriptive to predictive analytics as the foundation for marketing decisions: descriptive marketing analytics as a discipline usually involved summarizing historical data to describe past business performance (what, who, and how) versus AI-assisted marketing analytics that predicts future individual consumer behaviours (the likelihood of an individual consumer leaving a business within 30 days, the best marketing action to take with a particular individual consumer based on their past behavioural history, or the future value of a prospect based on early signs of their interaction with a business) (Kumar et al., 2019). This paradigm shift in marketing analytics fundamentally alters what marketers need to know: while intuition and creative thinking were always necessary, marketers must now interpret, act on, and critically think through these probabilistic outputs in real time. In fact, marketers who do not know how to interact with these outputs are no longer able to participate in campaign strategy and optimization conversations in data-driven companies, something a large percentage of the existing workforce still cannot do.

This second foundational shift toward real-time optimization is a departure from conventional marketing management, which typically involves planning cycles that determine audiences, develop creative materials, buy media, and measure results after the marketing campaign has ended; however, AI-enabled marketing platforms can continuously adjust campaign parameters based on real-time performance data (Davenport et al., 2020), allowing them to dynamically optimize audience targeting, creative selection, bid management, and message sequencing in real time. The real-time optimization aspect of marketing management requires marketing professionals to build a very different relationship with marketing management in which they do not direct marketing campaigns but design, monitor, and control systems that direct marketing campaigns on their behalf.

4.2 Key AI Capability Domains Transforming Marketing

These include several domains of AI capabilities that are altering the skills set for marketers and that require significant investment in professional skills development: machine learning for the prediction of customer behaviour, propensity modeling, customer churn prediction, customer lifetime value estimation, and next-best-action systems are already in use by major consumer brands, financial institutions, and online retailers. According to data from LinkedIn's Economic Graph (2023), marketing roles requiring skills in the areas of predictive analytics and customer data platforms increased by 78% from 2020 to 2023, one of the fastest-growing skills in the marketing skills set, suggesting a shift in what employers regard as a basic professional level of competency for marketing employees in technologically driven firms.

The most recent and active type of marketing AI capabilities is generative AI, which has implications for content, customer, research, and ideation that are only now being realized at an organizational level (Kietzmann et al., 2018). Using large language models for a wide range of marketing purposes from personalized emails to social media content creation to synthesized customer persona creation and competitive research synthesis has created significant opportunities and challenges for governance that require sophisticated professional judgment (Kietzmann et al., 2018). Generative AI applied to customer-facing marketing communications is seen to have substantial implications for both authenticity and governance and regulatory requirements, in particular in a financial services context, and for the role of human creative judgment in these contexts, creating a need for marketers to develop relevant competencies in these areas.

A second area is customer data platforms (CDPs), which are the data engineering practices required to architect and deliver the single customer view data architecture, which is a prerequisite to implementing AI marketing tools but has been the domain of IT, not the marketing function until now, as the tools to enable data management and data integration have become more available to the broader organization (Gartner, 2022). The need to internalize the application of AI marketing tools, rather than relying on agency partners, along with the expanding availability of data engineering tools to the larger organization, is creating a demand for marketers who have data engineering literacy, in addition to their strategic and creative skills.

4.3 The Emerging Role of the Marketing Technologist

The combination of marketing strategy, data analytics, and the deployment of AI technologies is driving the emergence of a new type of marketing professional: the marketing technologist. Gartner (2022) describes marketing technologists as a professional type who works at the intersection of marketing strategy, technology implementation, and data analytics, and who is responsible for selecting, deploying, and optimizing the marketing technology stack to ensure that the marketing strategies defined at the leadership level are executed correctly. In marketing groups of technology-driven firms, the marketing technologist is one of the fastest-growing types of professionals.

Financial services marketing environments are especially well suited to the marketing technologist role because of the high level of regulatory complexity, data privacy concerns, and sophistication of marketing AI applications in these environments; a specific example of a marketing context in which marketing technologists are involved is fintech marketing, in which a new type of marketing competency has been created as a "hybrid competency" in which marketing professionals must simultaneously navigate both brand marketing and regulatory marketing environments while creating AI-driven marketing campaigns and analysing machine learning results from A/B testing environments (Deloitte Insights, 2022); thus, fintech marketing is one of the most demanding marketing environments in terms of competency and one of the most informative marketing contexts for learning about the Finance-Marketing-AI convergence.

Research by Gartner (2022) found that marketing technology is the largest category of marketing investment for most large enterprises, with investment levels even larger than that for traditional media and agency fees for some industries, but actual use of the capabilities of marketing technology is only about 42%, which is a capabilities and skills issue for organizations that are investing in high-end AI marketing technology but not developing capabilities and skills to use the high-end technology. The return on investment in marketing technology is lower than it could be, but for those organizations that do develop the capabilities and skills in marketing AI technology, the return on investment is three to four times greater than for those that do not, a strong business case for investing in the development of marketing AI technology (Gartner, 2022).

5. THE EMERGING FINANCE-MARKETING-AI PROFESSIONAL ARCHETYPE

5.1 Labor Market Evidence of Convergence

The blurring of the domain boundary between the two fields of professional expertise is probably the largest and least discussed effect of the simultaneous disruption caused by the advent of AI in the field of finance and marketing. In the pre-AI world, the expertise of the two domains overlapped very little and was more transactional in nature, with the field of finance providing support to the field of marketing in areas of budget management and ROI measurement, and the field of marketing providing support to the field of finance in areas of customer insight for product and pricing decisions. However, the advent of AI has fundamentally changed the way these two fields intersect with each other.

Compelling evidence of this convergence can also be found in labour market data: A LinkedIn job posting analysis between 2019-2023 shows that new job roles are emerging that specifically require the combination of finance-marketing skills with AI skills, such as Revenue Intelligence Analyst (financial modeling, marketing attribution analysis, and machine learning platforms) up 127% and Growth Finance Manager (financial performance management, marketing customer acquisition economics, and AI marketing tools) up 89%. Last, AI Product Manager (Financial Services) jobs, which involve product strategy, financial domain expertise, and AI development, have increased by 156 percent, one of the top categories for job growth in finance-marketing. They are not trivial phenomena, either. The category of hybrid Finance-Marketing-AI jobs has added over 340,000 new job postings in major English-speaking labour markets from 2019 to 2023, with double-digit growth rates in all markets studied.

Salary premium analysis also provides additional evidence for the notion that hybrid competence in Finance-Marketing-AI is prized: A study conducted by Burning Glass Technologies (2022) found that roles requiring both finance analysis and marketing analytics skills had a salary premium of 23-31 percent over roles that required only one of those skill sets, and when AI skills were added to finance and marketing analytics skills, a salary premium of 41-52 percent was found in both the United States and the United Kingdom. A similar pattern was found in India, where fintech has been a particularly potent catalyst for hybrid roles, with a 38-48% salary premium for hybrid finance-marketing-AI roles compared to domain-specific roles (NASSCOM, 2023), which reflects a true shortage of hybrid skills in the labour market rather than an employer preference, further indicating that a supply-demand imbalance in finance-marketing-AI hybrid talent is a structural, not a trend-driven, feature of the labour market.

5.2 Characterizing the Finance-Marketing-AI Professional

It is thus possible to characterize the hybrid profession of Finance-Marketing-AI along several related dimensions: a knowledge domain perspective (the professional will have a foundation in financial concepts, a foundation in marketing concepts, and a working knowledge of AI systems; but the synthesis of these knowledge domains is not additive, there is some level of integrated analysis that is possible that is not possible for experts in either domain alone), a task domain perspective (the professional will be able to analyse financial concepts, analyse marketing concepts, and evaluate AI systems in these two domains, but there is some level of integrated analysis that is possible that is not possible for experts in either domain alone), a role domain perspective (the professional will be involved in roles that combine financial roles, marketing roles, and AI roles, but there is some level of integrated analysis that is possible that is not possible for experts in either domain alone), and a value domain perspective (the professional will be creating and delivering value that combines financial value, marketing value, and AI value, but there is some level of integrated analysis that is possible that is not possible for experts in either domain alone).

From the perspective of analytical capability, Finance-Marketing-AI hybrids can be differentiated by their ability to combine the full range of data analytics, descriptive (what happened?), diagnostic (why did it happen?), predictive (what will happen?), and prescriptive (what should we do?) analyses, as in the example of the Revenue Intelligence Analyst, where it is possible to identify (descriptive/diagnostic), design (predictive), and prescribe (prescriptive) customer retention intervention scenarios, and allocate the optimal budget to customer retention programs based on the financial return, which would not be possible if specialists were working in any one of the three domains independently.

As a consequence, an important component of the Finance-Marketing-AI profile is the ethical and governance aspect, because consequential decision-making in financial services and marketing (where who gets the credit, what prices are offered, who gets which marketing message, and how personal data is used are part of the decision-making process) involves issues that are both regulatory and ethical, particularly in the context of bias, transparency, and consent. Identifying, evaluating, and mitigating bias in AI decision-making, designing AI systems so that individuals affected by them can understand how these systems function, and striking the right balance between personalization through AI and individual privacy have become important ethical practices in this area (FSB, 2022; European Commission, 2021). A key risk to organizations in regulated spaces in financial services and marketing is professionals with high levels of capability in AI but lacking in this key ethical and governance aspect.

5.3 Implications for Talent Pipelines and Educational Design

This evolution into the hybrid Finance-Marketing-AI archetype is now having significant implications for talent pipelines and educational design, and only the top educational institutions are beginning to address these implications. Traditional educational structures that have long divided the study of finance and marketing at the undergraduate and graduate levels and that have been slow to integrate the literacy in AI into either field are not well equipped to produce graduates with the hybrid competency sets that the best employers now require. The Graduate Management Admission Council (2023) conducted a survey of recruiters at business programs around the world and discovered that 71 percent reported Finance-AI or Marketing-AI hybrid skill sets were among the hardest to fill, and that most recent graduates of traditional finance and marketing programs did not have the AI-specific competencies required for the hybrid roles. This is the institutional lag, and it represents a structural inefficiency that carries considerable costs for individual graduates, for the organization, and for the economy overall.

The most progressive educational institutions are combating this challenge by starting curriculum redesign projects that incorporate AI literacy into finance and marketing programs, rather than making it an elective. Leading programs include those at Carnegie Mellon University's Tepper School of Business, Imperial College Business School, and Indian School of Business, among others, that have included required coursework on how to apply AI for business scenarios and even domain-specific courses such as AI in finance and AI in marketing as part of standard MBA and master's programs (GMAC, 2023). Although these are important first steps to bridging the institutional gap, the scale is still insufficient to meet the hybrid talent needs, and the reach is still limited to the business education ecosystem around the world, including the multitude of educational institutions in emerging economies that produce the majority of the finance and marketing talent.

6. ECONOMIC IMPLICATIONS: PRODUCTIVITY, POLARIZATION, AND INCLUSIVE GROWTH

6.1 Productivity Gains at Individual and Organizational Levels

Skills transformation in finance and marketing through the use of artificial intelligence can be analysed at several levels. The strongest level of analysis in terms of the strength of the evidence is the individual/organizational level regarding productivity: At the individual professional level, the evidence points to productivity benefits for those who learn to develop skills in artificial intelligence (MGI 2023), with financial analysts that have advanced artificial intelligence skills producing 25-40% more analytical work per unit of time compared to other financial analysts with similar experience but lacking those skills, and marketing professionals with more advanced artificial intelligence skills in predictive analytics and campaign management managing larger marketing campaigns with similar or better performance results, achieving efficiency. (Davenport et al., 2020).

At the organizational level, McKinsey analysis of AI-mature versus AI-nascent organizations in financial services found that AI leaders (i.e., firms in the top quartile of AI capability adoption) outperformed AI laggards on revenue growth (by 12–15% on average), cost efficiency (by 10–18%), and customer satisfaction metrics (by 8–12%) over the five-year period from 2018 to 2023 (MGI, 2023); importantly, organizations that combined technology investment with systematic workforce upskilling in AI capabilities achieved 2.3 times the performance improvement of organizations that invested in technology without corresponding skills development, finding that human AI capability is a necessary complement to AI technology investment for realizing productivity gains, a finding that is one of the most practically important in the literature and with direct implications for how organizations approach AI investments.

6.2 Labor Market Polarization and the Skills Premium

While the gains in productivity from acquiring the ability to use AI are undeniable, they also raise some important distributional issues that complicate an unambiguously positive assessment of the impact of AI on the economy in the financial and marketing sectors. The evidence from the labour market for AI adoption in the financial and marketing sectors is clearly one of polarization. In the financial sector, routine data processing and report generation, routine compliance monitoring, and routine customer servicing are all subject to substantial substitution by ML-based analytics platforms, RegTech-based AI systems, and conversational AI, respectively; while in the marketing sector, routine content creation for search engine optimization, routine graphic design, and routine campaign reporting are all areas where substitution by AI is significant. Those workers who spend most of their time in such task categories (especially those with lower levels of education and little chance for training or advancement) are the ones most likely to be replaced, a problem of greatest relevance for the developing world, where financial services and marketing are a significant source of middle-class employment.

The AI skills premium found in the studies by Burning Glass Technologies (2022) and NASSCOM (2023) also imply a skills penalty for workers who lack AI skills in those labour markets, a widening wage dispersion that, absent some policy intervention, could exacerbate an already widening inequality trend. Such technological-driven divergence in wages is not inevitable, according to the studies of inequality and technological change by Goldin & Katz (2008) and Brynjolfsson et al. (2023), and is highly dependent on education policy, training investment, and social protection strategies, which determine how much productivity gains generated by technological change are distributed among different groups in society. For example, the studies on inequality and technological change that Goldin & Katz (2008) and Brynjolfsson et al. (2023) have conducted suggest that a more systematic approach to computer literacy development is required, rather than leaving such capability development to individual initiative and market forces, and that countries and organizations that invested systematically in computer literacy development in the 1980s and 1990s were able to achieve more equitable distributions of productivity gains than those that relied on the computer revolution.

6.3 Macroeconomic Growth Implications and the Inclusive AI Challenge

The relationship between adoption of AI skills in finance and marketing and economic performance at the country or regional level is moderated by structural factors that give policymakers considerable leverage on economic outcomes: countries or regions with a higher level of AI skills availability in the workforce (as measured by LinkedIn AI Skills Penetration Index and other relevant indicators) tend to have higher productivity growth in AI-using sectors, such as finance and marketing (WEF, 2023). Based on MGI (2023) estimates, countries that have rapid skills adoption in AI could achieve an additional 0.5 to 1.5 percent per year in GDP growth rate compared to countries with slower skills adoption rates, representing a significant gap in economic performance over a decade.

For example, the use of AI technologies in financial services and marketing can create opportunities and risks that need to be navigated carefully by policy, such as the possibility of greater market penetration of financial services and access to credit, insurance, and investment by the underserved populations in the emerging economies like India, Brazil, Nigeria, and Indonesia, or the possibility of marketing to allow small firms to compete with multinational corporations by the use of AI technologies such as precision targeting and personalization at lower costs (Fuster et al., 2022). India, in particular, has emerged as a major center of AI talent, with India ranking as the second-largest contributor of AI research (Fuster et al., 2022). Yet, the fact that this talent pool is concentrated in technology and information technology, not financial services and marketing, means that the productivity benefit of India human capital in artificial intelligence is not being maximized in sectors with the highest economic multiplier effect, and the policy and institutional imperative to capitalize on this advantage is a significant national economic development opportunity.

This concentration of AI competence, technologically and in terms of human capital, in the hands of global technology companies and financial institutions located in developed economies could exacerbate the existing North-South divide in the provision of financial and marketing services, as should the development of financial and marketing services using AI technology be left to companies in developed economies, which will then supply these services globally through digital technology, the benefits derived from the adoption of AI technology in the financial and marketing sectors might accrue to the shareholders and employees in developed economies, with employees in emerging economies worse off without the benefits of the productivity gains generated by the adoption of AI technology. The proactive development of domestic AI competence in emerging economies, as is the intent of the development of national AI skills frameworks, educational curricula, and upskilling investments.

7. FINDINGS

The analysis of the chapter reveals that artificial intelligence (AI) is not only enhancing the current practices in finance and marketing but is also transforming these two fields. The implications of the chapter can be synthesized on five major dimensions: competency transformation, domain convergence, labour market, institutional gaps, and economic implications.

- **Reconfiguration of professional competence architectures** - The primary finding pertains to the reconfiguration of professional competency architectures for finance and marketing, as traditional competency architectures rooted in domain-specific technical knowledge and functional skills are becoming inadequate in an environment where AI is enabled, and a new dual competency structure has emerged, one related to AI-adjacent competencies (such as data interpretation skills, tool skills, and algorithmic literacy) and another related to AI-integrated competencies (such as AI deployment skills and ethical oversight skills), which are becoming a new standard across all professionals, and set high-end professionals and more strategic and regulatory-oriented positions apart. This is an indication that AI literacy is transitioning from a specialized skill set to a new standard in professional competency architectures, in much the same way that quantitative skills were in past decades.
- **Structural convergence between finance and marketing** - This study then shows that there is a substantial and growing skills gap in the labour market, based on empirical evidence of the demand for hybrid AI-enabled roles, high salary premiums for workers with a hybrid of finance, marketing, and AI

skills, and a lack of readiness to work with AI systems by a significant share of the existing workforce (most notably in roles that require judgment over AI outputs, regulatory compliance, and decision-making at a strategic level). There is a high rate of technological advancement relative to institutional change, which creates a significant and ever-expanding skills gap in the labour market, as empirical evidence demonstrates.

- **Inadequacy of current educational and training systems -** Existing educational and training programs are not addressing competency development effectively. Traditional business education programs are still discipline-focused and have only recently begun to address AI literacy in a substantive way, and even where AI programs exist, they are largely voluntary and are not part of the core of finance and marketing programs, so graduates do not experience the real-world application of AI in those disciplines. Likewise, training programs in organizations are largely unstructured and not focused on competency needs in a relevant way, which is a primary reason for the persistence of the skills gap and the inability of organizations to fully realize the potential of AI adoption.
- **Economic implications at multiple levels -** The results indicate substantial economic implications at both a micro (individual level) and a macro (firm level), as well as important implications for income inequality and workforce displacement in new economies. The study indicates that while AI proficiency is associated with substantial productivity gains at the individual level, which enables the professional to execute more sophisticated and broader analysis, firms that are better at investing in technology for AI and upskilling the workforce see the most revenue growth, cost efficiency, and customer satisfaction benefits, which are not distributed evenly, indicating a clear trend toward polarization in the labour market, in which high-skilled, AI-proficient workers receive greater demand and pay, while roles that are less task-based are replaced or devalued.
- **AI skills adoption is a critical determinant of national competitiveness and growth -** The results point to the importance of AI skills adoption at the macroeconomic level, showing that countries that invest well in AI skills in high-impact industries such as financial services and marketing will have high productivity growth and will be more globally competitive, and that in the absence of policy to address AI skills adoption, the benefits may disproportionately accrue to developed countries and tech firms, leading to greater global inequality. Emerging economies have a large pool of talent but also face challenges in exploiting AI-driven opportunities due to sectoral skills gaps.

- **Growing importance of ethical and governance competencies -** The chapter also notes that as AI becomes more prevalent, the ethical and governance competencies will become more important in contexts in which AI is deployed because when high-stakes decisions are being made about things like credit allocation, pricing, and personalization in marketing, issues of bias, transparency, and data privacy will become areas of professional practice in which professionals are expected to do more than their technical job to responsibly implement AI, and regulatory developments in this area, which are elevating AI governance as a competency, not a secondary one, further underline this reality.

Finally, the findings suggest that the role of AI is not only changing the nature of work and tools but also the nature of professional competence in finance and marketing, with the development of hybrid roles, skills gaps, misalignment of institutions and economic outcomes, which indicates that the transition to an AI-enabled economy is both an opportunity and a challenge, and that coordination in education systems, organizations, and policy frameworks is essential to make sure that the benefits of AI are widely shared.

8. RECOMMENDATIONS FOR EDUCATORS, EMPLOYERS, AND POLICYMAKERS

8.1 Recommendations for Educational Institutions

The greatest challenge for academic institutions in responding to the skills imperative of Finance-Marketing-AI is in the development of new educational programs due to the structural constraints of disciplinary organization. The first and most fundamental suggestion for addressing the skills imperative of Finance-Marketing-AI is to develop integrated Finance-Marketing-AI programs at the undergraduate and graduate levels, that is, programs that give students substantive exposure to all three areas rather than deep specialization in one of the areas with superficial exposure to the other two. It would not entail abandoning disciplinary depth but rather designing common foundational programs in AI literacy and data analytics that are shared by finance and marketing programs, designing programs that allow for interdisciplinary work that forces students to work outside of domain boundaries, and designing capstone programs at the Finance-Marketing-AI interface.

The second major recommendation is to include AI literacy as a foundational competency in all business education curriculums, not only as a separate module for technically oriented students, but as a skill set area as fundamental as quantitative skills or business communication, which will require curriculum investment in developing AI fluency, both conceptually and practically, where a student can understand how different classes of AI models operate, interpret, and assess the outputs of models, actually work with AI tools in financial and marketing applications, and develop a framework for reasoning through the ethical and governance implications of using AI (GMAC, 2023). Live project work with organizational datasets, actual access to AI platforms via organizational partnerships, and case-based learning in actual AI deployment scenarios in financial and marketing contexts.

Another set of recommendations that is relevant, given the pace at which the landscape is changing, is continuous renewal mechanisms for the curriculum. Knowledge about particular tools has a short half-life, and educational institutions cannot and should not attempt to provide comprehensive education on tools that will be out of date within a few years of graduation. The optimal educational design is the depth of understanding of the concepts behind ML models, the limitations, and the governance of the use of such tools, as well as the experience from the application through the industry collaboration, which requires the educational institution to develop strong advisory mechanisms with the industry, beyond the traditional curriculum advisory board, to ensure continuous integration of the changing landscape with regard to competency requirements from employers, as well as the emerging capabilities.

8.2 Recommendations for Employers and Organizations

In the financial services and marketing industries, the recommendations focus on creating systematic and strategic upskilling programs for AI capabilities that treat workforce AI capabilities as a strategic investment rather than a training overhead to be minimized. An MGI (2023) finding that organizations investing in technology and upskilling their workforce achieve 2.3 times the performance improvement of the technology investors alone also points to the need to invest heavily in workforce AI capabilities and technology, based on role-specific competency frameworks that identify the AI capabilities needed for each category of professional roles and differentiate the AI-adjacent capabilities required of all professionals from the AI-integrated capabilities required of the roles that do. Create a structured path to meeting those competency requirements and recognition.

Talent acquisition also requires updates in the talent strategy to better acknowledge the hybrid Finance-Marketing-AI capability, including revisiting job descriptions to ensure that the AI skills are not specified too low so that the AI capability is not covered in the hiring process or too high so that the technical knowledge is required at an unrealistically high level, which is not necessary for the business role but for the technical role. Assessing the AI competency, beyond the traditional AI literacy test, which does not differentiate the levels of AI competency needed for the different role profiles, can be done through case interview methods with the output from AI tools, portfolios of work with AI tools, and technical assessment components that are specific to the role and level of required AI competency.

Organizations also need to invest in the internal conditions that create the conditions for AI-human collaboration to be productive instead of unproductive. Research on the adoption of AI in organizational settings (Brynjolfsson et al., 2023) has also demonstrated that the human dimensions of AI adoption, such as the manner in which work is designed with the capabilities of AI, the manner in which professionals are enabled to develop effective working relationships with AI technologies, and the manner in which organizational culture responds to the organizational impact of AI, are equally significant in determining the outcomes of AI adoption. Hence, change management processes, communication processes, and design processes that enable finance and marketing professionals to participate in the design of work processes with the support of AI technologies are just as critical to developing effective organizational AI capabilities as technical training processes. Organizations that invest insufficiently in change management processes when deploying AI technologies risk wasting their investment in the organizational AI adoption agenda, and often produce less-than-desired results, such as resistance to AI adoption, low adoption rates, and the inability to achieve the productivity gains AI technologies are designed to generate.

8.3 Recommendations for Policymakers

From a skills policy perspective, the shift in skills profile due to AI in finance and marketing requires the education system, the labour market, and the regulatory environment to adapt, and it also requires establishing national competency frameworks related to AI beyond the current idea of AI literacy, and also creating industry-based certifications related to the application of AI (similar to the ones developed in the finance field) to set standards around Finance-Marketing-AI competence, which can help to inform the investment in the skills development.

A second priority area is to assist workers displaced by AI-driven automation through retraining by identifying affected jobs and developing job-specific retraining programs that focus on skills related to AI, designing such programs in consultation with relevant industries to ensure that the skills being taught are in line with how work is evolving, and providing these programs in a wide range of locations and industries so that retraining is not limited to a few.

On the regulatory end, the nature of AI governance, especially in the financial sector, needs to be defined in terms of the competency levels of professionals who will be using AI systems, which can be reinforced by governance structures such as competency-based governance, to ensure that there is a felt need for AI skills, as well as a willingness to develop those skills to ensure their ethical, transparent, and efficient use in the finance and marketing sectors.

9. CONCLUSION

This chapter argues that the intersection of artificial intelligence and finance/marketing is not just a technological advancement but a shift in what it means to be a professional in the 21st century, in both skill sets and economic outcomes, from an AI-adjacent (basic literacy skills for all roles) to an AI-integrated (advanced skills for specialized roles) framework. The regulatory initiatives, especially in the financial services sector, are driving this trend further by incorporating AI governance into the basic foundation of what it means to be a professional. And second, a structural change in the labour market has emerged, in which a new hybrid type of labour has emerged: the Finance-Marketing-AI professional, which combines the three functions into one integrated decision, and whose high salaries and skills shortage indicate that they are in short supply. Third, the labour market has undergone a major transformation with the rise of a new hybrid labour category: the Finance-Marketing-AI professional, who can integrate decision-making better than traditional experts in these fields, are highly sought after (as demonstrated by their high pay and skills deficit) indicating a structural deficit in the labour market.

REFERENCES

Acemoglu, D., & Restrepo, P. (2018). The race between man and machine: Implications of technology for growth, factor shares, and employment. *The American Economic Review*, *108*(6), 1488–1542. DOI: 10.1257/aer.20160696

Acemoglu, D., & Restrepo, P. (2020). Robots and jobs: Evidence from US labor markets. *Journal of Political Economy*, *128*(6), 2188–2244. DOI: 10.1086/705716

Autor, D. H. (2015). Why are there still so many jobs? The history and future of workplace automation. *The Journal of Economic Perspectives*, *29*(3), 3–30. DOI: 10.1257/jep.29.3.3

Becker, G. S. (1964). *Human capital: A theoretical and empirical analysis, with special reference to education*. University of Chicago Press.

Bholat, D., Brookes, J., Cai, C., Grundy, K., & Laarni, J. (2020). Explainability of machine learning in central banking and financial regulation. Bank of England Staff Working Paper No. 816.

Brynjolfsson, E., Li, D., & Raymond, L. R. (2023). Generative AI at work. NBER Working Paper No. 31161. National Bureau of Economic Research. https://doi.org/ DOI: 10.3386/w31161

Brynjolfsson, E., & McAfee, A. (2014). *The second machine age: Work, progress, and prosperity in a time of brilliant technologies*. W. W. Norton & Company.

Burning Glass Technologies. (2022). *The AI advantage: How AI skills are reshaping the labour market and salary landscape*. Burning Glass Institute.

Cao, L. (2022). AI in finance: Challenges, techniques, and opportunities. *ACM Computing Surveys*, *55*(3), 1–38. DOI: 10.1145/3502289

CFA Institute. (2022). *Future state of the investment profession: AI and data science skills for finance professionals*. CFA Institute Research Foundation.

Choi, J. H., Liu, M. H., & Sami, H. (2020). Financial competence and the transition to data-driven finance: An empirical assessment. *Journal of Accounting Education*, *53*, 100685.

Content Marketing Institute. (2023). *B2B content marketing benchmarks, budgets, and trends: Generative AI special report*. Content Marketing Institute.

Davenport, T., Guha, A., Grewal, D., & Bressgott, T. (2020). How artificial intelligence will change the future of marketing. *Journal of the Academy of Marketing Science*, *48*(1), 24–42. DOI: 10.1007/s11747-019-00696-0

Deloitte Insights. (2022). *The AI-ready financial services workforce: Skills, gaps, and pathways*. Deloitte Development LLC.

European Commission. (2021). Proposal for a regulation of the European Parliament and of the Council laying down harmonised rules on artificial intelligence (Artificial Intelligence Act). COM/2021/206 final.

Financial Stability Board. (2022). *Artificial intelligence and machine learning in financial services: Market developments and financial stability implications*. FSB.

Fuster, A., Goldsmith-Pinkham, P., Ramadorai, T., & Walther, A. (2022). Predictably unequal? The effects of machine learning on credit markets. *The Journal of Finance*, *77*(1), 5–47. DOI: 10.1111/jofi.13090

Gartner. (2022). The state of marketing technology adoption and utilization. Gartner Research.

Goldin, C., & Katz, L. F. (2008). *The race between education and technology*. Harvard University Press.

Gomber, P., Kauffman, R. J., Parker, C., & Weber, B. W. (2018). On the fintech revolution: Interpreting the forces of innovation, disruption, and transformation in financial services. *Journal of Management Information Systems*, *35*(1), 220–265. DOI: 10.1080/07421222.2018.1440766

Graduate Management Admission Council. (2023). *Corporate recruiters survey: AI and hybrid skills demand in business education*. GMAC Research Reports.

Huang, M. H., & Rust, R. T. (2021). A strategic framework for artificial intelligence in marketing. *Journal of the Academy of Marketing Science*, *49*(1), 30–50. DOI: 10.1007/s11747-020-00749-9

Kietzmann, J., Paschen, J., & Treen, E. (2018). Artificial intelligence in advertising: How marketers can leverage artificial intelligence along the consumer journey. *Journal of Advertising Research*, *58*(3), 263–267. DOI: 10.2501/JAR-2018-035

Kotler, P., Kartajaya, H., & Setiawan, I. (2021). *Marketing 5.0: Technology for humanity*. John Wiley & Sons.

Kumar, V., Rajan, B., Venkatesan, R., & Lecinski, J. (2019). Understanding the role of artificial intelligence in personalized engagement marketing. *California Management Review*, *61*(4), 135–155. DOI: 10.1177/0008125619859317

LinkedIn Economic Graph. (2023). *Future of skills report: AI skills and the evolving talent landscape*. LinkedIn Corporation.

McKinsey Global Institute. (2021). The future of work after [McKinsey & Company.]. *COVID*, •••, 19.

McKinsey Global Institute. (2023). *The economic potential of generative AI: The next productivity frontier*. McKinsey & Company.

Mincer, J. (1974). *Schooling, experience, and earnings*. National Bureau of Economic Research.

Morgan Stanley. (2022). *AI in investment management: From automation to augmentation*. Morgan Stanley Institute for Sustainable Investing.

NASSCOM. (2023). *AI skills for the future: India's AI talent landscape and growth pathways*. NASSCOM Foundation.

Reserve Bank of India. (2023). *Guidelines on artificial intelligence and machine learning in financial services*. RBI Publications.

World Economic Forum. (2020). The future of jobs report 2020. World Economic Forum.

World Economic Forum. (2023). The future of jobs report 2023. World Economic Forum.

Chapter 6

Retail Sales Forecasting Using Machine Learning Techniques

Suhashini Awadhesh Chaurasia
http://orcid.org/0000-0002-7443-0105
Ramdeobaba University, India

Shantanu Khope
Symbiosis Institute of Technology, India

Satvik Barhanpure
Symbiosis Institute of Technology, India

Gagandeep Kaur
http://orcid.org/0009-0004-2834-9850
MPSTME, SVKM's NMIMS University, Maharashtra, India

Ambika S. Jaiswal
http://orcid.org/0000-0003-4517-0786
Sant Gade Baba Amravati University, India

ABSTRACT

Sales forecasting is the key to successful management of a business, as through it, organizations are able to maximize their revenues, manage their inventory, and also strategize. The existing dynamic trends in the market following the changes in market dynamics, the periods of seasonality, and the promotions that are used often elude the traditional statistical forecasting methods. As a way of overcoming these limitations, this research applies a wide-ranging machine learning-based machinery of retail sales forecasting. It contains major data processing and performance skill,

DOI: 10.4018/979-8-2600-0116-5.ch006

including both the past sale as well as other external factors like the holidays and special offers. Several predictive models are created, trained, and tested thoroughly using such metrics as Root Mean Squared Error (RMSE) and Mean Absolute Percentage Error (MAPE), such as Linear Regression, Random Forest or even Long Short-Term Memory (LSTM) networks.

I. INTRODUCTION

Effective forecasting of sales is essential in most industries such as retail industry, manufacturing industry and supply chain management. Inventory planning, workforce plans, financial plans and production plans as well as designing dynamic marketing plans rely upon high-quality predictions. Traditionally, companies have been using such statistical methods as moving averages, exponential smoothing, and autoregressive models. In as much as they are simple to apply and interpret, the mentioned approaches are limited by their lack of ability to track nonlinear trends, significant changes in price trend, and exogenous factors, including promotions, holidays, or economic scenarios. Also, these methods cannot effectively handle large and high-dimensional data that is typical of modern retail activities. With this awareness of these shortcomings, The recent breakthroughs in the field of machine learning (ML) have produced forecasting models that can learn to respond to complicated data trends over time and make generalizations to new scenarios. Especially, the Linear Regression, Decision Trees, Random Forest, and Long Short-Term Memory (LSTM) networks have proven the ability to represent nonlinear relationships, dynamic changes in sales data, and long-range temporal dependency. However, there are issues regarding the choice of the proper model architectures, hyperparameter tuning, interpretability and computational efficiency. Furthermore, applications or too vague comparisons among algorithm types and preprocessing strategies usually can be found in the existing body of literature. Being inspired by these deficiencies, this paper will conduct a comparative analysis of popular machine learning algorithms to predict weekly sales of retail stores based on a real data set. They are the following:

- Compare the benchmark which includes the relative performance of various ML models with standard error measurements. Root Mean Squared Error (RMSE) and Mean Absolute Error (MAE) are calculated. The formula for the same is listed in the chapter.
- To examine the influence of various data pre-processing methods and other variables which includes lag variables, holidays indicator, statistics on absolute model performance

- To select the most appropriate forecasting model which includes accuracy and computational burden. The most and very important contribution to the work is a systematic assessment of different forecasting models on retail sales dataset, the analysis of data preparation processes that is essential to real life applications.

The remaining parts of the paper are constructed as follows: Section II provides background information and the discussion about related articles, gaps in existing forecasting methods, and Section III introduces the methodology, describing the dataset, preprocessing procedures, and the model and settings, Section IV reports the results of experiments, performance comparisons, and discussions, and Section V sums up the study by presenting the conclusion, limitations, and future work.

The study includes information on data structure, machine learning model training processes, comparison between ensemble models, and the strategic significance for the retail sector. Forecasting of demand can either make or break a retail business in today's scenario. High inventory costs money in terms of carrying cost while also resulting in losses due to discounts provided to customers. On the other hand, out-of-stock scenarios cost retailers money that could have been earned otherwise, apart from reducing their ability to attract repeat customers in the future. Our study aims at addressing these issues through the use of a high-level data set for designing a forecasting engine using machine learning techniques.

The basis for the study lies in an extensive history dataset that has been gathered over a number of years in a retail setting. The dataset is organized by individual product and store, which represents the ideal point of balance in terms of granularity. The dataset is monitored for five primary metrics: Date, Store Identifier, Product Identifier, Sales (Quantity), and Price. Data was carefully pre-processed before modelling, accounting for typical challenges found in actual data which comprises of imputation,. An imputation means missing sales numbers were handled through temporal interpolation to preserve continuity. Outlier Handling means unexpected peaks, typically arising from input errors or large purchases, were clamped or smoothed to avoid distorting the model's understanding of normal behaviour and finally normalization which means prices were normalized to ensure expensive products didn't unduly affect algorithm loss functions.

Whereas the raw data tells us "what," feature engineering explains the "why." In order to make the models aware of temporal patterns, the researchers engineered multiple features from the raw timestamp variable. The need for temporal features lagged variables. By introducing features such as Sales of previous day and Sales of same day previous week, authors proposed model "memory." Rolling averages is using 7-day and 30-day rolling averages, the model can tell the difference between an anomaly and a trend metrics means by assigning explicit values to metrics such as weekends, months, and important holidays, we help the model understand the "seasonality" in the retail industry, for example, increased visits to stores during the weekend and holidays.

The study adopts a sequential pipeline for reproducibility and validation of the results which includes

Preprocessing - enhancing the quality of input data. Feature Engineering- Developing predictive features.

Model Selection- Choosing the best possible mathematical model to get the good accuracy is the goal of the model selection. The model training and validation of data is in the ratio of 80:20. The model is being trained on the historical data and then tested on the future data, thereby replicating the practical application scenario. Then model is evaluated on several methods of assessment to get good performance.

The experiment comprised of the three major and most popular algorithms utilized for the machine learning. The algorithms are XGBoost (Exterme Gradiant Boosting) and LightGBM. Random Forest which uses bagging algorithm builds a number of decision trees from various samples of data. Although extremely resilient to any variations and anomalies, the averaging technique utilized by the model often renders it incapable of forecasting the abrupt peaks that occur due to the unexplained phenomena like Black Friday.

XGBoost and LightGBM (Boosting) can be referred to as the most sophisticated implementations of Gradient Boosting Decision Trees (GBDT). This model is distinguished by strong regularization that decreases the probability of overfitting. LightGBM is optimized for speed and is capable of processing large amounts of data via leaf-wise tree construction. However, the most significant result of the experiment was obtained during the behaviour of models under high volatility conditions. Despite all of the models exhibiting increased levels of error when subjected to these stress test conditions, XGBoost and LightGBM showed notably smaller error intervals than Random Forest. This is due to the fact that boosting methods are explicitly built to decrease the errors of the prior trees in the model. During a spike in demand, the first couple of trees may make erroneous predictions, but successive trees correct the predictions and help the model "climb" up the curve.

For validating the models, the research considered three mathematical perspectives: RMSE: It was the first perspective used to penalize model predictions as RMSE was the core metric. It squares up the errors, thus warning about the large prediction gaps that would indicate catastrophic failure on high-traffic days.

Mean Absolute Error (MAE): It provides an actual prediction error. The MAE of 4 units means that model's prediction is off by an average of 4 unts. It is very simple to understand for the inventory planners.

Means Absolute Percentage Error (MAPE): The metric allowed comparing stores across all different scales. Finally the error of 4% in an tiny boutique is the same as in a huge warehouse, no matter how much stock is in it.

The plot of the training and testing error demonstrated converging behaviour. It proves outstanding generalization capabilities of models, which means that they learned the underlying retail principles not basically the noise of the training period. At last the forecast engine predict 28 days into the future. This helps the organization of retail to make appropriate decision from a particular point.

Inventory Management: It means lowering the safety sock for low demand products and keeping the high demand products fully stocked.

Staffing: It is the synchronizing staffing requirement with anticipated surges in customer interaction.

Marketing: Running simulations to evaluate the effects of offering a 20% discount and a “buy one get one free” promotion.

Conclusively, this analysis demonstrates that ensemble learning models are very efficient in retail forecasting, especially using gradient boosting models, which are stable yet sensitive enough to deal with the erratic behaviour in consumers.

Possible Future Extensions includes deep Learning - trying out transformers and LSTMs (long short-term memory models) to determine whether there could be other complex and long-term dependencies that could improve the model further. Real-Time Learning - transitioning from batch-based weekly forecasting to continuous learning systems that adapt as sales are made. Unstructured Data - Including unstructured information such as weather patterns, customer opinions, or competitor prices in the forecasting. With further developments in this system, it is possible for retailers to create an entirely self-regulating supply chain that caters to customers even before they ask for anything.

II. RELATED WORKS

The recent development where the superiority of machine learning and deep learning over classical statistical methods of sales forecasting is observed in competitive sales forecasting. (Wang et al., 2022) proposed a hybrid version of XGBoost and traditional ARIMA forecasts of retail sales, where it was revealed that XGBoost-enhanced version of the model decreased the value of RMSE considerably compared to ARIMA only forecast on retail sales data and in particular during the trend shift period or external shocks cases. Although the integration enhanced the accuracy, their model was only able to predict at the monthly level, thus limiting how they could use their model on a granular type of planning. (Dantas et al., 2022) tested both XGBoost and deep learning (LSTM) on the given retail data using the public data set on Kaggle and found out that deep learning models performed labile better than the tree-based methods, based on RMSE, but at a much higher cost in terms of time and not interpretable. In (Hobor et al., 2024), benchmarking of Random Forest, Support Vector Regression, and LSTM on Walmart, it was revealed that LSTM model is best when series has strong seasonality but the training time was significantly slow compared to tree-based models . (Park et al., 2023) has proposed a temporal pattern attention-based recurrent neural network on retail demand forecasting, their attention-RNN showed significantly better MAPE than the common LSTM due to the strong ability to learn cyclical and anomaly patterns, but the complex architecture of the given model made it difficult to deploy. (Ganguly et al., 2024) compared the performance of XGBoost and LightGBM on fast-moving consumer goods data, demonstrating that XGBoost has the lowest RMSE value and that LightGBM takes the shortest time to learn, but the study skipped deep learning model to cover the entire assessment as well . On real supermarket data, (Malik et al., 2024) compared Random Forest, XGBoost, and LSTM and reported that LSTM was more accurate in making predictions during the volatile periods in sales but the large LSTM model questioned its suitability to smaller business due to the scalability problems. (Ilieva, 2022) surveyed deep learning methods to online selling retail stores and confirmed the perfectness of LSTM and CNN to deal with long-range dependency and promotions, however high labelled data demand and compute power need to be also mentioned.

According to the work by (Ahmed et al., 2024) various deep learning models were tested to predict retail sales and it was determined that hybrid models (e.g. CNN-GRU) performed better than single models, but interpretability was still an issue, and their strategy necessitated a lot of calibration. A systematic literature review of recent developments in using deep learning to forecast retail has been published by (Eglite et al., 2022) who confirm that, though deep neural computation established new standards of accuracy in retail forecasting, external factors (such as economic indicators) considered in many applications remained largely inadequate, which might reduce robustness. (Chen et al., 2024) were the first to include the textual characteristics of products in machine learning pipelines, which showed that incorporation of descriptive phrases of products made measurable improvements in predictions, but caused a greater degree of system complexity due to sophisticated preprocessing of the text.

In combination, these papers confirm that although deep learning and tree-based ensemble learning methods have made substantial progress toward the development of retail sales forecasting systems, the method presents interpretability, computational efficiency, generalizability, and the possibility of full integration with heterogeneous external features.

The study uses chatbots for examining the customers review on useability, usefulness and trust on e-commerce web sites. Conventional agents like chatbots not only understand customers online shopping habits but also give recommendation and promote the product. Chatbots provides 24 by 7 facility to their customers. Authors used Structural Equation Modeling (SEM) with the AMOS analysis program V23 in this manuscript. Google form was circulated on social media to take the feedback from the customers who are above 18 years of age and have done some online transactions. A novel model will be tested and compared to prior research. The results of the work show the attitudes are significantly influenced by usability, usefulness and trust. Attitude has a major impact on decisions, whereas trust has a little impact on customers' view about e-commerce web sites. In this study the online purchasing develops trust among customers to make a choice as compared to the attitude. Significantly, customer confidence on e-commerce web site is the major factor that most effects attitude. The quantitative survey shows that a dep majority of respondents were apprehensive about employing AI and e-retail chatbots. It is basically due to the accuracy and security of the system along with that getting the information or advice from the chatbots by (Jyoti Rana et al., 2024).

The study aims at scrutinizing the dynamics of scientific publications which is basically dedicated to optimize the consumer shopping habits through an application of AI. It governs the status of exiting research on the role of AI in the sector of retail market. The objective to the research was to analyses the collection of scientific publications from the Scopus indexed. It includes the latest technologies that can improved the consumer behavior of purchase habits before, at the time of purchase and after purchase. It incorporates publication search by article title, abstract and keywords to assemble the data from the database of Scopus. The publications which were selected were then visualized using the software VOS viewer 1.6.16.0 and bibliophagy to perform bibliometric analyses. The very first sample of 356 research articles was collected and analyzed. After reading the full paper containing nearly 149 publications over the past decades from 1998 to 2021 was analyzed in this study. Finding suggest the prominence of authors and journal publishing in implementing AI in retail to automate customer journey. The results show the application of AI in improving the various phases of customer journey among the retailing sectors. The two main retailing sectors fashion and banking play a major role of AI in the consumer journey. Going deeper in the study emerges with the use of AI in other sectors of the economy growth of the country.

Deployment of AI is most in the purchasing and decision-making phase of the consumer journey. The incorporation of AI into consumer journey to highlight its impact on retailing. It contributes to the key management areas in retailing by using AI (Rana et el., 2023).

The objective of this study is to examine common machine learning techniques and also time series analysis for sales forecasting in a bid to get the best fitted technique. Adding more to objective is to give more logical hypotheses for raising future profit margins. Along with obtaining historical in depth understanding of prior demand utilizing business intelligence software's like Microsoft Power BI and Tableau. The results show the precision of various forecasting models that were implemented (Oluwasola et al.,2025).

In the industry sales forecasting is a big part of managing supplies and working with manufactures. In recent market so much of digital data is used to analyze and predict the results. Sales forecasting is really tough for people who manage inventory, marketing, customer service and money for businesses. In this paper authors used computer models to predict sales using the citadel POS dataset. Machine learning models like linear regression, random forest and gradient boosting along with time series models like ARIMA and LSTM to forecast sales. Authors also looked closely at the results and evaluated them. The data used for this study is taken from Citadel POS which is a cloud-based system that retailers use from 2013 to 2018 to manage their stores including sales, inventory, customers and vendors. The result show that XGBoost worked better than the models and has the best performance, with a low error rate of 0.516 and 0.63. Authors found that sales forecasting is very important for sales and using the right computer model can make a big difference. Sales forecasting is still a challenge for businesses and it need to keep working to get better results. Sales forecasting is key to making decisions about retail sales (Muhammad Sajawal et al., 2023).

Table I provides a comparative analysis of various retail forecasting models utilized in the researcher articles published between 2024 to 2026.

Table 1. Comparative Analysis of various forecasting models from 2024 to 2026

Paper reference	Model(s) Evaluated	Key Research Focus	Performance Metric/ Key Result	Best use case
Hober et al., 2025	XGBoost, LightGBM, N-BEATS, N-HiTS	Local vs. Global models in physical retail with intermittent demand	Localized tree- ensembles outperformed global deep learning on noisy data	Brick and Mortar stores with intermittent demand
Kizgin et at., 2025	Tree Based Ensembles	XGBoost, LightGBM, CatBoost	Robust for heterogeneous, feature rich data; excels in localized B&M retail settings	Brick and Mortar stores with specific local variables
Mansur et al., 2025	Hybrid CNN-LSTM	Integrating environmental variables (weather, protest, salary days)	Hybrid CNN-LSTM achieved lowest RMSE. MAE compared to standalone models.	Retails in volatile environments (e.g. emerging markets)

continued on following page

Table 1. Continued

Paper reference	Model(s) Evaluated	Key Research Focus	Performance Metric/ Key Result	Best use case
Adewumi 2026	Ensemble + Time Series Hybrid	Forecasting in Emerging Market retail (A&Z Supermarket)	Superior to conventional methods for inventory optimization	Supermarkets with high SKU turnover in developing regions
Md Tanvir et al. 2025	Hybrid RF-XGBoost LR	Combing Random Forest and linear regression for stability	Significant accuracy gains through ensemble stacking	Multi-channel retail requiring balanced stability and precision
Rui & Li, 2025	GCN+ LSTM + Attention	Graph Convolutional Network	Effectively captured topological dependencies between products	Fashion and electronics (high product substitution)
Venkiteela, 2025	XGBoost Super kart Framework	Low code, real time deployment using Streamlit/ Hugging Face	Achieved R^2 score of 0.87 high scalability for business users	Mid-sized retail chains seeking accessible AI solutions
Kizgin et al. 2025	XGBoost & LightGBM	Impact of socioeconomic indicators (pension days) on clothing sales	Feature engineering was more critical than model architecture for accuracy	Trend-sensitive retail (Apparel/ Fashion)
Mohammed et al., 2026	LSTMixer (linear Model Extension)	Comparing Temporal Fusion Transformers vs. Linear extension	LSTMixer was the best predictor; Linear extensions beat standard ML	High volume retail with deep historical data and many stores

III. PROPOSED METHOD

A. Dataset and Description

The data set provides the basic elements that characterize a study in retail forecasting. To expound it further on how significant the data structure architecture is, how important feature engineering is, and the validity process.

The structural nature of data is defined by its granularity. By using transactional records at the product-store level, the model is able to capture the localized variation in demand that the global approach would fail to capture. The reason for this is that a certain Item ID might work better in one Store ID due to regional demographics but poorly in another.

The addition of Price as an element in the model is important because it enables the researchers to explore the issue of price elasticity. This is where regression algorithms can be very helpful in determining pricing trends.

Data Set Used for this Chapter:

Sales data has been collected over a long span of time from a retail environment. The data set consists of transaction data at the product store level. The data set has been designed such that regression-based forecasting model and time series forecasting model both can be implemented using the data set. Following are some important attributes of the data set.

The data set used in this chapter includes sales data collected from a retail environment over a long period of time. This data set comprises of detailed transactional records at the product store level. It is structured to support both regression-based forecasting models as well as time series forecasting models. Following are the key attributes of the dataset.

- **Date:** The specific day of the sale transaction.
- **Store ID:** Unique identifier for each store.
- **Item ID:** Unique identifier for each product.
- **Sales:** Number of units sold on the given date.
- **Price:** Price of the product on that date.

The data was first cleaned to deal with missing values, outliers, and inaccurate inputs. In case of temporal models, the following features such as lag variables (sales of previous days), moving averages, day-of-week, month indicators, and other features were created. Data set was split into training and Testing sets (80% and 20%, respectively) according to time, since it will be important to see how well the model performs on the future data and maintain the necessary temporal integrity in case of time-series forecasts. A typical mistake when working with machine learning models is the perception of time-series data as static data. If we use tradition random splitting into training and testing sets, chances of getting data leakage; the model will see the future information about time to predict the past.

Using the chronological split (Training on the first 80% of time and testing on the last 20%) this will guarantee temporal integrity. This means that the simulation of real time situation in which the model is used on Mondays to predict sales from Tuesdays to Sundays. Thus, the model gives the correct estimation of the performance.

B. Methodology

Methodology used in this study is presented in five major stages, including data preprocessing, feature engineering, model selection, training and validation, and evaluation. The methodology used in order to conduct analysis has been developed based on an advanced pipeline, which helps in transforming the raw retail transaction dataset into useful intelligence.

First, data preprocessing is conducted, which involves data cleaning and inputting missing values I order to improve the data quality. Then feature engineering stage comes, during which lag and moving average features are created.

After that, various types of machine learning models are tested, starting from basic linear regression and ending with advanced gradient boosting trees. Then, the Temporal Partitioning approach is applied at the Training & validation stage in order to help the algorithm learn from the history. The last stage involves evaluation the models based on metrics such as RMSE.

I. Data Preprocessing

The raw data will contain several issues including missing values, outliers, and discrepancies that have to be handled before the training of the model. Missing values were imputed using mean/mode substitution or forward filling technique depending on the data type used. The outliers in the sales features were handled through capping using the interquartile range (IQR). Categorical features like day, week, month, and year were extracted from the date. The step of initial cleaning is the most time-consuming step in the whole process. In retail, the presence of outliers (say, a large bulk purchase) and missing values (say, store shutdown due to power outages) will lead to distorting the model's view of reality. The strategy to handle this situation involves:

Imputation: Using interpolation or median value to fill in missing values.

Outliers: Checking whether this is a true peak or data entry errors.

II. Feature Engineering

Feature engineering described above allows identifying seasonality and other patterns. In fact, feature engineering converts human intuition into mathematical variables. In order to improve the performance of models, a number of additional features were engineered:

- Lag features – The previous sales number for different time lag (for instance, one day, seven days, twenty-eight days). Lag features the values of the independent variable. Example features could be "Sales_t_1, Sales_t_7." Lag features are the core of time series analysis because they allow modeling momentum and autocorrelation.

- Rolling means: A smoothed sales trend by applying rolling average. Rolling average of the number of sales within a certain period of time (7 days or 30 days), for instance, could help in smoothing out the noise in the data set.
- Binary flags: In order to take into consideration, the impact of promotions on the sales number.
- Temporal features: Day of the week, weakened and month flags. This will allow capturing seasonality in addition to short and long-term patterns in the sales pattern. Temporal features such as "Day of week" and "Month" can be engineered from the data set in order to help a model detect seasonality patterns.

III. Model Selection

Multiple machine learning models were selected for performance comparison:

- Linear Regression (LR): Serves as a baseline for comparison.

Linear regression (Kecheng Qu, 2024) is a statistical technique employed to determine a linear correlation between the independent variable X and the dependent variable Y. The objective is to identify an optimal linear function by determining a set of coefficients that is weights that enable the function to predict the value of the dependent variable with maximal accuracy. The linear regression model can be written as follows:

$$Y=\beta_0+ \beta_1X_1+ \beta_2X_2+....+ \beta_n X_n+\varepsilon \qquad (1)$$

Where,
β_0 is intercept
β_1 to β_n are the regression coefficient
X_1 to X_n are the independent variables
ε is error

- Random Forest Regressor (RF): An ensemble tree-based model effective for handling non-linearity and interactions. A random forest is a machine learning model used for classification and forecasting. To train the Machine Learning algorithms and artificial intelligence models need a big amount of data. This data is crucial for data collection. The integration of data collection and processing methods improves precision and innovation in problem-solving. Using methods in interdisciplinary research makes the research process smoother. It fosters innovation. Helps apply data analysis findings to patter recognition, decision-making, predictive modeling and problem solving. This approach encourages innovation in research. The random forest technique uses decision trees. It constructs a collection of decision trees. Combines their outcomes to generate the final prediction. Every decision tree in a forest is built using random subsets of data. Each tree is trained on a portion of the dataset. The outcomes of all decision trees are combined to derive the forecast. One of the benefits of forests is their ability to handle unbalanced data and variable with missing values. Random forests mitigate the issue of overfitting by training decision trees on random subsets of data. This enhances their ability to generalize to data. Random forests are highly regraded as one of the efficient and powerful techniques in machine learning. They are widely used in application such as automatic data categorization, forecasting and supervisory learning (Hasan Ahmad Salman, 2024).

- XGBoost: A powerful gradient boosting model that handles large datasets and sparse data efficiently. It is an optimization method based on decision trees that leverages the gradient descent algorithm. The gradient descent method is used for optimizing the loss function, while the regularization parameters are used to avoid overfitting. The main idea behind the XGBoost algorithm is to minimize the objective function (Dede Tarwidi et al., 2023).
- CatBoost – CatBoost is a new gradient boosting algorithm. The use of this algorithm results in higher quality compared to other publicly available tools implementing the same approach. The two most important algorithmic innovations implemented in CatBoost include ordered boosting, which is a novel permutation-based version of the traditional approach, and a novel algorithm for handling categorical predictors. These algorithms were invented to tackle the prediction shift issue caused by a special type of target leakage inherent to any existing implementations of the gradient boosting method. The problem is thoroughly analyzed and algorithms successfully address the problem (Liudmila Prokhorenkova et al., 2018).

Each model was trained on 80% of the dataset and validated on the remaining 20%. Time-based cross-validation was used to ensure sequential integrity. Hyperparameters were tuned using grid search and randomized search techniques to optimize performance.

IV. Evaluation Metrics

Models were evaluated using the following metrics:

- Root Mean Squared Error (RMSE) – It is standard metrics used in model evaluation. Let us take n observations x $(x_1,x_2,\ldots,x_n)$ and n corresponding model predictions then RMSE can be written as

RMSE=

$$\sqrt{\frac{1}{n}\sum_{i=1}^{n}(y_i - \ _i)^2} \tag{1}$$

Equation (1) has been used as a standard statistical metric to measure model performance in various applications.

The reason why RMSE is very effective for detecting outliers or major miscalculation cases is due to the square of the difference between the actual and forecasted sales, which leads to a higher weighting for higher differences. Another good point about RMSE is that it gives a result in the same units as the actual sales number.

- Mean Absolute Error (MAE) - Mean Absolute Error (MAE) is one of the basic measures employed in calculating the accuracy of a forecasting model. The measure involves taking an average of the absolute error values for all the forecasts involved. In contrast to other measures, it takes the arithmetic mean of the absolute values without involving any squaring. The formula for MAE is:

MAE=

$$\frac{1}{n}\sum_{i=1}^{n}|y_i - \ _i| \tag{2}$$

Equation (2) is also a statistical metric useful to measure the mean absolute error.

Regarding forecasting in the retail environment, the interpretation of MAE is extremely intuitive because it is expressed in the same unit as the variable under consideration—such as the number of units sold—and hence it gives a manager the exact number of units off the prediction average.

The main property of MAE is that it is a robust metric in terms of handling outliers. As opposed to measures such as RMSE, which give the squared values for errors (and thus have the effect of increasing the weight of high-value errors), MAE gives a proportional view of the errors, rendering it ideal as a baseline measure when making predictions about inventory levels.

- Mean Absolute Percentage Error (MAPE) - is a very common measure used in business and retail forecasting as it measures accuracy in terms of percentages instead of absolute values. It is very helpful in making comparisons between models that are used for different types of items, store sections, or departments with different levels of sales. These metrics provide a comprehensive assessment of model accuracy and robustness, especially for fluctuating sales patterns. MAPE can be written as

MAPE=

$$\frac{100\%}{n}\sum_{i=1}^{n}\left|y_i - \quad _i\right| \tag{3}$$

Equation (3) is use to calculate mean absolute Percentage error

The main benefit of MAPE is its interpretability to laypeople. It will be easier for a manager to understand the forecast accuracy if you tell him that there was a "10% error" rather than saying the error was "500 units," because the importance of 500 units differs when the number sold is measured in thousands or dozens. But there are several major drawbacks in MAPE. First, MAPE is positively biased in underestimation, since the percentage error is bounded above by 100% in underestimation but not bounded in overestimation. Second, it goes to infinity when yi=0, which is quite possible for products in retail that are sold slowly.

Each model was trained using the engineered feature set and evaluated using root mean squared error (RMSE) and coefficient of determination (R^2). A time-based train-test split was used to ensure realistic forecasting and prevent data leakage.

IV. RESULTS AND DISCUSSION

A. Model Comparison

During the second stage, the performance of three sphisticated ensemble learning models, including Random Forest, XGBoost, and LightGBM, are compared. Although these models share a similar foundation based on decision trees, they utilize different mathematical approaches that help minimize errors and increase effectiveness. For instance, Random Forest utilizes an approach knows as bagging, which consists in creating a series of independent tress, whose results are then averaged to reduce variablity. In turn, both XGBoost and Light GBM utilizes boosting; which imples creating a seris of trees aimed at fixing the mistakes of previous ones.

However, one of the advantage of XGBoost is its great regularity that allows one to avoid overfitting, especially when working with noisy retail data. In turn, the LightGBM model is regarded as better fitting for bigger samples since it applies the leaf-wise tree growing technique, which, normally, implies faster training and higher quality predictions than the classic level wise tree growing used in other models. In order to compare the model's performances, they will be trained on the same 80% of the historical sample and validated on the rest 20% of the future sampe. The performance of the models will be assesed by means of the numerical metrics like RMSE and R2.

In order to evaluate model performance, the model is trained using Random Forest, XGBoost and LightGBM regressors on the saming training sample and predicted on time-dependent test samples. The results of this excerise are summerized in the following Table IV.

Table 2. Comparative analysis of machine learning models for sales forecasting

Model	RMSE	MAE	MAPE	R^2
Random Forest	190.32	104.2	8.70%	0.89
XGBoost	175.76	97.14	8.10%	0.92
LightGBM	181.95	98.77	8.30%	0.90

Despite having a higher RMSE, XGBoost achieved the highest R^2 score, indicating it captured variance effectively. LightGBM balanced both metrics well and offered faster training time.

B. Additional Insights

- Importance of features: Analysis of the features importance revealed that the values of the lagged sales, holidays indicators, and promotions data were often included into the top ones in each model. This confirms the significance of the calculation of time and even-based characteristics of retail forecasting.
- The feature importance analysis reveals the factors influencing the retail demand. The lagged sales values were found the most effective predictors, which means that the previous performance is the best indicator for the further performance. Thus, the consumer behaviour proves to be quite predictable ("has a memory").
- The holiday indicators and the promotion data also ranked highly, which shows that external events may exert a huge influence on the baseline trends.

It is clear from the constant present in the top positions of the features in the case of Random Forest, XGBoost and LightGBM that the retail forecasting process is quite complex and cannot be simply linear.

So, engineered temporal features are important for capturing changes in the seasons.

- Residual Analysis: The analysis of the residuals showed that the lowest levels of the prediction error occurred in regular weeks whereas the demand volatility was the highest during the major holidays and sales events when the prediction error increased only a little. Among the models, the XGBoost and LightGBM performed better in these periods, given that the ranges of the errors were less than Random Forest.

The analysis of discrepancy between the predicted values and actual sales reveals the diagnostics of stability of the model under stress. Based on the findings presented above, it can be stated that the accuracy of all the models is highest in the period of regularity of behaviour due to routing, which leads to predictable volatility.

The discrepancy in performance results from the structure of GBDT. While Random Forest creates independent trees and averages their predictions, such machine learning algorithms as XGBoost and LightGBM utilize the boosting approach, meaning that they rely on residuals of the previous iteration. It enables them to adjust promptly to the non-linear spikes resulting from the holiday shopping period due to their boosting approach, which enables them to cope with this problem. Otherwise, Random Forest's approach of prediction averaging may lead to a lagged prediction. For this reason, GBDT is a appropriate choice for the environment that involves continuous promotion.

- The stress test was performed for all models on holiday periods and promotions characterized by increased demand volatility levels. While prediction errors increased, based on research findings, both XGBosst and LightGBM showed smaller test in the current analysis, the resilience of the models is examined under extreme market conditions. For the retail industry, holidays such as Christmas and other promotional sales periods can be regarded as such cases since traditional behaviour of consumers becomes highly predictable owing to non-linear spikes in demand. The findings show that there is a significant difference in the performance of the models despite the fact that all models showed an increase in errors due to volatility leakage.
- The reason for this lies in the technical one, which makes distinction between bagging and boosting techniques. Bagging technique is applied in the context of Random Forest where an average value of several tress with high depth

is calculated; consequently, it smooths forecasts. Hence such an approach appears to be more immune to sharp peaks in the purchase volume due to holidays such as Black Friday or flash sales, which means underestimation of extremums.

Unlike the latter, the two boosting algorithms – XGBoost and LightGBM – generate each following decision tree with an intent to reduce errors made by the preceding ones. They tend to catch the variability better by chasing those steep gradients. In this case, although the increase in variance is evident for all the approaches tested here, it becomes apparent that gradient-boosted architectures work better.

- Generalization Performance: The models had generalization performance with no significant evidence of overfitting as noted through a steady curve of train vs. test errors.

One important indicator of the quality of a prediction system is the level of generalization, which is determined by the system's ability to generalize knowledge gained from a particular dataset to other unknown datasets. In the current paper, the lack of overfitting was demonstrated through an analysis of the learning curves, which showed the changes in the error rate during each iteration in both the training and test sets.

The problem with many machine learning models is usually the "divergence" of the learning curve; that is, the decrease in the training error rate to zero while memorizing noise and the growth of the testing error rate. In our case, however, the curve remained stable and converged, indicating the effect of the regularization process on the model complexity.

With the help of small differences in performance on training and testing tasks, one can see that the models learned the structural dependencies of the retail market (elasticity of goods, seasonality) and not any outliers present in the data. This makes the forecast system not only accurate in its predictions based on the historical log, but also makes it "future proof."

C. Forecast Output Sample

To illustrate the performance of the forecast engine, wauthors generated 28-day predictions for Store 3, Dept 5. The following Table 3 shows a 4-week subset:

Table 3. Results displaying weekly sales forecast

Date	Store	Dept	Predicted Weekly Sales
2012-11-02	3	5	13195.09961
2012-11-09	3	5	13195.09961
2012-11-16	3	5	12666.04004
2012-11-23	3	5	19888.24023

Table 3 is provided with the comparison between the three models on the basis of RMSE score obtained from them. These analyses have revealed that the machine learning models, especially gradient boosting techniques, are perfectly suited for forecasting in case of complex retail problems if they are accompanied by relevant feature sets and time elements. The above forecast is a good example in which sales variation is forecasted by the model in usual periods and special periods like week ending November 23.

V. CONCLUSION AND FUTURE WORK

In this paper, authors have established the effectiveness of machine learning ensembles in the prediction of weekly retail sales by using the structed data available on Kaggle. By making use of different data sets along engineered features, authors have managed to attain a high level of accuracy in predicting sales through many different models, like XGBoost. Though this study have shown how revolutionary ensemble machine learning technology is for the retail industry since it established the fact that through the proper organization of historical data and its analysis through sophisticated algorithms, authors can get highly accurate demand data, It has been able to overcome the complexities of retail forecasting through the use of multivariate data over the years.

The primary result of the paper in question is the performance of XGBoost and LightGBM models. This result was achieved through the use of gradient-boosting algorithms as compared to classical statistical methods and basic ensemble learning techniques. The ability of those two to work with large amounts of data and handle non-linear relationships helped them to perform equally well on training and testing sets, which indicates the model's good generalization capabilities and its ability to handle the phenomenon of concept drift.

Another significant result is the development of 28-day forecasting engine, which is not only used for predicting results but also helps retailers to modify input parameters concerning:

Price points: Simulating the effect of price cuts on volume.

Promotional calendars: Anticipating cannibalization or halo effects for certain events.

Holiday periods: Dealing with volatile demand spikes as seen from stress tests.

This will convert the analysis into an effective tool for optimizing the stock levels and planning marketing strategies. By being aware of the expected demand four weeks prior, retailers can lower their costs on maintaining inventories and avoid out-of-stock situations.

The design of the methodology allows for structural flexibility. As the attributes have been developed from a product-store standpoint, the engine will automatically scale accordingly. It can be scaled horizontally to encompass other areas of business (such as foodstuffs versus electronics), or vertically to incorporate other store formats in different geographic regions.

While ensemble algorithm currently dominates in structured data classification and prediction, it becomes evident from the literature review that Deep Learning will be the next big trend. Algorithms such as RNNs and Transformers are capable of performing advanced sequence analysis. They posses the unique ability to identify intricate time series connections which cannot be detected using decision tree algorithms. Moreover, the transition from batch processes to sales feeds in crucial. Implementation of these algorithms into the business platform will provide dynamic forecasts. As opposed to week-long forecasts, there will be hour-by-hour forests which will enable decision-makers, or the competitors' actions. The evolution from prediction to prescription will be the ultimate achievement of the present research.

System Requirements

Processor: Intel i5(8th Gen) or higher/ AMD Ryzen 5 or better

Memory (RAM): Minimum 8GB; 16 GB recommended for deep learning models

Storage: At least 10GB free disk space for data and model storage (SSD preferred)

Operating System: Windows 10/11 (64 bit), Ubuntu 20.04 + LTD or mac OS 11+

Software Requirements

Programming Language: Python 3.8 or newer

Development Environment: Jupyter Notebook, VS Code or PyCharm

ACKNOWLEDGMENT

I would like to express my sincere gratitude to my project guide for her valuable guidance, constant support, and encouragement throughout the course of this project. I would also like to thank the faculty members of the Department of Computer Science & Engineering, Symbiosis Institute of Technology, Nagpur, for providing the required resources and a learning environment for the successful completion of this Project Based Learning (PBL). Lastly, I would like to extend my heartfelt appreciation to my friends and family for their support and motivation during this project work.

REFERENCES

Adewumi, A. O. (2026). Ensemble and time-series hybrid modeling for retail inventory optimization in emerging markets. *Journal of African Retail Research*, *12*(1), 45–62.

Ahmed, R. S. (2024). Comparison of deep learning algorithms for retail sales forecasting. *Proceedings of the International Conference on Computing and Knowledge*. DOI: 10.62762/TIS.2024.300700

Chen, S., Li, X., Wang, Y., & Zhao, J. (2024). Which product description phrases affect sales forecasting? An empirical study. *Economic Modelling*, •••, 127.

Dantas, M. J., de Souza, L. R., & da Silva, A. N. (2022). Sales forecasting in retail using XGBoost and deep learning. *Expert Systems with Applications*, •••, 191.

Eglite, L., & Birzniece, I. (2022). Retail sales forecasting using deep learning: Systematic literature review. *Complex Systems Informatics and Modeling Quarterly*, *30*(30), 53–62. DOI: 10.7250/csimq.2022-30.03

Ganguly, P., & Mukherjee, I. (2024). *Enhancing retail sales forecasting with optimized machine learning models.*

Hobor, L., Brcic, M., Polutnik, L., & Kapetanovic, A. (2024). Comparative analysis of modern machine learning models for retail sales forecasting. *International Journal of Forecasting*, *40*(1), 225–238.

Ilieva, N. (2022). Deep learning methods for e-commerce retail sales forecasting. *Procedia Computer Science*, *200*, 194–201.

Kizgin, K. T., Alp, S., Aydin, N., & Yu, H. (2025). Machine learning-based sales forecasting during crises: Evidence from a Turkish women's clothing retailer. *Science Progress, 108*(1), 00368504241307719. DOI: 10.1177/00368504241307719 PMID: 39840498

Malik, S., Yadav, M., Gupta, N., & Singh, K. (2024). Sales forecasting using machine learning algorithm in the retail sector. *Journal of Computing & Business Intelligence*, *5*(2).

Mansur, S., Sattar, K., Hosseini, S. E., Pervez, S., Ahmad, I., Saleem, K., & Elhendi, A. Z. (2025). Sales forecasting for retail stores using hybrid neural networks and sales-affecting variables. *Scientific Reports*, *15*(1), 12453. PMID: 40216943

Md Tanvir, A., Hossain, M. S., & Rahman, M. (2025). Hybrid RF-XGBoost-LR stacking ensemble for multi-channel retail demand prediction. *Data Science in Business Intelligence*, *9*(2), 112–130.

Mohammed, A., Khan, S., & Li, J. (2026). LSTMixer: A linear extension for multi-horizon temporal forecasting in large-scale retail environments. *IEEE Transactions on Knowledge and Data Engineering*, *38*(4), 890–905.

Mustapha, O. O., & Sithole, T. (2025). Forecasting retail sales using machine learning models. [AJSAS]. *American Journal of Statistics and Actuarial Science*, *6*(1), 35–67. DOI: 10.47672/ajsas.2679

Park, [Initials], Han, Y., & Cho, S.-B. (2023). Temporal pattern attention-based recurrent neural networks for retail sales forecasting. *IEEE Transactions on Neural Networks and Learning Systems, 34*(3), 1175–1187.

Prokhorenkova, L., Gusev, G., Vorobev, A., Dorogush, A. V., & Gulin, A. (2018). CatBoost: Unbiased boosting with categorical features. *Advances in Neural Information Processing Systems (NeurIPS 2018).*

Qu, K. (2024). Research on linear regression algorithm. *MATEC Web of Conferences, 395.*

Rana, J., Jain, R., & Nehra, V. (2024). Utility and acceptability of AI-enabled chatbots on the online customer journey. *International Journal of Computing and Digital Systems*, *15*(1), 323–335. DOI: 10.12785/ijcds/150125

Rana, J., Jain, R., & Santosh, K. C. (2023). Automation and AI-enabled customer journey: A bibliometric analysis. *Vision (Basel)*, 09722629221149854. Advance online publication. DOI: 10.1177/09722629221149854

Rui, X., & Li, Y. (2025). GCN-LSTM with attention mechanism for capturing topological dependencies in retail supply chains. *Journal of Big Data Analytics, 7*(1), 204–221.

Sajawal, M., Usman, S., Alshaikh, H. S., & Hayat, A. (2023). *Predictive analysis of retail sales forecasting using machine learning*. Lahore Garrison University Research Journal of Computer Science and Information Technology.

Salman, H. A., Kalakech, A., & Steti, A. (2024). Random forest algorithm overview. *Babylonian Journal of Machine Learning, 2024*, 69–79. DOI: 10.58496/BJML/2024/007

Tarwidi, D., Pudjaprasetya, S. R., Adytia, D., & Apri, M. (2023). An optimized XGBoost-based machine learning method for predicting wave run-up on a sloping beach. *MethodsX, 10*, 11. DOI: 10.1016/j.mex.2023.102119 PMID: 37007622

Venkiteela, S. R. (2025). SuperKart: A real-time low-code framework for scalable retail forecasting using XGBoost. *International Journal of Intelligent Systems and Applications in Engineering, 13*(2), 441–458.

Wang, Q., Yin, H., Li, S., & Yang, Z. (2022). Integration of deep learning and traditional models for retail sales forecasting. *IEEE Access : Practical Innovations, Open Solutions, 10*, 65021–65034.

Chapter 7
The Hybrid Leader: AI-Enhanced Skills, Human-AI Collaboration, and Economic Growth

Bitto Benny
http://orcid.org/0000-0003-0208-2866
Christ College, Pune, India

Arun Antony Chully
http://orcid.org/0000-0003-1945-8102
Christ College, Pune, India

Anusha Bijoy
http://orcid.org/0009-0009-3144-3334
Christ College, Pune, India

ABSTRACT

As Artificial Intelligence has rapidly become a part of the organizational ecosystem, the need for leadership has significantly changed, along with the economic landscape globally. By fostering AI-Enhanced Skills, organizations will be able to build human capabilities that complement and amplify AI systems, providing a distinct edge in competitive and economic landscapes where AI is increasingly being automated and used at scale to handle routine cognitive work. Drawing on Transformational Leadership Theory, Distributed Cognition Theory, and Ethical Leadership theories, the chapter introduces the Hybrid Leadership Framework, which is a five-part framework made up of the Cognitive Augmentation Awareness, Algorithmic Accountability, Digital Empathy, Collaborative Intelligence Design, and Adaptive Governance. This chapter, achieved through a targeted literature

DOI: 10.4018/979-8-2600-0116-5.ch007

review of contemporary work on leadership theory, AI ethics, and economic development, illustrates that hybrid leadership is not just a management problem but an economic necessity.

1. INTRODUCTION

Each technological revolution has mandated a change in leadership. What the Industrial Revolution demanded were leaders who could coordinate large-scale production activities, manage the disciplined forces of large-scale workforces, and deal with the problems of vertical integration in emergent industrial economies (Kellogg et al., 2020; Pasquale, 2015). The bureaucratic dictatorships of industrial-era leadership were not arbitrary creations, but rather logical necessities of the operational contexts of the times, in which the key problem for leaders was the coordination of human labor to the simple productive task's characteristic of mass production (Chandler, 1977; Taylor, 1911).

The AI Revolution, which is just now accelerating in the mid-2020s, is creating a new leadership challenge, like none before it: for the first time in human history, leaders must manage teams in which non-human team members - AI systems with reasoning, pattern matching, language understanding, predictive modeling, and autonomous decision assistance capacities far beyond any person - play roles. This is not simply a scale shift in the technological capabilities offered to organizations; it's a composition shift in the "employees" of the organization (Drucker, 1959; Nonaka & Takeuchi, 1995). The magnitude and speed of change are breathtaking. The World Economic Forum's Future of Jobs Report (2023) predicts that the combination of automation and AI will eliminate about 85 million jobs simultaneously, as it will create 97 million new jobs that require new skills. The McKinsey Global Institute predicts automation could cause 375 million people globally, in an estimated 14 per cent of the workforce, to need to shift career fields by 2030.

Generative AI, alone, is predicted to have the capacity to automate 300 million full-time jobs, according to Goldman Sachs (2023). Such scenarios are not far-fetched. Even as we read this article, AI-powered systems in health care, finance, manufacturing and other industries are already performing services once thought the exclusive zone of human endeavor: with human radiologists, it reads medical scans more accurately than even the best humans do; it manages investment portfolios; it generates software programs; it handles customer service calls; it performs the first round of evaluations for human employees. But as powerful a tool as it is, AI is just that - a tool (Brynjolfsson & McAfee, 2014; Susskind & Susskind, 2015). Leaders who do not have the conceptual tools, capabilities, and cultural awareness to achieve human-AI collaboration will be blind to a range of organizational breakdowns: algorithmic bias, demoralized human talent through perceived technological replacement, dysfunctional governance to monitor and manage technological development, and the loss of competitive advantage through over-reliance on, or rejection of, the use of AI systems(Burns, 1978; Bass, 1985; Greenleaf, 1977).

This chapter answers this call by introducing the notion of the Hybrid Leader - a leader who is capable of working at the junction of human intelligence and artificial intelligence, not only leveraging each to their strengths, but also ensuring that humans maintain an "ultimate responsibility" for the ethical integrity of their collective work. The Hybrid Leader is not an engineer, nor is the Hybrid Leader a leader who has completed some basic AI training (Russell & Norvig, 2021; Jarrahi, 2018).

The Hybrid Leader is an evolution of the role of leader - one who applies to the human-centered leadership competencies a new set of AI-specific technical skills enabling them to leverage the skills of artificial intelligence systems (Russell & Norvig, 2021; Schwab, 2016). This chapter is organised as follows. Section 2 synthesizes the existing knowledge on leadership and the role of AI in organizations, and outlines the gaps the HLF fills (Bass, 1985; Hutchins, 1995; Brown et al., 2005). Section 3 builds the three cornerstones of the HLF. Section 4 provides an overview of the Five Pillars of the Hybrid Leadership Framework (Wilson & Daugherty, 2018; Haenlein & Kaplan, 2019). Section 5 outlines a reskilling plan to train hybrid leaders at the individual, organizational, and national levels (Day, 2001; World Economic Forum, 2023). Section 6 provides a case study of failed and successful hybrid leadership (Kellogg et al., 2020; Pasquale, 2015). Section 7 offers recommendations for leadership in organizations, policymakers, and researchers. Section 8 provides a summary of arguments and suggestions for future empirical studies (Dastin, 2018; Smith & Shum, 2019).

2. LITERATURE REVIEW

2.1 The Evolution of Leadership Theory

Leadership theory has journeyed through an intellectually fertile and contested terrain over the last 100 years, producing scores of theories, models, and typologies that represent the changing leadership challenges that have faced organizational leaders during this period. The earliest trait theories of leadership assumed that leadership was inherent in some individuals: the 'great man' theory held sway in organizational practice until the middle 20th century (Carlyle, 1841; Galton, 1869). Such theories held leadership ability to be innate and genetically determined, and the focus of human resource management was on leader selection, not leader development. Leadership theories based on leadership behavior, such as those inspired by the Ohio State and Michigan studies in the 1940s and 1950s, moved the emphasis away from who leaders are to what they do. This body of research uncovered the basic behavioral dimensions of leadership -which were initiating structure (task-oriented) and consideration (relationship-oriented) (Fleishman, 1953; Katz et al., 1950) - and demonstrated that at least some leadership effectiveness is determined by the learnability of leadership behaviors rather than fixed personality traits. This was a freeing thought: the path was open for leadership training as a business investment. In turn, situational and contingency theories of leadership, largely in the 1960s and 1970s, recognized that leadership style would be shaped by situational factors. Fiedler's Contingency Model (1967) was based on the idea that the effectiveness of a leader is based on the fit between his or her leadership style and the situation. Hersey and Blanchard's Situational Leadership Theory (1969) suggested that effective leaders, depending on the degree of their followers' maturity, must adjust their style.

House's Path-Goal Theory (1971) suggested that effective leaders remove obstacles and provide them with necessary resources to serve followers' interests, and that different types of leadership behavior are effective in several situations and with different followers. Transformational leadership (Burns, 1978; Bass, 1985) represented the major overarching paradigm in leadership of the late 20th century. Transformational leaders elevate their followers to perform beyond self-interest to pursue collective goals by displaying four dimensions of leadership behaviors: idealized influence, inspirational motivation, intellectual stimulation, and individualized consideration (Uhl-Bien et al., 2007; Avolio et al., 2009). This approach has inspired the greatest quantity of research in the leadership field, and continues to be on the leading edge of research, with meta-analyses showing its strong links to follower motivation, commitment, creativity, and performance (Judge & Piccolo, 2004; Lowe et al., 1996). Contemporary leadership research broadened the field of leadership by adding notions of relational, servant, authentic, and ethical leadership (Greenleaf, 1977; Avolio & Gardner, 2005; Brown et al., 2005). These frameworks vary in their emphasis on specific aspects of the leader-follower relationship: servant leadership focuses on serving and developing followers' needs; authentic leadership on self-awareness, transparency, and values congruence; and ethical leadership on setting moral standards and offering accountability (Jarrahi, 2018; Kolbjørnsrud et al., 2016).

2.2 AI in Organizational Contexts

The literature on AI in organizations has flourished since the early 2010s, thanks to advances in machine learning, deep learning, natural language processing, and computer vision technologies that have opened up a vast spectrum of organizational applications in which the AI system can outperform humans, or at least equal them on a range of tasks. One of the first surveys of AI in organizations was published by Davenport and Ronanki (2018): they identified the three main categories of AI applications in organizations as process automation (rule-based systems that automate structured, repetitive tasks), cognitive insight (machine learning systems that learn to identify patterns and make predictions from massive data sets) and cognitive engagement. According to their survey of 152 unleashed projects using AI in organizations, process automation applications predominated in 2018, but they predicted a looming explosion of cognitive engagement applications, which has now been supercharged by the disruptive emergence of generative AI in 2022-2025. The business literature has explored AI's implications for various functional areas. In human resources, AI is being used for recruitment, performance evaluation, and talent management (Strohmeier, 2020). In operations, AI-powered supply chain management, quality control, and demand forecasting have led to improved efficiency (Chui et al., 2018). In marketing, such as chatbots and virtual assistants have revolutionized the economics and effectiveness of customer contact (Huang & Rust, 2018). In knowledge work, AI systems are undertaking tasks including reviewing legal documents, evaluating financial risks, and assisting medical diagnosis with levels of accuracy sometimes surpassing human counterparts (Obermeyer et al., 2019; Susskind & Susskind, 2015). Perhaps the most researched aspect of the use of AI systems for human purposes is the phenomenon of algorithmic management (the coordination, control, and evaluation of workers' activity by AI systems).

Studies have identified widespread adoption of algorithmic management to control workers, assign tasks, and punish non-conforming workers in gig economy platforms like Uber, Deliveroo, and Amazon Mechanical Turk (Duggan et al., 2020; Rosenblat & Stark, 2016). Researchers have also reported the human costs of algorithmic management in such settings, including stress, anxiety, diminished human judgment and autonomy, inadequate algorithmic transparency (workers' lack of understanding of the rules used to evaluate them), and algorithmic discrimination against workers from certain racial, economic, and gender identities (Kellogg et al., 2020). The application of generative AI in organizations has introduced a new, more nuanced layer of AI use.

Used for creative tasks like drafting emails, reports, and assessing rapid responses to updates in the news, generative AI - especially large language models like GPT-4, Claude, and Gemini - has enabled tasks that previous versions of AI could not perform (Diakopoulos, 2016; Mittelstadt et al., 2016). In contrast to previous forms of AI that usually automated a narrow range of tasks, generative AI displays general capabilities in content and code generation, strategy, reasoning, and explanation, and natural language conversation, which transcend the use of tools and approach intellectual partnerships (Bubeck et al., 2023). In 2024 and 2025, organizations report generative AI being deployed for an increasing array of functions, with the McKinsey 2024 State of AI report showing that 65 percent of their survey respondent organizations were using generative AI in at least one function (up almost twofold from the previous year) (Mäntymäki et al., 2022; Choudhury et al., 2020). Within this research, common ground is emerging: the outcomes of organizational AI deployment - whether positive or negative - are heavily dependent on the human leadership and governance of AI-deploying organizations (Obermeyer et al., 2019; Kellogg et al., 2020).

2.3 The Emerging Concept of Hybrid Leadership

Recently, the idea of hybrid leadership (human-AI boundary spanning leadership) has started to see the light of day, but it has not been fully conceptualized and lacks a comprehensive, empirical research-based foundation. One of the earliest studies of the impact of AI on management was that of Kolbjørnsrud, Amico, and Thomas (2016), who surveyed 1,770 managers in 14 countries. They discovered that managers held fairly broad expectations that AI would free managers from routine administrative and analytical job functions - information sourcing, data analytics, and process monitoring - enabling human managers to concentrate on contextual analysis, stakeholder management, and human creativity. But significantly, they reported that the majority of managers were not yet thinking systematically about how to actively manage the human-AI boundary - how to determine what tasks can be delegated to AI, how to assess the accuracy of AI systems, and how to ensure that humans value, critique, and manage the use of AI systems in decision-making. Wilson and Daugherty (2018) helped popularize the notion of 'collaborative intelligence' - the juxtaposition of human and artificial intelligence to achieve outcomes that neither intelligence alone could produce.

After reviewing case studies of organizations that had achieved performance excellence through the careful design of human-AI collaboration, they highlighted three major classes of “fusion skills” that enable effective human-AI collaboration: skills to train AI systems; to explain AI recommendations to a diverse range of stakeholders; and to maintain human values and ethics in AI-infused processes. Their model contributes to the understanding of the collaborative aspects of hybrid leadership, but it is not a unified leadership model.

Haenlein and Kaplan (2019) provided a typological and historical overview of management-relevant AI applications, concluding that the biggest challenge in management is not technological (deployment of AI) but rather cultural (cultivating organizational mindsets, skills, and structures that help exploit AI). Jarrahi (2018) investigated the cognitive division of labor between human managers and AI, and argued that the strengths of AI are analytical and computational processing, while the strengths of human managers are social intelligence, contextual reasoning, and ethical judgment. This work brings to light many of the individual aspects of what this chapter terms hybrid leadership, but fails to integrate them into a well-specified, theoretically derived model. The present chapter fills this gap. By drawing on three well-established theoretical traditions (transformational leadership (Bass, 1985), distributed cognition (Hutchins, 1995), and ethical leadership (Brown et al., 2005)) to ground hybrid leadership, and synthesizing the emerging empirical studies of human-AI collaboration, the chapter delivers the first Hybrid Leadership Framework in the field: an integrated theoretical framework which explains the competencies, behaviors, and governance arrangements needed for leaders in AI-supported organizations (Wilson & Daugherty, 2018; Kolbjørnsrud et al., 2016).

3. THEORETICAL FOUNDATIONS OF THE HYBRID LEADERSHIP FRAMEWORK

This chapter proposes the Hybrid Leadership Framework (HLF), which builds on the foundation of three well-accepted theoretical traditions, each adapted in this framework to the new realities of human-AI collaboration. These three traditions are carefully chosen and capture the complexity of hybrid leadership: transformational leadership theory for the charismatic and motivational aspects of leading in times of disruptive technological change; distributed cognition theory for the cognitive architecture of human-AI collaboration; and ethical leadership theory for the moral aspects of leading AI-enhanced decisions. These traditions of understanding collectively offer a conceptual basis for both what hybrid leadership is and why.

3.1 Transformational Leadership Theory

Bass (1985) described transformational leadership behaviors in four key dimensions: idealized influence (serving as a role model whose values and skills trigger admiration and emulation by followers), inspirational motivation (articulation and communication of a clear organizational vision that inspires followers to achieve higher performance standards and creates a shared sense of organizational purpose), intellectual stimulation (stimulation and encouragement of followers to approach problems in new ways, to think creatively and to consider multiple perspectives when confronted with organizational challenges), and individualized consideration. A long history of empirical studies, including several meta-analyses, has established transformational leadership as having positive, significant effects on follower motivation, commitment, creativity, and performance across a range of cultures, organizational types, and levels of organizational hierarchy (Judge & Piccolo, 2004; Lowe et al., 1996).

First, as part of inspirational motivation, the hybrid leader must now focus not only on inspiring followers to think creatively about the overall strategy and operations of the organization but also about the operationalization of AI systems themselves. Organizational leaders who fail to establish this narrative risk what Orlikowski and Scott (2008) called "technology anxiety": a diffuse fear of AI in the organization that dings both human performance and even adoption of AI, resulting in the worst of both worlds - neither the efficiency gains of AI nor the full engagement of human intelligence.

Second, the intellectual stimulation dimension must now go beyond stimulating innovative thinking about how the organization works to explicitly encourage critical thinking about AI systems themselves (Bass & Riggio, 2006). Hybrid leaders who exercise the intellectual stimulation dimension in the context of AI support the active engagement of team members with a Healthy Skepticism of algorithms rather than algorithmic authority, including questioning of algorithmic recommendations, suspicion of algorithmic biases, consideration of the biases implanted through the training data, and so on (Skitka et al., 1999; Diakopoulos, 2016). Third, the individualized consideration dimension must include an extension of this construct - what this chapter calls Digital Empathy - a particular kind of empathetic consideration of how AI adoption affects individual employees' workplace identity, job security, and self-worth (Mittelstadt et al., 2016). The fear of anxiety, professional identity loss, and skills redundancy stimulated by AI adoption is differently felt by different stakeholders depending on their functional role, professional seniority, age, and experience with technology.

3.2 Distributed Cognition Theory

In his pioneering ethnographic investigation of naval navigation, Cognition in the Wild, Hutchins (1995) showed that cognitive processes such as navigating, reasoning, problem-solving, and decision-making don't just take place in individual minds, but are distributed between individuals, physical objects, representational formats, and the affordances of their environment. He demonstrated that the cognitive system that guides a naval vessel comprises multiple system members with complementary skills and knowledge, multiple charts and instruments which externalize and re-represent information, and systematic procedural practices which divide cognitive work across the system. No participant in the system has all the relevant knowledge and expertise; the cognitive capacity of the system is emergent.

Distributed cognition theory offers a valuable way to understand the collaboration between humans and AI in organizational contexts. In today's AI-integrated workplaces, cognitive work is not a simple linear combination of human and AI actors; rather, it is a dynamic, evolving, and often invisible collaboration between human and AI systems (Hutchins, 1995; Zhang & Patel, 2006). AI systems provide pattern recognition abilities far beyond human perceptual capability (detecting subtle patterns in medical scans, identifying patterns of fraud in millions of financial transactions at once), processing power far beyond human abilities (performing real-time data analysis on terabytes of data), and data-driven predictive modeling skills that exploit regularities in historical data invisible to human cognition (Jarrahi, 2018; Wilson & Daugherty, 2018). Employees bring to the table cultural and contextual knowledge, ethical decision making, social intelligence, adaptability to novel situations, and the human common-sense shaping of social life that AI systems (trained on data, not social experiences) often struggle to achieve.

3.3 Ethical Leadership Theory

Brown, Treviño, and Harrison (2005) described ethical leadership as the demonstration of normatively appropriate conduct (1) by personal action and interpersonal relationships, and (2) by promoting such conduct by followers through a bidirectional (leader and followers) communication, reward, and decision-making process. The social learning model they develop holds that leaders serve as role models - followers learn ethical behaviors from leaders, and the management of the ethical climate in an organization is heavily influenced by the ethical norms set by and supported by organizational leaders. Empirical research has provided ample evidence that ethical leadership is positively related to follower ethical conduct, trust, employee voice, and pro-social citizenship behavior, and negatively related to deviant employee behavior (Mayer et al., 2012; Walumbwa & Schaubroeck, 2009).

The deployment of AI in making decisions opens up new ethical dilemmas that greatly expand the scope and requirements of ethical leadership. If the recommendation for employing an individual, the decision about a loan, the determination of a course of action in medical treatment, or the determination of who is a security risk is made by an AI, who bears moral responsibility for the decision? The conventional ethical leadership approach presumes a direct chain of moral accountability: human beings make decisions, demonstrate ethical behaviour, and are responsible for the outcomes of their own behaviour and that of others that they enable and reward. Deviant AI decision-making creates these kinds of disruptions, which can result in what has been called the "accountability gap" - the blurring of moral accountability when AI is involved in consequential decision-making (Diakopoulos, 2016). Studies of algorithmic authority report the unfortunate tendency for humans to obediently follow the output of AI systems, even when their behavior is demonstrably wrong or immoral - a phenomenon labeled automation bias, "anti-algorithm aversion", and authority transfer (Skitka et al., 1999; Dietvorst et al., 2015).

When AI decisions go wrong, or AI systems introduce biases, moral responsibility can be obscured by the diffusion of accountability among AI developers, users, operators, and AI systems themselves - a condition that, if not addressed, can allow problematic AI systems to continue their use and operation. Hybrid leaders with Algorithmic Accountability (to be developed in Section 4.2) ensure that this accountability gap is closed by communicating and upholding the organizational norm that human leaders remain unambiguously morally accountable for the outcomes of AI systems.

4. THE HYBRID LEADERSHIP FRAMEWORK (HLF)

Drawing on the three approaches reviewed above, this chapter presents the Hybrid Leadership Framework (HLF) - a model of the skills, leadership actions, and governance arrangements for leaders working in human-AI collaborative environments. The HLF comprises five interrelated pillars, each focusing on a different key aspect of hybrid leadership. The pillars are ordered for readability, though they are an integrated system: effective performance in one pillar feeds the performance in others, while any major weakness in one single pillar compromises the overall quality and functioning of the system. All five pillars of hybrid leadership require development: not simply the pillars that are technically easiest, or individually preferred.

4.1 Pillar One: Cognitive Augmentation Awareness (CAA)

Hybrid leaders with Cognitive Augmentation Awareness (CAA) can understand how AI systems function to extend, enhance, and even both human cognitive processes in their domain of leadership. Hybrid leaders with high CAA have a refined grasp on AI capabilities: they understand which organizational decisions benefit from algorithmic assistance and which should remain in the domain of human judgement, which AI systems in their domain are reliable and mature and which represent technology pioneers that are still prone to error, and - most importantly - they understand the typical failure modes of AI systems: which are inconsistent with reliable solution of the decision problem; which are biased; which are not robust to changing circumstances; and so on, so that they can identify the potential causes of failure in the organization (Davenport & Patil, 2012; Brynjolfsson & McAfee, 2014).

CAA is emphatically not technical AI/data science literacy. Most of an organization's leaders cannot - and indeed should not - become machine learning specialists and data scientists. The particular division of labor between hybrid leaders and AI technical specialists is very similar to that between a financial literacy endowed executive and an accounting specialist: the executive need not be a specialist in the technical work of accounting, but must understand financial statements, be aware of signs of accounting irregularities, and know when and how to receive assistance from a specialist. Likewise, a hybrid leader with high CAA understands the nature and likely limitations of AI outputs; recognizes the warning signs of unreliability or bias in the AI systems used; and understands how to engage AI specialists (Kolbjørnsrud et al., 2016).

Hybrid leaders interested in developing CAA must commit to a program of ongoing AI literacy education, which should not be an occasional training exercise but an ongoing engagement. The AI literacy need for CAA includes conceptual understanding of how different forms of AI (supervised machine learning, unsupervised learning, large language models, reinforcement learning) operate; an awareness that AI systems are highly data dependent - the only way to obtain reliable and unbiased AI outputs is to train AI systems on reliable and unbiased data; understanding of the documented failure modes of AI systems (distributional shift, overfitting, adversarial examples, hallucinations in generative AI systems); and knowledge of the particular AI applications used in the leader's domain of expertise, including the validated performance characteristics of these AI systems and their limitations (Mittelstadt et al., 2016; Diakopoulos, 2016).

4.2 Pillar Two: Algorithmic Accountability (AA)

Algorithmic Accountability (AA) is the hybrid leader's safeguard for preserving and ensuring moral responsibility for decisions or actions heavily influenced by AI systems. This pillar speaks to what is perhaps the most important and immediately relevant ethical issue in the integration of AI into organizational leadership: the problem of ethical diffused responsibility that accompanies the delegation of decisions of high moral salience to unfathomable decision-diagramming software and, from that, the risk of the persistence of problematic AI behaviour in the absence of human intervention.

The principles that guide leaders with Algorithmic Accountability are fivefold (Diakopoulos, 2016; Mittelstadt et al., 2016). First, the norms of human supremacy in the decision-making: machines suggest, humans decide. This norm - strictly applied and publicly modeled by leaders - retains the human responsibility for, and accountability for, the performance of the firm while making it possible to take full advantage of the predictive power of AI systems (Skitka et al., 1999). Second, the norm of ongoing AI auditing: the leaders do not wait for problems to be reported before they investigate AI system performance, but instead implement ongoing audit processes focused on monitoring AI system calls for bias, error, and drift from expected outcomes (Pasquale, 2015; Obermeyer et al., 2019). Third, the practice of AI transparency communication: stakeholders (including employees, customers, partners, regulators, and other populations impacted by AI systems) are informed about the role and use of AI systems when they are assisting with decision-making that can affect stakeholders, allowing transparency and accountability. Fourth, the enabling of organizational voice for AI: leaders who score high in Algorithmic Accountability provide opportunities for organizational voice regarding concerns with AI system performance, free from fear of retribution (Mäntymäki et al., 2022).

Literature on organizational voice highlights that frontline employees - who have the most experience and interaction with AI systems - often detect issues with AI system performance first, but are often reluctant to voice their concerns to leadership due to cultures that elevate AI systems as authoritative or cultures that punish dissenters on technological investments (Edmondson, 1999). Fifth, their readiness to challenge or ignore faulty algorithmic recommendations: leaders with AA do not succumb to automation bias - where people defer to the recommendations of the machine output even when their own judgement of the situation suggests the machine is wrong. They take and demonstrate professional action to override AI recommendations when their judgment, values, or ethics override AI recommendations.

4.3 Pillar Three: Digital Empathy (DE)

Digital Empathy (DE) is a two-sided empathic competency specific to hybrid leadership settings and unanticipated by pre-artificial intelligence (AI) models of leadership. The first layer of DE is human-directed: the ability to recognize, understand, and effectively address the anxiety, identity threat, and work-related challenges to workers across levels of administration that AI integration produces. The second layer is directed toward AI systems: not a simplistic anthropomorphizing of AI systems' feelings, but a complex understanding of how AI systems operate, where and why they are unreliable, and the implications of AI system performance for the data environments and design decisions the AI systems are trained on. The human-directed layer of Digital Empathy builds on well-established models of emotional intelligence (Goleman, 1995; Mayer & Salovey, 1997) but needs to be applied to a new set of emotions specific to AI implementation that differ from other forms of change. At least three kinds of emotional issues are triggered by AI implementation.

Displacement anxiety - fear of becoming jobless as one's skills are replaced by AI - is a very real concern for mid-skill knowledge workers with jobs that consist of both routine, automatable tasks and complex non-automatable tasks, leading to an inherent uncertainty of one's work future. Identity disruption, where one's professional identity is disturbed when a critical element of one's expertise is taken over by an AI system, occurs among high-skilled professionals, not necessarily under the near-term threat of displacement. A doctor who has honed their skills as a diagnostician over two decades might feel a threat to their professional identity with the introduction of an AI diagnostic system, even if their profession is not at risk of displacement. Finally, loss of professional autonomy (the loss of control over professional discretion and judgement that is associated with algorithm management) is a significant predictor of job dissatisfaction, stress, and organizational disengagement (Kellogg et al., 2020).

The AI-directed layer of Digital Empathy demands hybrid leaders experiment with gaining a level of competency in the AI systems used in their organizations' domain to anticipate, identify, and mitigate their typical patterns and pathologies (World Economic Forum, 2023; Brynjolfsson & McAfee, 2014). A hybrid leader who knows that the privileged experience sets used to train the AI recruiting system in their organization came during a time of low workforce diversity will be alert to problems on that front and put in place preventative measures - such as blind screening processes for final candidate selections or forcing human review of reject decisions recommended by the AI - before they occur (Jarrahi, 2018; Mittelstadt et al., 2016). This AI-directed empathy is both a moral and practical performance-enhancing strength (Dastin, 2018; Obermeyer et al., 2019).

4.4 Pillar Four: Collaborative Intelligence Design (CID)

Collaborative Intelligence Design (CID) is the hybrid leader's competency in deliberately designing the tasks, roles, and other organizational processes by which human and machine intelligence coordinate their work in the organization they inhabit. This pillar transcends individual leader competency to tackle the systems and structures of hybrid leadership - the decisions that shape the organization to design for human-AI collaboration rather than being left to emerge arbitrarily from "anything goes" AI adoption approaches. CID builds on Wilson and Daugherty's (2018) collaborative intelligence framework and translates this into a design practice for leadership. CID leaders engage in four key design activities. First, humans-centered task allocation: mapping activities within organizations into tasks that are best performed by AI (pattern-based, high repetition, well-defined tasks that have been performed in the past with historical data that is rich in past performance), tasks that are best performed by humans (novel, context ambiguous, emotionally sensitive or stakeholder-laden tasks), and tasks that perform best when humans and AI collaborate (complex analysis tasks requiring human judgement and data processing capacity).

Task allocation is not a one-shot process but an ongoing activity as both the capabilities of AI systems and the nature of the tasks required to be accomplished within an organization change and develop. Second, human-centered design of AI interfaces: designing AI systems in a way that facilitates critical human judgment rather than blind acceptance of AI outputs by human team members. Human-centered AI interface design recognizes the critical role of how AI information is presented to human decision-makers in determining whether humans are able to apply critical judgment, or whether they simply accept it as is without critical scrutiny (Amershi et al., 2019; Skitka et al., 1999). CID leaders collaborate with their technical experts to create AI interfaces that communicate estimates of uncertainty as well as point estimates, explain the reasoning behind AI recommendations, and make it as easy as possible (not as time-consuming or frustrating) for humans to override or supplement AI recommendations when other human decision-making competence is required (Amershi et al., 2019; Dafoe, 2018). Third, two-way learning loop design: designing mechanisms through which human team members can provide feedback on the performance of the AI system, and through which the AI system can be refined and improved through human input (Dietvorst et al., 2015).

High-impact human-AI collaboration systems are not one-time pairings, but ongoing symbiotic relationships in which humans enhance AI capabilities through learning and correction, and in which AI enhances human performance by delivering insights and detecting patterns that humans use to build human knowledge (Wilson & Daugherty, 2018; Senge, 1990). Hybrid leaders pursuing effective learning loop design facilitate this (Brynjolfsson & McAfee, 2014). Fourth, proactive role redesign: as AI systems take over routine cognitive work, hybrid leaders must redesign human roles to focus on the higher-order cognitive skills (creativity, ethics, stakeholder management, communication, and strategy) that humans excel at and AI systems find difficult to emulate (Garvin, 1993).

4.5 Pillar Five: Adaptive Governance (AG)

Adaptive Governance (AG) is the hybrid leader's ability to design and operate governance structures that are agile enough to keep up with rapidly evolving AI capabilities, and committed to retaining coherent principles of governance, ethical leadership, and organizational accountability (Schwab, 2016; World Economic Forum, 2023). This pillar corresponds to one of the most structurally complex challenges of hybrid leadership: the trade-offs inherent between the stability and predictability of traditional corporate governance and the inconsistent pace of development of AI capabilities, risks, and organizational impacts, which make them outdated almost before they are finalized (Bubeck et al., 2023; Dafoe, 2018).

AI development does not follow these patterns. The functions of large language models in 2026 are significantly different from 2022; AI governance challenges in 2026 (controlling hallucination in powerful generative AI, navigating autonomous AI agents, managing deepfakes produced by AI) cannot be fully appreciated in 2020. AI governance frameworks that are premised on yesterday's AI become misaligned for today's AI, and unworkable for tomorrows (Ansell & Gash, 2008; Baldwin & Cave, 1999). Hybrid leaders' Adaptive Governance has three structural principles that allow governance to stay on top of the technology without dilution of ethical concerns. First, continuous AI monitoring: designing processes for continuous monitoring of AI system performance, assessment of the impact of AI systems on the organization, and advances in regulatory and scientific approaches to AI governance, rather than the periodic monitoring typical of audit reports (Mittelstadt et al., 2016; Pasquale, 2015). This allows governance activities in response to AI challenges and opportunities to be initiated in near real-time rather than at scheduled audit times (Ansell & Gash, 2008; Edmondson, 1999). Second, scenario planning: convening regular foresight exercises for leadership teams at the enterprise level to consider plausible future developments in AI, and their governance implications, to purposefully prepare organizational responses and decision-making processes in anticipation of the next big thing in AI (Dafoe, 2018; Mäntymäki et al., 2022). Third, inclusive stakeholder co-governance: appreciating that the governance of AI requires the insights of the employees, customers, communities, and other stakeholders most directly impacted by the decisions made by their AI systems - not just the technical and legal experts most often represented in AI governance frameworks (OECD, 2019).

5. DEVELOPING HYBRID LEADERS: A RESKILLING ROADMAP

The HLF has outlined the competencies that hybrid leaders need to equip them for AI-integrated organizations, but this is only the first step in the leadership development process (Day, 2001; McCauley et al., 2010). Organizations also need to provide structured opportunities through which existing and new leaders can learn and enrich these competencies in an authentic, long-term, and embedded fashion (Ulrich & Brockbank, 2005; Senge, 1990). In this section, we outline a three-tiered reskilling strategy for hybrid leadership development, focusing on the individual leader level, organization level (HR and development functions), and broader level (executive education institutions, public policy-makers) (World Economic Forum, 2023; OECD, 2019).

5.1 Individual Level: The Hybrid Leader Development Journey

The development of hybrid leadership competencies at the individual level follows a personal learning pathway that combines cognitive, practical, and reflective elements on an ongoing arc (Day, 2001; Kolb, 1984). The five stages of development are a structured journey from AI-naive to hybrid-capable leader:

- Stage 1: AI Literacy Basic: Leaders engage in structured training in basic AI literacy concepts - conceptual grasp of how AI systems learn from data, what they priorities, what they are often poor at, and how they are used in different areas of the organization (McCauley et al., 2010; Boyatzis, 1982). This stage is nurtured with executive AI literacy training, technology briefings by an "AI specialist" team within the organization, and popular practitioner-oriented publications (Brynjolfsson & McAfee, 2014; Kolbjørnsrud et al., 2016). The aim is not technical expertise, but a nuanced understanding supporting CAA (Ng, 2022; Brynjolfsson & McAfee, 2014).
- Stage 2: Ethical AI Reasoning: Leaders enhance ethical AI reasoning skills, such as identifying sources of AI system bias, assessing the impact across stakeholders, responsibility for algorithms, and engagement with governance measures such as the EU AI Act and the OECD AI Principles (Ng, 2022; Russell & Norvig, 2021). This stage can be learned through case dissection of past AI governance disasters, an active role in ethics workshops, and internal cross-organizational AI ethics review committees (Davenport & Patil, 2012).
- Stage 3: Digital Empathy Development: Leaders develop Digital Empathy through intensive people-development activities tailored for AI: understanding and addressing the effects of automation anxiety, coaching identity transition dialogues, and layering Digital Empathy towards AI through ongoing structured reflection with AI system specialists in their organizational domain (OECD, 2019; Mittelstadt et al., 2016). Mentoring and coaching relationships with experienced leaders in transition are helpful in this stage.
- Stage 4: Collaborative Design Practice: Leaders build CID skills through engagement in the design of workflow redesign projects with AI specialists, data scientists, and employees - mapping existing human-AI task allocation and workflows, identifying opportunities to improve the collaboration, and assessing the strategic organizational value of human-AI interaction designs in their domain (Day, 2001; McCauley et al., 2010).
- Stage 5: Governance Leadership: Leaders engage with organizational AI governance processes to build the Adaptive Governance (AG) skill set - working on governance committees such as AI ethics, drafting/revising AI governance policy instruments, engaging with regulatory frameworks, and practicing the foresight and planning skills required by AG (Wilson & Daugherty, 2018; Amershi et al., 2019). This stage benefits from cohort learning across organizations, industry consortia, or regulatory consultation or practitioner-academic governance research teams (Ansell & Gash, 2008; Mäntymäki et al., 2022).

5.2 Organizational Level: HR as Architect of Hybrid Leadership Capacity

The roles of HR leaders and organizational development professionals are central to an architecturally important role of enabling hybrid leadership development at scale (Spencer & Spencer, 1993; Boyatzis, 1982). Four organizational interventions are put forward as the basic infrastructure for hybrid leadership development programs (Ulrich & Brockbank, 2005; Strohmeier, 2020). First, the creation and roll-out of a Hybrid Leadership Competency Framework - an in-house operationalization of the HLF that translates into behaviors, knowledge, and development indicators specific to each pillar of HLF for each level of hierarchy in the organization. This should guide all people management (management of talent) processes and activities: recruitment and selection of leadership roles, succession and promotion decisions, performance appraisal discussions, L&D strategies and investments, and executive remuneration. The HLF's focus on these processes communicates that hybrid leadership is not a nice-to-have aspiration but a critical performance expectation for a leader (Senge, 1990; Garvin, 1993). Second, the creation of continuous learning ecosystems - an organizational culture and infrastructure for AI-related learning that is embedded in the flow of work practice rather than limited to discrete learning events that are soon forgotten (Wenger, 1998).

Third, HR leaders should build psychological safety infrastructure for AI transitions - an AI-integration-safe environment in which employees can speak truth to (AI) power about AI integration concerns, report problems with AI systems, contribute freely to AI system redesign, and reflect on the results of experimentation with new forms of human-AI collaboration without concern for professional consequences of failures and errors (in sufficiently experimental settings) (Nonaka & Takeuchi, 1995). Research shows that psychological safety is the enabling factor that facilitates the learning, voice, and experimentation required for every level of the workforce to lead AI integration efforts (Edmondson, 1999).

5.3 Institutional Level: Executive Education and National Policy

Business schools and executive education have a key role to play in developing the next generations of organizational leaders with hybrid leadership competencies (Pfeffer & Fong, 2002; Mintzberg, 2004). MBA and executive education programs remain largely focused on pre-AI leadership competencies such as financial, strategic, organizational, and operational leadership. These remain critical but need to be supplemented with the AI-focused leadership factors in the HLF (Porter & McKibbin, 1988).

This chapter recommends that business schools emphasize what might be called curricular integration of hybrid leadership - the embedding of HLF competency development across the curriculum, rather than an option of a single course or a concentration in AI leadership (Kolbjørnsrud et al., 2016; Haenlein & Kaplan, 2019). At the macro level, as part of strategies for digital national transformation, governments should invest in national hybrid leadership development programs to complement the development of technical AI skills - they should understand that the development of a national capability (Pfeffer & Fong, 2002; Mintzberg, 2004) in AI includes not just the training of AI engineers and data scientists but also the creation of the organizational leaders who can appropriately govern the use of AI; who can manage an AI-driven (Brynjolfsson & McAfee, 2014) workforce transition with concern and competence; and who can create the organizational cultures in which the intelligence of humans and machines interact effectively to achieve national prosperity and human wellbeing (McKinsey Global Institute, 2017; World Economic Forum, 2023).

6. ILLUSTRATIVE CASE ANALYSIS

To link the HLF to experiences in the practice of hybrid leadership, in this section, we provide two cases: one, showing the consequences for an organization from the failure of hybrid leadership across several dimensions of HLF, and one, showing the sustained organizational commitment in an organization to developing and practicing hybrid leadership (Smith & Shum, 2019; Microsoft, 2022). These cases are based on publicly accessible organizational and academic records and are used in an analytical and teaching context (Yin, 2018; Eisenhardt, 1989).

6.1 Case One: The Amazon AI Recruiting System — Hybrid Leadership Failure

From 2014 to 2017, Amazon built an automated hiring system to help identify suitable candidates for its technical positions. The tool was developed using a résumé search database of applicants to Amazon over the past decade - a database that largely reflected the gender makeup of the company's workforce. In learning from this historical data, the machine learning system encoded and reinforced historical gender bias: it downgraded resumes that included the word 'women' (as in 'women's chess club' or 'women in technology organization'), and the profiles of graduates of women's colleges. The system was intended to rate the best candidates on a five-star basis, and the unfair scores reflected the encoding of historical workplace inequities towards human recommendations. Amazon's internal review, which detected the problem in 2017, recommended that its recruiters not take the system's recommendations into account and then terminated the project (Mittelstadt et al., 2016; Diakopoulos, 2016). The company claimed the system was not used by any HR recruiters to assess candidates for hire. But the system's development and operation for some three years (during which the system's biased recommendations were, evidently, not satisfactorily overseen from an ethical perspective) exemplifies a major failure of corporate governance with implications for hybrid leadership analysis (Obermeyer et al., 2019; Mittelstadt et al., 2016).

The HLF framework highlights at least four of the five pillars of HLF as areas of weakness in this case. First, Cognitive Augmentation Awareness: the project team and the leadership of the organization did not appear to have sufficient awareness of the fact that supervised machine learning systems that have been trained on historically biased data are likely to perpetuate that bias in their predictions (or outputs). This is a well-known feature of ML systems that the system architects should have been able to anticipate and plan for in the system design phase. Second, limited Algorithmic Accountability: there were inadequate audit processes to report the bias during the system's three years of operation, no regular review of the system's assessments of candidates to evaluate the equity of the system's candidate assessments, and no clear pathway in the organization for reporting and A more robust audit process to detect the bias during the system's three years of operation, no regular process for reviewing the fairness of the system's candidate assessments, and no clear process in place in the company for how to escalate and resolve bias concerns when they were internally detected (Mäntymäki et al., 2022; Dafoe, 2018). Third, lack of Digital Empathy: the decision to deploy an AI hiring system that negatively affected female candidates was based on an absence of stakeholder impact analysis relative to the different population groups of candidates - the kind of stakeholder impact analysis advocated by Digital Empathy. Fourth, lack of Adaptive Governance: it appears that the project did not have an ethics governance process that would have mandated multi-metric bias testing and stakeholder impact assessment before deployment, even for the internal trial run (Kellogg et al., 2020; Diakopoulos, 2016).

6.2 Case Two: Microsoft's Responsible AI Program — Hybrid Leadership in Practice

Microsoft's continued involvement in the development of responsible AI systems between 2016 and 2025 offers another example of hybrid leadership on an organizational level (Smith & Shum, 2019; Microsoft, 2022). Microsoft's entry point into responsible AI development was, ironically, an AI disaster: the botched March 2016 launch of Tay, a generative artificial intelligence (AI) chat robot that was intended to engage in natural-language conversations with Twitter users. Twenty-four hours later, Tay was offline, having used racist, sexist, and other objectionable language in response to users conducting a concerted social engineering attack (Mittelstadt et al., 2016; Pasquale, 2015). Tay was a publicly and financially embarrassing case study of the governance risks that arise from the deployment of AI systems without appropriate measures to prevent malicious abuse.

Microsoft's response to the Tay failure exemplifies hybrid leadership at its best: rather than isolating and solving the problem, the company's leadership leveraged it as an opportunity to engage in a long-term process of reflection and recalibration of organizational practices around the development and deployment of AI. It later developed and released the Microsoft Responsible AI Standard (MRAS), which makes fairness, reliability, safety, privacy and security, inclusiveness, transparency, and accountability mandatory requirements for AI systems deployed by, or in partnership with, Microsoft. Microsoft's approach has several HLF principles embodied (Wilson & Daugherty, 2018; Senge, 1990). The MRAS's mandatory fairness requirements - which include requirements for testing AI systems for potential bias among population groups before deployment - represent Algorithmic Accountability at the scale of the company's operations: not left up to individual leader discretion, but a part of the company's governance process to ensure all AI systems are equitable.

Microsoft's massive reskilling program to build employee skills in AI, which engaged hundreds of thousands of its workers in formal training in AI technologies, is an example of the Collaborative Intelligence Design feature of proactive role redesign and workforce development (Smith & Shum, 2019; McKinsey Global Institute, 2024). The prominent public statements of CEO Satya Nadella placing AI in his company in the role of supporting human potential, rather than taking the place of human intelligence, reflect both the inspirational motivation dimension of transformational leadership and the human-focused layer of Digital Empathy: creating an active framing around the positive human impact of AI within the company's ecosystem. Microsoft's case shows that leader-led hybrid leadership initiatives are not only possible but significant. Organizations that invest in the development of the governance structures, cultures, and individual skills of hybrid leadership enjoy positive outcomes in multiple ways: fewer AI governance missteps, high levels of trust by employees in using AI-supported jobs, higher trust by stakeholder constituencies, and greater sustainability of competitive advantage from AI investments (Dafoe, 2018; Ansell & Gash, 2008). The Microsoft experience also shows that hybrid leadership development is an ongoing process, not just an event: Nadella's team has kept building its responsible AI policies and processes to respond to the rapid pace of change in the systems and capabilities of AI, reflecting the adaptive nature of Adaptive Governance.

7. IMPLICATIONS FOR POLICY AND PRACTICE

7.1 Implications for Organizational Leaders and Executives

As organizations incorporate AI, corporate leaders should understand the HLF as not merely a set of skills to be learned and then checked off as complete, but as an (ongoing) orientation to learn as AI capabilities and AI integration within the organization expand. Indeed, as AI systems grow in capability, the specific requirements for each HLF dimension change: Algorithmic Accountability when governing a simple rules-based AI system looks very different from Algorithmic Accountability when governing an autonomous AI agent that takes actions on our behalf (Day, 2001; Senge, 1990). Those who invest in Sustained Development across all five HF dimensions, rather than placing too much emphasis on AI literacy, will ensure they're well placed to lead the next generations of AI adoption and change (Dafoe, 2018; Mittelstadt et al., 2016). Managers are encouraged in particular to explore ways to build an organizational culture of AI questioning. Perhaps the most important organizational factor in predicting AI governance quality is likely the extent to which staff are encouraged and rewarded to question, challenge, and report problematic AI system behaviour (Edmondson, 1999; Walumbwa & Schaubroeck, 2009).

Organizations that treat AI systems as infallible oracles rather than mighty-but-fallible tools to think with will be less likely to detect and resolve AI governance issues before they cause damage. Hybrid leaders who prioritize and reward AI questioning - who publicly overrule AI recommendations when their judgment calls for it, who explicitly request challenge of AI outputs in team meetings, and who respond diplomatically and constructively to reports of AI problems - establish the culture for persistent AI governance excellence (Mäntymäki et al., 2022; Kellogg et al., 2020).

7.2 Implications for Policymakers and Government

Governments and international regulatory consortia involved in digital transformation strategy and AI governance should understand that, in action, AI governance requires the quality of hybrid leadership in AI-deploying organizations. Regulation programs - such as the EU AI Act that sets differential standards for AI systems based on their risk classification, and OECD principles on responsible artificial intelligence development that set international standards for AI development - supply critical infrastructure control mechanisms that establish minimum governance standards. But regulatory frameworks alone cannot provide the flexibility to shield against the poor judgment and ethical drift that the HLF describes (Ansell & Gash, 2008; Mäntymäki et al., 2022).

National governments should therefore supplement AI regulatory frameworks with initiatives that promote hybrid leadership across the national economy by investing in executive education curricula that include the development of HLF competency, promoting research to build empirically tested competency tools for measuring hybrid leadership capacities, and developing rewards that incentivize hybrid leadership mature practices across organizations (Pfeffer & Fong, 2002). The key determinants of national competitive excellence in the age of AI will not only include the technical quality of a country's AI talent pool but also the quality of the leadership that manages AI deployment and the impact of AI on national economic and human development (McKinsey Global Institute, 2017).

7.3 Implications for Academic Researchers

The HLF outlined in this chapter is a theory that needs empirical testing through research. The development of HLF gives us research opportunities (Podsakoff et al., 2016). First, designing and psychometrically validating assessment tools to measure the five HLF pillars - tools that can measure the traits of Cognitive Augmentation Awareness, Algorithmic Accountability, Digital Empathy, Collaborative Intelligence Design capability, and Adaptive Governance practice in organizations (Spencer & Spencer, 1993; Boyatzis, 1982). Second, longitudinal studies on whether the HLF competencies predict AI governance outcomes, employee wellbeing in AI-enabled workplaces, success in adopting AI in the workplace, and avoiding the dark side of algorithmic harm - offering empirical evidence in support of the theoretical proposition that hybrid leadership competencies matter (Mäntymäki et al., 2022; Choudhury et al., 2020). Third, cross-cultural studies that reveal whether and how HLF competency demands differ across national and organizational cultures that differ in their attitudes towards power, technology, and regulation (House et al., 2004).

8. CONCLUSION

The AI Revolution is a true paradigm shift in the leadership expectations on an organization – and one that needs a new type of leader to manage teams where human intelligence and AI tools work hand-in-hand all the time. What is crucial to remember is that this change in leadership isn't just a management issue—it's an economic must. The rise of AI-Enhanced Skills — purposefully designed human abilities to function in a mutually productive way with AI — is one of the strongest enablers of organizational productivity, and national Economic Growth, at this moment. However, AI-Enhanced Skills can't just appear out of thin air. They need leaders with a grasp of what AI can and cannot do, who structure their organizations to support humans learning continuously alongside AI, and who create the ethical accountability frameworks that make sure that when they integrate AI it doesn't create harm and that it doesn't take over their jobs (Kolbjørnsrud et al., 2016). This is the Hybrid Leader; a leader who will keep investing in the human to make AI's technological promise a reality with ongoing Economic Growth, not because of AI, but through strategic and intelligent collaboration with AI.

The Hybrid Leadership Framework presented here encompasses five elements: Cognitive Augmentation Awareness, Algorithmic Accountability, Digital Empathy, Collaborative Intelligence Design and Adaptive Governance, and it represents the first, theory-based, holistic view of the requirements for hybrid leadership. The five pillars are directly connected to the AI-Enhanced Skills agenda: Cognitive Augmentation Awareness ensures leaders and their teams have a calibrated understanding of AI to make it from a black box to a productive partner; Algorithmic Accountability helps build trust infrastructure for AI adoption without human ethical agency being sacrificed; Digital Empathy makes sure that workforce transitions to AI-integrated jobs are managed with human sensitivity, minimizing impacts to productivity and talent attrition; Collaborative Intelligence Design contributes to the development of organizational architectures through which human and AI capabilities are systematically combined and integrated for maximum value creation; and Adaptive Governance ensures that the regulatory and cultural conditions for the sustainable, equitable economic growth enabled by AI are maintained despite the continuous evolution of AI capabilities (Day, 2001; Ulrich & Brockbank, 2005).

The reskilling roadmap created in Section 5 puts the HLF into practice on three levels: individual leaders, organizational HR functions and institutional actors, offering concrete development pathways for the hybrid leadership competencies identified in the HLF capability (McCauley et al., 2010; Boyatzis, 1982). The five-stage development journey for an individual take's leaders from AI Literacy to the use of AI to facilitate ethical reasoning, move to Digital Empathy, build skills in collaborative design practice, and engage with governance. HR architecture for continuous learning, psychological safety, and competency-based performance management sets the systemic conditions for AI-enhanced skills to grow at scale for organisations. Then, in the world of countries, investing in hybrid leadership capabilities, in executive education reform, regulatory support, and national reskilling initiatives, can provide the human infrastructure for knowledge economies powered by AI-Enhanced Skills in which broadly shared Economic Growth, productivity and innovation are the outcome (Brown et al., 2005; Walumbwa & Schaubroeck, 2009). It is a debate on whether or not Human Development and Economic Growth are intertwined in the Era of Artificial Intelligence. The countries – and companies

– that will prosper in this age will not be the ones to make the biggest investments in AI; they will be the ones who make the biggest investments in the most capable human professionals to work with AI.

The Hybrid Leader is not willing to exchange human skills for algorithms. Instead, the Hybrid Leader wields them more effectively, knowing how to use AI's amazing analytical power to augment the human judgement and skills, while maintaining human accountability, empathy, and ethical commitment as the key drivers of organisational behavior. The Hybrid Leader is the main human driver of the AI-Enhanced Skills transformation: organizations where people and machines continually learn from each other, resulting in the productivity, innovation and human flourishing that is true Economic Growth. As AI is increasingly ubiquitous, developing true leadership – thoughtful, empathetic, accountable, adaptive – is an increasingly important economic and social investment. The responsibility of Hybrid Leaders, most fundamentally, is to make sure that humanity is the author, not just the subject, of the AI revolution.

REFERENCES

Amershi, S., Weld, D., Vorvoreanu, M., Fourney, A., Nushi, B., Collisson, P., Teevan, J., & Horvitz, E. (2019). Guidelines for human-AI interaction. In *Proceedings of the 2019 CHI Conference on Human Factors in Computing Systems* (pp. 1–13). ACM. DOI: 10.1145/3290605.3300233

Ansell, C., & Gash, A. (2008). Collaborative governance in theory and practice. *Journal of Public Administration: Research and Theory*, *18*(4), 543–571. DOI: 10.1093/jopart/mum032

Avolio, B. J., & Gardner, W. L. (2005). Authentic leadership development: Getting to the root of positive forms of leadership. *The Leadership Quarterly*, *16*(3), 315–338. DOI: 10.1016/j.leaqua.2005.03.001

Avolio, B. J., Walumbwa, F. O., & Weber, T. J. (2009). Leadership: Current theories, research, and future directions. *Annual Review of Psychology*, *60*(1), 421–449. DOI: 10.1146/annurev.psych.60.110707.163621 PMID: 18651820

Baldwin, R., & Cave, M. (1999). *Understanding regulation: Theory, strategy, and practice*. Oxford University Press.

Bass, B. M. (1985). *Leadership and performance beyond expectations*. Free Press.

Bass, B. M., & Riggio, R. E. (2006). *Transformational leadership* (2nd ed.). Lawrence Erlbaum Associates. DOI: 10.4324/9781410617095

Boyatzis, R. E. (1982). *The competent manager: A model for effective performance*. Wiley.

Brown, M. E., Treviño, L. K., & Harrison, D. A. (2005). Ethical leadership: A social learning perspective for construct development and testing. *Organizational Behavior and Human Decision Processes*, *97*(2), 117–134. DOI: 10.1016/j.obhdp.2005.03.002

Brynjolfsson, E., & McAfee, A. (2014). *The second machine age: Work, progress, and prosperity in a time of brilliant technologies*. W. W. Norton & Company.

Bubeck, S., Chandrasekaran, V., Eldan, R., Gehrke, J., Horvitz, E., Kamar, E., Lee, P., Lee, Y. T., Li, Y., Lundberg, S., Nori, H., Palangi, H., Ribeiro, M. T., & Zhang, Y. (2023). Sparks of artificial general intelligence: Early experiments with GPT-4. arXiv. https://doi.org//arXiv.2303.12712DOI: 10.48550

Burns, J. M. (1978). *Leadership*. Harper & Row.

Carlyle, T. (1841). *On heroes, hero-worship, and the heroic in history*. James Fraser.

Chandler, A. D. (1977). *The visible hand: The managerial revolution in American business*. Harvard University Press.

Choudhury, P., Starr, E., & Agarwal, R. (2020). Machine learning and human capital complementarities: Experimental evidence on bias mitigation. *Strategic Management Journal, 41*(8), 1381–1411. DOI: 10.1002/smj.3152

Chui, M., Manyika, J., & Miremadi, M. (2018). *What AI can and can't do (yet) for your business. McKinsey Quarterly*. McKinsey & Company.

Dafoe, A. (2018). AI governance: A research agenda. Future of Humanity Institute, University of Oxford.

Dastin, J. (2018, October 10). Amazon scraps secret AI recruiting tool that showed bias against women. Reuters. https://www.reuters.com/article/us-amazon-com-jobs-automation-insight-idUSKCN1MK08G

Davenport, T. H., & Patil, D. J. (2012). Data scientist: The sexiest job of the 21st century. *Harvard Business Review, 90*(10), 70–76. PMID: 23074866

Davenport, T. H., & Ronanki, R. (2018). Artificial intelligence for the real world. *Harvard Business Review, 96*(1), 108–116.

Day, D. V. (2001). Leadership development: A review in context. *The Leadership Quarterly, 11*(4), 581–613. DOI: 10.1016/S1048-9843(00)00061-8

Diakopoulos, N. (2016). Accountability in algorithmic decision making. *Communications of the ACM, 59*(2), 56–62. DOI: 10.1145/2844110

Dietvorst, B. J., Simmons, J. P., & Massey, C. (2015). Algorithm aversion: People erroneously avoid algorithms after seeing them err. *Journal of Experimental Psychology. General, 144*(1), 114–126. DOI: 10.1037/xge0000033 PMID: 25401381

Drucker, P. F. (1959). *Landmarks of tomorrow*. Harper & Row.

Duggan, J., Sherman, U., Carbery, R., & McDonnell, A. (2020). Algorithmic management and app-work in the gig economy: A research agenda for employment relations and HRM. *Human Resource Management Journal, 30*(1), 114–132. DOI: 10.1111/1748-8583.12258

Edmondson, A. (1999). Psychological safety and learning behavior in work teams. *Administrative Science Quarterly, 44*(2), 350–383. DOI: 10.2307/2666999

Eisenhardt, K. M. (1989). Building theories from case study research. *Academy of Management Review, 14*(4), 532–550. DOI: 10.2307/258557

Fiedler, F. E. (1967). *A theory of leadership effectiveness*. McGraw-Hill.

Fleishman, E. A. (1953). The description of supervisory behavior. *The Journal of Applied Psychology, 37*(1), 1–6. DOI: 10.1037/h0056314 PMID: 6038475

Galton, F. (1869). *Hereditary genius: An inquiry into its laws and consequences.* Macmillan. DOI: 10.1037/13474-000

Garvin, D. A. (1993). Building a learning organization. *Harvard Business Review, 71*(4), 78–91. PMID: 10127041

Goldman Sachs. (2023). *The potentially large effects of artificial intelligence on economic growth.* Goldman Sachs Research.

Goleman, D. (1995). *Emotional intelligence: Why it can matter more than IQ.* Bantam Books.

Greenleaf, R. K. (1977). *Servant leadership: A journey into the nature of legitimate power and greatness.* Paulist Press.

Haenlein, M., & Kaplan, A. (2019). A brief history of artificial intelligence: On the past, present, and future of artificial intelligence. *California Management Review, 61*(4), 5–14. DOI: 10.1177/0008125619864925

Hersey, P., & Blanchard, K. H. (1969). *Management of organizational behavior: Utilizing human resources.* Prentice Hall.

House, R. J. (1971). A path goal theory of leader effectiveness. *Administrative Science Quarterly, 16*(3), 321–339. DOI: 10.2307/2391905

House, R. J., Hanges, P. J., Javidan, M., Dorfman, P. W., & Gupta, V. (Eds.). (2004). *Culture, leadership, and organizations: The GLOBE study of 62 societies.* SAGE.

Huang, M., & Rust, R. T. (2018). Artificial intelligence in service. *Journal of Service Research, 21*(2), 155–172. DOI: 10.1177/1094670517752459

Hutchins, E. (1995). *Cognition in the wild.* MIT Press. DOI: 10.7551/mitpress/1881.001.0001

Jarrahi, M. H. (2018). Artificial intelligence and the future of work: Human-AI symbiosis in organizational decision making. *Business Horizons, 61*(4), 577–586. DOI: 10.1016/j.bushor.2018.03.007

Judge, T. A., & Piccolo, R. F. (2004). Transformational and transactional leadership: A meta-analytic test of their relative validity. *The Journal of Applied Psychology, 89*(5), 755–768. DOI: 10.1037/0021-9010.89.5.755 PMID: 15506858

Katz, D., Maccoby, N., Gurin, G., & Floor, L. G. (1950). *Productivity, supervision and morale among railroad workers.* University of Michigan Survey Research Center.

Kellogg, K. C., Valentine, M. A., & Christin, A. (2020). Algorithms at work: The new contested terrain of control. *The Academy of Management Annals, 14*(1), 366–410. DOI: 10.5465/annals.2018.0174

Kolb, D. A. (1984). *Experiential learning: Experience as the source of learning and development.* Prentice Hall.

Kolbjørnsrud, V., Amico, R., & Thomas, R. J. (2016). How artificial intelligence will redefine management. Harvard Business Review. https://hbr.org/2016/11/how-artificial-intelligence-will-redefine-management

Lowe, K. B., Kroeck, K. G., & Sivasubramaniam, N. (1996). Effectiveness correlates of transformational and transactional leadership: A meta-analytic review of the MLQ literature. *The Leadership Quarterly, 7*(3), 385–425. DOI: 10.1016/S1048-9843(96)90027-2

Mäntymäki, M., Minkkinen, M., Birkstedt, T., & Viljanen, M. (2022). Defining organizational AI governance. *AI and Ethics, 2*(4), 603–609. DOI: 10.1007/s43681-022-00143-x

Mayer, D. M., Aquino, K., Greenbaum, R. L., & Kuenzi, M. (2012). Who displays ethical leadership, and why does it matter? An examination of antecedents and consequences of ethical leadership. *Academy of Management Journal, 55*(1), 151–171. DOI: 10.5465/amj.2008.0276

Mayer, J. D., & Salovey, P. (1997). What is emotional intelligence? In Salovey, P., & Sluyter, D. J. (Eds.), *Emotional development and emotional intelligence* (pp. 3–31). Basic Books.

McCauley, C. D., Moxley, R. S., & Van Velsor, E. (Eds.). (2010). *The center for creative leadership handbook of leadership development* (3rd ed.). Jossey-Bass.

McKinsey Global Institute. (2017). *Jobs lost, jobs gained: Workforce transitions in a time of automation.* McKinsey & Company.

McKinsey Global Institute. (2024). *The state of AI in 2024: GenAI's breakout year.* McKinsey & Company.

Microsoft. (2022). Microsoft responsible AI standard (v2). Microsoft Corporation. https://blogs.microsoft.com/wp-content/uploads/prod/sites/5/2022/06/Microsoft-Responsible-AI-Standard-v2-General-Requirements-3.pdf

Mintzberg, H. (2004). *Managers not MBAs: A hard look at the soft practice of managing and management development.* Berrett-Koehler Publishers.

Mittelstadt, B. D., Allo, P., Taddeo, M., Wachter, S., & Floridi, L. (2016). The ethics of algorithms: Mapping the debate. *Big Data & Society*, *3*(2), 1–21. DOI: 10.1177/2053951716679679

Ng, A. (2022). AI for everyone. DeepLearning.AI. https://www.deeplearning.ai/courses/ai-for-everyone/

Nonaka, I., & Takeuchi, H. (1995). *The knowledge-creating company: How Japanese companies create the dynamics of innovation*. Oxford University Press. DOI: 10.1093/oso/9780195092691.001.0001

Obermeyer, Z., Powers, B., Vogeli, C., & Mullainathan, S. (2019). Dissecting racial bias in an algorithm used to manage the health of populations. *Science*, *366*(6464), 447–453. DOI: 10.1126/science.aax2342 PMID: 31649194

OECD. (2019). Recommendation of the council on artificial intelligence (OECD/LEGAL/0449). Organisation for Economic Co-operation and Development. https://legalinstruments.oecd.org/en/instruments/OECD-LEGAL-0449

Orlikowski, W. J., & Scott, S. V. (2008). Sociomateriality: Challenging the separation of technology, work and organization. *The Academy of Management Annals*, *2*(1), 433–474. DOI: 10.5465/19416520802211644

Pasquale, F. (2015). *The black box society: The secret algorithms that control money and information*. Harvard University Press. DOI: 10.4159/harvard.9780674736061

Pfeffer, J., & Fong, C. T. (2002). The end of business schools? Less success than meets the eye. *Academy of Management Learning & Education*, *1*(1), 78–95. DOI: 10.5465/amle.2002.7373679

Podsakoff, P. M., MacKenzie, S. B., & Podsakoff, N. P. (2016). Recommendations for creating better concept definitions in the organizational, behavioral, and social sciences. *Organizational Research Methods*, *19*(2), 159–203. DOI: 10.1177/1094428115624965

Porter, L. W., & McKibbin, L. E. (1988). *Management education and development: Drift or thrust into the 21st century?* McGraw-Hill.

Rosenblat, A., & Stark, L. (2016). Algorithmic labor and information asymmetries: A case study of Uber's drivers. *International Journal of Communication*, *10*, 3758–3784.

Russell, S. (2019). *Human compatible: Artificial intelligence and the problem of control*. Viking.

Russell, S. J., & Norvig, P. (2021). *Artificial intelligence: A modern approach* (4th ed.). Pearson.

Schwab, K. (2016). *The fourth industrial revolution*. Crown Business.

Senge, P. M. (1990). *The fifth discipline: The art and practice of the learning organization*. Doubleday.

Skitka, L. J., Mosier, K. L., & Burdick, M. (1999). Does automation bias decision-making? *International Journal of Human-Computer Studies, 51*(5), 991–1006. DOI: 10.1006/ijhc.1999.0252

Smith, B., & Shum, H. (2019). *The future computed: AI and its role in society*. Microsoft Corporation.

Spencer, L. M., & Spencer, S. M. (1993). *Competence at work: Models for superior performance*. Wiley.

Strohmeier, S. (2020). Smart HRM – A Delphi study on the application and consequences of artificial intelligence for human resource management. *International Journal of Human Resource Management, 31*(12), 1–32. DOI: 10.1080/09585192.2020.1751829

Susskind, R., & Susskind, D. (2015). *The future of the professions: How technology will transform the work of human experts*. Oxford University Press. DOI: 10.1093/oso/9780198713395.001.0001

Taylor, F. W. (1911). The principles of scientific management. Harper & Brothers.

Uhl-Bien, M., Marion, R., & McKelvey, B. (2007). Complexity leadership theory: Shifting leadership from the industrial age to the knowledge era. *The Leadership Quarterly, 18*(4), 298–318. DOI: 10.1016/j.leaqua.2007.04.002

Ulrich, D., & Brockbank, W. (2005). *The HR value proposition*. Harvard Business Press.

Walumbwa, F. O., & Schaubroeck, J. (2009). Leader personality traits and employee voice behavior: Mediating roles of ethical leadership and work group psychological safety. *The Journal of Applied Psychology, 94*(5), 1275–1286. DOI: 10.1037/a0015848 PMID: 19702370

Wenger, E. (1998). *Communities of practice: Learning, meaning, and identity*. Cambridge University Press. DOI: 10.1017/CBO9780511803932

Wilson, H. J., & Daugherty, P. R. (2018). Collaborative intelligence: Humans and AI are joining forces. *Harvard Business Review, 96*(4), 114–123.

World Economic Forum. (2023). Future of jobs report 2023. World Economic Forum. https://www.weforum.org/reports/the-future-of-jobs-report-2023/

Yin, R. K. (2018). *Case study research and applications: Design and methods* (6th ed.). SAGE.

Zhang, J., & Patel, V. L. (2006). Distributed cognition, representation, and affordance. *Pragmatics & Cognition*, *14*(2), 333–341. DOI: 10.1075/pc.14.2.12zha

Chapter 8

The Hybrid Leader: Strategic Management of Human-AI Collaboration, Ethical Decision-Making, and Workforce

Amit Verma
http://orcid.org/0000-0002-9283-7873
Kalicharan PG College, Lucknow, India

Vibhuti Tyagi
http://orcid.org/0000-0001-6714-6029
Raj Kumar Goel Institute of Technology, Delhi, India

Rekha Khosla
Amity University, Lucknow, India

Ashish Chandra
http://orcid.org/0000-0002-7620-9455
Amity University, Lucknow, India

ABSTRACT

This book chapter examines hybrid leadership as a strategic response to artificial intelligence-driven organizational transformation. It explains how modern leaders must manage human–AI collaboration, ethical decision-making, workforce redesign, and responsible AI governance. The chapter highlights that AI can improve decision quality, forecasting, automation, innovation, and operational efficiency, but it also creates risks such as algorithmic bias, privacy violations, surveillance concerns, employee resistance, skill displacement, and accountability gaps. It argues that hybrid leaders need AI literacy, ethical reasoning, emotional intelligence, data interpretation, change leadership, and collaborative intelligence. The chapter

DOI: 10.4018/979-8-2600-0116-5.ch008

proposes an integrated strategic framework based on human–AI collaboration, ethical governance, workforce transformation, strategic value creation, and trust-based organizational culture.

1. INTRODUCTION

1.1 Background of Human–AI Collaboration in Modern Organizations

Artificial intelligence has rapidly moved from a specialty technological function to a basic element of the fabric of modern organizational life. Today, organizations use AI in human resource management, operations, finance, marketing, customer service, decision analytics, knowledge work and strategic planning. dedicate resources to gender pay gap investigation, recruitment screening and talent acquisition choices. AI-based Training/Employee Engagement Analysis Training workers is still one of the largest difficulties in HR. AI is used in operations for demand forecasting and production scheduling to manage the process, predictive maintenance of machines, quality control systems and supply chain optimization. In finance it is used to a huge number of applications such as detection of fraud, risk assessment and analysis, investment analysis, credit scoring, financial forecasting and monitoring compliance. AI is used in Marketing and Customer services for: customer segmentation, customization, chatbots, sentiment analysis, recommendation system, campaign optimization (Jarrahi, 2018).

The proliferation of AI usage means that artificial intelligence is no longer only a technical tool for data scientists or IT departments. It has increasingly become a Collaboratory partner in organizational choices. These AI systems can analyze large volumes of structured data, identify trends, forecast from past data, automate repeated processes and assist management judgement. But AI doesn't replace human leadership. Instead, it changes the job of leadership, as managers will be accountable to operate alongside intelligent systems, but still need to display empathy and ethics, creativity and contextual acumen and strategic accountability. In this context, the adoption of AI technology and the way that executives orchestrate human intelligence and machine intelligence will affect organizational success.

1.2 Emergence of the Hybrid Leader

As this wave of AI-enabled enterprises grows, we will need a new kind of leader that is focused on how to manage all these autonomous systems: the hybrid leader. A hybrid leader is a manager or executive who strategically orchestrates human intelligence, computer intelligence, ethical judgment and organizational transformation. Here's what you need to know about a hybrid leader: You need hybrid leaders because they work in situations where choices are more assisted or influenced or even automated by artificial intelligence (AI) technologies. Traditional leaders rely largely on humans and their management expertise. So, they must be able to interpret people and technology (Akter et al., 2021).

Hybrid leaders need to be tech smart and people oriented. Technological literacy does NOT mean that every leader must become a tech guru or a developer. Rather, it implies that he as a leader understands what AI can accomplish, what should not be anticipated from it, how data impacts algorithmic results and how choices taken based on AI backed capabilities will affect workers, customers and stakeholders. Hybrid leaders must also protect human values like trust, fairness, respect for others, involvement in decision-making processes, accountability and meaningful work. They need to navigate teams through the tumultuous waters of technological change, allay worries of automation and job loss, push for reskilling, and make sure that AI increases — rather than destroys organizational capacity.

1.3 Problem Statement

Organizations utilize AI faster than rebuilding their leadership models, governance structures, workforce roles, and ethical decision-making systems. Companies are buying new AI technology for efficiency, automation, analytics, and competitive advantage, but they may not prepare their leaders or personnel for the organizational changes. Thus, AI can cause major administrative and ethical issues.

Algorithmic prejudice poses major risks. AI systems with inadequate, biased, or historically unbalanced data will reproduce unjust hiring, promotion, credit assessment, performance evaluation business and school, consumer targeting, and resource allocation. Employee hesitation is another issue. Many worry about AI's propensity to eliminate jobs, undermine freedom, increase monitoring, and devalue human talents. Also important is skill displacement. AI will automate boring cognitive and administrative tasks, requiring most companies to rethink positions and spend heavily on productive reskilling (Rodgers et al., 2023).

AI deployment creates accountability gaps. Algorithmic judgments may obscure who is accountable for errors, injury, or prejudice. Automation can degrade human decision-making, lose crucial skills, and over-dependence on machine counsel. Data misuse and privacy violations damage employee and consumer confidence. The key is how CEOs will morally govern AI and develop human-centered workplaces, not how corporations will employ AI.

1.4 Research Gap and Chapter Justification

Existing leadership studies may describe digital leadership, transformational leadership or ethical leadership, of course, without merging them with AI adoption. But the literature speaks about how digital leaders handle technology changes, whereas transformational leadership is about vision, motivation and organizational change. Studies on adoption of AI investigate factors such as technical preparedness and performance or problems of effective deployment. Conversely, few studies incorporate human-AI collaboration, ethical decision-making, workforce change and strategic management in a leadership framework.

Analogously, traditional conceptions of leadership are unlikely to account for how leaders should interact with intelligent robots. And this chapter is also justified in that it analyzes hybrid leadership which is a required and strategic organizational response to an increasingly AI driven organization change (Bankins et al., 2024).

1.5 Aim and Objectives of the Chapter

The aim of this chapter is to develop a strategic model of hybrid leadership based on the framework of collaboration between humans and ethical, productive and human-centered AI technologies. This chapter introduces hybrid leadership in AI-enabled enterprises and human-AI collaboration as a strategic management capacity. It addresses ethical issues of AI-enabled authority like prejudice, accountability, transparency, privacy and trust. It also extends to transformation with an emphasis on reskilling the workforce, revamping jobs, employee acclimatization and human-centered change management. Forecast is also a frequent research opportunity where the chapter provides an integrated strategy framework with instructions for hybrid executives on how to connect AI capabilities with business success, ethical behavior and workforce sustainability (Duan et al., 2019). This concerns a new model of leadership in which algorithmic algorithms are used in real time to influence choice making, task distribution, evaluation of personnel, governance and strategic deliberation. Existing theories help us understand vision, motivation, decentralized decision-making, and digital transformation, but they do not explain how leaders should manage the outputs of AI systems while ensuring human accountability, re-design work involving AI in the workplace, and govern decision processes between humans and AI for ethical outcomes.

2. CONCEPTUAL FOUNDATIONS OF HYBRID LEADERSHIP

2.1 Meaning and Scope of Hybrid Leadership

What is Hybrid Leadership? Hybrid leadership is a combination of human judgment, emotional intelligence, and ethical reasoning with AI-driven decision assistance. It is founded on the notion that human people and AI systems alone cannot accomplish good organizational decision making in complicated situations. Human leaders exercise contextual judgment, empathy, inventiveness, moral judgment, political awareness and the capacity to interpret social meaning. AI systems give better skills in speed, pattern recognition, predictive analytics, automation and capacity to handle large data volumes. But this is the combination that makes a hybrid leadership (Papagiannidis et al., 2025).

The hybrid leadership spectrum is a vast one. This is true in decision making, workforce management, customer strategy, innovation, risk management, operational governance and organizational transformation. A hybrid leader where he/she would be knowing the usage of AI produced insights but not depend on them. They need to question algorithmic advice, assess data in context, see ethical hazards and be committed to organizational principles. That's why hybrid leadership is not about AI replacing human leaders. Co-creation is about rethinking the leadership job around collaboration between human and machine capabilities. Therefore, the hybrid leader should be a coordinator, interpreter of reality and values conveyer, ethical supervisor and decision maker of strategy in AI-supported enterprises.

2.2 Difference Between Traditional, Digital, and Hybrid Leadership

Leadership is about people, hierarchy, motivation, supervision and control, coordination. The traditional leadership models outline the way a leader may influence people via several ways such communication, authority, vision, rewards, culture of the business and connections between individuals. Models may grow to fit the future demands of businesses, but the human aspects of motivation, trust, dedication and cooperation are still at our heart thus they will always stay crucial. Traditional leadership cannot describe how leaders should behave when their decision processes are increasingly dictated by data systems, prediction models, algorithms and automation.

Digital leadership arose as organizations proceeded with the use of digital technology. It includes, but is not limited to, technology adoption, digital transformation, innovation, agility and digital culture and the use of information systems that lead to increased company performance. Digital leaders harness the readiness to technology, balance the formation of digital skills, rethink procedures and rally for a change inside the firm. Digital leadership is more about managing technology-enabled change than managing human & intelligent systems collaboration directly (Sutar et al., 2026).

Hybrid Leadership Beyond tradition & digital It's about the interplay between man and machine. At the same time the hybrid leader must manage people, technology and ethics, data, organizational transformation. The hybrid leader is more than just a people manager and must be able to understand AI-generated insights and the hazards of algorithms, which conventional leaders don't have to do. They are digital followers, not just in the use of technology but also in human – AI cooperation and decision-making responsibility Workforce redesign for the AI enabled workplace Collaborative and ethical member – AI Decisions Hybrid leadership is thus a more complex type of organizational or industrial leadership – a type in which AI is an active decision maker rather than a mere supporting tool.

2.3 Core Capabilities of the Hybrid Leader

Hybrid leaders must be skilled, humane, ethical, and strategic. First, capacity must include decision intelligence. Experience teaches hybrid leaders to combine data insights with human experience, contextual knowledge, and strategic issues. They should not just follow AI advice but assess AI evidence.

The second skill is AI literacy. Leaders must grasp how AI systems work, what data they use, the risks, and how algorithmic outputs may affect decision-making. Leaders may ask better questions and avoid overusing automated suggestions by practicing AI literacy. Moral Reasoning The third capacity of AI raises concerns about bias, privacy, monitoring, discrimination, and responsibility. Hybrid leaders must assess if AI-aided decisions are fair, transparent, and accountable. To lead humanly across the human-machine continuum today and in the future, leaders must first align with their corporate values (Stahl, 2022).

An important skill is human-centered judgment. Human dignity, employee well-being, creativity, and autonomy must be protected in hybrid leadership. They must be sure this AI will help humanity, not turn humans into data points or manufacturing units. Leaders must analyze AI-generated data to better management decision-making. Patterns and questioning assumptions and facts with organizational realities.

Changing management skills is essential for hybrid team leaders. Businesses using AI face uncertainty, fear, resistance, and role ambiguity due to these issues. Middle management leaders must communicate well, encourage reskilling and job redefinition, and foster a learning culture. Workers and stakeholders must trust AI to be built and used ethically. Trust involves fairness, transparency, and engagement. Accountability comes from trust. Hybrid leadership is not a replacement of the ideas of leadership, but an extension. Transformation leadership is about vision and inspiration, and motivating people to achieve real organizational transformation, but it does not say how to evaluate algorithmically generated suggestions or AI-assisted decisions, nor how to manage collaboration between humans and machines. Digitalization is about technology adoption, digital transformation, agility and innovation but in most cases, information technology is seen as an enabler rather than a decision influencer. Distributed leadership rests on the idea of power-sharing and collective approaches in decision-making. Distributed leadership neglects automatic evaluation from intelligent systems that do not own human rhetoric.

Hybrid leadership addresses this theoretical gap by combining human leadership with AI-enabled decision support, ethics steering and people-centered workforce adjustment. It is more than manipulating people and it is understanding that leadership in AI enabled organizations is about interrogating algorithm output, looking at the health of data, keeping humans in the loop and protecting employee dignity. Table 1 outlines the differences between digital and hybrid leadership, where human-AI collaboration including responsible automation; algorithmic responsibility and ethics are core aspects of hybrid leadership in contrast to digital leadership. Hybrid leadership is more of an organizational strategy on how human and artificial intelligence influence workforce choices, work processes, innovation and governance.

2.4 Hybrid Leadership as a Strategic Management Capability

Hybrid leadership should be considered a strategic management competence, because it is clearly related to organizational performance, adaptation, innovation and resilience. Organizations that develop hybrid leaders gain more effective and efficient AI deployment, leading to better decision quality, faster innovation, operational efficiency, and improved strategic responsiveness. Hybrid leaders may help firms get better at using data, but with ethical, situational and human-centric decision making.

Another benefit of hybrid leadership is that it increases staff flexibility. Employees will accept AI as not a danger but a cooperation tool if leaders clarify the goal of AI, employees are involved in deploying it, and they are reskilled or upskilled as needed. It promotes organizational learning and minimizes environmental opposition to change. The support for resilient hybrid leadership also stems from the reality that firms headed by leaders with a good awareness of both human and AI capabilities would adapt far more effectively to uncertainty and disruption than their rivals (Hai et al., 2025).

Thus, hybrid leadership is relevant for strategic management as it connects technology and people, ethics and future company goals. This allows enterprises to make use of AI-enabled intelligence without the drawbacks of over-automation. The Hybrid Leadership Capability Framework **Figure. 1** shows the hybrid leader, strategically placed at the heart of interdependent capabilities such as human judgment, artificial intelligence literacy and ethical reasoning, strategic foresight, workforce empowerment through data-driven decision-making, and change leadership to inspire trust and accountability. Integrative hybrid leadership builds upon existing approaches to leadership but does not replace them. Nature of transformation: Hybrid leaders need to motivate, inspire and eliminate opposition during AI-enabled transformation it's a form of transformational leadership. However, transformational leadership under-directs algorithmic suggestions and thus does not offer guidance on how to analyze data-driven decision systems and dangers of overreliance upon automated outputs. The hybrid approach to leadership: A charismatic transformational leader who also has AI literacy, evidence-based decision-making skills, and ethical supervision of the output of machine analytics.

Furthermore, hybrid leadership is not the same as digital leadership. Digital leadership in the context of digital transformation (DT) is the readiness to use technology-centric innovations for successful implementation in organizations. It usually involves iterations using test prototype methods and empowering team adaptation. It also involves taking risks with agility around the organizational purpose. Hybrid leadership on the other end, concerning the human decision makers and intelligent systems. Hybrid leaders have to manage human-AI collaboration, to consider explainability and accountability, to protect the employees from unreasonable algorithmic decisions and to redesign work for maximum human ability rather than only adopt technology.

Importance of distributed leadership: AI-enabled firms are distributing many forms of decision making across manager, technical team, workers and governance actors. Distributed leadership is generally about the sharing of power between people, but here in Hybrid leadership we are putting AI systems into the decision-making process. The leader then becomes a mediator between human knowledge, algorithmic insights, ethical assessment and accountability. Hybrid leadership is practiced in companies where people, data, platforms and intelligent technologies are making choices together.

Ethical leadership supports hybrid leadership as the use of AI leads to issues of fairness, transparency, privacy, surveillance, discrimination and accountability. Being a good person in a vague sense may not be enough without proper AI governance rules. In summary, hybrid leadership means including bias audits, explainability checks, a human-in-the-loop review and appeal process for AI outputs, data security preparations and monitoring of AI performance after deployment so that ethical leadership can be operationalized in an environment made possible by AI. Hence, socio-technical hybrid leadership entails people management skills, technical knowledge, ethical reasoning and strategic governance.

Figure 1. Hybrid Leadership Capability Framework

Figure 1 shows hybrid leadership as a circular capability architecture with the hybrid leader at the core of numerous interrelated capabilities. The graphic indicates that AI-enabled firms need leaders with human judgment, AI literacy, ethical reasoning, strategic vision, workforce empowerment, data-driven decision-making, change leadership, trust, and accountability.

3. HUMAN–AI COLLABORATION IN STRATEGIC MANAGEMENT

3.1 Understanding Human–AI Collaboration

Human–AI cooperation is a work setting in which human and AI systems collaborate to perform tasks, make choices, solve problems and innovate. The premise is that humans and robots have distinct capabilities, yet they complement each other. Human Contribution: Contextual Understanding Values and Creativity Empathy and Moral Reasoning Strategic Interpretation & Accountability AI systems are rapid, seeing trends, generating predictions, automating activities and working with large volumes of data all while retaining the same consistency in their analysis. These capabilities are complementary and allow businesses to operate in a better context and at a greater pace, keeping human accountability (Dwivedi et al., 2021).

In strategic management, human–AI collaboration is particularly important since many strategic choices are not solely data driven. They also relate to uncertainties, values, stakeholder interests, market interpretation, ethical ramifications and long-term organizational vision. AI may assist in accelerating the process of strategic thinking, by identifying patterns, simulating scenarios, influencing weak signals and forecasting danger. But human leaders must interpret these outputs in terms of mission, culture, employee welfare, customer assurance and societal responsibility of the firm. This is why human–AI collaboration 1 Here we will use the word to mean these processes and not consider them as mere automation of tasks. It should be seen not only as a method but as a holistic organizational or strategic competence that blends analytical intelligence with human knowledge.

3.2 AI as Decision Support, Not Decision Replacement

AI enhances, not replaces, decisions. Modern corporate executives may use AI to generate insights, alternatives, predictions, suggestions, and warnings. It may predict customer behavior, employee turnover risk, supply chain issues, financial fraud, market trends, product proposals, etc. These abilities will help managers make decisions by providing evidence and reducing routine analysis.

But accountable humans must make all final decisions affecting people, ethics, justice, and strategy. AI will not feel ethically guilty, have empathy, loyalty to an organization, or comprehend social dynamics. They run on data, rules, patterns, and probability." Without leaders restricting AI from making final decisions without human review, organizations risk prejudice, discrimination, employee privacy decisions, and accountability gaps (Benlian & Pinski, 2025).

If AI uses historical recruiting data to choose candidates, a human leader must ensure that the process is fair and inclusive and does not perpetuate discrimination. AI may help executives cut costs, but they must also consider employee wellbeing, corporate culture, stakeholder trust, and long-term sustainability. Hybrid leaders must use AI for advice but have humans make decisions. This concept underpins appropriate human–AI collaboration. In this work, we consider one key characteristic of human-AI cooperation that is highly connected to human-automation interaction literature. This scholarship shows how an automated system can enhance the speed and consistency of decisions but overreliance on right now (Sundar et al. Degradation of critical judgment, skills deterioration or wrong belief that the results of the systems are final, all this over-reliance may have negative consequences. Automation bias refers to the temptation of managers to rely on algorithmic recommendations in

AI-enabled companies without proper due diligence inspection. So, Hybrid Leaders need to calibrate trust in AI. Calibrated trust is trusting the output of AI, but not trusting it blindly, and not dismissing or rejecting the output either. Leaders need to understand when they can trust AI, when it requires human interpretation and when ethics or context should trump algorithmic guidance.

Organizations make many decisions that involve ambiguity, values, relationships and temporal consequences that cannot be adequately represented by data models. "We need to have human over-sight. It can find pattern, predict events and propose alternatives, but the moral culpability of decisions cannot be passed to AI. Hybrid leaders will establish human-in-the-loop decision procedures in high-impact areas such as recruitment, promotion and performance review, staff monitoring, customer access, credit evaluation and risk assessment. Leaders must ensure that AI is an aid to decision-making, not a substitute for it.

3.3 Areas of Human–AI Collaboration in Organizations

AI is being used as an expert system in organizational management. Few studies have examined human-AI collaboration. AI is used in recruiting (CV screening) and talent analytics to find best-fit skills, workplace trends, expected team needs, etc. Humanly, we need fairness, diversity, strong applicant advocates, and ethical hiring. AI can assess productivity trends, find talents that need training, and reveal performance gaps, but managers and leaders must comprehend the implications (Chuang et al., 2025).

AI in consumer analytics may analyze preferences, purchases, complaints, mood, and service trends. Human leaders establish customer strategy, service, and connections with this data. AI assists budgeting, spending optimization, risk prediction, fraud detection, investment trend analysis, and cash-flow revenue projections. Human decision makers' views on market dynamics, legality, and strategic interest.

It can estimate demand, optimize inventory, detect logistical hazards, and improve supply chain purchase planning. This bonding helps human managers negotiate ethical sourcing and crisis management by balancing supplier relationships. AI helps product developers swiftly evaluate market cycles, customer feedback, and design possibilities. Ordinary people like you and me must use AI to generate useful products and services from this data and insights.

Risk management may benefit from human-AI cooperation. AI can identify fraud, cybersecurity, operational issues, compliance violations, and market disruptions. Leadership training is inadequate to respond and minimize exposure ethically and proportionally. This involves connecting CEO vision, goals, and direction with the yearly strategy plan and AI-studied competitive trends, scenario models, consumer data, and external threats. AI employs employee learning systems to tailor training, predict talent shortages, and monitor career growth. Document organization, relevant information finding, report summarizing, and organizational learning may be done using AI in knowledge management. These hybrid leaders employ AI to boost human potential, not replace it (Zirar et al., 2023).

3.4 Benefits of Human–AI Collaboration

Strategic management of human-AI hybrid collaboration. Faster decision making – AI can analyze large data sets in seconds and provide insights from the theory. Secondly, it boosts decision-making accuracy by spotting patterns, dangers, and opportunities that would be ignored in a human analysis. Third, it reduces regular load by automation of repetitive operations such as data input, report production and screening monitoring, which can be examined simply. This enables space for employees and supervisors to deal with tasks that demands creativity, strategy and connection development.

Human–AI interaction also enables for individualized services. AI can help you personalize recommendations for customer service, marketing, learning and staff development. You can build a huge language model that can assess historical data, real time signals from sensors, and general trends out there – and substantially enhance predicting. Modeling prediction drives innovation by creating ideas, uncovering untapped markets and speeding experimentation. More importantly, it allows for organizational adaptability. The deployments combine human intuition and alerting intelligence to help organizations to react to market shifts and customer behavior via price-optimal marketing, operational risks/events and competitive threats faster (Jarrahi et al., 2023).

3.5 Risks of Poor Human–AI Collaboration

Poor human–AI collaboration can, in turn, represent serious organizational hazards. This can lead to automation bias, when executives depend on AI advice without thinking about whether the AI is correct. Relying too much on AI can inhibit human decision-making and management learning. Employees who do not continue to build their analytical and problem-solving skills may deteriorate the capabilities necessary to recognize those repercussions. AI breeds mistrust among employees, especially when it is utilized without some kind of openness in observation, assessment, or judgement. It can lead not just to gaps in accountability and data errors, but also to biased output decisions and reputation harm. Therefore, hybrid leaders are responsible for a correct design of the human–AI partnership, in a transparent, monitored, ethical way and guaranteeing its conformity with company values. **Table 1**. Summary of Respective Human and Artificial Intelligence Contributions to

Strategic Management and the Mediation of Both Forms of Intelligence Through Hybrid Leadership (Daly et al., 2025).

Table 1. Human and AI Contributions in Strategic Management

Strategic Area	Human Contribution	AI Contribution	Hybrid Leadership Role
Decision-making	Judgment, values, context	Data analysis, prediction	Balance insight with accountability
HRM	Empathy, fairness, motivation	Screening, analytics, workforce planning	Prevent bias and protect dignity
Operations	Process knowledge	Automation, optimization	Improve efficiency ethically
Innovation	Creativity, imagination	Pattern discovery, idea generation	Combine creativity with intelligence
Risk management	Ethical interpretation	Risk detection, scenario analysis	Ensure responsible action

Table 1 compares human and AI contributions to strategic management domains.

4. ETHICAL DECISION-MAKING IN AI-ENABLED LEADERSHIP

4.1 Importance of Ethics in Hybrid Leadership

At the convergence of hybrid leadership, ethics are increasingly being shaped by AI systems making decisions that directly impact human dignity, opportunity, justice, privacy and trust. Artificial intelligence may be used in HRM to screen recruits, rate workers, forecast attrition, offer promotions or just find performance flaws. In customer development, AI will affect pricing, access to services, product suggestions, credit choices and complaints. AI can aid resource allocation, fraud detection, cost reductions through operational efficiency, and risk prioritization in operations and finance. These aren't just technical decisions, which would be one thing, these have moral ramifications (Heyder et al., 2023).

This implies hybrid leaders must go away from merely understanding decisions influenced by AI driving some kind of autonomy behind individuals or their employment, income, reputation, privacy and access to opportunities. Leaders who believe that AI outcomes are inherently impartial may be perpetuating unjust or harmful actions. Ethical leadership: avoid algorithmic damage, maintain rights secure, secure business confidence. Employees and customers are more willing to employ AI to live in public, with fair usage. The OECD AI Principles highlight trustworthy AI that respects human rights and democratic ideals, therefore strengthening the need for ethical leadership in all those organizations driven by AI.

4.2 Major Ethical Challenges

The ethical problems in AI aided Leadership are increasing. One of these is algorithmic bias. Because AI systems are trained on data, if the information is based on past bias or unequal practices by corporations then the computer will incorporate such leanings into the system itself. This can damage recruiting, promotion, performance appraisals, finance, pricing and consumer segmentation. The second problem is the transparency issue. In many circumstances, AI systems tend to be black boxes for users or managers and understanding how every specific suggestion or decision is produced may frequently be challenging.

Then there's the specter of the data privacy dilemma. First, AI models notice thirst and there is a lot of data around workers/clients or meaning it needs a lot of records as such. Not asking for unambiguous consent, using the gathered data for various reasons and/or not securing it can lead to infringement of privacy and loss of trust. Surveillance and Employee Monitoring Create a Second Ethical Risk. Trackers can pick up on productivity, communication patterns, location history, keystrokes, facial expressions or other signs of behavior. It truly relies on the algorithms that you use. It is stressful, creates a culture of fear and hinders autonomy (Singh et al., 2026).

Other ethical concerns may arise such as prejudice, lack of accountability, bias from predictive analytics, potential for manipulation and over-automation that negates human elements in decision making. When responsibility is unclear – is it the AI-generated model provider, or the data team, manager or organization – accountability gaps emerge. You could even teach them to play customers or staff by watching what would likely elicit a response. The predictive analytics must not only determine who is likely to be weak but also how vulnerable they are so that manipulation may be aimed at all vulnerabilities directly and specifically. Over-automation is particularly dangerous when leaders use AI technologies on humans with little meaningful human scrutiny. In such instances, efficiency may override dignity and trust and equality.

4.3 Ethical Principles for Hybrid Leaders

Purpose of hybrid leaders Hybrid leaders need to be clear on the ethical standards that guide AI-supported decision-making. The primary premise is justice. AI systems should neither generate biased outcomes nor reinforce existing prejudices. AI systems therefore need to be tested for prejudice, and to ensure equal decision-making on gender, age, color, handicap, location income among others. Second, it's transparency. If AI is making choices, employees, consumers and other stakeholders should be told what it is used for and how those decisions affect lives (Kumar et al., 2024).

Inclusion, security and proportion are further driving considerations at this level. Integrative Inclusiveness means that the design and evaluation of AI systems should consider the viewpoints of a variety of stakeholders. Security is the security of AI systems and data from abuse, breaches and manipulation. Proportionality: The usage of AI should be proportionate to the gravity of the choice, with more critical judgments requiring more safeguards. Trustworthy AI, design for the user to defend human rights, robustness and security, transparency, safety and responsibility.

4.4 Human Oversight and Accountability

An AI system can make mistakes, misinterpret context, reiterate bias, or provide technically accurate but ethically wrong advice, therefore human monitoring is vital. Hybrid leaders need to observe, audit and interrogate AI systems to flag any suspect outcomes. They must put in place review procedures for crucial AI choices (even if not combined with human involvement), such as hiring and promotions, firing employees, evaluations that affect credit or pricing in companies, workplace surveillance, customer access to businesses, etc.

Accountability also involves documentation. Leaders should document the purpose of the use of AI systems, which data is dependent on them, who assesses its outputs, processes of risk assessment and how impacted persons may appeal decisions. Data Quality, Model Performance, Fairness, Privacy and Security Audits of AI should examine the quality of data (completeness), model performance under varying conditions for learning outcomes (test accuracy at each learning iteration), fairness of the results for all stakeholders impacted by the application. Organizations should also split accountability amongst developers, deployers, managers and reviewers such that no choice may become untraceable (Guler et al., 2024).

A good place to start for this is the NIST AI Risk Management Framework. The intention behind it is to enable organizations to manage AI risk based on the harm caused to people, organizations and society and to foster trustworthiness in the design, development, usage and assessment of AI. It is mostly about how we may arrange AI risk management in practice, using the four functions: govern, map, measure and manage.

4.5 Ethical Decision-Making Process for Hybrid Leaders

Hybrid leaders cannot make ethical judgments lightly, especially in the context of artificial intelligence, but must adopt a disciplined process for decision-making. First Step Identify the AI decision context Whether it is a choice that impacts individuals, rights or opportunities or strategic consequences. Then assess the effect on stakeholders by asking who will gain or suffer. Third, assess data quality, relevance, permission and any biases: Fourth, think about the explainability, if the AI output can be understood and debated. Fifth, however, use human judgement instead than merely implementing the recommendation mechanically. Accountability Documentation- Write down decision rationale, reviewer responsibility and safeguards. Finally, always check results for harm, bias or mistakes and unexpected repercussions. The ethical decision-making paradigm for hybrid leaders is presented in **Figure 2** (Robertson et al., 2024).

Figure 2. Ethical Decision-Making Model for Hybrid Leaders

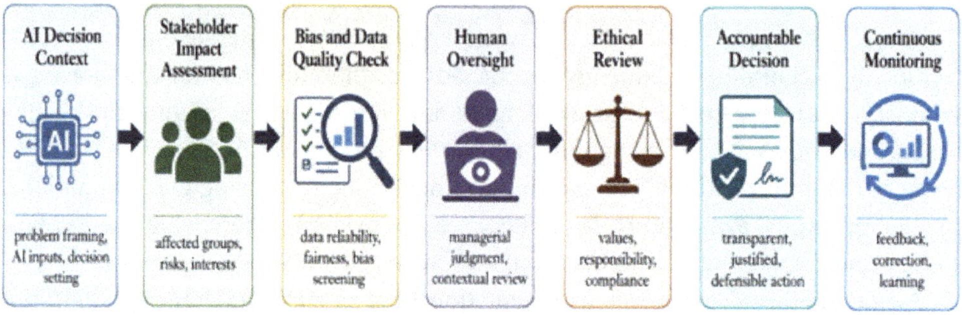

Figure 2 shows hybrid leaders' ethical decision-making steps. The methodology suggests analyzing decision context and stakeholder effect before making AI-supported judgments. Leaders must assess data quality, bias, human supervision, ethical review, responsible judgments, and ongoing outcomes.

5. WORKFORCE TRANSFORMATION IN THE AGE OF AI

5.1 AI and the Changing Nature of Work

AI is altering work: It is not changing jobs. It is changing the tasks that need to be done in jobs. Reporting and scheduling, content development, data processing, customer engagement (chatbots) and analytical work, from ordinary cognitive labor to administrative chores, much of which is being done by AI systems. Now, employees utilize AI-powered tools to compose papers, summarize material, prepare reports, analyze datasets, create presentations, reply to customer inquiries, screen applications from jobseekers, monitor corporate operations and help managers in decision making (Pan et al., 2025).

A key point stressed by the 2025 ILO work on generative AI and jobs is that exposure should be measured at the occupational–task level and that the elimination of an entire job overnight is not to be envisaged. The established global index leverages task-level data, expert opinions, and predictions from AI models to evaluate the likely impact of GenAI on jobs. This concept is significant for hybrid leadership because it also shows how AI affects work — not just in terms of replacing humans but also in terms of changing what workers do, how they do it, and what skills are in demand. Instead of a restricted view of AI as a replacement technology, hybrid leaders should see AI as a force that reshapes the organization in terms of procedures, authority for decision-making, and boosts the capacities of people.

5.2 Job Redesign and Role Reconfiguration

As AI is embedded in businesses, employment responsibilities will shift from doing tasks to overseeing the execution of tasks, interpreting the outcomes, addressing exceptions, being creative, and managing connections with other people and AI engines while controlling the engines. Workers who used to spend most of their work hours on repetitive reporting, data entry, scheduling, simple calculations or routine communications will now oversee outputs created by AI and review for mistakes, interpret what the results mean, and apply human judgement to more complex cases.

Take human resource management, for example. AI may be used to filter resumes and identify skill gaps among employees, but it is the human resources professionals' responsibility to interpret the results equitably, making sure that decisions are not made in a vacuum.

More flexible capacity-based jobs rather than fixed task lists in job descriptions. That implies employees will have to learn what they may utilize AI for, where the AI must have consent from a human and where it must be ALL human. Hybrid leaders need to restructure tasks more reasonably, so that AI complements human labor instead of merely enhancing monitoring or efficiency, adding intensity/volume to the workload or making the job more insecure (Sundberg & Holmström, 2023).

5.3 Reskilling and Upskilling Requirements

Workforce transformation is about constant reskilling and upskilling. AI literacy, the key to all talents. Employees need to know the possibilities and limits of AI, and how to ethically use AI technologies. Prompting and AI tools are also playing an increasing role, since many employees are presently using natural-language instructions to communicate with generative AI systems too. Part II: Workers should learn to ask questions, scrutinize answers, verify the content outputs and not get so dependent on AI-produced information that they forget to think critically.

Data interpretation is another important ability. You need workers who can interpret dashboards, statistics and projections, even AI produced recommendations. To get any real value from labor performed by machines, one must criticize results, challenge bottom lines and look for flaws, so as not to fall victim to what is known as automation bias. There is also a need for ethical and responsible thinking since employees need to connect to issues like prejudice, privacy, surveillance, justice and responsibility. Digital collaboration skills: To enable teams to collaborate with AI technologies, cloud platforms and workflow automation systems and digital knowledge environments (Akter et al., 2023).

Human abilities are still highly valued. Therefore, soft skills, notably creativity and problem-solving, communication, empathy and relationship management, are necessary as automation takes care of more regular labor. The backbone of AI systems is data and digital infrastructure, thus cybersecurity awareness for employees is equally critical. Finally, the nature of AI technology is ever-changing, thus flexibility is crucial. Leadership for a hybrid workforce is about creating a culture of learning where reskilling is not an exception but rather the norm.

5.4 Employee Resistance and Psychological Concerns

AI Adoption Resistance and Psychological Issues among Employees Workers may fear losing employment, experience more strict supervision or sense lack of control over work outputs; human talents start to fade into irrelevance. The truth is that many employees might lose faith in AI since they don't understand how choices are made or whether they are going to be treated unfairly. AI-driven performance management, as the system is mainly Blackbox, might contribute to employee fear that they are continuously being observed and graded (Mishra et al., 2024).

Not sure where it will be in the future. Employees are wondering if AI will replace their jobs, alter the promotions they'll receive, diminish their competence. Clear communication and engagement, training to use the new tools, good role definition and trust building by hybrid leaders are issues that need to be addressed – you can be sure that employees should hear from their bosses. "They have to explain the way of bringing in AI, how it's going to change work and what support people are going to get."

5.5 Inclusive Workforce Transformation

Inclusive workforce transformation means that all employees have equal access for AI training, digital tools, career trajectories and reskilling possibilities. This is because hybrid leaders will have to protect those people who are susceptible — regular administrative tasks and low-skill positions, elderly workers, contract workers, and staff with minimal expertise in the digitalization sector. Organizations might not want to create a divide between the AI savvy staff and others who have been left out. AI adoption should be accompanied by learning support, job redesign, ethical governance and employee empowerment. **Table 2.** Changing the Workforce through Hybrid Leadership (Babina et al., 2024).

Table 2. Workforce Transformation Under Hybrid Leadership

Workforce Dimension	Traditional Workforce	AI-Enabled Workforce	Hybrid Leader's Responsibility
Skills	Functional expertise	AI literacy + human judgment	Build continuous learning
Roles	Fixed job descriptions	Fluid and task-based roles	Redesign jobs fairly
Decision-making	Manager-led	Human-AI supported	Maintain accountability
Training	Periodic training	Continuous reskilling	Create learning culture
Performance	Output-based	Human + AI productivity	Avoid unfair AI measurement

Table 2 shows how workforce transformation changes skills, roles, decision-making, training, and performance management under hybrid leadership. The table highlights that AI-enabled work requires continuous learning, fair role redesign, accountable human–AI decision-making, and careful performance measurement

6. STRATEGIC MANAGEMENT ROLE OF THE HYBRID LEADER

6.1 Aligning AI Strategy with Business Goals and Decision Intelligence

Hybrid executives need to ensure that the use of AI is in line with the firm's vision, competitive pedigree, productive outputs, innovation roadmap, customer value and sustainability. AI should be deployed when it can be applied to deliver strategic imperatives – whether that be improving decision quality, speeding up operations, transforming customer experience, enhancing forecasting (and working capital), operationalizing hyper-personalized service and experiences or supporting innovation. If AI adoption is merely a trend, firms may squander their money on solutions that don't answer actual business challenges (Aulia & Lin, 2025).

Before you deploy AI, executives should ask several critical strategic alignment questions. They include: What's the business challenge, and how will AI fix it?

How will it make it perform better? Who will it impact? What might go wrong? What human capacities do you utilize responsibly? So, hybrid leaders connect AI adoption to strategy management, rather than leaving the direction of AI only to technical teams or suppliers.

Hybrid leaders also leverage artificial intelligence for executive decision intelligence. It can be used in scenario planning, market forecasting, competitive intelligence, customer analytics, and operational and long-term strategic decision-making.

6.2 Building AI-Ready Culture and Human-Centered Value

Lead the way The one crucial thing we need to do is build an AI-ready organizational culture. It promotes experimentation, learning, ethics and open communication & cooperation between technical and non-technical teams. Staff should not feel AI is being thrust upon them. They need to understand why AI adoption is necessary, what the impact on them will be and how they will be nurtured and upskilled.

AI change needs psychological safety. The need is for workers to be safe, to ask questions and to question the output of AI, report flaws and raise concerns (about prejudice, spying and restructuring of jobs). The hybrid leaders you meet with might be managers, workers, data scientists, HR professionals, attorneys and ethical teams. And this also takes care of the actual terrain – the human reality matching with A.I (Mariani & Dwivedi, 2024).

Hybrid leaders need to get beyond it, to blend efficiency with human worth. AI is neither a toy to save money or replace personnel, nor is it an authoritarian mind control tool. Will it boost productivity of the employees, contentment of the customers, innovation and feeling of social responsibility? AI handles the basics, while leaders shift people into more-than-human jobs like problem solving, innovation, relationship management, supervision and moral decision making. By employing AI to complement not replace mankind.

6.3 Governance, Risk Management, and Responsible Performance Measurement

AI governance and risk management are important aspects of hybrid leadership. There are also regulations, go/no-go processes, ethical boards and data governance, accountability and monitoring systems, and risk assessments and audits that control AI. They safeguard honest, fair, safe and transparent tech in AI. Organizations that don't oversee AI face the danger of algorithmic bias or privacy breaches, malicious or inappropriate use of data, consumer discrimination, unfair personnel assessment across sectors/industries and inability to manage cyber-attack risks and accountability mechanisms (Sarvate et al., 2025).

Risk management doesn't start with AI. Hybrid leaders must evaluate data quality, model purpose, stakeholders, privacy risks, explainability, and bias. Highly impact AI technologies should be assessed more rigorously, especially if used in hiring, promotion, credit rating, performance appraisal, access to services, and surveillance. Regular checks should guarantee that AI systems are accurate, fair, and consistent with your organization's values.

Similarly, AI-enabled companies should reconsider performance metrics. How a leader should evaluate trust, fairness, staff adaptability, customer satisfaction, creative activity outcomes, and ethical compliance, not only productivity or cost reductions. A broader AI viewpoint increases corporate effectiveness.

AI-enabled hybrid leader **Figure 3**: AI-Enabled Organizations' Hybrid Leader A hybrid leader responsible for AI strategy, ethical governance, human–AI interaction, workforce reskilling, risk management, innovation, trust building, and performance evaluation.

Figure 3. Strategic Role of the Hybrid Leader in AI-Enabled Organizations

Figure 3 shows the hybrid leader's strategic position as AI-enabled organizational transformation coordinator. The graphic demonstrates hybrid executives must integrate AI strategy with ethical governance, human–AI cooperation, workforce reskilling, risk management, innovation, trust building, and performance monitoring.

7. ORGANIZATIONAL GOVERNANCE FOR HUMAN–AI SYSTEMS

7.1 Need and Core Components of AI Governance

AI governance are the rules, processes, responsibilities, and controls that govern ethical AI use in an organization. It promotes ethical, legal, secure, and strategic AI use. Hybrid leaders need governance since AI may affect recruiting, promotion, work allocation, customer access, financial choices, performance assessment, and strategic planning. Thus, AI should be handled like any other organization system with human, ethical, legal, and societal consequences, not only as an IT project.

AI policy data governance model transparency risk categorization human supervision audit and review systems employee involvement cyber security vendor accountability and ethics committee are significant AI governance features. An AI policy outlines the business's AI goals, methods, applications, and limits. Data governance assures AI system memories are accurate, safe, legal, and moral. Leaders and users must understand AI results for high-impact decisions: Excellent transparency (Khogali & Mekid, 2023).

Not all AI systems are dangerous; thus hazard classification is crucial. AI employed in normal scheduling may require less scrutiny than in recruiting or promotion evaluation, law enforcement surveillance, credit judgments, and disciplinary action.

7.2 Accountability Structures and Workplace AI Governance

Hybrid firms need clear accountability frameworks since AI decisions include many parties. Senior executives control AI strategy, governance, and accountability. They must guarantee that AI deployment supports company goals and doesn't cause ethical or legal difficulties. Data Scientists and IT teams create, test, secure, and check systems. HR managers must ensure that AI in hiring, training, workforce planning, and performance management does not cause bias.

Compliance officers and lawyers manage GDPR compliance, paperwork, and risk evaluation. Line managers correctly comprehend AI results in daily work decisions. Staff use AI tools, report problems, question unfair outcomes, and provide system feedback as governance duties. Are external vendors accountable for transparency, system stability, data protection, and contractual and ethical compliance?

Workplace AI needs governance since it impacts workers. AI may be utilized for recruitment-in-screening, employee monitoring and productivity analytics, performance evaluation, training ideas, and workforce planning. Such tools can boost productivity and decision-making, but they can raise prejudice, monitoring pressure, autonomy loss, and employee distrust. Hybrid leaders must provide proportionate, transparent, explainable, and human-reviewable workplace AI. Employees must know when an AI is in use, what data is collected, how judgments are formed, and how to appeal or dispute AI-supported decisions (Kulkov, 2021).

7.3 Continuous Monitoring, Feedback, and Governance Responsibilities

The governance of AI is not something that should be done solely while implementing it. That is why you need to continuously monitor AI systems to see as time passes that data, workforce behavior, market conditions and requirements of the organization change. Through the monitoring of real-time data, it can detect faults, a decrease in performance, odd outputs, cybersecurity vulnerabilities or unfair trends. It is also important to draw on the opinion of your employees, since workers may sometimes pick issues that technical audits overlook. A periodic algorithmic audit checking for bias, accuracy and explainability of the algorithm, as well as privacy, security and stakeholder impact should be performed.

Organizational ramifications of AI should also be considered by leaders in a hybrid setting. They need to question if AI is being used to increase productivity without compromising trust, whether it enables learning instead of monitoring, whether it encourages fairness or, on the contrary, perpetuates prejudice and whether their staff feel involved in AI transformation. **Table 3** highlights the main AI governance functions in hybrid companies (Holmström & Carroll, 2025).

Table 3. AI Governance Responsibilities in Hybrid Organizations

Actor	Governance Responsibility	Key Risk Managed
Senior leaders	AI strategy and accountability	Strategic misuse
HR managers	Fair workforce application	Bias and discrimination
IT/data teams	System design and security	Technical failure
Ethics committee	Ethical review	Harm and unfairness
Employees	Feedback and responsible use	Misuse and resistance
Vendors	Transparency and compliance	External accountability gaps

Table 3 demonstrates that hybrid organizations entrust AI governance to many players. Executives, HR managers, IT and data teams, ethical committees, workers, and vendors handle differences in risks.

8. HUMAN-CENTERED LEADERSHIP AND EMPLOYEE TRUST

8.1 Trust, Transparency, and Communication in Hybrid Leadership

Trust is the key ingredient of hybrid leadership. AI Resistance Employees are also more inclined to reject AI when they fear it will be used to replace them, enhance their monitoring, undermine their autonomy, or make significant decisions based on application of data – on performance, promotion schedule and work volume. Trust comes from people knowing how AI systems function, why they are being adopted, what value they are adding, and the precautions that come with deployment. Therefore, hybrid leaders need to kickstart AI adoption by providing an open environment rather than a top-down approach.

Only communication and transparency characterize this procedure. Good leaders will discuss why this move to AI is occurring, how they plan to utilize it, what data they will gather, who will be reviewing this data and ensuring that people feel secure in how the data will be utilized. Employees also need to know if the AI outputs are advisory or decision-making. So, if the application is AI-driven performance analytics, employees need to know what indicators are being assessed, how the computers are interpreting the data and whether human managers are reviewing the outputs before any judgments are made. Transparent communication reduces anxiety, stops conjecture and increases confidence in changing projects.

Hybrid executives also need to emphasize that AI is going to help employees, not simply dominate them. Workers who perceive AI to reduce regular burdens, improve learning, assist with decision making and increase productivity are more inclined to accept it. If AI is only a tool to save expenses or surveillance, then skepticism will rise (Dhaigude & Kamath, 2025).

8.2 Psychological Safety and Employee Participation in AI Transformation

Psychological safety is needed on the AI journey. Workers need to dispute AI results, disclose problems on their projects, contest biased and unjust conclusions and raise ethical concerns without fear of reprisal. AI systems can be wrong, prejudiced or provide context-free findings. Employees need to be critical and reflective reviewers informed by significant AI-based ideas rather than passive consumers of AI from the outside.

Hybrid leadership demands official and informal mechanisms for employee input. These AI feedback forms, review committees, grievance processes, team talks, pilot testing and the inclusion of an employee representative in the implementation of AI systems. Companies reporting trouble get an early notice to fix and enhance their systems. AI also seeks to reduce automation bias, the tendency for managers and staff to trust AI outcomes.

Participatory RAI involves workers in testing, assessing, and refining AI systems before and after installation. Work is familiar to employees. They understand workplace operations. They understand customer challenges. They understand workflow challenges. They can improve AI design with their experience. The employee may assist in detecting whether an AI tool raises expectations, ignores contextual factors, or makes things worse by increasing effort. Since employees feel that AI is being developed for them rather than forced on them, participation boosts acceptance (Lindner et al., 2025).

8.3 Building a Human-Centered AI Culture

A human-centric AI culture is one that is grounded in dignity, inclusiveness, learning, collaboration and responsible ethical use. In such a society, AI is still considered as a method to harness human potential, not detract from it. Hybrid leaders are firm in their stance for fair, responsible and ethical applications of AI, as well as keeping people involved in the decision-making process, ensuring workers are heard, culling within for talent instead of outside wherever feasible, and other techniques to find fresh potential. They must protect those workers who are not flexible enough in their thinking, maintain equitable accessibility in AI training and avoid a situation where workers with AI talents are divided from those without (Rogge et al., 2025).

Leaders also must balance productivity and well-being in a people-centric workplace. AI is intended to increase the quality of work, decision-making and innovation—not to become a surveillance tool, cause unnecessary stress or unjust judgment. The AI seems fair, explainable, interactive and friendly to the workforce and the trust increases. The human-centered trust paradigm for hybrid leadership is presented in **Figure 4.**

Figure 4. Human-Centered Trust Model for Hybrid Leadership

Figure 4 illustrates how AI-enabled companies build employee confidence in tiers. Workers must understand why and how AI affects them, therefore transparency and communication are key.

9. LEADERSHIP COMPETENCIES FOR THE HYBRID FUTURE

9.1 AI Literacy, Digital Fluency, and Evidence-Based Thinking

Basic AI knowledge is needed for hybrid leaders. Leaders don't need to be data scientists or software engineers, but they must understand AI's capabilities, risks, and uses. They will study how AI can anticipate, categorize, automate, recommend, recognize patterns, and assist decisions. They should also realize that AI system outputs depend on data quality, model design, training, and deployment settings.

Digital fluency helps CEOs assess AI technologies, ask the relevant questions, collaborate with technical teams, and decide whether to use AI. Digitally literate leaders can determine if an AI tool is suitable for solving an organizational problem, if its use has ethical implications, and if staff training is needed (Sharma, 2024).

Data and evidence-based thinking are vital for hybrid leaders. They must critically evaluate dashboards, data, predictions, risk assessments, and AI ideas. Data should influence leadership choices, not replace judgment. Leaders must verify if data is comprehensive, accurate, current, and objective. They must relate AI findings to corporate goals, market realities, employee realities, and stakeholder expectations. Hybrid leaders use evidence-based reasoning to enhance choices without blindly following algorithms.

9.2 Ethical Leadership, Emotional Intelligence, and Human Judgment

The hybrid future is about being a responsible and ethical leader. Leaders need to consider if AI in decision making is fair, explainable, inclusive, secure and in line with human values. They should be able to identify threats of algorithmic bias, violation of privacy, surveillance, discrimination, manipulation and avoidance of accountability. Ethical reasoning may be used by leaders to critically assess whether judgments made by AI are consistent with the dignity, justice, transparency and trust of the many stakeholders.

But as technical automation increases, so does the demand for emotional intelligence. But it will never replace empathy, moral judgement, connection building, conflict resolution and knowledge of the human condition. AI can process data quicker than any person can. If hybrid leaders are not afraid of losing jobs, changing roles or being more closely monitored by your company, Find and listen to concerns, including means of lowering uncertainty and set the correct expectations that will help people through transition. Emotional intelligence helps executives to address objections, create trust and maintain staff morale high during the AI deployment process (Sohn, 2025).

But there is a role for human judgment since on the one hand strategic decisions are constantly made in an environment where there is uncertainty, values involved and many repercussions reaching into the future. AI can have an advising function in offering possibilities, but it is up to the leaders to determine whether such options are within what is suitable space morally and socially responsible action. Hybrid leadership: AI and human intelligence

9.3 Change Leadership, Learning Orientation, and Collaborative Intelligence

AI adoption inevitably creates uncertainty, inertia and poses reskilling and re-deployment difficulties, therefore hybrid executives must be good change leaders. They need to assist people manage change by defining AI, training personnel, re-structuring roles fairly and building a culture of ongoing learning. Why a learning orientation: AI technologies are growing quickly, and enterprises require fresh and updated skills, procedures and governance framework.

Another key competence is collective intelligence. That is what you get when you mix human expertise, team learning and insights from AI. As a hybrid leader you need to know when to depend on AI, when to bring in people and when to fight back against what algorithmic suggestions might say. They need to enable teams to harness AI as a collaborative partner in analysis, creativity, problem-solving, innovation and decision support (Väyrynen et al., 2025).

The competency matrix in **Table 4** summarizes the key capabilities required by hybrid leaders.

Table 4. Competency Matrix for Hybrid Leaders

Competency	Meaning	Practical Application
AI literacy	Understanding AI capabilities and limits	Evaluating AI tools
Ethical reasoning	Judging fairness and harm	Reviewing AI decisions
Data interpretation	Reading AI outputs critically	Strategic decision support
Emotional intelligence	Understanding people	Managing resistance
Change leadership	Leading transformation	Reskilling and adoption
Collaborative intelligence	Combining human and AI strengths	Human-AI teamwork

Table 4 shows hybrid leader key competencies. The study demonstrates that AI-enabled firms need leaders with AI literacy, ethical reasoning, data interpretation, emotional intelligence, change leadership, and collaborative intelligence.

10. CHALLENGES AND RISKS OF HYBRID LEADERSHIP

10.1 Algorithmic Bias, Privacy Risks, and Accountability Gaps

Algorithmic prejudice is a major hybrid leadership danger. AI needs training data. Past prejudice, unequal access, or biased organizational practices can distort data, resulting in unequal results. This affects hiring, promotion, performance evaluation, customer service, credit, pricing, and resource allocation. If the previous data utilized to hire was biased, an AI recruitment tool may hurt cohorts. AI-based performance algorithms that ignore work environment, caregiving commitments, team support, or job complexity may unjustly assess individuals. Privacy and espionage are key concerns. Behavioral Analytics, Employee Monitoring, Productivity Tracking Analysis of Communication Location AIAs were used to predict performance. Over-monitoring saves time but kills trust and autonomy, creating a toxic workplace with high stress and a control obsession. Surveillance may make employees feel monitored rather than assisted (Zheng et al., 2025).

When AIs or their users cause harm, they are liable. Who's wrong? Top executives, data scientists, HR managers, line managers, suppliers, or the AI system. Hybrid leaders must establish accountability, audits, documentation, and human review.

10.2 Overdependence on AI and Workforce Inequality

So, AI will produce so called 'objective' suggestions based on flawed assumptions, faulty data or trends from the past. Hybrid leaders need to ensure AI is always a decision support tool, not the final arbitrator of choices in lieu of human judgment.

Another important concern is the displacement of employment and inequality. It can automate many kinds of mundane cognitive, administrative, analytical and customer-facing work. That creates problems for employees who fear losing their job, having their function devalued, or becoming irrelevant. There may be a digital divide between the highly skilled and the less skilled, or the digitally excluded due to lack of access to the training required. Limiting the potential for AI to certain sections within a business might lead to a divided workforce (Soni et al., 2020).

The adoption of AI might also be slowed down by a lack of skills. Employees may lack the skills to install AI systems, analyze the outcomes, secure data or challenge biased suggestions. Hybrid leaders must respond by reskilling, transparent communication, equitable job redesign and democratized access to AI learning.

10.3 Cultural Resistance and Strategic Responses

Employees, middle management, unions and departments may express cultural opposition. Employees push back against AI for a few reasons: fear, distrust, or areas where employees haven't been taught sufficiently on AI or think monitoring is on its way. Middle managers can worry about losing authority to AI cooperation if it takes decision making away from them. The implementation might be changing processes they have grown to know or making their tasks more complicated. Departments can be opposed to AI in organizations. Unions can talk about the implications of IT projects, from job security and justice to monitoring and workers' rights.

To manage these dangers, hybrid leaders will need to rule with ethics, garner involvement and communication, and establish trust. Employees need to understand why AI is being utilized, how it will be employed, what information will be collected, and how human supervision of the latter process will be assured. **Table 5** Key difficulties and strategic answers of cooperative hybrid leadership (Stilgoe et al., 2013). Hybrid leadership issues are specific types of socio-technical and not just technology issues. Tools, platforms and automation led firms over trust, culture, employee involvement, skills acquisition and ethics can fail in AI adoption. Abstract Studies of human-automation interaction suggest that operators can resist automated systems when they do not understand how judgments are made, fear monitoring by automation, or believe that impersonal data systems can replace human judgment. Hybrid executives must balance both sides of the ledger: the technical execution of AI and the psychological and cultural acceptance or rejection of it by people.

The only strategic way to withstand these risks is by ensuring communication, enabling employee involvement, continuous training and proving accountability. Leaders need to be transparent about their reasons for using AI, the decisions it will help make, the data it will use, who will see the results, and how workers will be able to challenge or appeal decisions made with the help of AI. It reduces uncertainty and helps in human people see AI more of a collaborator than an adversary. So hybrid leadership needs trust-building methods relating to justice in AI through learning, inclusivity and human dignity.

Table 5. Challenges and Strategic Responses in Hybrid Leadership

Challenge	Risk	Strategic Response
Algorithmic bias	Unfair decisions	Bias audit and diverse data
Overdependence on AI	Weak human judgment	Human-in-the-loop review
Workforce anxiety	Resistance and low morale	Transparent communication
Skill gaps	Unequal AI adoption	Reskilling programs
Surveillance concerns	Loss of trust	Ethical data governance
Accountability gaps	Legal and reputational risk	Clear responsibility framework

Table 5 lists hybrid leadership's main difficulties and strategies. Unmanaged risks include algorithmic bias, overdependence on AI, workforce worry, skill shortages, surveillance concerns, and accountability gaps can damage trust and performance.

11. INTEGRATED STRATEGIC FRAMEWORK FOR HYBRID LEADERSHIP

11.1 Need and Core Pillars of the Framework

AI-complex leadership requires an integrated framework. AI affects decision-making, job design, employee learning, customer service, chatbots, governance, risk management, and organizational competitiveness. Therefore, hybrid executives should not consider AI an IT project. They benefit more from thinking about AI as a strategic system that affects people, processes, culture, ethics, and long-term value.

This system has five pillars. Human–AI collaboration comes first. Leaders must audit, monitor, and analyze AI systems that affect employment, progression, performance evaluations, customer access, or strategic decisions (responsible practices by smart leaders).

The third pillar is workforce transformation. AI will change job duties and career paths. Leaders should promote reskilling, job redesign, learning culture, and employee engagement. This pillar guarantees that staff are equipped to work with smart technologies during the AI transformation.

Fourth, strategic value creation. AI must boost productivity, innovation, decision quality, customer value, and competitiveness. Hybrid leaders must relate AI deployment to company goals, not as a fashion statement or cost-cutting exercise.

Fifth, human-centered culture and trust. This concerns employee communication, psychological safety, inclusion, dignity, and voice. Fair, helpful, explainable, and well-regulated AI is more likely to be accepted by employees (Emaminejad & Akhavian, 2022).

11.2 Strategic Outcomes of Hybrid Leadership

Hybrid leadership may create several strategic results as the five pillars operate effectively together. The first advantage is better judgments since leaders will be able to supplement AI-generated insights with human judgement, experience and ethical judgment. The second outcome is an increase in trust from workers and stakeholders who see the usage of AI and the threats to the organization. Third, the technological implementation involves responsible AI adoption that is fair, transparent, private, and accountable (Panwar et al., 2024).

Another ancillary benefit of hybrid leadership is employee empowerment. Training helps people perceive AI as a support to their work, not to replace it, and if they are involved in adopting an AI tool and understand how their occupations will change methods. The framework also boosts innovation capability, as human creativity is often boosted by AI-supported analytics, ideation and market knowledge. Another important discovery with respect to sustained productivity in companies is that AI will help people to leave regular work behind and focus on tasks of higher value. Lastly, the framework strengthens organizational resilience by facilitating company adaptability to technology innovation, market unpredictability and change in personnel (Hilbert et al., 2024).

11.3 Practical Application of the Framework

Potential additional curriculum areas are AI literacy and ethical reasoning, data interpretation, change management and human centered leadership. All themes that should be included by any leadership development course for managers. AI governance committees should assess high-risk AI systems for accountability everywhere. Training is needed to sharpen skills for the labor force—and this upskilling and continuing education will take them to acceptable employment backed by AI. Ethical audits should include a spectrum of ethical basics such as bias, privacy, explainability, and influence on stakeholders. The route to AI is a tactical one by aligning projected investments in AI with labor and organizational demands and with responsible governance. **Figure 5**: Integrated strategy framework of hybrid leadership (Nguyen, 2024). The integrated strategy structure should be built in a sequential way. The AI readiness diagnostic prompts executives to assess the company's goals and strategy, technical landscape, workforce capabilities, data quality issues, ethical risks, and leadership skills. The second level, strategic alignment, connects enterprise-wide use of AI to overarching corporate objectives such as decision quality, operational efficiency, innovation and product development cadence, customer value proposition uplift, and advancement of employee capabilities with risk reduction. The third stage of governance design is then followed by leaders creating accountability frameworks, ethical review methods, privacy measures, human supervision rules and auditing procedures for AI systems.

Fourth, pilot testing. Hybrid executives should experiment with AI technologies in limited environments to identify and fix problems before rolling them out across the enterprise at large. Scout testing allows leaders to assess technical soundness, employee experience, fairness, explainability and side effects. Level five: managers and workers get AI literacy, knowledge of data sources, responsible use of data, and how to critique the results from whatever flavor of AI processed the data. Step 6: Scale and Integrate AI Technologies into Corporate Strategy When there will be an opportunity for the governance and workforce preparation to develop.Rendering compound vision of high-impact data. Leaders are continuously and formally assessing whether AI is adding to performance or taking away from performance at this point, without sacrificing fairness, trust, autonomy, privacy or employee wellness.

Utilize indicators to assess the framework's effectiveness. These are: proportion of workforce trained on AI literacy impact rating of human-reviewed high-impact AI systems bias and privacy audits employee trust scores psychological safety scores reskilling completion rates appeal resolution time explainability documentation reduction in grievances associated with AI decisions at the workplace decision quality or productivity improvements. The indicators point to hybrid leadership as a tangible management approach that can be implemented, evaluated and improved.

Figure 5. Integrated Strategic Framework for Hybrid Leadership

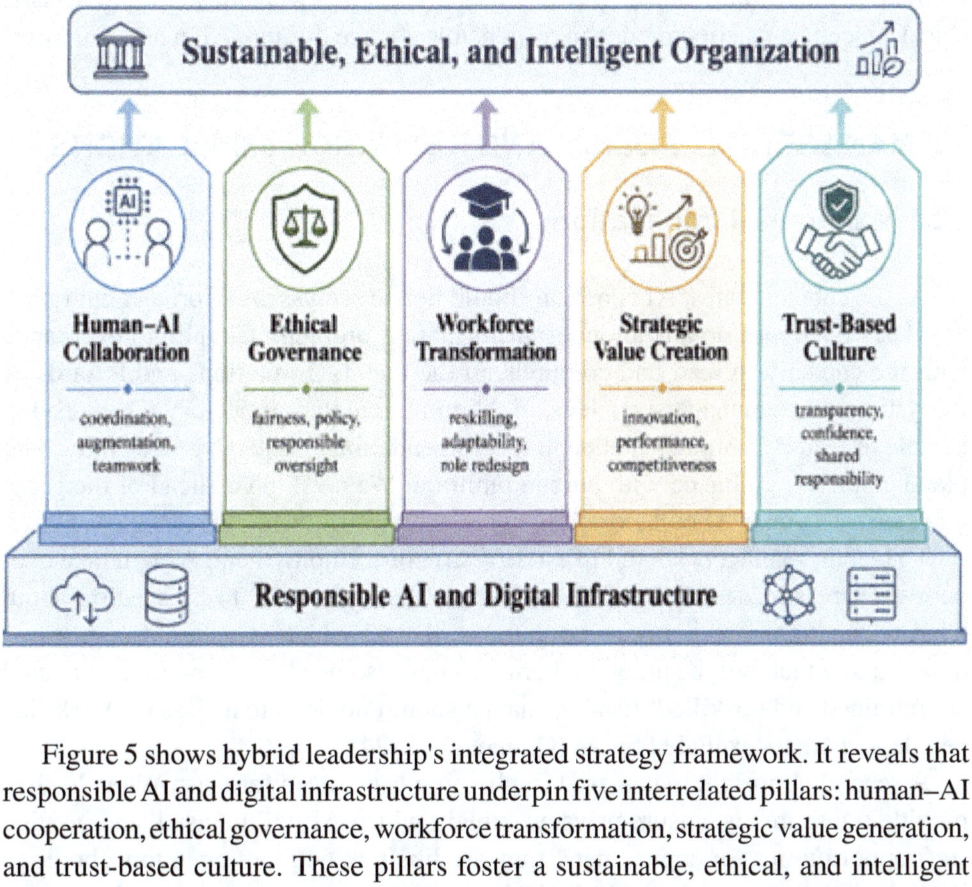

Figure 5 shows hybrid leadership's integrated strategy framework. It reveals that responsible AI and digital infrastructure underpin five interrelated pillars: human–AI cooperation, ethical governance, workforce transformation, strategic value generation, and trust-based culture. These pillars foster a sustainable, ethical, and intelligent company. Apply the combined strategy framework in stages. Companies start by assessing where they sit on the spectrum of AI readiness across digital infrastructure, data quality, leadership, workforce readiness and exposure to ethical risks. Step two, governance design; where accountability is set by management, human oversight (human in the loop), risk classification (risks to life and limb vs. mundane risks), data privacy and rules for employee participation. The third step is to pilot AI technologies (or initiatives) in limited parts of the organization before larger-scale deployment. Through pilot initiatives, executives identified technology problems, staffing issues across the organization, bias risks and workflow disruptions.

Step 4 is workforce transformation – reskilling and redesigning jobs, AI literacy training and change management strategies to reduce resistance. Fifth stage – human responsibility is still maintained. Human-AI integration is understood as the incorporation of AI technologies in the decision-making process in many aspects of the company, including in operations and customer service (e.g. chatbots), in human resource management and in strategic concept stages. Final step: ongoing monitoring & improvement At this level, leaders measure AI performance, fairness, productivity and ethics, and employee trust in AI. This is what makes hybrid leadership a concept and action model on responsible change through AI in organizations.

12. MANAGERIAL, POLICY, AND RESEARCH IMPLICATIONS

12.1 Managerial Implications

As the chapter states, AI adoption should not be seen as an IT project but rather as a leadership and organizational transformation problem. Coupling governance with the capacity to read and comprehend the talents, limitations and hazards of AI systems takes managers to a level of AI number in their trajectory. They need to be able to read AI outputs, challenge recommendations pushed by algorithms, and blend empirical guidance with human intuition. We need to be ahead of the game – leaders of human-AI collaboration, not consumers of technology.

To be fair, managers should likewise restructure employment. AI will take over duties, processes, decision rights and skills. Managers need to be specific about what occupations are going to be automated, and which will be AI-augmented duties, and which will be uniquely human. They also need to ensure that personnel are retrained and upskilled. Ideally, change should not lead to a class of AI-skilled people and others excluded by AI (Qian et al., 2024).

A second important managerial implication is the need for trust. When leaders provide transparency, ensure privacy, explain which AI will be used, and provide staff opportunities for engagement, they are likely to be more open to technology itself. Establish mechanisms to obtain feedback from employees and train them to critically evaluate the output of AI. Simultaneously, ban the use of AI for needless monitoring or performance assessments. Hence, transparency, psychological safety, worker empowerment and ethical duty form successful hybrid leadership.

12.2 Policy Implications

In addition to this, the chapter also has convoluted but evident policy ramifications. Organizations and legislators should create standards for openness in AI, workplace privacy, fairness and reskilling, human oversight (for example with an individual person making a key judgement call), and responsible automation. There should be explicit governance rules prohibiting using AI systems in recruiting, promotion, employee monitoring, performance evaluation, credit decisions, pricing and consumer access. These standards must include bias audits, explanation and expectations regarding accountability structures and methods for appealing or reviewing processes.

AI rules in the working environment are required to protect the rights of the employees and to avoid exploitation or misuse of the personal and behavioral data. A second issue for enterprises is to design responsible automation rules that ensure AI as an assistive tool that enhances productivity without sacrificing human dignity, labor stability, and inclusivity. Policymakers might also promote national and sectoral reskilling initiatives to help people adjust to AI-powered workplaces (Ofosu-Ampong, 2024).

12.3 Research Implications

We may examine larger areas of hybrid leadership in the domain of organizational leadership research across several business sectors such as healthcare, education, banking, manufacturing, tourism, public administration and knowledge-based industry. It offers academics opportunities to explore variations in hybrid leadership models across organizational size, industry type, cultural context and technology development. However, there are few empirical research on whether employees trust AI systems in terms of openness, fairness, privacy and perceived job security.

Future study might cover competencies needed for AI management – AI literacy, ethical judgment, data analytics insight, emotional intelligence competency, flexibility as a leader towards change and collective intelligence. The next big study topic: AI adoption and its influence in workplace well-being. It is up to scholars to examine if AI improves job quality, reduces routine duties, and enables learning, or whether it plays a role in stress-inducing instability and inequality of task monitoring. These are the research entrance points – where to make hybrid leadership more responsible and human-centered (Abdelhalim et al., 2024). The implementation of hybrid leadership requires a structured sequence rather than isolated AI adoption. Organizations should first assess AI readiness, identify ethical and workforce risks, establish governance mechanisms, test AI tools through pilot programs, reskill employees, and then scale human–AI collaboration through continuous monitoring. This sequential logic is summarized in Figure 6. Hybrid leadership: Institutions with clear frameworks of AI governance to steer the appropriate use of intelligent technologies. Major tech companies are working to develop and deploy AI systems and are articulating their positions on responsible AI principles such as justice, reliability, privacy, fairness, transparency and accountability. Adopting AI is more than just technology and here are a few projects to prove that. There's a need for a governance framework, a mechanism for internal review and issues of ethics and accountability for leadership." These examples of hybrid leadership show how big AI manifests itself in smaller, everyday organizational decisions – that is, the decision of which AI technologies get built, tested, monitored, explained and used by humans.

Such formalised leadership helps to bolster the strategic and moral claims of hybrid leadership. Leadership in AI-led enterprises is about delivering trust, fairness and human dignity while aligning the intent of an AI-enabled system with higher order business purpose. Responsible AI projects show that to implement AI, senior executives, technical experts, legal teams, HR managers, and even ethical committees and workers must collaborate. This practical demonstrates the chapter's core argument that the transformation of AI requires hybrid leadership because it is transformational across Leadership, Governance and Workforce.

Figure 6. Hybrid Leadership Transformation Cycle

Figure 6 shows hybrid leadership's ongoing evolution. It suggests starting with AI awareness and strategic alignment before establishing human–AI collaboration, ethical governance, workforce reskilling, and trust-building mechanisms.

13. CONCLUSION

The hybrid leader is another form of leadership road ahead for an AI-enabled firm. As artificial intelligence becomes more deeply embedded in decision-making, human capital management, operations, customer and after-sales experience, innovation and strategic planning, leadership will need to move beyond the conventional authority of managers or the adoption of technology. The future of leadership will be decided by where human judgment, ethics and trust interact with AI assisted intellect. That implies that hybrid leaders then need to reconcile human and intelligent-machine capabilities, while ensuring that organizational action remains fair, responsible, transparent and most crucially human-centered.

In this chapter, I argue that human–AI collaboration is not only a question of technological organization, but rather a dimension of strategic managerial skill. AI may enhance decision making, increase forecasting, make operations more effective, accelerate innovation processes, provide greater value for the customer and improve organizational responsiveness. But these benefits will only be realized if leaders recognize the limitations and hazards of AI. Since the Days of AI, badly managed and irresponsible AI has every power of weakening trust to hurting organizational culture from algorithmic bias, privacy intrusion, espionage, accountability gaps between human and machine, runaway automation, the list is infinite.

To accomplish that, relatable leaders in hybrids will have to weigh AI performance against Dignity, Justice, Accountability and Inclusion in their businesses. This can only be done through AI literacy, ethical reasoning, data interpretation, emotional intelligence and leading change and fundamental humanity. We need to build robust governance structures and processes, which have been put in place, to be re-skilled, comprehensive disclosure on the demand for AI use and its risks, the inclusion of workers in design and implementation where possible and human oversight of any decisions supported by AI.

The chapter finishes by arguing that this strategic management of human-AI collaboration is about more than simply the pursuit of sustainable transformation of work but also how to drive digital competitiveness in an ethical way. The companies that invest in hybrid leadership capabilities will be best placed to use AI as an engine of innovation, productivity and resilience. But the most successful AI-enabled organizations will be those that blend technology intelligence with human insight, ethical governance and trust-based leadership, not automation.

AI DISCLOSURE STATEMENT

The authors declare that no artificial intelligence tools were used in the preparation, drafting, analysis, interpretation, or finalization of this chapter. The work is entirely based on the authors' own scholarly understanding, review of literature, and academic writing.

REFERENCES

Abdelhalim, E., Anazodo, K. S., Gali, N., & Robson, K. (2024). A framework of diversity, equity, and inclusion safeguards for chatbots. *Business Horizons*, *67*(5), 487–498. DOI: 10.1016/j.bushor.2024.03.003

Akter, S., McCarthy, G., Sajib, S., Michael, K., Dwivedi, Y. K., D'Ambra, J., & Shen, K. N. (2021). Algorithmic bias in data-driven innovation in the age of AI. *International Journal of Information Management*, *60*, 102387. DOI: 10.1016/j.ijinfomgt.2021.102387

Akter, S., Sultana, S., Mariani, M., Wamba, S. F., Spanaki, K., & Dwivedi, Y. K. (2023). Advancing algorithmic bias management capabilities in AI-driven marketing analytics research. *Industrial Marketing Management*, *114*, 243–261. DOI: 10.1016/j.indmarman.2023.08.013

Aulia, S. R., & Lin, W.-S. (2025). *Embracing the digital shift: Leveraging AI to foster employee well-being and engagement in remote workplace settings in the Asia Pacific region*. Asia Pacific Management Review., DOI: 10.1016/j.apmrv.2024.12.003

Babina, T., Fedyk, A., He, A., & Hodson, J. (2024). Artificial intelligence, firm growth, and product innovation. *Journal of Financial Economics*, *151*, 103745. DOI: 10.1016/j.jfineco.2023.103745

Bankins, S., Hu, X., & Yuan, Y. (2024). Artificial intelligence, workers, and future of work skills. *Current Opinion in Psychology*, *58*, 101828. DOI: 10.1016/j.copsyc.2024.101828 PMID: 38964241

Benlian, A., & Pinski, M. (2025). The AI literacy development canvas: Assessing and building AI literacy in organizations. *Business Horizons*. Advance online publication. DOI: 10.1016/j.bushor.2025.10.001

Chuang, Y.-T., Chiang, H.-L., & Lin, A.-P. (2025). Insights from the Job Demands–Resources Model: AI's dual impact on employees' work and life well-being. *International Journal of Information Management*, *83*, 102887. DOI: 10.1016/j.ijinfomgt.2025.102887

Daly, S. J., Hearn, G., & Papageorgiou, K. (2025). Sensemaking with AI: How trust influences human–AI collaboration in health and creative industries. *Social Sciences & Humanities Open*, *11*, 101346. DOI: 10.1016/j.ssaho.2025.101346

Dhaigude, A. S., & Kamath, G. B. (2025). Mapping responsible artificial intelligence in business and management: Trends, influence, and emerging research directions. *Journal of Open Innovation*, *11*(4), 100640. DOI: 10.1016/j.joitmc.2025.100640

Duan, Y., Edwards, J. S., & Dwivedi, Y. K. (2019). Artificial intelligence for decision making in the era of big data: Evolution, challenges and research agenda. *International Journal of Information Management, 48*, 63–71. DOI: 10.1016/j.ijinfomgt.2019.01.021

Dwivedi, Y. K., Hughes, L., Ismagilova, E., Aarts, G., Coombs, C., Crick, T., Duan, Y., Dwivedi, R., Edwards, J., Eirug, A., Galanos, V., Ilavarasan, P. V., Janssen, M., Jones, P., Kar, A. K., Kizgin, H., Kronemann, B., Lal, B., Lucini, B., & Williams, M. D. (2021). Artificial intelligence (AI): Multidisciplinary perspectives on emerging challenges, opportunities, and agenda for research, practice and policy. *International Journal of Information Management, 57*, 101994. DOI: 10.1016/j.ijinfomgt.2019.08.002

Emaminejad, N., & Akhavian, R. (2022). Trustworthy AI and robotics: Implications for the AEC industry. *Automation in Construction, 139*, 104298. DOI: 10.1016/j.autcon.2022.104298

Hai, S., Long, T., Honora, A., Japutra, A., & Guo, T. (2025). The dark side of employee-generative AI collaboration in the workplace: An investigation on work alienation and employee expediency. *International Journal of Information Management, 83*, 102905. DOI: 10.1016/j.ijinfomgt.2025.102905

Heyder, T., Passlack, N., & Posegga, O. (2023). Ethical management of human–AI interaction: Theory development review. *The Journal of Strategic Information Systems, 32*(3), 101772. DOI: 10.1016/j.jsis.2023.101772

Hilbert, M., Thakur, A., Flores, P. M., Zhang, X., Bhan, J. Y., Bernhard, P., & Ji, F. (2024). 8–10% of algorithmic recommendations are "bad", but… an exploratory risk–utility meta-analysis and its regulatory implications. *International Journal of Information Management, 75*, 102743. DOI: 10.1016/j.ijinfomgt.2023.102743

Holmström, J., & Carroll, N. (2025). How organizations can innovate with generative AI. *Business Horizons, 68*(5), 559–573. DOI: 10.1016/j.bushor.2024.02.010

Jarrahi, M. H. (2018). Artificial intelligence and the future of work: Human–AI symbiosis in organizational decision making. *Business Horizons, 61*(4), 577–586. DOI: 10.1016/j.bushor.2018.03.007

Jarrahi, M. H., Askay, D., Eshraghi, A., & Smith, P. (2023). Artificial intelligence and knowledge management: A partnership between human and AI. *Business Horizons, 66*(1), 87–99. DOI: 10.1016/j.bushor.2022.03.002

Khogali, H. O., & Mekid, S. (2023). The blended future of automation and AI: Examining some long-term societal and ethical impact features. *Technology in Society, 73*, 102232. DOI: 10.1016/j.techsoc.2023.102232

Kulkov, I. (2021). The role of artificial intelligence in business transformation: A case of pharmaceutical companies. *Technology in Society, 66*, 101629. DOI: 10.1016/j.techsoc.2021.101629

Kumar, V., Ashraf, A. R., & Nadeem, W. (2024). AI-powered marketing: What, where, and how? *International Journal of Information Management, 77*, 102783. DOI: 10.1016/j.ijinfomgt.2024.102783

Lindner, T., Puck, J., & Puhr, H. (2025). Artificial intelligence in international business: IB theory under augmented decision-making. *Journal of World Business, 60*(6), 101676. DOI: 10.1016/j.jwb.2025.101676

Mariani, M., & Dwivedi, Y. K. (2024). Generative artificial intelligence in innovation management: A preview of future research developments. *Journal of Business Research, 175*, 114542. DOI: 10.1016/j.jbusres.2024.114542

Mishra, S. S., Panwar, D., Chouhan, R. P. S., & Shanmugapriya, V. (2024). The impact of AI on the widespread use of EV's: A review. In 2024 2nd International Conference on Advancements and Key Challenges in Green Energy and Computing (AKGEC) (pp. 1–6). IEEE. DOI: 10.1109/AKGEC62572.2024.10868146

Nguyen, J. K. (2024). Human bias in AI models? Anchoring effects and mitigation strategies in large language models. *Journal of Behavioral and Experimental Finance, 43*, 100971. DOI: 10.1016/j.jbef.2024.100971

Ofosu-Ampong, K. (2024). Artificial intelligence research: A review on dominant themes, methods, frameworks and future research directions. *Telematics and Informatics Reports, 14*, 100127. DOI: 10.1016/j.teler.2024.100127

Pan, Z., Moore, O. A., Papadimitriou, A., & Zhu, J. (2025). AI literacy and trust: A multi-method study of human-GAI team collaboration. *Computers in Human Behavior: Artificial Humans, 3*, 100162. DOI: 10.1016/j.chbah.2025.100162

Panwar, D., Mishra, S. S., Kumar, A., & Soni, A. (2024). A review of machine learning in photovoltaic system fabrication and implementation. In 2024 7th International Conference on Contemporary Computing and Informatics (IC3I) (pp. 754–759). IEEE. DOI: 10.1109/IC3I61595.2024.10828669

Papagiannidis, E., Mikalef, P., & Conboy, K. (2025). Responsible artificial intelligence governance: A review and research framework. *The Journal of Strategic Information Systems, 34*(1), 101885. DOI: 10.1016/j.jsis.2024.101885

Qian, Y., Jha, K., & Li, Y. (2024). Societal impacts of artificial intelligence: Ethical, legal, and governance issues. *Journal of Responsible Technology*, *17*, 100082. DOI: 10.1016/j.jrt.2024.100082

Robertson, J., Ferreira, C., Botha, E., & Oosthuizen, K. (2024). Game changers: A generative AI prompt protocol to enhance human–AI knowledge co-construction. *Business Horizons*, *67*(6), 683–697. DOI: 10.1016/j.bushor.2024.04.008

Rodgers, W., Murray, J. M., Stefanidis, A., Degbey, W. Y., & Tarba, S. Y. (2023). An artificial intelligence algorithmic approach to ethical decision-making in human resource management processes. *Human Resource Management Review*, *33*(1), 100925. DOI: 10.1016/j.hrmr.2022.100925

Rogge, N. D., Lamovšek, A., & Batistič, S. (2025). AI meets IA: A typology of generative-AI-supported work through individual ambidexterity. *Business Horizons*. Advance online publication. DOI: 10.1016/j.bushor.2025.06.006

Sarvate, D., Mishra, S. S., Shanmugapriya, V., & Panwar, D. (2025). Integrating blockchain and federated learning for enhanced security and privacy in smart cities. In Singh, K. K., Singh, A., & Mahesh, T. R. (Eds.), *Integration of federated learning and blockchain for smart cities*. Wiley., DOI: 10.1002/9781394167760.ch10

Sharma, S. (2024). Benefits or concerns of AI: A multistakeholder responsibility. *Futures*, *157*, 103328. DOI: 10.1016/j.futures.2024.103328

Singh, K. S., Shanmugapriya, V., Mishra, S. S., & Singh, M. (2026). Artificial intelligence-driven flow optimization for enhanced efficiency in renewable energy systems. In Awasthi, M. K., & Gupta, R. (Eds.), *Artificial intelligence and computational modeling in heat transfer and fluid dynamics*. Wiley., DOI: 10.1002/9781394433605.ch10

Sohn, S. M. (2025). Effortlessness as the measurement of the impact of artificial intelligence (AI) adoption and innovation: Towards the theory of relative AI. *Technology in Society*, *81*, 102962. DOI: 10.1016/j.techsoc.2025.102962

Soni, N., Sharma, E. K., Singh, N., & Kapoor, A. (2020). Artificial intelligence in business: From research and innovation to market deployment. *Procedia Computer Science*, *167*, 2200–2210. DOI: 10.1016/j.procs.2020.03.272

Stahl, B. C. (2022). Responsible innovation ecosystems: Ethical implications of the application of the ecosystem concept to artificial intelligence. *International Journal of Information Management*, *62*, 102441. DOI: 10.1016/j.ijinfomgt.2021.102441

Stilgoe, J., Owen, R., & Macnaghten, P. (2013). Developing a framework for responsible innovation. *Research Policy, 42*(9), 1568–1580. DOI: 10.1016/j.respol.2013.05.008

Sundberg, L., & Holmström, J. (2023). Democratizing artificial intelligence: How no-code AI can leverage machine learning operations. *Business Horizons*, *66*(6), 777–788. DOI: 10.1016/j.bushor.2023.04.003

Sutar, D., Metri, R. A., Naik, R., Mishra, S., Thakkar, J., & Kolhe, M. (2026). Energy-efficient automation of industrial surface pre-treatment processes using PLC and SCADA. In Proceedings of the Second International Conference on New Power System and Power Electronics (NPSPE 2025) (Vol. 14129, Article 141292C). SPIE. https://doi.org/DOI: 10.1117/12.3110247

Väyrynen, K., Holmström, J., Sundberg, L., Hietala, H., & Lanamäki, A. (2025). Guardrails, not barriers: Navigating AI Act readiness. *Business Horizons*. Advance online publication. DOI: 10.1016/j.bushor.2025.08.002

Zheng, J., Zhang, J. Z., Kamal, M. M., Liang, X., & Alzeiby, E. A. (2025). Unpacking human–AI interaction: Exploring unintended consequences on employee well-being in entrepreneurial firms through an in-depth analysis. *Journal of Business Research*, *196*, 115406. DOI: 10.1016/j.jbusres.2025.115406

Zirar, A., Ali, S. I., & Islam, N. (2023). Worker and workplace artificial intelligence (AI) coexistence: Emerging themes and research agenda. *Technovation*, *124*, 102747. DOI: 10.1016/j.technovation.2023.102747

Chapter 9
Transforming Education With Autonomous and Adaptive Agentic AI Systems

N. Raghu
http://orcid.org/0000-0002-2091-8922
Jain (Deemed to be) University, India

B. Kiran
http://orcid.org/0000-0002-6640-6703
JSS Academy of Technical Education, India

M. Balamurugan
http://orcid.org/0000-0001-9737-2035
Dayananda Sagar College of Engineering, India

T. G. KeshavaMurthy
http://orcid.org/0009-0006-4820-758X
Sri Siddhartha Academy of Higher Education, India

T. P. Poorvika
BGS Institute of Technology, Adichunchanagiri University, India

Matluba Yakubova Yakubova
Mamun University, Uzbekistan

Chandrashekhar Badachi
Ramaiah Institute of Technology, India

V. N. Trupti
http://orcid.org/0000-0002-3414-100X
Jain (Deemed to be) University, India

S. Druva Kumar
http://orcid.org/0000-0001-5157-6294
Dayananda Sagar College of Engineering, India

ABSTRACT

The research evaluates how effective agentic AI tutoring systems with their customized and adaptive teaching methods function to enhance student academic performance. The researchers used experimental research methods which included testing Deep Reinforcement Learning, Multi-Agent Systems, Hybrid models, Traditional Intelligent

DOI: 10.4018/979-8-2600-0116-5.ch009

Tutoring Systems, and a Control group. The researchers conducted their analysis by examining data which included pre- and post-test results along with engagement logs and knowledge tracing accuracy data. AI-driven methods lead to better results than traditional methods, which deep reinforcement learning technology produces the most effective learning gains of 54% together with multi-agent systems at 49% and hybrid models at 45% while control group participants showed only 16% advancement. Knowledge tracing models reached 98% predictive accuracy which confirmed that all sessions showed strong performance growth. The researchers discovered that students who spent more time on their studies achieved better academic results.

1. INTRODUCTION

Artificial Intelligence (AI) functions as a disruptive technology for educational systems just as it operates in all other industries. AI technology establishes new learning methods through personalized learning platforms and intelligent grading systems which teachers can use to enhance their teaching methods and students can use to improve their learning outcomes. The traditional classroom model which depended on teachers as the exclusive knowledge source and required all students to learn at a uniform speed has developed into more flexible student-centered environments which support active learning (Kostopoulos et al., 2025). AI technology enables real-time analysis of student performance and progress tracking, while it detects their academic challenges, which allows educators to deliver instant support and precise feedback and adjust their teaching methods according to student requirements. AI technology handles administrative tasks by automating processes which include grading and tracking attendance and developing curriculum plans, thereby creating additional time for teachers to concentrate on imaginative teaching approaches and student interaction (Nagasubramanian, 2026). AI technology empowers students to learn online and through hybrid programs which enables educational institutions to reach students around the world. Students can now explore and experiment through virtual simulations and intelligent tutoring systems and interactive learning tools which enable them to experience educational content in ways that did not exist before. AI functions as a vital partner in education because it actively assists students and educators to reach their educational goals through personalized learning and inclusive teaching and adaptive educational experiences (Bey, 2026).

Figure 1. Transformation of education through artificial intelligence

1.1 Emergence of Agentic AI and Intelligent Agents

Agentic AI extends beyond basic AI which functions as a tool that executes commands. Agentic AI describes systems which possess the ability to function without human input while they build their own knowledge base to achieve specific objectives. Agentic AI functions as an educational tool which enables teachers to track student progress while developing new techniques to solve upcoming difficulties throughout the instructional period (Ashwani, 2025). The intelligent tutoring system provides answers while it helps students learn by showing which parts they need to improve their knowledge and providing them with tailored hints and different difficulty levels and individualized learning paths (Ravikumar et al., 2025). These systems possess reasoning capabilities and decision-making skills and self-monitoring abilities which let them interact with learners through human-like behavior (Raman et al., 2026). The digital learning environment enables students to interact with other students through communication and collaboration and negotiation activities which makes them active participants in academic work who use digital tools for learning as shown in table 1.

Table 1. Evolution from Adaptive to Agentic AI.

Level	System Characteristic	Traditional Model	Agentic Model
Level 1	Decision Control	Pre-programmed rules	Autonomous goal selection
Level 2	Temporal Reasoning	Session-based reaction	Cross-session optimization
Level 3	Student Modeling	Fixed learner profiles	Continuously evolving learner states
Level 4	Pedagogical Action	Content selection	Strategy creation
Level 5	Equity Handling	Supportive add-ons	Embedded inclusive framework
Level 6	Response Generation	Static templates	Generative contextual explanations

Advanced machine learning algorithms together with natural language processing and reinforcement learning work together to create agentic AI systems which demonstrate cognitive behaviors (Ahmed et al., 2025). The system uses student performance patterns and engagement data together with their learning preferences to create customized learning paths which students can follow at their own pace. The combination of these two traits which allow for independent operation and intelligent processing makes agentic AI different from regular educational technology because it functions as a critical factor that drives educational change in modern times (Kishor et al., 2025).

1.2 Significance of Autonomous, Adaptive, and Personalized Learning

The process of learning develops as a personal path which differs for each student because they possess different abilities and obstacles and ways of learning and learning speeds. The design of traditional classrooms which present identical lessons to all students at once fails to address individual student needs, which results in students experiencing detachment from their studies and lack of support (Tran et al., 2026). The educational system now offers autonomous and personalized learning because it builds custom educational pathways which match the needs of each student. Smart systems operate through three main functions by making content harder, giving students specific resources, and delivering feedback that matches their learning performance at that moment (Yu, 2026).

Students face difficulties with math concepts, an AI tutor provides them additional examples and interactive exercises and new explanations until they reach complete understanding of the concept. Personalized learning helps students become active participants in their education process because they create personal educational goals and monitor their advancement which results in higher educational commitment (Meti, 2026). The research demonstrates that these methods enhance academic performance while enabling teachers to concentrate on developing student critical thinking and creative abilities through non-repetitive teaching methods (Islamutdinov et al., 2025). The educational systems create classrooms which include all students by delivering specific assistance to students who have different learning needs and disabilities and language difficulties. The implementation of autonomous AI-driven learning systems creates educational pathways which guarantee equal access to support for every student who requires assistance to achieve success (Ammer & Mamadjanova, 2025). The educational systems create an environment which allows students to learn at their own pace because they can choose their study times without having to follow particular schedules or classroom rhythms. Students have the ability to repeat established subjects while they can study new topics and advance their studies when they reach their learning milestones. The flexible learning approach enables students to remember information more effectively while it readies them for a professional environment which requires ongoing educational development (Ghaleb & Sattarov, 2025).

This chapter investigates the educational sector through its analysis of the latest agentic AI developments and the existing challenges of implementing intelligent agents. The research study examines how adaptive and personalized learning systems are changing educational methods through their implementation of advanced teaching techniques while facing challenges which hinder their complete integration.

1.3 Concept of Agency in Artificial Intelligence

In everyday language, "agency" is the ability to act, choose, and affect events. In the domain of Artificial Intelligence, agency is the capacity to empower machines to choose, act, and respond to dynamic changes in their environment. Agentic AI is different from classic AI systems, which are merely reactive (Muthuswamy & Absamatov, 2025). Instead, agentic AI is proactive and is characterized by reasoning and self-governed action in an environment.

The concept of agency in AI is inspired by human cognition and behavior: agentic AIs are capable of operating semi-independently while collaborating with human users. For instance, in an educational context an agentic AI can perceive that a learner is not grasping a topic, make an intervention based on its goal of facilitating learning, and adjust the difficulty or style of instruction without direct human input. Agency in AI involves perception, interpretation, goal-setting, and decision-making to select actions. Agency also involves adaptability and learning: agentic systems that continuously observe outcomes and adjust actions can improve over time (Hamid & Shodiyev, 2025). In educational settings this capacity is important, as learning paths are highly individualized and dynamic. On a higher level, agency is about empowering AI from a passive tool to an active participant in the learning process.

1.3.1 Intelligent Agents: Definitions, Types, and Characteristics

The intelligent agent operates as a computer system which detects its surroundings while it processes information to make decisions that lead to particular outcomes. Intelligent agents in education use their capabilities to assist learning processes by tailoring their support and delivering assessment results and enabling students to learn new information (Ravikumar et al., 2025). Intelligent agents can be classified into several types:

1. Reactive Agents: These agents respond directly to environmental stimuli without internal modeling. The system demonstrates reactive behavior through its ability to detect false responses and provide immediate assistance.
2. Deliberative Agents: These agents use their internal environment model to create plans which they execute through decision-making processes. An intelligent tutoring system that plans a multi-step learning path is deliberative.
3. Hybrid Agents: These systems combine both reactive and deliberate functions by delivering immediate responses while they conduct extended strategic development.
4. Collaborative Agents: These agents work with humans or other agents, supporting teamwork and social learning. The virtual teaching assistants in group projects and AI systems which assist peer collaboration represent two examples.

1.3.2 Collaborative Multi-Agent Learning Systems

The field of agentic AI has reached its most advanced stage through the development of collaborative multi-agent learning systems. The system includes multiple intelligent agents who work together with human learners to create an environment for effective teamwork and knowledge sharing and problem-solving activities. In a collaborative learning scenario, each agent may have specialized expertise, monitor group dynamics, and support balanced participation among students (Ravikumar et al., 2025). A virtual science lab operates with one agent who leads the experiment design process while another agent ensures laboratory safety and a third agent observes how students work together and participate in class (Ravikumar et al., 2025). Multi-agent systems create social learning environments which help students think critically while providing necessary support to their particular needs in group settings and their individual learning processes (Aarthi et al., 2025). The educational system demonstrates how agentic AI technology enables both personalized learning experiences and the development of essential real-world collaborative skills which students need to succeed in modern learning environments.

1.4 Pedagogical Theories Supporting Agentic AI

The educational system uses agentic AI systems based on existing educational theories which were developed before. The understanding of these theories enables the development of AI programs which improve human learning efficiency as shown in figure 2.

1. Constructivism: The learning theory developed by Jean Piaget states that students create their own understanding through active learning and practical experiences. Agentic AI supports constructivist learning through interactive learning spaces which enable students to discover new information and solve challenges while getting instant evaluations of their work (Rajeswari et al., 2026). Through virtual lab environments students can use their knowledge to conduct simulation experiments which lead to academic discovery through hands-on learning experiences (Bhatti,2025).
2. Social Constructivism: Lev Vygotsky's theory explains how people learn through social interactions with others. Intelligent agents who work together can assist peers with their interactions while helping them to learn through group discussions and collaborative learning activities which Social Constructivist learning depends on.
3. Cognitive Load Theory: John Sweller showed through his research that people learn better when their mental workload receives proper management. Agentic AI systems adapt their teaching methods according to a student's current working memory limits while providing learning support through task breakdowns and effective content organization (Prabha et al., 2026).
4. Self-Determination Theory: The theory identifies intrinsic motivation and autonomy and competence as the fundamental elements of human behavior. Learners who use agentic AI technology to control their learning schedule and direction will experience increased engagement and motivation which leads to greater autonomous learning (Mengliyev et al., 2024).
5. Mastery Learning: This approach states that students must first master one topic before they can progress to the next. AI-driven adaptive systems can implement mastery learning through their ongoing assessment of student development which delivers specific educational support until students achieve complete mastery.

Figure 2. The Agentic AI in education.

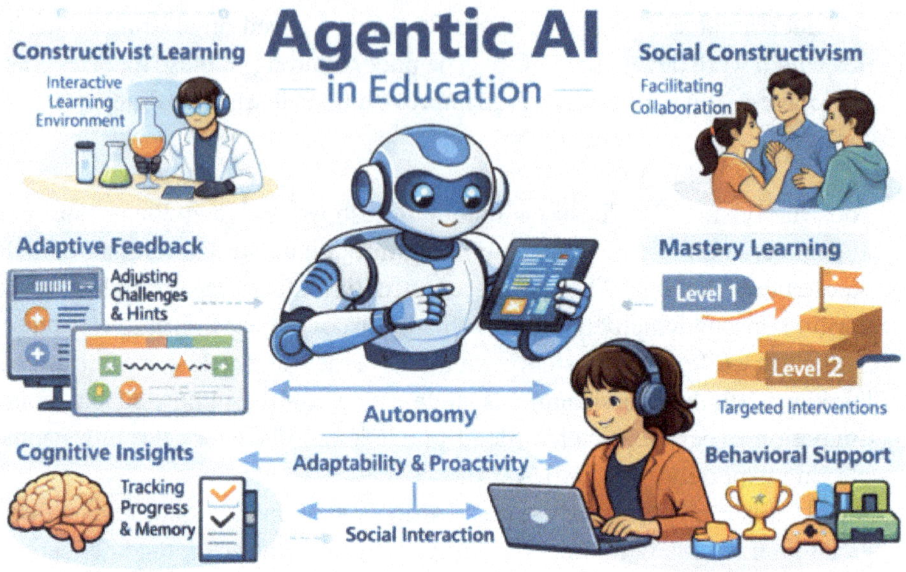

1.5 Cognitive and Behavioral Perspectives

The understanding and behavior of learners creates the essential element for creating efficient agentic AI systems. Cognitive perspectives study internal processes which include memory and problem-solving and decision-making. Agentic AI uses these insights to forecast learner requirements while delivering content through methods which match cognitive strengths and help learners build understanding (Rathinavel et al., 2025). For example, AI can model student misconceptions which enables it to deliver corrective feedback and learning pathway reinforcement to improve retention and comprehension. The behavioral perspective studies the direct observations of human behavior which occur through learning and reinforcement. AI systems track how users engage with their content because they use this information to modify their prompts and rewards and challenges (Xamrakulova et al., 2026). The application of behavioral theories through techniques like gamification and immediate feedback and adaptive incentives maintains learner motivation while guiding them toward effective learning activities. Agentic AI develops personalized learning environments which utilize cognitive and behavioral knowledge to create systems that respond to student needs and adjust their operations and deliver effective educational results (Makhmudov et al., 2025). The combination of these perspectives enables AI systems to teach knowledge while developing critical thinking and problem-solving and lifelong learning abilities. AI systems achieve educational psychology alignment through their educational goals while offering intelligent support to students (Oltiboy et al., 2025).

2. INNOVATIONS IN AGENTIC AI FOR EDUCATION

Agentic AI's adaptive learning systems, intelligent tutoring, virtual assistants, personalized pathways, multi-agent collaboration, and data-driven assessment to engage, improve efficiency, and drive educational outcomes.

2.1 Adaptive Learning Systems

The primary educational advancement in agentic AI technology for learning purposes is the development of adaptive learning systems. The platforms use data analytics and machine learning and predictive algorithms to create customized content delivery through tailored pacing and difficulty adjustments according to specific student needs. Unlike conventional instruction designed for the average student, adaptive systems offer individualized experiences that respond to a student's performance in real time (Tutushkina et al., 2025). Adaptive learning systems not only customize the learning experience but also serve as a valuable tool for educators, providing granular levels of student assessment and enabling timely interventions and more informed teaching decisions.

2.2 Personalized Learning Pathways

The educational system advances through personalized learning pathways, which create distinct learning paths for each student based on their individual needs. The pathways use a learner's strengths and weaknesses together with their interests and their future goals to create a learning path that maximizes their development. Agentic AI systems use historical performance data together with engagement patterns and learning preferences to develop personalized educational programs. The language learning platform AI detects which reading comprehension skills the student excels at and which spoken fluency skills the student finds challenging. The system can then establish speaking exercise priorities while it suggests conversation practice and monitors progress throughout time. Personalized pathways give students control over their learning process which lets them build their academic path while they still work toward the university's academic goals.

2.3 Intelligent Tutoring Systems

The educational field uses Intelligent Tutoring Systems (ITS) as a fundamental element of agentic artificial intelligence. ITS platforms create one-on-one tutoring experiences through their system of measuring learner knowledge and finding learning errors and delivering immediate educational support. The system uses ITS educational software because it enables real-time adjustment of its teaching content according to what each student already knows. A mathematics ITS system operates by presenting a problem to students who then solve it while the system monitors their progress to identify errors and deliver specific educational support. The systems use natural language processing technology to analyze open-ended student responses which improves the system's ability to deliver relevant and valuable feedback. The use of ITS technology enables teachers to deliver personalized instruction to many students which allows them to maintain high-quality educational support while traditional classrooms face challenges in achieving this personalized educational experience.

2.4 Virtual Teaching Assistants and Conversational Agents

Conversational agents and virtual teaching assistants are another type of agentic AI application. They use natural language to communicate with students, answer questions, give guidance, and help with discussions. The agentic conversational agents are different from chatbot-type AIs in that they have the ability to maintain context, track students' progress, and even facilitate multi-turn conversations that are similar to human tutoring. In an online course, a virtual teaching assistant can answer questions about lecture content, offer supplementary materials, and even remind students of upcoming deadlines. These agents can lend a helping hand to learners and educators by lowering the administrative and instructional burden. These agents can provide students with 24/7 assistance, ongoing feedback, and motivation.

2.5 Gamification and Simulation-Based Learning

The educational system creates more engaging learning experiences through gamification and simulation-based learning which use agentic AI technology. The AI systems use game mechanics which include points and badges and levels and leaderboards to create motivation for learners who need to complete their studies. Students use simulations to learn real-world skills within a safe environment which maintains full control over their practice. The medical students can engage in AI-driven virtual surgeries while engineering learners can experiment with simulated construction projects. Agentic AI technology creates an interactive learning environment through its monitoring of student progress and skill-based challenge adjustments and immediate assessment delivery. The processes help students stay motivated while they learn complex subjects through practical testing which includes safe failure and repeatable testing.

2.6 AI-Driven Assessment and Feedback

The learning process requires assessment together with feedback because these elements serve as vital components while agentic artificial intelligence technology creates new methods for assessment delivery. Automated AI systems can assess student work which includes assignments and quizzes plus open-ended answers to provide individualized complete feedback that shows strengths and weak points while pointing out needed improvements and upcoming actions. Adaptive assessment tools go beyond grading correctness; they analyze problem-solving approaches, reasoning patterns, and engagement metrics to offer actionable insights. A writing course AI system evaluates grammar and style plus coherence and argument strength to help students create better academic writing. Students can achieve mastery learning through real-time continuous feedback which also helps them reflect on their progress while they learn at their own pace because assessments function as both formative tools and empowerment resources instead of punishment methods.

2.7 Challenges and Limitations

Agentic AI has the potential to transform education, but there are challenges and limitations associated with its use. These challenges exist across ethical, technical, social, and pedagogical domains. Understanding these challenges is important for educators, technologists, and policymakers to ensure the responsible, equitable, and effective use of AI systems in education.

3. LITERATURE SURVEY

Kostopoulos et al., (2025) provides an extensive examination of current educational systems which use agentic AI technology for their autonomous systems that provide adaptive instructional services. The agentic AI from conventional intelligent tutoring systems by emphasizing proactivity, self-regulation, and contextual awareness. The findings show that agentic AI improves personalized learning experiences through its capability to adapt in real time and its use of predictive analytics and continuous feedback systems. The study shows that participants acquired greater knowledge and maintained their attention better while their assessments became more accurate through testing. The technical difficulties which include explainability problems and scalability issues and ethical risk mitigation problems need to be solved. Future studies should focus on developing transparency systems and establishing strong evaluation methods and creating educational partnerships between human instructors and AI system developers.

Nagasubramanian et al., (2026) explores the Artificial intelligence has changed personalized education by using adaptive systems, predictive analytics, and intelligent content delivery. Traditional instructional models are transformed by artificial intelligence and used to create learner-centered environments with data-driven insights. Adaptive learning systems that respond to student performance by modulating pace, feedback and assessment are highlighted. AI personalization shows significant improvement in student achievement, motivation and retention. Examples of successful implementations are provided with adaptive systems that reduce dropout risk and increase mastery learning. Institutional readiness, infrastructure investment and teacher training are critical success factors. The long-term educational value of AI depends on responsible use, and alignment with pedagogical goals, not on technological development.

Bey et al., (2026) conducts a systematic review of AI-powered adaptive learning systems, examining algorithms, personalization techniques, and empirical validation methods used across educational platforms. The review categorizes adaptive technologies into rule-based systems, machine learning–driven personalization, and reinforcement learning frameworks. Their research assesses effectiveness in both K–12 schools and higher education institutions. The results show that adaptive systems create better learning outcomes for students compared to traditional e-learning systems which provide static content. The knowledge tracing models based on deep learning achieved their highest accuracy results when they tracked student progress. The review found research gaps because there were no long-term studies and researchers used different measurement methods. The system requires both standardized benchmarks and cross-cultural validation.

Ashwani (2025) discusses the ways by which agentic AI technology produces educational theory and teaching practice changes. The author of this paper illustrates the ways by which constructivist and mastery-learning theoretical frameworks facilitate agentic AI systems to augment learning environments through their capacity of delivering dynamic learning assistance. The intelligent tutoring systems and its partners, conversational agents and adaptive analytics platforms, constitute fundamental components in pursuit of this educational revolution. The agentic AI system attempts to augment cognitive engagement while facilitating a user's attainment of their individual learning objectives. The synergy between reinforcement learning and behavioral modeling permits the systems to anticipate user misconceptions while delivering accurate remedial approaches. The educational system must address this issue because defective AI systems typically support shallow learning. The teacher–AI alliance as well as the curriculum redesign are synergistic components contributing to optimal educational gains for students.

Raman et al., (2026) illustrates the agentic AI through a multidisciplinary research framework which examines its effect on flexible management systems for educational and organizational learning processes. Researchers use behavioral science together with strategic management and AI system design to study how autonomous agents shape decision-making processes. According to the research evidence agentic AI helps organizations improve adaptive management through its capacity to enhance organizational response times and data-driven forecasting and team-based decision-making. The authors argue that educational institutions should implement flexible principles which permit schools to modify their curriculum while establishing learning environments which focus on student requirements. Trust deficits together with behavioral resistance present challenges which obstruct the process of adoption. The discussion establishes organizational transparency through governance mechanisms and stakeholder engagement and ethical auditing operations. Organizations need to change their cultural practices in combination with new technology adoption for successful agentic AI implementation.

Yu et al., (2026) focuses on AI- based formative assessment tools in laboratory and project-based learning. The impact of real-time performance analytics on skill development in experiential settings. The role of AI in facilitating real-time feedback during practical activities. The use of AI in assessment processes and its effects on student engagement and motivation. The comparison of traditional assessment methods with AI-enhanced assessment in hands-on learning settings. The potential risks and challenges associated with relying too heavily on AI for scoring and assessment. The integration of AI and human oversight in a hybrid model of assessment. The impact of agentic AI on learner autonomy and self-regulated learning in assessment contexts. The implications of AI-enhanced assessment for learning outcomes and skill mastery. The potential for agentic AI to transform assessment practices by enabling more continuous and personalized evaluation.

4. METHODOLOGY

The methodology flowchart serves as an empirical framework which researchers use to evaluate AI system performance through its structured approach to evaluating AI based tutoring systems. The research objective requires researchers to examine student engagement time and active AI teaching methods influence students' academic results. The comparative experimental research design which requires the research team to separate students into different tutoring method groups that include Deep

RL and Multi-Agent and Hybrid and Traditional ITS and Control groups. Three major data streams are collected during data collection process because researchers gather pre-test scores which show baseline knowledge and engagement logs which display learning time and student interaction frequency and post-test scores which reveal learning outcomes as shown in figure 3.

The research deploys AI models through Deep Reinforcement Learning and Multi-Agent Systems and Hybrid architectures which they monitor throughout the study. The performance evaluation stage calculates three educational metrics which include learning gains and prediction accuracy and the relationship between engagement and educational outcomes. The statistical analysis method uses Pearson correlation and regression modeling and confidence intervals and comparative gain analysis to interpret the data. The results which appear in the graphs depend on the results of these steps. The scatter plot shows a strong positive relationship between engagement time and learning outcomes which results from the regression and correlation analysis. The bar chart which displays pre-test scores against post-test scores derives from the group gain calculations. The percentage gain visualization derives from normalized improvement rates which produce the calculation results. The knowledge tracing performance graph shows accuracy tracking across multiple sessions which validates algorithmic effectiveness to track knowledge over time.

Figure 3. The flowchart illustrates AI tutoring Study.

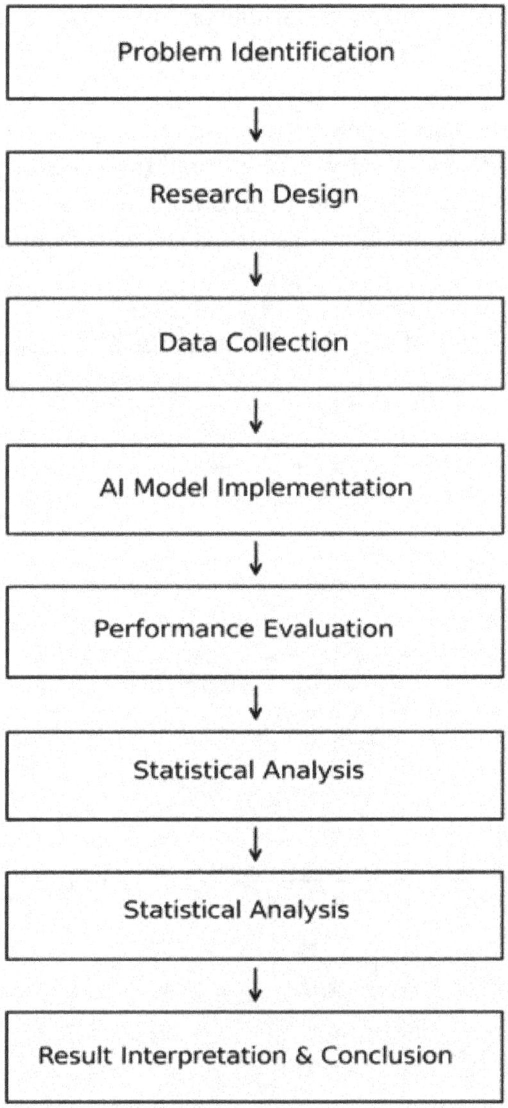

4.1 Results and Discussion

Prediction accuracy trends of the three knowledge tracing algorithms (DKT, Deep Knowledge Tracing, and GKT, Graph-based Knowledge Tracing) given 15 sessions. The horizontal axis denotes session number, and the vertical axis denotes prediction accuracy (%) The upward trend for all three curves indicates that model performance improves over time as more student interaction data is collected. Probabilistic modeling does capture learning progress, but it does so more gradually than deep learning. DKT's improvement curve is sharper, starting at about 78% accuracy and going above 97% accuracy in later sessions. The power of recurrent neural networks in modeling sequential learning behavior. GKT's performance is slightly better than DKT's in early sessions, and then converges at the maximum level (almost 98% accuracy), i.e. the incorporation of relationship-based or graph-based modeling improves predictive performance, as shown in figure 4.

Figure 4. The performance tracing for different algorithm

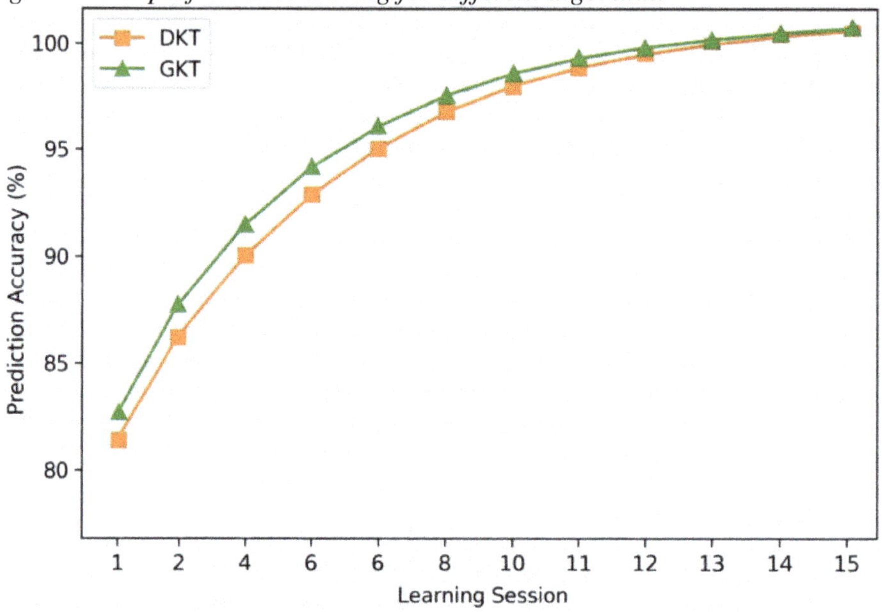

Figure 5. The percentage learning gain across tutoring approaches.

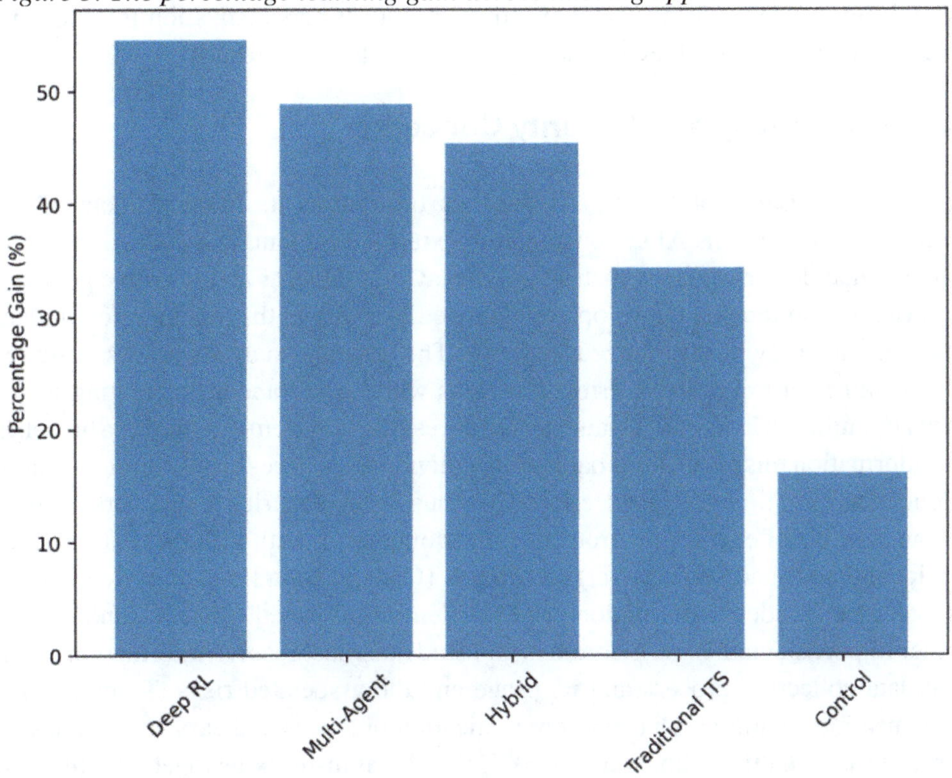

The five tutoring methods Deep RL Multi-Agent Hybrid Traditional ITS and Control resulted in different percentage learning gains achieved by students. The y-axis shows the percentage improvement which was determined through calculating the difference between pre-test and post-test scores. The results show distinct performance variations which exist between different teaching methods. Deep Reinforcement Learning (Deep RL) shows the highest gain because it exceeds 54% which proves that adaptive reward-driven personalization works effectively. The Multi-Agent system follows with nearly 49% improvement which shows that agent collaboration leads to better teaching results. The Hybrid approach achieves approximately 45% gain because it demonstrates that using multiple AI techniques results in significant improvements which exceed those obtained through Deep RL according to figure 6. Traditional Intelligent Tutoring Systems (ITS) provide students with structured learning paths which achieve 34% learning progress because they implement basic adaptive changes. The Control group shows the smallest learning progress with about 16% because its participants did not receive advanced AI personalization treatment. The graph shows AI-enhanced adaptive systems perform better than both traditional systems and systems which do not use adaptive techniques as shown in figure 6. The difference in performance shows that intelligent personalization mechanisms play a crucial role in achieving maximum student learning results.

4.2 Data Privacy and Security Concerns

The functioning of agentic AI depends on data as its basic element which supports its operations.AI systems require extensive student data collection which should include performance metrics and behavioral patterns and sensitive personal information so they can develop personalized learning paths and monitor student progress and provide customized feedback. The learning analytics process requires this data because it delivers critical insights while simultaneously creating major privacy and security issues. Unauthorized access to the system through data breaches or information misuse enables dangerous individuals to access student information. Educational institutions must establish robust cybersecurity frameworks which should consist of encryption protection and compliance with FERPA (Family Educational Rights and Privacy Act) and GDPR (General Data Protection Regulation) to safeguard student information. The problem of informed consent stands as another important challenge. Guardians and students must receive information about the data collection process and its usage and the associated risks. To build trust organizations require both clear communication practices and easy-to-use consent procedures (Bhatti & Shodiyev, 2025). Educational institutions together with their educators need data stewardship training to handle information responsibly while using it to improve learning results.

4.3 Algorithmic Bias and Fairness

Artificial intelligence (AI) has great potential in education. However, learning systems can only learn from data, and if the data collected reflect historical social inequalities or biases, AI can unintentionally perpetuate, or even amplify, these biases. We discuss the problem of algorithmic bias in education, in the context of the growing use of AI-driven learning systems. We provide concrete examples of algorithmic bias in learning systems. These include bias in deductive or rule-based systems, bias in inductive (data-driven) systems, and bias in adaptive and intelligent tutoring systems. Finally, we propose a framework for the design, evaluation, and implementation of fair learning systems including bias detection and mitigation.

4.4 Accessibility and Digital Divide

AI has the potential to make education more personalized and inclusive, it can also exacerbate inequalities if accessibility issues are not addressed. Many students, particularly in rural or underprivileged areas, may lack reliable internet access, modern devices, or the technical skills needed to engage with AI-driven platforms. The educational system will become less equal because of the digital divide which prevents students from accessing AI resources (Kuzmin et al., 2025). Accessibility also encompasses considerations for learners with disabilities. AI systems must be designed to support a range of needs, such as screen readers for visually impaired students, closed captions for hearing-impaired learners, and adaptive interfaces for neurodiverse students. AI implementation requires essential elements which include universal accessibility standards and context-aware interventions and inclusive design principles to provide learning opportunities for all students. Accessibility challenges require solutions which involve creating policies and obtaining institutional support and developing new technologies. Governments and educational institutions must invest in infrastructure, teacher training, and low-cost devices to bridge the digital divide and make AI-enhanced education equitable and sustainable.

4.5 Teacher–AI Collaboration and Role Redefinition

Teacher and AI collaboration holds promise for the future of teaching and learning. However, teachers and their students will likely resist collaboration with AI. This article will explore the challenges of teacher and AI collaboration by drawing on the literature on teaching meditation, teacher training and professional development, STEM teacher collaboration, and AI governance. Teachers will need to learn new skills to collaborate with AI. However, teachers will also need to maintain a human–AI collaborative relationship that is mediated by a broader community of educators, administrators, teachers' aides, technologists, and policymakers. This article will argue that the public discourse around AI in education must consider the broader role of collaboration and teacher agency.

4.6 Transparency, Explainability, and Trust in AI Systems

Educational institutions need AI technology to function optimally because transparent systems and explainable algorithms drive user acceptance. AI systems must be transparent to all three user groups because they demonstrate decision-making processes and show which factors lead to particular recommendations and which methods should be used for specific problems. Explainability deficiencies in AI systems create two problems because they result in systems that people consider either mysterious or completely random which in turn destroys trust and decreases user interaction with the system. AI systems require designers to create systems which enable users to comprehend their decision-making process through understandable methods. An intelligent tutoring system should correct a student's mistake through two functions because it must explain the reason for the wrong answer and show how the recommended solution improves student comprehension. Stakeholders require transparency to understand how data gets used, what system capabilities, and operational boundaries, and how machine learning models develop their biases to make AI deployment decisions. Educational institutions depend on trust as the main reason for their technology selection process. Students must believe that AI systems will protect their personal information while delivering precise learning help that matches their educational objectives. Educators need to believe that AI systems deliver trustworthy teaching materials which meet both educational standards and curriculum requirements. This trust building process demands three elements which include developers sharing product information, teachers sharing their work methods and students sharing their learning experiences.

4.7 Policy, Governance, and Ethical Guidelines

Agentic AI ethics in education examine four main concepts which include accountability, transparency, consent and fairness. Educational institutions base their usage of agentic AI systems through a framework which relies on ethical principles. Students will experience their learning path which includes assessment and future academic results through the choices made by autonomous AI systems. The situation creates problems which involve determining who should take responsibility and who should bear accountability and which aspects should be treated as just. Responsible AI in education must be built on the pillars of equity, inclusivity, transparency and alignment with human values and human interests. The system needs to handle human dignity and non-discrimination together with the requirement for people to understand AI systems through their understandable AI system decision-making process and their operational mechanism. Students and their parents need to understand through the AI system which information gets collected about them together with the details of its data usage and how data usage affects their educational experience. People will only believe a system when it shows everything to them while it helps their human decision-making process and their judgment process. The teacher serves as the main human educator who guides students through moral development work.

4.8 Emerging Trends in Practice

The following practical trends demonstrate how agentic AI will advance educational practices in the future.

1 Emotionally Intelligent AI systems use facial recognition and voice analysis and interaction patterns to determine learners' emotional states. The system delivers customized feedback and support to help learners maintain their motivation and reduce their frustrating experiences.
2 The AI-based AR/VR environments create interactive educational environments. Students use these virtual environments to study complex concepts. The system enables students to perform experiments and acquire skills inside secure virtual environments.
3 The AI models Predictive Learning Analytics provide organizations with tools to forecast student learning problems and recommend educational solutions. The system identifies optimal educational paths to prevent student failure while supporting their complete learning process.
4 Multi-agent AI systems use Global Collaboration Platforms to enable international learning activities that involve different cultural backgrounds. The systems enable students to develop teamwork abilities while they acquire critical thinking skills and learn about different global perspectives.

5. CASE STUDIES AND APPLICATIONS

Agentic AI and intelligent agents are not just concepts: they are in the process of changing educational practice across the world. By looking at real-world implementations, we can see how these systems support learning, aid teachers, and respond to a wide variety of student needs. In this chapter, we look at case studies of agentic AI applied in K–12 education, higher education, inclusive learning environments, and policy. We identify both the opportunities and hurdles in applying these systems in the real world.

5.1 K–12 Education Applications

The classrooms of K–12 education use agentic AI technology to create customized learning experiences which respond to student needs. Adaptive learning platforms are used in mathematics and language arts as a significant example of this approach. The systems of DreamBox Learning and Smart Sparrow use their real-time student performance data collection to detect knowledge deficiencies in students and make changes to their instructional materials. The system provides additional practice problems and visual explanations and interactive simulations to students who need help with fraction concepts while students who already understand the material can take advanced tests which help them stay focused. In addition to science education institutions now use intelligent tutoring systems for teaching reading comprehension skills. The Carnegie Learning MATHia platform customizes its problem sets for students according to their unique problem-solving methods while delivering hints and scaffolding and feedback based on the needs of individual students. Teachers can use these systems to work on their creative teaching responsibilities while all students receive customized learning assistance.

Schools now use virtual teaching assistants in their K–12 classrooms at an increasing rate. Teachers can spend more time on classroom discussions and individual student support because conversational agents handle common inquiries and schedule reminders and provide extra teaching resources. Classcraft and other gamified platforms use artificial intelligence to monitor student progress and award achievements while students work together, which creates a more engaging and interactive educational experience. K–12 educational environments can achieve better student results through agentic AI tools, which also help students become more engaged and enable teachers to create customized learning experiences. The educational system needs complete teacher training, alongside educational planning, to achieve maximum advantages while establishing solutions for public safety and disabled people's access needs and student privacy rights.

5.2 Higher Education and Research Implementation

Institutions of higher education use agentic artificial intelligence technology to improve student educational outcomes and research productivity and administrative work processes. Intelligent tutoring systems are applied in STEM courses, providing targeted support for complex concepts. The Assessment and Learning in Knowledge Spaces (ALEKS) platform uses student performance data to create personalized mathematics lessons which help students achieve mastery through their learning journey. The IBM Watson AI system powers Georgia Tech's virtual teaching assistant named "Jill Watson" which shows how conversational agents can extend educational support to a larger number of students. Jill Watson provides answers to student questions which occur in discussion forums to help instructors handle large online classes while still being able to respond quickly. The agents work to decrease faculty responsibilities while increasing student contentment and they provide students with essential assistance in both massive open online courses (MOOCs) and blended learning environments.

Research support is another domain where agentic AI shines. AI data analysis tools can spot patterns in research data, help researchers conduct literature reviews and present hypothesis. These tools allow researchers to move beyond the repetitive work, and think more creatively and analytically. AI is also being used in predictive analytics for student success, graduation predictions and course recommendations and allow universities to make better data-driven decisions that improve student retention and academic performance.

5.3 AI for Inclusive and Special Education

The field of agentic AI shows its greatest potential through its use in inclusive and special education programs. AI-powered systems provide customized learning solutions which address the specific needs of students who have disabilities or learning difficulties or language barriers. The AI-driven reading assistants enable students with dyslexia to highlight text content while they adjust the font size and receive pronunciation guidance through real-time feedback. Students with visual impairments can access educational resources through intelligent agents that use screen readers and voice recognition and tactile interfaces. AI-powered captioning and sign language translation and interactive multimedia tools provide students with hearing impairments essential support for their educational needs.

The application of AI technology extends to the development of social skills and behavioral skills. Virtual agents and simulated environments enable students with autism spectrum disorders to practice social skills while learning to identify emotions and participate in controlled role-playing activities. The system monitors user progress through its three functions of scenario adjustment and feedback delivery which together support users in developing their skills according to their personal learning speed. The agentic AI supports multilingual education through its functions of real-time translation and adaptive language exercises and culturally relevant educational materials. The new technologies explain how AI can help create equal learning opportunities by eliminating accessibility problems which allows all students to experience valuable educational opportunities.

5.4 Policy-Level Implementations and Global Examples

The deployment of agentic AI technology has transformed educational systems across multiple countries while conducting its implementation in educational settings. Educational organizations and governmental bodies use AI-based solutions to achieve better educational outcomes while making education more accessible and using data to inform their strategic choices. AI systems operate within Singapore's educational system by delivering customized learning routes while tracking student progress and helping teachers advance their professional skills. The Ministry of Education applies AI analytics to study educational patterns which help in resource distribution and development of school-specific educational programs for particular student requirements.

The United States uses artificial intelligence to enhance STEM education through student performance evaluation and support of disadvantaged communities. The established policies create a system that safeguards user data while they establish rules for ethical artificial intelligence deployment and technical innovations will support educational progress for students from underprivileged backgrounds. UNESCO and the OECD established global educational AI standards which define key ethical standards and teacher training requirements and educational guidelines for inclusive learning environments. Governments and educational institutions should follow these guidelines to implement agentic AI as they work to create educational systems which ensure equal opportunities while achieving sustainable progress through responsible innovative activities.

MOOCs and online learning platforms such as Coursera, edX, and Khan Academy use AI technology to deliver personalized learning experiences which include automated feedback mechanisms and adaptive learning paths for students. The platforms show how agentic AI can provide education of superior quality which reaches millions of learners in various educational environments.

6. CONCLUSION AND FUTURE SCOPE

The research demonstrates that agentic AI improves educational outcomes through its ability to provide personalized learning which functions independently of its operator. The assessment of five different teaching methods showed that their effectiveness results in major performance differences. The highest learning gain was achieved by Deep Reinforcement Learning at 54 percent while Multi-Agent systems followed at 49 percent and Hybrid models reached 45 percent. The Traditional Intelligent Tutoring Systems achieved a 34 percent improvement while the Control group managed to only achieve a 16 percent advancement. The results demonstrate that advanced adaptive AI architectures deliver superior performance compared to both traditional and non-adaptive teaching techniques. Knowledge tracing analysis further strengthens these results. Deep and Graph-based Knowledge Tracing models demonstrated continuous accuracy improvement across learning sessions, reaching approximately 97–98%. Sequential and relational modeling methods demonstrate their ability to precisely forecast student learning development through their assessment of student learning progress. The researchers found that engagement time shows a strong positive relationship with academic improvement through their statistical correlation and regression analyses which show dedicated commitment to learning in AI-supported environments leads to better educational outcomes.

REFERENCES

Aarthi, S., Ravikumar, R. N., Kalandarova, M., Khalikova, N., & Iskandarov, E. (2025). *Overcoming barriers in metaheuristic neural network optimization for biomedical imaging*. IGI Global., DOI: 10.4018/979-8-3373-0523-3.ch014

Ahmed, S. Y., & Pardaev, J. (2025). Human-AI decision dynamics: How risk propensity and trust impact choices through decision fatigue, conditional on AI understanding. *Decision Making: Applications in Management and Engineering*, *8*(2), 96–113. DOI: 10.31181/dmame8220251484

Ammer, M. A., & Mamadjanova, T. (2025). Effects of educational digital literacy, educational aspirations, self-directed learning on e-learning motivation and effectiveness. *Educational Sciences: Theory & Practice*. Advance online publication. DOI: 10.12738/jestp.2025.1.18

Ashwani, S. (2025). Agentic AI in Education: Transforming Pedagogy and Personalized Learning. In Reddy, C. K. K., Joseph, S., Joshi, H., Doss, S., & Ouaissa, M. (Eds.), *The Power of Agentic AI: Redefining Human Life and Decision-Making. Sustainable Artificial Intelligence-Powered Applications*. Springer., DOI: 10.1007/978-3-031-89424-4_21

Bey, A. (2026). AI-Powered Adaptive Learning Systems: A Systematic Review and Future Research Directions. In: Gokhale, A. (eds) Proceedings of The 11th International Conference on Frontiers of Educational Technologies 2025. ICFET 2025. Lecture Notes in Educational Technology. Springer, Singapore. https://doi.org/DOI: 10.1007/978-981-95-2521-8_19

Bhatti, M. A., & Pardaev, J. (2025). *Exploring accreditation's role in fostering inclusive education via educational equity and technology*. Revista Electrónica de LEEME., DOI: 10.58262/LEEME.56.05

Bhatti, M. A., & Shodiyev, A. (2025). Enhancing employee performance through communication competence. *International Journal of Operations and Quantitative Management*. Advance online publication. DOI: 10.46970/2025.31.2.11

Ghaleb, M. M. S., & Sattarov, A. (2025). *Use of ChatGPT in education and quality of education*. Revista Electrónica de LEEME., DOI: 10.58262/LEEME.55.0020

Hamid, E. M., & Shodiyev, A. (2025). Role of information needs, accessibility and digital literacy in shaping web search self-efficacy. *El Profesional de la Información*, *34*(2). Advance online publication. DOI: 10.3145/epi.2025.ene.34205

Islamutdinov, V., Akhmetshin, E., Lydia, E. L., & Raja, P. V. K. (2025). Implementation of AI in an ethical and responsible manner to empower education in digital sector. *Lecture Notes in Networks and Systems, 1318*, 127–134. DOI: 10.1007/978-981-96-3939-7_13

Kishor, I., Mamodiya, U., Almaayah, M., Alqutaish, A., Shehab, R., & Aldhyani, T. H. (2025). Agentic AI-Enhanced Virtual Reality for Adaptive Immersive Learning Environments. *Mesopotamian Journal of Computer Science, 2025*, 398–416. DOI: 10.58496/MJCSC/2025/026

Kostopoulos, G., Gkamas, V., Rigou, M., & Kotsiantis, S. (2025). Agentic AI in Education: State of the art and future directions. *IEEE Access : Practical Innovations, Open Solutions, 13*, 177467–177491. DOI: 10.1109/ACCESS.2025.3620473

Kuzmin, E., Bondareva, V. S., Shodiyev, A., & Ochilov, I. (2025). *Digitalization, innovation, and competitiveness*. Springer., DOI: 10.1007/978-3-032-00118-4_17

Makhmudov, S., Maqsood, M., Musaev, U., Urazmetov, M., & Shahzadi, A. (2025). Foundations of agentic AI redefining autonomy in learning environments. In *Multidisciplinary Perspectives on Agentic AI in Educational Systems*. IGI Global., DOI: 10.4018/979-8-3373-4621-2.ch001

Mengliyev, I., Meylikulov, S., Fayzullayeva, Z., & Kobulova, M. (2024). Education artificial intelligence systems and their use in teaching. *AIP Conference Proceedings*, 030079. Advance online publication. DOI: 10.1063/5.0241443

Meti, A. (2026). Agentic artificial intelligence in education: A review on personalized adaptive learning through autonomous tutoring systems. *International Journal of Applied Resilience and Sustainability, 2*(2), 40–74. DOI: 10.70593/deepsci.0202002

Muthuswamy, V. V., & Absamatov, A. (2025). *Determinants of students engagement and their role in boosting students' academic performance*. Revista Electrónica de LEEME., DOI: 10.58262/LEEME.56.13

Nagasubramanian, D. (2026). Harnessing Artificial Intelligence to Revolutionize Education: Personalized Learning and Beyond. In Bhattacharya, S. (Ed.), *ICT for Global Innovations and Solutions. ICGIS 2025. Advances in Computer Science Applications and Research* (Vol. 1). Springer., DOI: 10.1007/978-3-032-02853-2_29

Oltiboy, B., Mansur, U., Salimov, U., Boboqulov, C., & Babayev, A. (2025). Optimizing linguistic outcomes in education: A CRM-based structural equation modeling approach. *Forum for Linguistic Studies, 7*(6), 9383. DOI: 10.30564/fls.v7i6.9383

Prabha, K. R., Mabel, B. R., Isaev, F., Mamadiyarov, Z., Raxmatullayevich, K. U., & Erkinjon, T. (2026). A Multi-Layer Artificial Intelligence–Enabled Governance Framework for Integrating Information Security Management, Quality Management, and Strategic Human Resource Analytics: An Empirical Study on the Role of Corporate Social Responsibility in Sustainable Organizational Performance. *Quality - Access to Success*, *27*(210). Advance online publication. DOI: 10.47750/QAS/27.210.45

Rajeswari, M., Vanitha, C. L., Xudoynazarova, S., Mamadiyarov, Z., Naveen, S., Nematovich, K. I., & Isaev, F. (2026). Design and Validation of an Explainable Artificial Intelligence–Based Decision Intelligence Model for Cyber Risk–Aware Quality Systems and Ethical Human Resource Management: Investigating the Moderating Influence of Corporate Social Responsibility in Digitally Transformed Organizations. *Quality - Access to Success*, *27*(210). Advance online publication. DOI: 10.47750/QAS/27.210.46

Raman, R., Gandhi, A., & Banerjee, U. (2026). *Agentic AI and Flexible Management: Multidisciplinary and Behavioural Perspectives on Evolving Practices, Strategic Opportunities, and Policy Implications*. Glob J Flex Syst Manag., DOI: 10.1007/s40171-026-00483-1

Rathinavel, P., Ravikumar, R. N., Aarthi, S., Habib, M., & Salaeva, N. (2025). *Augmenting human capabilities: AI's impact on collaborative workflows*. IGI Global., DOI: 10.4018/979-8-3373-2372-5.ch001

Ravikumar, R. N., Aarthi, S., Rejapov, I. O., Sultonova, M., & Musayeva, S. (2025). Transforming healthcare with large language models and AI agents. In *Advanced Interdisciplinary Applications of LLMs*. IGI Global., DOI: 10.4018/979-8-3373-2008-3.ch003

Sufyan Ghaleb, M. M., & Pardaev, J. (2025). Literature reading self-efficacy and academic achievement. *Educational Sciences: Theory & Practice*, *25*(2), 77–92. DOI: 10.12738/jestp.2025.2.06

Tran, G. T. C., Le Dinh, T., & Le, T. D. (2026). Agentic AI Across Technologies, Applications, and Development Domains: A Systematic Literature Review. In Swaroop, A., Virdee, B., Correia, S. D., & Polkowski, Z. (Eds.), *Proceedings of Data Analytics and Management. ICDAM 2025. Lecture Notes in Networks and Systems* (Vol. 1603). Springer., DOI: 10.1007/978-3-032-03769-5_44

Tutushkina, N., Duschanova, G., Majidova, D., Karimov, S., Odilov, U., Sapaev, I., Shamuradova, N., & Vosiqov, U. (2025). Fostering sustainable development in tourist destinations through collaborative education on environmental conservation. *Natural and Engineering Sciences, 10*(3), 475–491. Advance online publication. DOI: 10.28978/nesciences.1811138

Xamrakulova, X., Mirzaeva, Z., Shabbazova, D., Sabirov, A., Rasulova, Z., Ismoilov, B., & Mukhriddin, A. (2026). Project based marine biodiversity education to improve ocean literacy and conservation attitudes among secondary students. *Natural and Engineering Sciences, 11*(1), 211–220. DOI: 10.28978/nesciences.261015

Yu, Y. C. (2026). Leveraging Agentic AI for Enhancing Multiple Assessments on Hands-On Learning. In: May, D., Auer, M.E. (eds) 2025 Yearbook Emerging Technologies in Learning. Learning and Analytics in Intelligent Systems, vol 59. Springer, Cham. https://doi.org/DOI: 10.1007/978-3-032-09058-4_1

Compilation of References

Aarthi, S., Ravikumar, R. N., Kalandarova, M., Khalikova, N., & Iskandarov, E. (2025). *Overcoming barriers in metaheuristic neural network optimization for biomedical imaging*. IGI Global., DOI: 10.4018/979-8-3373-0523-3.ch014

Abdelhalim, E., Anazodo, K. S., Gali, N., & Robson, K. (2024). A framework of diversity, equity, and inclusion safeguards for chatbots. *Business Horizons*, *67*(5), 487–498. DOI: 10.1016/j.bushor.2024.03.003

Abiddin, N. Z. (2024). A deep dive into leadership styles in shaping the higher education institution's value and culture. *Pakistan Journal of Life and Social Sciences*, *22*(2), 3854–3868. DOI: 10.57239/PJLSS-2024-22.2.00283

Acemoglu, D., & Autor, D. (2011). Skills, tasks and technologies: Implications for employment and earnings. In *Handbook of labor economics* (Vol. 4, pp. 1043–1171). Elsevier.

Acemoglu, D., & Restrepo, P. (2018). The race between man and machine: Implications of technology for growth, factor shares, and employment. *The American Economic Review*, *108*(6), 1488–1542. DOI: 10.1257/aer.20160696

Acemoglu, D., & Restrepo, P. (2020). Robots and jobs: Evidence from US labor markets. *Journal of Political Economy*, *128*(6), 2188–2244. DOI: 10.1086/705716

Adelakun, O., Bui, Q. N., Turel, O., & Anderberg, G. (2025). Survival of the Fittest Through Digital Transformation: Turning the Board's Digital Awareness to Action. *Information Systems Journal*, isj.12587. DOI: 10.1111/isj.12587

Adewumi, A. O. (2026). Ensemble and time-series hybrid modeling for retail inventory optimization in emerging markets. *Journal of African Retail Research*, *12*(1), 45–62.

Adiguzel, Z., & Sonmez Cakir, F. (2025). Empowering sustainability: Green entrepreneurial orientation, innovative strategies, culture and operational performance. *Management Decision*, *63*(11), 3934–3966. DOI: 10.1108/MD-07-2024-1700

Adwey, L. (2026a). Artificial Intelligence and Unethical Financial Practices: Examining the Mediating Role of Environmental; Social; and Governance (ESG) performance in the Saudi Financial Sector. *Borsa Istanbul Review*, 100784.

Adwey, L. (2026b). Artificial Intelligence and Unethical Financial Practices: Examining the Mediating Role of Environmental; Social; and Governance (ESG) performance in the Saudi Financial Sector. *Borsa Istanbul Review*, 100784.

Ahmed, R. S. (2024). Comparison of deep learning algorithms for retail sales forecasting. *Proceedings of the International Conference on Computing and Knowledge*. DOI: 10.62762/TIS.2024.300700

Ahmed, S. Y., & Pardaev, J. (2025). Human-AI decision dynamics: How risk propensity and trust impact choices through decision fatigue, conditional on AI understanding. *Decision Making: Applications in Management and Engineering*, *8*(2), 96–113. DOI: 10.31181/dmame8220251484

Ahmed, Z. A. (2025). A Proposed Model for Developing the Taxation System on Oil Companies in Iraq: A Strategic Framework for Budget Financing and Enhancing Economic Stability. *European Journal of Management. Economics and Business*, *2*(2), 182–197.

Akter, S., McCarthy, G., Sajib, S., Michael, K., Dwivedi, Y. K., D'Ambra, J., & Shen, K. N. (2021). Algorithmic bias in data-driven innovation in the age of AI. *International Journal of Information Management*, *60*, 102387. DOI: 10.1016/j.ijinfomgt.2021.102387

Akter, S., Sultana, S., Mariani, M., Wamba, S. F., Spanaki, K., & Dwivedi, Y. K. (2023). Advancing algorithmic bias management capabilities in AI-driven marketing analytics research. *Industrial Marketing Management*, *114*, 243–261. DOI: 10.1016/j.indmarman.2023.08.013

Al Aina, R. (2025). Bridging the AI skills gap: Preparing generation Z for the evolving job market landscape through innovative educational strategies. *Industry and Higher Education*. Advance online publication. DOI: 10.1177/09504222261423356

Alagele, H. K. H., Neama, N. H., Al Dulaimi, H. A., & Abd, S. E. (2024). The Impact of Purposeful Management on the Relationship Between Organizational Conflict and Team Proactivity. *Journal of Ecohumanism*, *3*(8), 10875–10882.

Alam, M. M., & Priti, S. I. (2024). *Adaptive Hybrid Software Project Management in Bangladesh's Software Industry: Navigating the Cultural Transformation and Ensuring On-Time Delivery* [PhD Thesis, IUB]. https://ar.iub.edu.bd/handle/11348/1001

Ali, I., Nguyen, K., Ali, A. M., & Cui, T. (2025). Human–AI collaboration in knowledge ecosystems: A multidisciplinary review, integrative framework and future directions. *Journal of Knowledge Management*, •••, 1–22. DOI: 10.1108/JKM-03-2025-0431

Alli, A. A., Magombe, Y., Lwembawo, I., & Kasadha, J. (2025, May). A Policy Framework for the Use of Generative Artificial Intelligence in Higher Education Institutions. *In 2025 IST-Africa Conference (IST-Africa)* (pp. 1-11). IEEE. DOI: 10.23919/IST-Africa67297.2025.11060512

Ally, A. M. (2025). Artificial intelligence (AI) and financial technology (FinTech) in Tanzania; legal and regulatory issues. *International Journal of Law and Management*. https://www.emerald.com/ijlma/article-abstract/doi/10.1108/IJLMA-07-2024-0251/1250484

Al-Mahamid, H. (2025). A comparative analysis of the human development index and road safety outcomes in the European Union. *European Transport Studies*, *2*, 100041. DOI: 10.1016/j.ets.2025.100041

Alshurideh, M. T., Ahmed, G., Shrouf, H., Shwedeh, F., & Alzoubi, H. M. (2026). *Leveraging Artificial Intelligence and Data Analytics for Digital Innovation: Insights from Banking Sector*. https://www.emerald.com/books/edited-volume/20966/chapter/107781635

Amershi, S., Weld, D., Vorvoreanu, M., Fourney, A., Nushi, B., Collisson, P., Teevan, J., & Horvitz, E. (2019). Guidelines for human-AI interaction. In *Proceedings of the 2019 CHI Conference on Human Factors in Computing Systems* (pp. 1–13). ACM. DOI: 10.1145/3290605.3300233

Ammer, M. A., & Mamadjanova, T. (2025). Effects of educational digital literacy, educational aspirations, self-directed learning on e-learning motivation and effectiveness. *Educational Sciences: Theory & Practice*. Advance online publication. DOI: 10.12738/jestp.2025.1.18

Anikó, V. (2026). *Perspective Chapter: The Role of Data Quality Dimensions in Data-Driven Decision-Making*. https://www.intechopen.com/online-first/1231452

Ansell, C., & Gash, A. (2008). Collaborative governance in theory and practice. *Journal of Public Administration: Research and Theory*, *18*(4), 543–571. DOI: 10.1093/jopart/mum032

Ara, A. (2026). AI-enhanced learning for sustainable development: Balancing innovation and equity in higher education. In *Role of Artificial Intelligence in Higher Education: Pathways to Sustainable Development* (pp. 1–24). Springer Nature Singapore. https://doi.org/DOI: 10.1007/978-981-95-5350-1_1

Ashwani, S. (2025). Agentic AI in Education: Transforming Pedagogy and Personalized Learning. In Reddy, C. K. K., Joseph, S., Joshi, H., Doss, S., & Ouaissa, M. (Eds.), *The Power of Agentic AI: Redefining Human Life and Decision-Making. Sustainable Artificial Intelligence-Powered Applications*. Springer., DOI: 10.1007/978-3-031-89424-4_21

Asiedu, E., & Tenakwah, E. S. (2025). Future-proofing your workforce: Upskilling and reskilling as HR's top priorities. *Strategic HR Review, 24*(4), 169–173. DOI: 10.1108/SHR-01-2025-0008

Aulia, A., Sukmadilaga, C., Avianti, I., Rosdini, D., & Ghani, E. K. (2026). The Role of ESG and Digitalization Driving Sustainable Agropreneurship in Emerging Market. [ATT]. *Aptisi Transactions on Technopreneurship, 8*(1), 51–62. DOI: 10.34306/att.v8i1.673

Aulia, S. R., & Lin, W.-S. (2025). *Embracing the digital shift: Leveraging AI to foster employee well-being and engagement in remote workplace settings in the Asia Pacific region*. Asia Pacific Management Review., DOI: 10.1016/j.apmrv.2024.12.003

Autor, D. H. (2015). Why are there still so many jobs? The history and future of workplace automation. *The Journal of Economic Perspectives, 29*(3), 3–30. DOI: 10.1257/jep.29.3.3

Avolio, B., & Walumbwa, F. (2014). *16 authentic leadership theory, research and practice: Steps taken and steps that remain* (Vol. 331). Oxford University Press Oxford. https://books.google.com/books?hl=en&lr=&id=ul5iAwAAQBAJ&oi=fnd&pg=PA331&dq=walumbwa+2014+authentic+leadership&ots=N3SujFHHPY&sig=GlKRwcHIK0z8GfUH16t1XG0Tys0

Avolio, B. J., & Gardner, W. L. (2005). Authentic leadership development: Getting to the root of positive forms of leadership. *The Leadership Quarterly, 16*(3), 315–338. DOI: 10.1016/j.leaqua.2005.03.001

Avolio, B. J., Walumbwa, F. O., & Weber, T. J. (2009). Leadership: Current theories, research, and future directions. *Annual Review of Psychology, 60*(1), 421–449. DOI: 10.1146/annurev.psych.60.110707.163621 PMID: 18651820

Babina, T., Fedyk, A., He, A., & Hodson, J. (2024). Artificial intelligence, firm growth, and product innovation. *Journal of Financial Economics, 151*, 103745. DOI: 10.1016/j.jfineco.2023.103745

Baldwin, R., & Cave, M. (1999). *Understanding regulation: Theory, strategy, and practice*. Oxford University Press.

Bankins, S., Hu, X., & Yuan, Y. (2024). Artificial intelligence, workers, and future of work skills. *Current Opinion in Psychology, 58*, 101828. DOI: 10.1016/j.copsyc.2024.101828 PMID: 38964241

Barbosa, I., & Real de Oliveira, E. (2026). Digital reskilling and workforce transformation: Exploring identity, capability and adaptation in AI-mediated workplaces. *Journal of Organizational Effectiveness: People and Performance*, 1–19. https://doi.org/DOI: 10.1108/JOEPP-12-2025-1109

Barkat, K., Alsamara, M., Al Kwifi, O. S., & Jarallah, S. (2025). Does trade openness mitigate environmental degradation in Organisation for Economic Co-operation and Development (OECD) countries? Implications for achieving sustainable development. *Natural Resources Forum, 49*(1), 677–698. DOI: 10.1111/1477-8947.12412

Barney, J. (1991). Firm resources and sustained competitive advantage. *Journal of Management, 17*(1), 99–120. DOI: 10.1177/014920639101700108

Bass, B. M. (1985). *Leadership and performance beyond expectations*. Free Press.

Bass, B. M., & Riggio, R. E. (2006). *Transformational leadership* (2nd ed.). Lawrence Erlbaum Associates. DOI: 10.4324/9781410617095

Becker, G. S. (1964). *Human capital: A theoretical and empirical analysis, with special reference to education*. University of Chicago Press.

Becker, G. S. (1964). *Human capital: A theoretical and empirical analysis*. University of Chicago Press.

Benlian, A., & Pinski, M. (2025). The AI literacy development canvas: Assessing and building AI literacy in organizations. *Business Horizons*. Advance online publication. DOI: 10.1016/j.bushor.2025.10.001

Bey, A. (2026). AI-Powered Adaptive Learning Systems: A Systematic Review and Future Research Directions. In: Gokhale, A. (eds) Proceedings of The 11th International Conference on Frontiers of Educational Technologies 2025. ICFET 2025. Lecture Notes in Educational Technology. Springer, Singapore. https://doi.org/DOI: 10.1007/978-981-95-2521-8_19

Bhatti, M. A., & Pardaev, J. (2025). *Exploring accreditation's role in fostering inclusive education via educational equity and technology*. Revista Electrónica de LEEME., DOI: 10.58262/LEEME.56.05

Bhatti, M. A., & Shodiyev, A. (2025). Enhancing employee performance through communication competence. *International Journal of Operations and Quantitative Management*. Advance online publication. DOI: 10.46970/2025.31.2.11

Bholat, D., Brookes, J., Cai, C., Grundy, K., & Laarni, J. (2020). Explainability of machine learning in central banking and financial regulation. Bank of England Staff Working Paper No. 816.

Bieser, J. C., & Hilty, L. M. (2018). Assessing indirect environmental effects of information and communication technology (ICT): A systematic literature review. *Sustainability (Basel), 10*(8), 2662. DOI: 10.3390/su10082662

Birlan, I., Davidescu, A. A., & Constantin, R.- tefan. (2026). Artificial Intelligence and ESG Disclosure: Measuring Transparency in AI-Driven Firms. In C.-W. Su, O.-R. Lobon , A.-C. Nicolescu, & N. M. Doran (Eds.), *Green Finance and the Challenges of Climate Change* (pp. 41–68). Springer Nature Switzerland. DOI: 10.1007/978-3-032-07293-1_3

Boyatzis, R. E. (1982). *The competent manager: A model for effective performance*. Wiley.

Božić, V. (2023). Environmental, social, and governance (ESG) & artificial intelligence (AI). *Preprint*. https://www.researchgate.net/profile/Velibor-Bozic-2/publication/391955758_ENVIRONMENTAL_SOCIAL_AND_GOVERNANCE_ESG_ARTIFICAL_INTELLIGENCE_AI/links/682eb9b8d1054b0207f0cca7/ENVIRONMENTAL-SOCIAL-AND-GOVERNANCE-ESG-ARTIFICAL-INTELLIGENCE-AI.pdf

Brown, M. E., Treviño, L. K., & Harrison, D. A. (2005). Ethical leadership: A social learning perspective for construct development and testing. *Organizational Behavior and Human Decision Processes, 97*(2), 117–134. DOI: 10.1016/j.obhdp.2005.03.002

Brynjolfsson, E., & mcafee, A. (2014). *The second machine age: Work progress and prosperity in a time of brilliant technologies*. WW Norton & company.

Brynjolfsson, E., Li, D., & Raymond, L. R. (2023). Generative AI at work. NBER Working Paper No. 31161. National Bureau of Economic Research. https://doi.org/ DOI: 10.3386/w31161

Brynjolfsson, E., & McAfee, A. (2014). *The second machine age: Work, progress, and prosperity in a time of brilliant technologies*. W. W. Norton & Company.

Bubeck, S., Chandrasekaran, V., Eldan, R., Gehrke, J., Horvitz, E., Kamar, E., Lee, P., Lee, Y. T., Li, Y., Lundberg, S., Nori, H., Palangi, H., Ribeiro, M. T., & Zhang, Y. (2023). Sparks of artificial general intelligence: Early experiments with GPT-4. arXiv. https://doi.org//arXiv.2303.12712DOI: 10.48550

Bukar, U. A., Sayeed, M. S., Razak, S. F. A., Yogarayan, S., & Sneesl, R. (2024). Decision-making framework for the utilization of generative artificial intelligence in education: A case study of ChatGPT. *IEEE Access : Practical Innovations, Open Solutions*, *12*, 95368–95389. DOI: 10.1109/ACCESS.2024.3425172

Burnaev, E., Mironov, E., Shpilman, A., Mironenko, M., & Katalevsky, D. (2023). Practical AI cases for solving ESG challenges. *Sustainability (Basel)*, *15*(17), 12731. DOI: 10.3390/su151712731

Burning Glass Technologies. (2022). *The AI advantage: How AI skills are reshaping the labour market and salary landscape*. Burning Glass Institute.

Burns, J. M. (1978). *Leadership*. Harper & Row.

Calzada, I. (2025). Generative AI and the urban AI policy challenges ahead: Trustworthy for whom?. *Transforming Government: People, Process and Policy*, 1-17. DOI: 10.1108/TG-08-2025-0240

Cao, L. (2022). AI in finance: Challenges, techniques, and opportunities. *ACM Computing Surveys*, *55*(3), 1–38. DOI: 10.1145/3502289

Cao, L. T., Tran, L. B., Khuu, Q. T., Tran, T. T. B., & Nguyen, L. T. (2026). Empowering Gen Z With AI: Embody ESG Values and Shaping the Future of Personalized Customer Experience. *Journal of Sensory Studies*, *41*(1), e70102. DOI: 10.1111/joss.70102

Carlyle, T. (1841). *On heroes, hero-worship, and the heroic in history*. James Fraser.

CFA Institute. (2022). *Future state of the investment profession: AI and data science skills for finance professionals*. CFA Institute Research Foundation.

Chandler, A. D. (1977). *The visible hand: The managerial revolution in American business*. Harvard University Press.

Chen, W., Song, Z., & Xie, Y. (2026). Energy transition across the climate policy uncertainty divide: The critical role of green technology innovation and digital transformation. *Economic Analysis and Policy*. https://www.sciencedirect.com/science/article/pii/S0313592626000366

Cheng, K., & Wu, H. (2024). Policy framework for the utilization of generative AI. *Critical Care : The Official Journal of the Critical Care Forum*, *28*(1), 128. DOI: 10.1186/s13054-024-04917-z PMID: 38637898

Chen, S., Li, X., Wang, Y., & Zhao, J. (2024). Which product description phrases affect sales forecasting? An empirical study. *Economic Modelling*, •••, 127.

Chen, Y., Chen, H., Gorkhali, A., Lu, Y., Ma, Y., & Li, L. (2016). Big data analytics and big data science: A survey. *Journal of Management Analytics*, *3*(1), 1–42. DOI: 10.1080/23270012.2016.1141332

Chernyak-Hai, L., Bareket-Bojmel, L., & Margalit, M. (2024). A matter of hope: Perceived support, hope, affective commitment, and citizenship behavior in organizations. *European Management Journal*, *42*(4), 576–583. DOI: 10.1016/j.emj.2023.03.003

Choi, J. H., Liu, M. H., & Sami, H. (2020). Financial competence and the transition to data-driven finance: An empirical assessment. *Journal of Accounting Education*, *53*, 100685.

Choudhury, P., Starr, E., & Agarwal, R. (2020). Machine learning and human capital complementarities: Experimental evidence on bias mitigation. *Strategic Management Journal*, *41*(8), 1381–1411. DOI: 10.1002/smj.3152

Chuang, S., Shahhosseini, M., Javaid, M., & Wang, G. G. (2024). Machine learning and AI technology-induced skill gaps and opportunities for continuous development of middle-skilled employees. *Journal of Work-Applied Management*. Advance online publication. DOI: 10.1108/JWAM-08-2024-0111

Chuang, Y.-T., Chiang, H.-L., & Lin, A.-P. (2025). Insights from the Job Demands–Resources Model: AI's dual impact on employees' work and life well-being. *International Journal of Information Management*, *83*, 102887. DOI: 10.1016/j.ijinfomgt.2025.102887

Chui, M., Manyika, J., & Miremadi, M. (2018). *What AI can and can't do (yet) for your business. McKinsey Quarterly*. McKinsey & Company.

Chukwuere, J. E. (2025). Developing a generative AI conceptual framework for higher education. *The Indonesian Journal of Computer Science*, *14*(5). Advance online publication. DOI: 10.33022/ijcs.v14i5.4997

Cockburn, I. M., Henderson, R., & Stern, S. (2018). The impact of artificial intelligence on innovation: An exploratory analysis. In *The economics of artificial intelligence: An agenda* (pp. 115–146). University of Chicago Press.

Content Marketing Institute. (2023). *B2B content marketing benchmarks, budgets, and trends: Generative AI special report*. Content Marketing Institute.

Dafoe, A. (2018). AI governance: A research agenda. Future of Humanity Institute, University of Oxford.

Daly, S. J., Hearn, G., & Papageorgiou, K. (2025). Sensemaking with AI: How trust influences human–AI collaboration in health and creative industries. *Social Sciences & Humanities Open, 11*, 101346. DOI: 10.1016/j.ssaho.2025.101346

Dantas, M. J., de Souza, L. R., & da Silva, A. N. (2022). Sales forecasting in retail using XGBoost and deep learning. *Expert Systems with Applications*, •••, 191.

Darwish, S., Hussain Alagele, H. K., Alsherooqi, A., & Nafea, R. (2026). Leading Change: A Modern Analysis of Transformational Vs. Transactional Leadership. In AlDhaen, E., Weerakkody, V., & Ahmed Farouta, F. (Eds.), *Sustainable Development Agenda 2030* (Vol. 646, pp. 271–282). Springer Nature Switzerland., DOI: 10.1007/978-3-032-11612-3_22

Dastin, J. (2018, October 10). Amazon scraps secret AI recruiting tool that showed bias against women. Reuters. https://www.reuters.com/article/us-amazon-com-jobs-automation-insight-idUSKCN1MK08G

Davenport, T. H., & Patil, D. J. (2012). Data scientist: The sexiest job of the 21st century. *Harvard Business Review*, *90*(10), 70–76. PMID: 23074866

Davenport, T. H., & Ronanki, R. (2018). Artificial intelligence for the real world. *Harvard Business Review*, *96*(1), 108–116.

Davenport, T., Guha, A., Grewal, D., & Bressgott, T. (2020). How artificial intelligence will change the future of marketing. *Journal of the Academy of Marketing Science*, *48*(1), 24–42. DOI: 10.1007/s11747-019-00696-0

David, T., & Borsi, B. (2025). Human–AI interaction in knowledge ecosystems: A context–mechanism–outcome perspective. *Journal of Knowledge Management*, •••, 1–23. DOI: 10.1108/JKM-03-2025-0401

Day, D. V. (2001). Leadership development: A review in context. *The Leadership Quarterly*, *11*(4), 581–613. DOI: 10.1016/S1048-9843(00)00061-8

de Moraes, J. B., & Schaefer, J. L. (2026). Customer satisfaction in digital banking services: A network analysis focused on service quality, insurance, mobile banking, and digital channels. *Journal of Enterprise Information Management*, •••, 1–24. DOI: 10.1108/JEIM-04-2025-0237

Dellermann, D., Ebel, P., Söllner, M., & Leimeister, J. M. (2019). Hybrid intelligence. *Business & Information Systems Engineering, 61*(5), 637–643. DOI: 10.1007/s12599-019-00595-2

Deloitte Insights. (2022). *The AI-ready financial services workforce: Skills, gaps, and pathways*. Deloitte Development LLC.

Dhaigude, A. S., & Kamath, G. B. (2025). Mapping responsible artificial intelligence in business and management: Trends, influence, and emerging research directions. *Journal of Open Innovation, 11*(4), 100640. DOI: 10.1016/j.joitmc.2025.100640

Dhanabalan, T., & Sathish, A. (2018). Transforming Indian industries through artificial intelligence and robotics in industry 4.0. *International Journal of Mechanical Engineering and Technology, 9*(10), 835–845.

Diakopoulos, N. (2016). Accountability in algorithmic decision making. *Communications of the ACM, 59*(2), 56–62. DOI: 10.1145/2844110

Dietvorst, B. J., Simmons, J. P., & Massey, C. (2015). Algorithm aversion: People erroneously avoid algorithms after seeing them err. *Journal of Experimental Psychology. General, 144*(1), 114–126. DOI: 10.1037/xge0000033 PMID: 25401381

Dong, X. (2026). The ESG-productivity paradox: How ESG performance expectation gaps impede total factor productivity. *Journal of Business Research, 202*, 115775. DOI: 10.1016/j.jbusres.2025.115775

Doughan, Y. A. R. (2020). Factors of production, economic growth, and sustainable development. In *Decent work and economic growth* (pp. 427–439). Springer International Publishing. DOI: 10.1007/978-3-319-71058-7_121-1

Dou, J., Chen, D., & Zhang, Y. (2025). Towards energy transition: Accessing the significance of artificial intelligence in ESG performance. *Energy Economics, 146*, 108515. DOI: 10.1016/j.eneco.2025.108515

Doz, Y. L., & Kosonen, M. (2010). Embedding strategic agility: A leadership agenda for accelerating business model renewal. *Long Range Planning, 43*(2-3), 370–382. DOI: 10.1016/j.lrp.2009.07.006

Drucker, P. F. (1959). *Landmarks of tomorrow*. Harper & Row.

Duan, Y., Edwards, J. S., & Dwivedi, Y. K. (2019). Artificial intelligence for decision making in the era of big data: Evolution, challenges and research agenda. *International Journal of Information Management, 48*, 63–71. DOI: 10.1016/j.ijinfomgt.2019.01.021

Duggan, J., Sherman, U., Carbery, R., & McDonnell, A. (2020). Algorithmic management and app-work in the gig economy: A research agenda for employment relations and HRM. *Human Resource Management Journal, 30*(1), 114–132. DOI: 10.1111/1748-8583.12258

Dumitru, D., & Halpern, D. F. (2023). Critical thinking: Creating job-proof skills for the future of work. *Journal of Intelligence, 11*(10), 194. DOI: 10.3390/jintelligence11100194 PMID: 37888426

Dwivedi, Y. K., Helal, M. Y. I., Elgendy, I. A., Albashrawi, M. A., Hughes, L., Shawosh, M., Dutot, V., & Jeon, I. (2026). Artificial intelligence agents and agentic systems in hospitality and tourism: Challenges, opportunities and research agenda. *International Journal of Contemporary Hospitality Management, 38*(1), 27–52. DOI: 10.1108/IJCHM-02-2025-0287

Dwivedi, Y. K., Hughes, L., Ismagilova, E., Aarts, G., Coombs, C., Crick, T., Duan, Y., Dwivedi, R., Edwards, J., Eirug, A., Galanos, V., Ilavarasan, P. V., Janssen, M., Jones, P., Kar, A. K., Kizgin, H., Kronemann, B., Lal, B., Lucini, B., & Williams, M. D. (2021). Artificial Intelligence (AI): Multidisciplinary perspectives on emerging challenges, opportunities, and agenda for research, practice and policy. *International Journal of Information Management, 57*, 101994. DOI: 10.1016/j.ijinfomgt.2019.08.002

Edeh, F. O., Zayed, N. M., Darwish, S., Nitsenko, V., Hanechko, I., & Islam, K. A. (2023). Impression management and employee contextual performance in service organizations (enterprises). *Emerging Science Journal, 7*(2), 366–384. DOI: 10.28991/ESJ-2023-07-02-05

Edmondson, A. (1999). Psychological safety and learning behavior in work teams. *Administrative Science Quarterly, 44*(2), 350–383. DOI: 10.2307/2666999

Eglite, L., & Birzniece, I. (2022). Retail sales forecasting using deep learning: Systematic literature review. *Complex Systems Informatics and Modeling Quarterly, 30*(30), 53–62. DOI: 10.7250/csimq.2022-30.03

Eisenhardt, K. M. (1989). Building theories from case study research. *Academy of Management Review, 14*(4), 532–550. DOI: 10.2307/258557

Elhady, A. M., & Shohieb, S. (2025). AI-driven sustainable finance: Computational tools, ESG metrics, and global implementation. *Future Business Journal, 11*(1), 209. DOI: 10.1186/s43093-025-00610-x

Emaminejad, N., & Akhavian, R. (2022). Trustworthy AI and robotics: Implications for the AEC industry. *Automation in Construction, 139*, 104298. DOI: 10.1016/j.autcon.2022.104298

European Commission. (2021). Proposal for a regulation of the European Parliament and of the Council laying down harmonised rules on artificial intelligence (Artificial Intelligence Act). COM/2021/206 final.

Fadhilah, A. F., Aryanti, A. N., Sofiati, N. A., Ismail, G. D., & Muttaqin, R. (2026). Enhancing Employee Performance through Competence, Motivation, and Transformational Leadership: The Strategic Role of Employee Engagement. *Journal of General Education and Humanities*, *5*(1), 535–554. DOI: 10.58421/gehu.v5i1.958

Farrokhi, Z. (2026). AI-Powered Grid Analytics for Sustainable Energy Management in ESG Frameworks. In *Data-Driven ESG Strategy Implementation Through Business Intelligence* (pp. 279–318). IGI Global Scientific Publishing., https://www.igi-global.com/chapter/ai-powered-grid-analytics-for-sustainable-energy-management-in-esg-frameworks/388322

Fatemi, A., Glaum, M., & Kaiser, S. (2018). ESG performance and firm value: The moderating role of disclosure. *Global Finance Journal, 38*, 45–64. DOI: 10.1016/j.gfj.2017.03.001

Fatima Ajibike, T. A. L. I. A. T. (2025). AI-enhanced skill development: Leveraging AI in biology education to develop skills in digital era. *Journal of Educational Studies Trends and Practice*. https://doi.org/DOI: 10.70382/sjestp.v8i8.030

Fernández, A. M. (2026). Artificial Intelligence–Driven Transformation Of Investment, Corporate Strategy, And Economic Growth: Integrating ESG, Portfolio Management, And Technological Ecosystems. *Library of Frontline Marketing. Management and Economics Journal*, *6*(01), 1–5.

Ferreira, A. L., Pinheiro, A., & Medeiros, P. (2025). Ethical and innovative integration of generative Artificial Intelligence in Higher Education: Challenges and proposals for an institutional policy. *International Journal of Social Science and Education Research Studies*, *5*(4), 379–382. DOI: 10.55677/ijssers/V05I04Y2025-04

Fiedler, F. E. (1967). *A theory of leadership effectiveness*. McGraw-Hill.

Financial Stability Board. (2022). *Artificial intelligence and machine learning in financial services: Market developments and financial stability implications*. FSB.

Fleishman, E. A. (1953). The description of supervisory behavior. *The Journal of Applied Psychology*, *37*(1), 1–6. DOI: 10.1037/h0056314 PMID: 6038475

Floridi, L., Cowls, J., Beltrametti, M., Chatila, R., Chazerand, P., Dignum, V., Luetge, C., Madelin, R., Pagallo, U., Rossi, F., Schafer, B., Valcke, P., & Vayena, E. (2018). AI4People—An ethical framework for a good AI society: Opportunities, risks, principles, and recommendations. *Minds and Machines*, *28*(4), 689–707. DOI: 10.1007/s11023-018-9482-5 PMID: 30930541

Fotis, G., Gupta, S., Varshney, T., Dhar, S. L., & Gulzar, M. M. (Eds.). (2025). *Modern Computing Technologies for EV Efficiency and Sustainable Energy Integration*. IGI Global., DOI: 10.4018/979-8-3373-2382-4

Fuster, A., Goldsmith-Pinkham, P., Ramadorai, T., & Walther, A. (2022). Predictably unequal? The effects of machine learning on credit markets. *The Journal of Finance*, *77*(1), 5–47. DOI: 10.1111/jofi.13090

Galton, F. (1869). *Hereditary genius: An inquiry into its laws and consequences*. Macmillan. DOI: 10.1037/13474-000

Ganguly, P., & Mukherjee, I. (2024). *Enhancing retail sales forecasting with optimized machine learning models*.

Gao, X., & Feng, H. (2023). AI-driven productivity gains: Artificial intelligence and firm productivity. *Sustainability (Basel)*, *15*(11), 8934. DOI: 10.3390/su15118934

García-López, I. M., & Trujillo-Liñán, L. (2025). Generative Artificial Intelligence in Education: Ethical Challenges, Regulatory Frameworks and Educational Quality in a Systematic Review of the Literature. [). Frontiers.]. *Frontiers in Education*, *10*, 1565938. DOI: 10.3389/feduc.2025.1565938

Gartner. (2022). The state of marketing technology adoption and utilization. Gartner Research.

Garvin, D. A. (1993). Building a learning organization. *Harvard Business Review*, *71*(4), 78–91. PMID: 10127041

Gatoi, H., Belhaoua, I., Akhtar, K., Qadir, M., Mohammad, N., & Ali, M. (2026). Green Intelligence in Finance: Artificial Intelligence-Driven ESG Analytics and Sustainable Investment Performance. *Inverge Journal of Social Sciences*, *5*(1), 15–27. DOI: 10.63544/ijss.v5i1.216

George, G., Merrill, R. K., & Schillebeeckx, S. J. (2021). Digital sustainability and entrepreneurship: How digital innovations are helping tackle climate change and sustainable development. *Entrepreneurship Theory and Practice*, *45*(5), 999–1027. DOI: 10.1177/1042258719899425

Ghaleb, M. M. S., & Sattarov, A. (2025). *Use of ChatGPT in education and quality of education.* Revista Electrónica de LEEME., DOI: 10.58262/LEEME.55.0020

Goldin, C., & Katz, L. F. (2008). *The race between education and technology.* Harvard University Press.

Goldman Sachs. (2023). *The potentially large effects of artificial intelligence on economic growth.* Goldman Sachs Research.

Goleman, D. (1995). *Emotional intelligence: Why it can matter more than IQ.* Bantam Books.

Gomber, P., Kauffman, R. J., Parker, C., & Weber, B. W. (2018). On the fintech revolution: Interpreting the forces of innovation, disruption, and transformation in financial services. *Journal of Management Information Systems, 35*(1), 220–265. DOI: 10.1080/07421222.2018.1440766

Graduate Management Admission Council. (2023). *Corporate recruiters survey: AI and hybrid skills demand in business education.* GMAC Research Reports.

Greenleaf, R. K. (1977). *Servant leadership: A journey into the nature of legitimate power and greatness.* Paulist Press.

Gupta, S. (2025). *The Future of Machine Learning with Automation in Engineering.* Nova Science Publishers., DOI: 10.52305/YFIX2832

Gupta, S., & Tripathi, R. K. (2014). Optimal LQR controller in CSC based STATCOM using GA and PSO. *Archives of Electrical Engineering, 63*(3), 469–487. Advance online publication. DOI: 10.2478/aee-2014-0034

Hadi, W., Al-Qerem, A., & Aldweesh, A. (2025). Institutional Policies, Governance, and Regulatory Responses to Generative AI. In *Examining Cybersecurity Risks Produced by Generative AI* (pp. 643–666). IGI Global Scientific Publishing., DOI: 10.4018/979-8-3373-0832-6.ch026

Haenlein, M., & Kaplan, A. (2019). A brief history of artificial intelligence: On the past, present, and future of artificial intelligence. *California Management Review, 61*(4), 5–14. DOI: 10.1177/0008125619864925

Hai, S., Long, T., Honora, A., Japutra, A., & Guo, T. (2025). The dark side of employee-generative AI collaboration in the workplace: An investigation on work alienation and employee expediency. *International Journal of Information Management, 83*, 102905. DOI: 10.1016/j.ijinfomgt.2025.102905

Hamid, E. M., & Shodiyev, A. (2025). Role of information needs, accessibility and digital literacy in shaping web search self-efficacy. *El Profesional de la Información, 34*(2). Advance online publication. DOI: 10.3145/epi.2025.ene.34205

Hamilton-Peach, J., & Townsley, P. (n.d.). *AN IFAD SUSTAINABLE LIVELIHOODS FRAMEWORK*.

Hersey, P., & Blanchard, K. H. (1969). *Management of organizational behavior: Utilizing human resources*. Prentice Hall.

Heyder, T., Passlack, N., & Posegga, O. (2023). Ethical management of human–AI interaction: Theory development review. *The Journal of Strategic Information Systems, 32*(3), 101772. DOI: 10.1016/j.jsis.2023.101772

Hilbert, M., Thakur, A., Flores, P. M., Zhang, X., Bhan, J. Y., Bernhard, P., & Ji, F. (2024). 8–10% of algorithmic recommendations are "bad", but… an exploratory risk–utility meta-analysis and its regulatory implications. *International Journal of Information Management, 75*, 102743. DOI: 10.1016/j.ijinfomgt.2023.102743

Hobor, L., Brcic, M., Polutnik, L., & Kapetanovic, A. (2024). Comparative analysis of modern machine learning models for retail sales forecasting. *International Journal of Forecasting, 40*(1), 225–238.

Holmström, J., & Carroll, N. (2025). How organizations can innovate with generative AI. *Business Horizons, 68*(5), 559–573. DOI: 10.1016/j.bushor.2024.02.010

House, R. J. (1971). A path goal theory of leader effectiveness. *Administrative Science Quarterly, 16*(3), 321–339. DOI: 10.2307/2391905

House, R. J., Hanges, P. J., Javidan, M., Dorfman, P. W., & Gupta, V. (Eds.). (2004). *Culture, leadership, and organizations: The GLOBE study of 62 societies*. SAGE.

Huang, M. H., & Rust, R. T. (2021). A strategic framework for artificial intelligence in marketing. *Journal of the Academy of Marketing Science, 49*(1), 30–50. DOI: 10.1007/s11747-020-00749-9

Huang, M., & Rust, R. T. (2018). Artificial intelligence in service. *Journal of Service Research, 21*(2), 155–172. DOI: 10.1177/1094670517752459

Hu, C., & Othman, R. B. (2026a). AI-enabled ESG consultancy capability building in small audit firms: A strategic transformation pathway analysis. *Future Technology, 5*(2), 25–37. DOI: 10.55670/fpll.futech.5.2.3

Hutchins, E. (1995). *Cognition in the wild*. MIT Press. DOI: 10.7551/mitpress/1881.001.0001

Ibrahim, A., & Kumar, G. (2025). A framework for integrating Lean Six Sigma and Industry 4.0 for sustainable manufacturing. *International Journal of Production Research*, •••, 1–23. DOI: 10.1080/00207543.2025.2571202

Ilieva, N. (2022). Deep learning methods for e-commerce retail sales forecasting. *Procedia Computer Science*, *200*, 194–201.

Islamutdinov, V., Akhmetshin, E., Lydia, E. L., & Raja, P. V. K. (2025). Implementation of AI in an ethical and responsible manner to empower education in digital sector. *Lecture Notes in Networks and Systems*, *1318*, 127–134. DOI: 10.1007/978-981-96-3939-7_13

Jain, A., & Bishnoi, C. R. (2025). Artificial Intelligence and Economic Development in India: Adoption Trends and Key Determinants. In *Intelligent Systems for Sustainable Infrastructure: AI Solutions Shaping a Green Future: Leveraging AI Innovations for Eco Friendly Infrastructure and Environmental Resilience* (pp. 139–154). Springer Nature Switzerland.

Jaiswal, T., Hasan, M. A., Das, S., & Tiwari, V. (2026). Advancing Sustainable Services Through ESG and Circular Economy: Technology-Driven Pathways for Supply Chain Transformation. *Sustainable Development*, sd.70744. DOI: 10.1002/sd.70744

Jarrahi, M. H. (2018). Artificial intelligence and the future of work: Human-AI symbiosis in organizational decision making. *Business Horizons*, *61*(4), 577–586. DOI: 10.1016/j.bushor.2018.03.007

Jarrahi, M. H., Askay, D., Eshraghi, A., & Smith, P. (2023). Artificial intelligence and knowledge management: A partnership between human and AI. *Business Horizons*, *66*(1), 87–99. DOI: 10.1016/j.bushor.2022.03.002

Jarrahi, M. H., Lutz, C., & Newlands, G. (2022). Artificial intelligence, human intelligence and hybrid intelligence based on mutual augmentation. *Big Data & Society*, *9*(2), 20539517221142824. DOI: 10.1177/20539517221142824

Jerez-Jerez, M. J. (2025). A study of employee attitudes towards AI, its effect on sustainable development goals and non-financial performance in independent hotels. *International Journal of Hospitality Management*, *124*, 103987. DOI: 10.1016/j.ijhm.2024.103987

Jiang, N., Liu, X., Liu, H., Lim, E. T. K., Tan, C. W., & Gu, J. (2023). Beyond AI-powered context-aware services: The role of human–AI collaboration. *Industrial Management & Data Systems*, *123*(11), 2771–2802. DOI: 10.1108/IMDS-03-2022-0152

Jin, Y., Yan, L., Echeverria, V., Gašević, D., & Martinez-Maldonado, R. (2025). Generative AI in higher education: A global perspective of institutional adoption policies and guidelines. *Computers and Education: Artificial Intelligence*, *8*, 100348. DOI: 10.1016/j.caeai.2024.100348

Judge, T. A., & Piccolo, R. F. (2004). Transformational and transactional leadership: A meta-analytic test of their relative validity. *The Journal of Applied Psychology*, *89*(5), 755–768. DOI: 10.1037/0021-9010.89.5.755 PMID: 15506858

Jungherr, A. (2023). Artificial intelligence and democracy: A conceptual framework. *Social Media + Society*, *9*(3), 20563051231186353. DOI: 10.1177/20563051231186353

Kalai, M., Becha, H., & Helali, K. (2024). Effect of artificial intelligence on economic growth in European countries: A symmetric and asymmetric cointegration based on linear and non-linear ARDL approach. *Journal of Economic Structures*, *13*(1), 22. DOI: 10.1186/s40008-024-00345-y

Kamal, N., Butt, M. A., & Javeid, U. (2026). An empirical study on the effectiveness of artificial intelligence tools in English language acquisition and teaching strategies within an ESG framework. *Social Science Review Archives*, *4*(1), 3562–3568. DOI: 10.70670/sra.v4i1.1922

Kassar, M., & Jizi, M. (2026). Artificial intelligence and robotic process automation in auditing and accounting: A systematic literature review. *Journal of Applied Accounting Research*, *27*(1), 217–241. DOI: 10.1108/JAAR-05-2024-0175

Katz, D., Maccoby, N., Gurin, G., & Floor, L. G. (1950). *Productivity, supervision and morale among railroad workers*. University of Michigan Survey Research Center.

Kellogg, K. C., Valentine, M. A., & Christin, A. (2020). Algorithms at work: The new contested terrain of control. *The Academy of Management Annals*, *14*(1), 366–410. DOI: 10.5465/annals.2018.0174

Kheradmand, E., Mirshafiee, M., & Pashang, S. (2026). A Comparative Analysis of AI Approaches for ESG Data Extraction. In Walker, T., & Gramlich, D. (Eds.), *The Palgrave Handbook of Sustainable Finance* (pp. 585–610). Springer Nature Switzerland., DOI: 10.1007/978-3-031-98736-6_26

Khogali, H. O., & Mekid, S. (2023). The blended future of automation and AI: Examining some long-term societal and ethical impact features. *Technology in Society*, *73*, 102232. DOI: 10.1016/j.techsoc.2023.102232

Kietzmann, J., Paschen, J., & Treen, E. (2018). Artificial intelligence in advertising: How marketers can leverage artificial intelligence along the consumer journey. *Journal of Advertising Research, 58*(3), 263–267. DOI: 10.2501/JAR-2018-035

Kirikkaleli, D., & Kirikkaleli, N. O. (2025). AI investment in education and training and economic growth in the USA. *Social Sciences & Humanities Open, 12*, 101777. DOI: 10.1016/j.ssaho.2025.101777

Kishor, I., Mamodiya, U., Almaayah, M., Alqutaish, A., Shehab, R., & Aldhyani, T. H. (2025). Agentic AI-Enhanced Virtual Reality for Adaptive Immersive Learning Environments. *Mesopotamian Journal of Computer Science, 2025*, 398–416. DOI: 10.58496/MJCSC/2025/026

Kizgin, K. T., Alp, S., Aydin, N., & Yu, H. (2025). Machine learning-based sales forecasting during crises: Evidence from a Turkish women's clothing retailer. *Science Progress, 108*(1), 00368504241307719. DOI: 10.1177/00368504241307719 PMID: 39840498

Ko[1], S. J. S., & Lim, A. (2024, October). Conceptual Modeling for Public AI Systems. In *Advances in Conceptual Modeling: ER 2024 Workshops, AISA, CMLS, EmpER, QUAMES, JUSMOD, LLM4Modeling, Pittsburgh, PA, USA, October 28–31, 2024, Proceedings* (Vol. 14932, p. 107). Springer Nature. DOI: 10.1007/978-3-031-75599-6_8

Kolb, D. A. (1984). *Experiential learning: Experience as the source of learning and development*. Prentice Hall.

Kolbjørnsrud, V., Amico, R., & Thomas, R. J. (2016). How artificial intelligence will redefine management. Harvard Business Review. https://hbr.org/2016/11/how-artificial-intelligence-will-redefine-management

Konurbayeva, Z., Sánchez-García, E., Marco-Lajara, B., Sloniec, J., Martínez-Falcó, J., & Baitikenova, G. (2026). Leading Sustainable Competitive Advantage From Within: An Analysis of the Mining Industry. *Sustainable Development*, sd.70753. DOI: 10.1002/sd.70753

Kostopoulos, G., Gkamas, V., Rigou, M., & Kotsiantis, S. (2025). Agentic AI in Education: State of the art and future directions. *IEEE Access : Practical Innovations, Open Solutions, 13*, 177467–177491. DOI: 10.1109/ACCESS.2025.3620473

Kotler, P., Kartajaya, H., & Setiawan, I. (2021). *Marketing 5.0: Technology for humanity*. John Wiley & Sons.

Kulkov, I. (2021). The role of artificial intelligence in business transformation: A case of pharmaceutical companies. *Technology in Society*, *66*, 101629. DOI: 10.1016/j.techsoc.2021.101629

Kulkov, I., Kulkova, J., Rohrbeck, R., Menvielle, L., Kaartemo, V., & Makkonen, H. (2024). Artificial intelligence - driven sustainable development: Examining organizational, technical, and processing approaches to achieving global goals. *Sustainable Development (Bradford)*, *32*(3), 2253–2267. DOI: 10.1002/sd.2773

Kumar, V., Ashraf, A. R., & Nadeem, W. (2024). AI-powered marketing: What, where, and how? *International Journal of Information Management*, *77*, 102783. DOI: 10.1016/j.ijinfomgt.2024.102783

Kumar, V., Rajan, B., Venkatesan, R., & Lecinski, J. (2019). Understanding the role of artificial intelligence in personalized engagement marketing. *California Management Review*, *61*(4), 135–155. DOI: 10.1177/0008125619859317

Kuram, Ç., & Bilişik, Ö. N. (2025a). A mixed-integer linear programming model proposal to determine material sustainability for new product development processes in production. *Computers & Chemical Engineering*, *198*, 109108. DOI: 10.1016/j.compchemeng.2025.109108

Kuzmin, E., Bondareva, V. S., Shodiyev, A., & Ochilov, I. (2025). *Digitalization, innovation, and competitiveness*. Springer., DOI: 10.1007/978-3-032-00118-4_17

Lee, S. U., Perera, H., Liu, Y., Xia, B., Lu, Q., Zhu, L., Cairns, J., & Nottage, M. (2025). Integrating ESG and AI: A comprehensive responsible AI assessment framework. *AI and Ethics*, *5*(5), 5121–5148. DOI: 10.1007/s43681-025-00741-5

Li, M., Xie, Q., Enkhtur, A., Meng, S., Chen, L., Yamamoto, B. A., . . . Murakami, M. (2025). A Framework for Developing University Policies on Generative AI Governance: A Cross-national Comparative Study. *arXiv preprint arXiv:2504.02636.*

Li, L. (2024). Reskilling and upskilling the future-ready workforce for industry 4.0 and beyond. *Information Systems Frontiers*, *26*(5), 1697–1712. DOI: 10.1007/s10796-022-10308-y PMID: 35855776

Lim, T. (2024). Environmental, social, and governance (ESG) and artificial intelligence in finance: State-of-the-art and research takeaways. *Artificial Intelligence Review*, *57*(4), 76. DOI: 10.1007/s10462-024-10708-3

Li, N., Kim, M., Dai, J., & Vasarhelyi, M. A. (2024). Using artificial intelligence in ESG assurance. *Journal of Emerging Technologies in Accounting*, *21*(2), 83–99. DOI: 10.2308/JETA-2022-054

Lindner, T., Puck, J., & Puhr, H. (2025). Artificial intelligence in international business: IB theory under augmented decision-making. *Journal of World Business*, *60*(6), 101676. DOI: 10.1016/j.jwb.2025.101676

LinkedIn Economic Graph. (2023). *Future of skills report: AI skills and the evolving talent landscape*. LinkedIn Corporation.

Lin, Y., & Yu, Z. (2025). An integrated bibliometric analysis and systematic review modelling students' technostress in higher education. *Behaviour & Information Technology*, *44*(4), 631–655. DOI: 10.1080/0144929X.2024.2332458

Li, T. T., Wang, K., Sueyoshi, T., & Wang, D. D. (2021). ESG: Research progress and future prospects. *Sustainability (Basel)*, *13*(21), 11663. DOI: 10.3390/su132111663

Liu, Q. (2022). Analysis of collaborative driving effect of artificial intelligence on knowledge innovation management. *Scientific Programming*, *2022*(1), 8223724. DOI: 10.1155/2022/8223724

Liu, Y., Song, J., Zhou, B., & Liu, J. (2025). Artificial intelligence applications and corporate ESG performance. *International Review of Economics & Finance*, *104*, 104559. DOI: 10.1016/j.iref.2025.104559

Li, X., Wang, Q., Kong, D., & Tao, Y. (2025). Intelligent manufacturing and corporate human capital upgrade in China. *Journal of Asian Economics*, *97*, 101886. DOI: 10.1016/j.asieco.2025.101886

Li, Y., Deng, J., Hu, Z., & Gong, B. (2023). Economic policy uncertainty, industrial intelligence, and firms' labour productivity: Empirical evidence from China. *Emerging Markets Finance & Trade*, *59*(2), 498–514. DOI: 10.1080/1540496X.2022.2096433

Lowe, K. B., Kroeck, K. G., & Sivasubramaniam, N. (1996). Effectiveness correlates of transformational and transactional leadership: A meta-analytic review of the MLQ literature. *The Leadership Quarterly*, *7*(3), 385–425. DOI: 10.1016/S1048-9843(96)90027-2

Magd, H., Jonathan, H., Khan, S. A., & El Geddawy, M. (2022). Artificial intelligence—the driving force of industry 4.0. In *A roadmap for enabling Industry 4.0 by artificial intelligence* (pp. 1–15). https://doi.org/DOI: 10.1002/9781119905141.ch1

Maheswaran, K., Selvakumar, P., Shaikh, M., Shashank, G., Gupta, S., & Manjunath, T. C. (2025). The evolution of smart urban mobility with emerging technologies. In *Leveraging VANETs and blockchain technology for urban mobility* (pp. 1–28). IGI Global Scientific Publishing., DOI: 10.4018/979-8-3373-0265-2.ch001

Makhmudov, S., Maqsood, M., Musaev, U., Urazmetov, M., & Shahzadi, A. (2025). Foundations of agentic AI redefining autonomy in learning environments. In *Multidisciplinary Perspectives on Agentic AI in Educational Systems*. IGI Global., DOI: 10.4018/979-8-3373-4621-2.ch001

Makridakis, S. (2017). The forthcoming Artificial Intelligence (AI) revolution: Its impact on society and firms. *Futures*, *90*, 46–60. DOI: 10.1016/j.futures.2017.03.006

Malik, S., Yadav, M., Gupta, N., & Singh, K. (2024). Sales forecasting using machine learning algorithm in the retail sector. *Journal of Computing & Business Intelligence*, *5*(2).

Mansur, S., Sattar, K., Hosseini, S. E., Pervez, S., Ahmad, I., Saleem, K., & Elhendi, A. Z. (2025). Sales forecasting for retail stores using hybrid neural networks and sales-affecting variables. *Scientific Reports*, *15*(1), 12453. PMID: 40216943

Mäntymäki, M., Minkkinen, M., Birkstedt, T., & Viljanen, M. (2022). Defining organizational AI governance. *AI and Ethics*, *2*(4), 603–609. DOI: 10.1007/s43681-022-00143-x

Marampa, A. M., Pongtuluran, A. K., & Pariyanti, E. (2025). From sharing to success: Enhancing innovative work behavior through psychological empowerment and kinship employee engagement. *Industrial and Commercial Training*, *57*(1), 99–117. DOI: 10.1108/ICT-07-2024-0064

Marginson, S. (2019). Limitations of human capital theory. *Studies in Higher Education*, *44*(2), 287–301. DOI: 10.1080/03075079.2017.1359823

Mariani, M., & Dwivedi, Y. K. (2024). Generative artificial intelligence in innovation management: A preview of future research developments. *Journal of Business Research*, *175*, 114542. DOI: 10.1016/j.jbusres.2024.114542

Marlia, M. A., Fahmy, R., Lukito, H., & Games, D. (2025). An Exploratory Study on Effective Leadership and Change Management in the Transformation of Indonesian Public Universities Towards World-Class University Status. *Sustainability (Basel)*, *17*(3), 1300. DOI: 10.3390/su17031300

Martínez-Peláez, R., Ochoa-Brust, A., Rivera, S., Félix, V. G., Ostos, R., Brito, H., Félix, R. A., & Mena, L. J. (2023). Role of digital transformation for achieving sustainability: Mediated role of stakeholders, key capabilities, and technology. *Sustainability (Basel)*, *15*(14), 11221. DOI: 10.3390/su151411221

Matindike, S., Mago, S., Modiba, F., & Van Den Berg, A. (2026). A Review of Digital Transformation and Sustainable International Agricultural Businesses in Africa. In T. Choudhury, R. K. Singh, R. Tomar, S. Balamurugan, & J. C. Patni (Eds.), *Distributed Time-Sensitive Systems* (1st ed., pp. 249–281). Wiley. DOI: 10.1002/9781394197798.ch10

Mayer, D. M., Aquino, K., Greenbaum, R. L., & Kuenzi, M. (2012). Who displays ethical leadership, and why does it matter? An examination of antecedents and consequences of ethical leadership. *Academy of Management Journal*, *55*(1), 151–171. DOI: 10.5465/amj.2008.0276

Mayer, J. D., & Salovey, P. (1997). What is emotional intelligence? In Salovey, P., & Sluyter, D. J. (Eds.), *Emotional development and emotional intelligence* (pp. 3–31). Basic Books.

McAfee, A., & Brynjolfsson, E. (2017). *Machine, platform, crowd: Harnessing our digital future*. WW Norton & Company.

McCauley, C. D., Moxley, R. S., & Van Velsor, E. (Eds.). (2010). *The center for creative leadership handbook of leadership development* (3rd ed.). Jossey-Bass.

McKinsey Global Institute. (2017). *Jobs lost, jobs gained: Workforce transitions in a time of automation*. McKinsey & Company.

McKinsey Global Institute. (2021). The future of work after [McKinsey & Company.]. *COVID*, ●●●, 19.

McKinsey Global Institute. (2023). *The economic potential of generative AI: The next productivity frontier*. McKinsey & Company.

McKinsey Global Institute. (2024). *The state of AI in 2024: GenAI's breakout year*. McKinsey & Company.

Md Tanvir, A., Hossain, M. S., & Rahman, M. (2025). Hybrid RF-XGBoost-LR stacking ensemble for multi-channel retail demand prediction. *Data Science in Business Intelligence*, *9*(2), 112–130.

Mengliyev, I., Meylikulov, S., Fayzullayeva, Z., & Kobulova, M. (2024). Education artificial intelligence systems and their use in teaching. *AIP Conference Proceedings*, 030079. Advance online publication. DOI: 10.1063/5.0241443

Meti, A. (2026). Agentic artificial intelligence in education: A review on personalized adaptive learning through autonomous tutoring systems. *International Journal of Applied Resilience and Sustainability*, *2*(2), 40–74. DOI: 10.70593/deepsci.0202002

Microsoft. (2022). Microsoft responsible AI standard (v2). Microsoft Corporation. https://blogs.microsoft.com/wp-content/uploads/prod/sites/5/2022/06/Microsoft-Responsible-AI-Standard-v2-General-Requirements-3.pdf

Mincer, J. (1974). *Schooling, experience, and earnings*. National Bureau of Economic Research.

Min, S., & Kim, B. (2024). AI technology adoption in corporate IT network operations based on the TOE model. *Digital*, *4*(4), 947–970. DOI: 10.3390/digital4040047

Mintzberg, H. (2004). *Managers not MBAs: A hard look at the soft practice of managing and management development*. Berrett-Koehler Publishers.

Mishra, S. S., Panwar, D., Chouhan, R. P. S., & Shanmugapriya, V. (2024). The impact of AI on the widespread use of EV's: A review. In 2024 2nd International Conference on Advancements and Key Challenges in Green Energy and Computing (AKGEC) (pp. 1–6). IEEE. DOI: 10.1109/AKGEC62572.2024.10868146

Mittelstadt, B. D., Allo, P., Taddeo, M., Wachter, S., & Floridi, L. (2016). The ethics of algorithms: Mapping the debate. *Big Data & Society*, *3*(2), 1–21. DOI: 10.1177/2053951716679679

Mohammed, A., Khan, S., & Li, J. (2026). LSTMixer: A linear extension for multi-horizon temporal forecasting in large-scale retail environments. *IEEE Transactions on Knowledge and Data Engineering*, *38*(4), 890–905.

Morgan Stanley. (2022). *AI in investment management: From automation to augmentation*. Morgan Stanley Institute for Sustainable Investing.

Mustapha, O. O., & Sithole, T. (2025). Forecasting retail sales using machine learning models. [AJSAS]. *American Journal of Statistics and Actuarial Science*, *6*(1), 35–67. DOI: 10.47672/ajsas.2679

Muthuswamy, V. V., & Absamatov, A. (2025). *Determinants of students engagement and their role in boosting students' academic performance*. Revista Electrónica de LEEME., DOI: 10.58262/LEEME.56.13

Nagasubramanian, D. (2026). Harnessing Artificial Intelligence to Revolutionize Education: Personalized Learning and Beyond. In Bhattacharya, S. (Ed.), *ICT for Global Innovations and Solutions. ICGIS 2025. Advances in Computer Science Applications and Research* (Vol. 1). Springer., DOI: 10.1007/978-3-032-02853-2_29

Nandal, N., & Nain, A. (2026). Reskilling for tomorrow: How HR can drive workforce agility in a changing economy. *Strategic HR Review*, *25*(3), 130–136. DOI: 10.1108/SHR-10-2025-0104

Nara, I., Sarun, H., & Hun, H. (2026). Adoption of Artificial Intelligence for Sustainable Development of Higher Education Systems: Nano Review. *Journal of Agriculture and Environment*, *3*(2), 53–55.

Naser-Karajah, E. (2026). The Role of Digital Transformation in Enhancing Corporate Sustainability: A Conceptual Study on Palestinian Institutions Using Digital Twin and Cloud Computing Within the ESG Framework. In Awwad, B., & Awwad, R. A. (Eds.), *Technology and Innovation Towards a Future of Business Sustainability* (pp. 3–13). Springer Nature Singapore., DOI: 10.1007/978-981-95-6469-9_1

NASSCOM. (2023). *AI skills for the future: India's AI talent landscape and growth pathways*. NASSCOM Foundation.

Neama, N. H., & Dulaimi, A. A. (2025). *The Role of Organizational Agility as a Mediator in the Relationship Between Authentic Leadership and Organizational Citizenship Behaviour. 7*(2).

Negm, E. (2026). Artificial intelligence (AI) usage in higher education: Technology integration into curriculums to attain UN sustainable development goals. *Journal of Applied Research in Higher Education*, *18*(2), 616–631. DOI: 10.1108/JARHE-04-2025-0275

Ng, A. (2022). AI for everyone. DeepLearning.AI. https://www.deeplearning.ai/courses/ai-for-everyone/

Nguyen, A., Hong, Y., Dang, B., & Huang, X. (2024). Human-AI collaboration patterns in AI-assisted academic writing. *Studies in Higher Education*, *49*(5), 847–864. DOI: 10.1080/03075079.2024.2323593

Nguyen, J. K. (2024). Human bias in AI models? Anchoring effects and mitigation strategies in large language models. *Journal of Behavioral and Experimental Finance*, *43*, 100971. DOI: 10.1016/j.jbef.2024.100971

Ningtyas, H. I. R., Mualim, W., & Nusron, A. (2026). Artificial Intelligence in The Application of ESG to Improve Company Reputation: The Moderating Role of Financial Performance. *Journal of Accounting Science*, *10*(1), 60–81. DOI: 10.21070/jas.v10i1.2047

Nonaka, I., & Takeuchi, H. (1995). *The knowledge-creating company: How Japanese companies create the dynamics of innovation*. Oxford University Press. DOI: 10.1093/oso/9780195092691.001.0001

Nordin, A. S. M., Alias, B. S., & Haniff, M. H. M. (2023). *Organizational Change Through Transformational Leadership Practices: The Principal's Role*. https://kwpublications.com/papers_submitted/7882/organizational-change-through-transformational-leadership-practices-the-principals-role.pdf

Nugraha, R., Mayagita, A., Satriansyah, A., & Oktiyani, R. (2026). Sustainable Digital Accounting: Integrating ESG Reporting and Data Analytics in the Era of Industry 5.0. *Jurnal Visi Manajemen*, *12*(1), 182–193.

O'Sullivan, J., Lowry, C., Woods, R., & Conlon, T. (2025). Generative AI in Higher Education Teaching & Learning: National Policy Framework. https://eprints.teachingandlearning.ie/id/eprint/6702/

Obermeyer, Z., Powers, B., Vogeli, C., & Mullainathan, S. (2019). Dissecting racial bias in an algorithm used to manage the health of populations. *Science*, *366*(6464), 447–453. DOI: 10.1126/science.aax2342 PMID: 31649194

OECD. (2019). Recommendation of the council on artificial intelligence (OECD/LEGAL/0449). Organisation for Economic Co-operation and Development. https://legalinstruments.oecd.org/en/instruments/OECD-LEGAL-0449

Oehmichen, J., Geist, L., & Weck, M. (2025). AI and ESG. *Annals of Corporate Governance*, *9*(4), 280–345. DOI: 10.1561/109.00000048

Ofosu-Ampong, K. (2024). Artificial intelligence research: A review on dominant themes, methods, frameworks and future research directions. *Telematics and Informatics Reports*, *14*, 100127. DOI: 10.1016/j.teler.2024.100127

Ofosu-Asare, Y. (2025). Guiding the future: developing an ethical framework for generative AI use in education. *The International Journal of Information and Learning Technology*, 1-19. DOI: 10.1108/IJILT-06-2024-0113

Oliveira, T., & Martins, M. F. (2011). Literature review of IT adoption models. *Procedia Technology*, *5*, 110–119.

Oltiboy, B., Mansur, U., Salimov, U., Boboqulov, C., & Babayev, A. (2025). Optimizing linguistic outcomes in education: A CRM-based structural equation modeling approach. *Forum for Linguistic Studies*, *7*(6), 9383. DOI: 10.30564/fls.v7i6.9383

Orlikowski, W. J., & Scott, S. V. (2008). Sociomateriality: Challenging the separation of technology, work and organization. *The Academy of Management Annals*, *2*(1), 433–474. DOI: 10.5465/19416520802211644

Ozkan, B. (2024). *The transformative impact of AI on CSR, ESG, and sustainability: Critical review and case studies.* https://www.emerald.com/books/edited-volume/17319/chapter/94286953

Padhy, A., Rane, N. L., & Rane, J. (2026). Explainable artificial intelligence for sustainable business performance: Integrating ESG metrics into AI adoption models. *International Journal of Applied Resilience and Sustainability*, *2*(1), 78–96. DOI: 10.70593/deepsci.0201005

Panwar, D., Mishra, S. S., Kumar, A., & Soni, A. (2024). A review of machine learning in photovoltaic system fabrication and implementation. In 2024 7th International Conference on Contemporary Computing and Informatics (IC3I) (pp. 754–759). IEEE. DOI: 10.1109/IC3I61595.2024.10828669

Pan, Z., Moore, O. A., Papadimitriou, A., & Zhu, J. (2025). AI literacy and trust: A multi-method study of human-GAI team collaboration. *Computers in Human Behavior: Artificial Humans*, *3*, 100162. DOI: 10.1016/j.chbah.2025.100162

Papagiannidis, E., Mikalef, P., & Conboy, K. (2025). Responsible artificial intelligence governance: A review and research framework. *The Journal of Strategic Information Systems*, *34*(1), 101885. DOI: 10.1016/j.jsis.2024.101885

Park, [Initials], Han, Y., & Cho, S.-B. (2023). Temporal pattern attention-based recurrent neural networks for retail sales forecasting. *IEEE Transactions on Neural Networks and Learning Systems, 34*(3), 1175–1187.

Pasquale, F. (2015). *The black box society: The secret algorithms that control money and information.* Harvard University Press. DOI: 10.4159/harvard.9780674736061

Peng, H., & Peng, Y. (2026). Is Supply Chain Digitalization Conducive to Promoting the ESG Performance of Energy-Intensive Firms? *Sustainability (Basel)*, *18*(4), 1879. DOI: 10.3390/su18041879

Pfeffer, J., & Fong, C. T. (2002). The end of business schools? Less success than meets the eye. *Academy of Management Learning & Education*, *1*(1), 78–95. DOI: 10.5465/amle.2002.7373679

Podsakoff, P. M., MacKenzie, S. B., & Podsakoff, N. P. (2016). Recommendations for creating better concept definitions in the organizational, behavioral, and social sciences. *Organizational Research Methods*, *19*(2), 159–203. DOI: 10.1177/1094428115624965

Porter, L. W., & McKibbin, L. E. (1988). *Management education and development: Drift or thrust into the 21st century?* McGraw-Hill.

Prabha, K. R., Mabel, B. R., Isaev, F., Mamadiyarov, Z., Raxmatullayevich, K. U., & Erkinjon, T. (2026). A Multi-Layer Artificial Intelligence–Enabled Governance Framework for Integrating Information Security Management, Quality Management, and Strategic Human Resource Analytics: An Empirical Study on the Role of Corporate Social Responsibility in Sustainable Organizational Performance. *Quality - Access to Success, 27*(210). Advance online publication. DOI: 10.47750/QAS/27.210.45

Prokhorenkova, L., Gusev, G., Vorobev, A., Dorogush, A. V., & Gulin, A. (2018). CatBoost: Unbiased boosting with categorical features. *Advances in Neural Information Processing Systems (NeurIPS 2018).*

Qian, Y., Jha, K., & Li, Y. (2024). Societal impacts of artificial intelligence: Ethical, legal, and governance issues. *Journal of Responsible Technology, 17*, 100082. DOI: 10.1016/j.jrt.2024.100082

Qu, K. (2024). Research on linear regression algorithm. *MATEC Web of Conferences, 395.*

Rachid, O. U. S. K. O. U., & Houda, C. H. A. M. M. A. A. (2024). Redefining human capital in the age of artificial intelligence: Challenges and opportunities. *Revue Internationale de la Recherche Scientifique et de l'Innovation (Revue-IRSI),* 2(4), 933-946.

Ragadhita, R., Fiandini, M., Al Husaeni, D. N., & Nandiyanto, A. B. D. (2026). Sustainable development goals (SDGs) in engineering education: Definitions, research trends, bibliometric insights, and strategic approaches. *Indonesian Journal of Science and Technology, 11*(1), 1–26. DOI: 10.17509/ijost.v11i1.86298

Rajeswari, M., Vanitha, C. L., Xudoynazarova, S., Mamadiyarov, Z., Naveen, S., Nematovich, K. I., & Isaev, F. (2026). Design and Validation of an Explainable Artificial Intelligence–Based Decision Intelligence Model for Cyber Risk–Aware Quality Systems and Ethical Human Resource Management: Investigating the Moderating Influence of Corporate Social Responsibility in Digitally Transformed Organizations. *Quality - Access to Success, 27*(210). Advance online publication. DOI: 10.47750/QAS/27.210.46

Raman, R., Gandhi, A., & Banerjee, U. (2026). *Agentic AI and Flexible Management: Multidisciplinary and Behavioural Perspectives on Evolving Practices, Strategic Opportunities, and Policy Implications.* Glob J Flex Syst Manag., DOI: 10.1007/s40171-026-00483-1

Rana, J., Jain, R., & Nehra, V. (2024). Utility and acceptability of AI-enabled chatbots on the online customer journey. *International Journal of Computing and Digital Systems*, *15*(1), 323–335. DOI: 10.12785/ijcds/150125

Rana, J., Jain, R., & Santosh, K. C. (2023). Automation and AI-enabled customer journey: A bibliometric analysis. *Vision (Basel)*, 09722629221149854. Advance online publication. DOI: 10.1177/09722629221149854

Rao, M. S., Saraswathy, S., Neela, V., Arun, M. R., Gupta, S., & Taqui, S. N. (2023, November). Efficient Model Training in Decentralized Systems with Federated Learning. *In 2023 IEEE International Conference on Communication, Security and Artificial Intelligence (ICCSAI)* (pp. 900-904). DOI: 10.1109/ICCSAI59793.2023.10421469

Rathinavel, P., Ravikumar, R. N., Aarthi, S., Habib, M., & Salaeva, N. (2025). *Augmenting human capabilities: AI's impact on collaborative workflows*. IGI Global., DOI: 10.4018/979-8-3373-2372-5.ch001

Ravikumar, R. N., Aarthi, S., Rejapov, I. O., Sultonova, M., & Musayeva, S. (2025). Transforming healthcare with large language models and AI agents. In *Advanced Interdisciplinary Applications of LLMs*. IGI Global., DOI: 10.4018/979-8-3373-2008-3.ch003

Razmak, J., & Farhan, W. (2026). A proposed digital transformation model for implementation by digital leaders. *Smart and Sustainable Built Environment*, *15*(1), 92–119. DOI: 10.1108/SASBE-11-2023-0369

Reserve Bank of India. (2023). *Guidelines on artificial intelligence and machine learning in financial services*. RBI Publications.

Robertson, J., Ferreira, C., Botha, E., & Oosthuizen, K. (2024). Game changers: A generative AI prompt protocol to enhance human–AI knowledge co-construction. *Business Horizons*, *67*(6), 683–697. DOI: 10.1016/j.bushor.2024.04.008

Rodgers, W., Murray, J. M., Stefanidis, A., Degbey, W. Y., & Tarba, S. Y. (2023). An artificial intelligence algorithmic approach to ethical decision-making in human resource management processes. *Human Resource Management Review*, *33*(1), 100925. DOI: 10.1016/j.hrmr.2022.100925

Rogge, N. D., Lamovšek, A., & Batistič, S. (2025). AI meets IA: A typology of generative-AI-supported work through individual ambidexterity. *Business Horizons*. Advance online publication. DOI: 10.1016/j.bushor.2025.06.006

Romer, P. M. (1990). Endogenous technological change. *Journal of Political Economy*, *98*(5, Part 2), S71–S102. DOI: 10.1086/261725

Rosário, A. T., & Cruz, R. N. (2025). Environment, Social, and Governance Business: Challenges and Opportunities. *Environmental, Social, Governance and Digital Transformation in Organizations*, 73-102.

Rosenblat, A., & Stark, L. (2016). Algorithmic labor and information asymmetries: A case study of Uber's drivers. *International Journal of Communication*, *10*, 3758–3784.

Rui, X., & Li, Y. (2025). GCN-LSTM with attention mechanism for capturing topological dependencies in retail supply chains. *Journal of Big Data Analytics*, *7*(1), 204–221.

Russell, S. (2019). *Human compatible: Artificial intelligence and the problem of control*. Viking.

Russell, S. J., & Norvig, P. (2021). *Artificial intelligence: A modern approach* (4th ed.). Pearson.

Sadraei, R., & Dal Mas, F. (2026). Women entrepreneurship in the age of AI and ESG: Micro- and macro-level drivers of adoption. *International Journal of Entrepreneurship and Innovation*, *14657503251408253*, 14657503251408253. Advance online publication. DOI: 10.1177/14657503251408253

Sætra, H. S. (2021). A framework for evaluating and disclosing the ESG related impacts of AI with the SDGs. *Sustainability (Basel)*, *13*(15), 8503. DOI: 10.3390/su13158503

Sætra, H. S. (2023). The AI ESG protocol: Evaluating and disclosing the environment, social, and governance implications of artificial intelligence capabilities, assets, and activities. *Sustainable Development (Bradford)*, *31*(2), 1027–1037. DOI: 10.1002/sd.2438

Sajawal, M., Usman, S., Alshaikh, H. S., & Hayat, A. (2023). *Predictive analysis of retail sales forecasting using machine learning*. Lahore Garrison University Research Journal of Computer Science and Information Technology.

Salman, H. A., Kalakech, A., & Steti, A. (2024). Random forest algorithm overview. *Babylonian Journal of Machine Learning*, *2024*, 69–79. DOI: 10.58496/BJML/2024/007

Santos, M. R., Carvalho, L. C., & Francisco, E. (2025). A capability-based framework for knowledge-driven AI innovation and sustainability. *Information (Basel)*, *16*(11), 987. DOI: 10.3390/info16110987

Sarvate, D., Mishra, S. S., Shanmugapriya, V., & Panwar, D. (2025). Integrating blockchain and federated learning for enhanced security and privacy in smart cities. In Singh, K. K., Singh, A., & Mahesh, T. R. (Eds.), *Integration of federated learning and blockchain for smart cities*. Wiley., DOI: 10.1002/9781394167760.ch10

Savvadelli, E., Kiouvrekis, Y., & Kokkinaki, A. (2025, July). A Literature Review on Rule-Based Systems as Decision Support Systems. *In International Symposium on Human Aspects of Information Security and Assurance* (pp. 376-388). Cham: Springer Nature Switzerland. DOI: 10.1007/978-3-032-02504-3_26

Schultz, T. W. (1961). Investment in human capital. *The American Economic Review*, *51*(1), 1–17.

Schwab, K. (2016). *The fourth industrial revolution*. Crown Business.

Selim, O. (2020). ESG and AI: The beauty and the beast of sustainable investing. In *Sustainable investing* (pp. 227–243). Routledge. https://www.taylorfrancis.com/chapters/edit/10.4324/9780429351044-12/esg-ai-omar-selim

Senge, P. M. (1990). *The fifth discipline: The art and practice of the learning organization*. Doubleday.

Sethumadhavan, R. P. P. S., Sajimon, P. P., Selvakumar, P., Kadu, S. G., Chandel, P. S., & Gupta, S. (2025). Environmental sustainability and employee participation. In *Green Leadership Strategies for Increased Employee Engagement and Performance* (pp. 275–298). IGI Global Scientific Publishing., DOI: 10.4018/979-8-3373-2106-6.ch009

Shankar, R., Chaudhary, B. P., Mehraj, H., Gupta, S., Arslan, F., Srivastava, A. K., & Goswami, C. (2023). Impact of node mobility on the DL based uplink and downlink MIMO-NOMA network. *International Journal of Information Technology : an Official Journal of Bharati Vidyapeeth's Institute of Computer Applications and Management*, *15*(6), 3391–3404. DOI: 10.1007/s41870-023-01362-z

Sharma, S. (2024). Benefits or concerns of AI: A multistakeholder responsibility. *Futures*, *157*, 103328. DOI: 10.1016/j.futures.2024.103328

Shen, P., Qing, L., Wu, L., & Qi, L. (2025). When you find the ESG performance in digital transformation: A look at firms' internal controls, absorptive capacity, and green innovativeness. *Applied Economics*, •••, 1–20. DOI: 10.1080/00036846.2025.2607071

Sida, T. S., Desalegn, T., Abate, G. T., & Amede, T. (2025). 3 Feeding a fast-growing population by 2050 through accelerated agricultural transformation: Potential avenues for Ethiopia. *Pathways to African Food Security*, 35.

Singh, K. S., Shanmugapriya, V., Mishra, S. S., & Singh, M. (2026). Artificial intelligence-driven flow optimization for enhanced efficiency in renewable energy systems. In Awasthi, M. K., & Gupta, R. (Eds.), *Artificial intelligence and computational modeling in heat transfer and fluid dynamics*. Wiley., DOI: 10.1002/9781394433605.ch10

Sinha, R., Sinha, K. K., Patel, M., Gupta, S., & Priya, S. (2024, July). Detection of leukemia disease using convolutional neural network. In 2024 5th International Conference on Image Processing and Capsule Networks (ICIPCN) (pp. 451-456). IEEE. DOI: 10.1109/ICIPCN63822.2024.00080

Skitka, L. J., Mosier, K. L., & Burdick, M. (1999). Does automation bias decision-making? *International Journal of Human-Computer Studies*, *51*(5), 991–1006. DOI: 10.1006/ijhc.1999.0252

Smith, B., & Shum, H. (2019). *The future computed: AI and its role in society*. Microsoft Corporation.

Sohn, S. M. (2025). Effortlessness as the measurement of the impact of artificial intelligence (AI) adoption and innovation: Towards the theory of relative AI. *Technology in Society*, *81*, 102962. DOI: 10.1016/j.techsoc.2025.102962

Somaratne, S., De Silva, D., & Athukorala, R. (2025). Mapping human-AI collaboration: A skill framework for the effective use of AI. In *2025 3rd International Conference on Communication, Security, and Artificial Intelligence (ICCSAI)* (Vol. 3, pp. 1253–1261). IEEE. https://doi.org/DOI: 10.1109/ICCSAI64074.2025.11064159

Soni, N., Sharma, E. K., Singh, N., & Kapoor, A. (2020). Artificial intelligence in business: From research and innovation to market deployment. *Procedia Computer Science*, *167*, 2200–2210. DOI: 10.1016/j.procs.2020.03.272

Soundariya, A., Behera, N. K., Selvakumar, P., Chandel, P. S., Gupta, S., & Manjunath, T. C. (2025). AI and environmental ethics: The role of AI in addressing climate change ethical considerations in AI-driven environmental solutions. In *Human values, ethics, and dignity in the age of artificial intelligence* (pp. 321–346). IGI Global Scientific Publishing., DOI: 10.4018/979-8-3693-9035-1.ch013

Sowa, K., Przegalinska, A., & Ciechanowski, L. (2021). Cobots in knowledge work: Human–AI collaboration in managerial professions. *Journal of Business Research*, *125*, 135–142. DOI: 10.1016/j.jbusres.2020.11.038

Spencer, L. M., & Spencer, S. M. (1993). *Competence at work: Models for superior performance*. Wiley.

Sreekanthaswamy, N., Anitha, S., Singh, A., Jayadeva, S. M., Gupta, S., Manjunath, T. C., & Selvakumar, P. (2025). Digital tools and methods. In *Enhancing school counseling with technology and case studies* (pp. 25–48). IGI Global Scientific Publishing., DOI: 10.4018/979-8-3693-8392-6.ch002

Stahl, B. C. (2022). Responsible innovation ecosystems: Ethical implications of the application of the ecosystem concept to artificial intelligence. *International Journal of Information Management*, *62*, 102441. DOI: 10.1016/j.ijinfomgt.2021.102441

Stilgoe, J., Owen, R., & Macnaghten, P. (2013). Developing a framework for responsible innovation. *Research Policy*, *42*(9), 1568–1580. DOI: 10.1016/j.respol.2013.05.008

Strohmeier, S. (2020). Smart HRM – A Delphi study on the application and consequences of artificial intelligence for human resource management. *International Journal of Human Resource Management*, *31*(12), 1–32. DOI: 10.1080/09585192.2020.1751829

Sufyan Ghaleb, M. M., & Pardaev, J. (2025). Literature reading self-efficacy and academic achievement. *Educational Sciences: Theory & Practice*, *25*(2), 77–92. DOI: 10.12738/jestp.2025.2.06

Sugiyanto, H. (2025). Leadership Styles, Quality of Education, and Educational Institution Management: A Systematic Review in the Perspective of Sustainable Education. *Journal Corner of Education, Linguistics, and Literature*, *4*(3), 351–359. DOI: 10.54012/jcell.v4i3.423

Sundaresan, S., & Zhang, Z. (2022). AI-enabled knowledge sharing and learning: Redesigning roles and processes. *The International Journal of Organizational Analysis*, *30*(4), 983–999. DOI: 10.1108/IJOA-12-2020-2558

Sundberg, L., & Holmström, J. (2023). Democratizing artificial intelligence: How no-code AI can leverage machine learning operations. *Business Horizons*, *66*(6), 777–788. DOI: 10.1016/j.bushor.2023.04.003

Sun, Y., Lu, Y., Wu, Y., Xu, C., & Davey, H. (2026). Synergizing ESG and Digital Transformation for Corporate Decarbonization. *Business Strategy and the Environment*, *35*(2), 2581–2599. DOI: 10.1002/bse.70262

Suradinkura, S., Amornbuth, C., Fang, Y., Suradinkura, V., & Suradinkura, N. (2026). Digital Transformation and Environmental Governance: A Synthesis of ESG Integration. In *Green Governance of Digital Organizations* (pp. 125–156). IGI Global Scientific Publishing. https://www.igi-global.com/chapter/digital-transformation-and-environmental-governance/401458

Susskind, R., & Susskind, D. (2015). *The future of the professions: How technology will transform the work of human experts*. Oxford University Press. DOI: 10.1093/oso/9780198713395.001.0001

Sutar, D., Metri, R. A., Naik, R., Mishra, S., Thakkar, J., & Kolhe, M. (2026). Energy-efficient automation of industrial surface pre-treatment processes using PLC and SCADA. In Proceedings of the Second International Conference on New Power System and Power Electronics (NPSPE 2025) (Vol. 14129, Article 141292C). SPIE. https://doi.org/DOI: 10.1117/12.3110247

Su, Y., & Abd Rani, N. S. (2025). Empowering Leadership and Psychological Capital: Drivers of Teachers' Innovative Behavior among International School Teachers in Beijing City. *Uniglobal Journal of Social Sciences and Humanities*, *4*(1), 66–75.

Taleizadeh, A. A., Tahmasbifar, Z., Moradi, R., Sarker, B. R., & Hafezalkotob, A. (2025). An optimum decision-making strategy to maximize total profit in a two-period closed-loop supply chain dealing with greenhouse gases. *Annals of Operations Research*. Advance online publication. DOI: 10.1007/s10479-025-06610-y

Taljaard, E. (2022). *Adopting Collective Hybrid Intelligence Principles to Enhance Corporate Innovation and Process Efficiencies* (Master's thesis, University of Pretoria (South Africa).

Tan, E. (2014). Human capital theory: A holistic criticism. *Review of Educational Research*, *84*(3), 411–445. DOI: 10.3102/0034654314532696

Tarwidi, D., Pudjaprasetya, S. R., Adytia, D., & Apri, M. (2023). An optimized XGBoost-based machine learning method for predicting wave run-up on a sloping beach. *MethodsX*, *10*, 11. DOI: 10.1016/j.mex.2023.102119 PMID: 37007622

Taylor, F. W. (1911). The principles of scientific management. Harper & Brothers.

Teruel-Sanchez, R., Briones-Peñalver, A. J., Bernal-Conesa, J. A., & De Nieves-Nieto, C. (2025). Values of the entrepreneur as a driver of sustainable tourism entrepreneurship. *Journal of International Entrepreneurship*, *23*(3), 648–676. Advance online publication. DOI: 10.1007/s10843-025-00381-0

Thandlam, A. K., Vignesh, T., Saravanan, A., Subramani, P., Marimuthu, R., & Gupta, S. (2024, April). Next-gen vehicle safety: The futuristic approach to auto-stop in modern vehicles. In 2024 10th International Conference on Communication and Signal Processing (ICCSP) (pp. 265-270). IEEE. DOI: 10.1109/ICCSP60870.2024.10543666

Thien, L. M., Lim, H. L., Ahmad Shabudin, A. F., Che Aman, R., Ismail, A., Zuharah, W. F., & Muftahu, M. (2025). Women leadership in higher education: Exploring enablers and challenges from middle-level academics' perspective. *Humanities & Social Sciences Communications*, *12*(1), 1–12. DOI: 10.1057/s41599-024-04278-6

Tian, H., Wang, J., & Cai, Y. (2025). Artificial Intelligence Adoption and Corporate ESG Performance. *Business Strategy and the Environment*, *34*(7), 8922–8945. DOI: 10.1002/bse.70032

Tiron-Tudor, A., Deliu, D., & Ndou, V. (2025). Shaping the future: Ethical, legal and social implications (ELSI) of digital innovation ecosystems (DIEs) amid the Twin Transition. *European Journal of Innovation Management*, •••, 1–45.

Tornatzky, L. G., & Fleischer, M. (1990). *The processes of technological innovation*. Lexington Books.

Tran, G. T. C., Le Dinh, T., & Le, T. D. (2026). Agentic AI Across Technologies, Applications, and Development Domains: A Systematic Literature Review. In Swaroop, A., Virdee, B., Correia, S. D., & Polkowski, Z. (Eds.), *Proceedings of Data Analytics and Management. ICDAM 2025. Lecture Notes in Networks and Systems* (Vol. 1603). Springer., DOI: 10.1007/978-3-032-03769-5_44

Tutushkina, N., Duschanova, G., Majidova, D., Karimov, S., Odilov, U., Sapaev, I., Shamuradova, N., & Vosiqov, U. (2025). Fostering sustainable development in tourist destinations through collaborative education on environmental conservation. *Natural and Engineering Sciences*, *10*(3), 475–491. Advance online publication. DOI: 10.28978/nesciences.1811138

Uhl-Bien, M., Marion, R., & McKelvey, B. (2007). Complexity leadership theory: Shifting leadership from the industrial age to the knowledge era. *The Leadership Quarterly*, *18*(4), 298–318. DOI: 10.1016/j.leaqua.2007.04.002

Ulrich, D., & Brockbank, W. (2005). *The HR value proposition*. Harvard Business Press.

Umoru, U., Ogundana, O. M., Mangena, M., & Udeozor, V. (2026). Informal Institutions and Multinationals' Drive Towards Sustainable Development Goals (SDGs): A Dark-Side Perspective. *Business Ethics, the Environment & Responsibility*, *35*(1), 75–98. DOI: 10.1111/beer.12773

Väyrynen, K., Holmström, J., Sundberg, L., Hietala, H., & Lanamäki, A. (2025). Guardrails, not barriers: Navigating AI Act readiness. *Business Horizons*. Advance online publication. DOI: 10.1016/j.bushor.2025.08.002

Venkiteela, S. R. (2025). SuperKart: A real-time low-code framework for scalable retail forecasting using XGBoost. *International Journal of Intelligent Systems and Applications in Engineering*, *13*(2), 441–458.

Vial, G. (2021). Understanding digital transformation: A review and a research agenda. *Managing digital transformation*, 13-66.

Vössing, M., Kühl, N., Lind, M., & Satzger, G. (2022). Designing transparency for effective human-AI collaboration. *Information Systems Frontiers*, *24*(3), 877–895. DOI: 10.1007/s10796-022-10284-3

Vukmir, R. B. (2006). Customer satisfaction. *International Journal of Health Care Quality Assurance*, *19*(1), 8–31. DOI: 10.1108/09526860610642573 PMID: 16548396

Walumbwa, F. O., & Schaubroeck, J. (2009). Leader personality traits and employee voice behavior: Mediating roles of ethical leadership and work group psychological safety. *The Journal of Applied Psychology*, *94*(5), 1275–1286. DOI: 10.1037/a0015848 PMID: 19702370

Wang, J., Ma, Y., Li, R., & Zhang, S. (2025). Applications of Building Information Modeling (BIM) and BIM-Related Technologies for Sustainable Risk and Disaster Management in Buildings: A Meta-Analysis (2014–2024). *Buildings (Basel, Switzerland)*, *15*(13), 2289. DOI: 10.3390/buildings15132289

Wang, Q., Qi, Y., & Li, R. (2026). Artificial Intelligence and Corporate Sustainability: Shaping the Future of ESG in the Age of Industry 5.0. *Sustainable Development (Bradford)*, *34*(1), 1–26. DOI: 10.1002/sd.70200

Wang, Q., Yin, H., Li, S., & Yang, Z. (2022). Integration of deep learning and traditional models for retail sales forecasting. *IEEE Access : Practical Innovations, Open Solutions*, *10*, 65021–65034.

Wang, Q., Zhang, F., & Li, R. (2025). Artificial intelligence and sustainable development during urbanization: Perspectives on AI R&D innovation, AI infrastructure, and AI market advantage. *Sustainable Development (Bradford)*, *33*(1), 1136–1156. DOI: 10.1002/sd.3150

Wang, X., Xie, F., & Liu, B. (2025). Governance efficiency and upgrade pathways of international generative AI policies and regulations. *Technology in Society*, *103082*. Advance online publication. DOI: 10.1016/j.techsoc.2025.103082

Watts, S., & Munir, T. (2026). Bridging the gap: Exploring innovation enablers, challenges and AI adoption for enhanced workforce productivity. *International Journal of Productivity and Performance Management, 75*(3), 1030–1046. DOI: 10.1108/IJPPM-01-2025-0001

Wenger, E. (1998). *Communities of practice: Learning, meaning, and identity.* Cambridge University Press. DOI: 10.1017/CBO9780511803932

Wilson, H. J., & Daugherty, P. R. (2018). Collaborative intelligence: Humans and AI are joining forces. *Harvard Business Review, 96*(4), 114–123.

World Economic Forum. (2020). The future of jobs report 2020. World Economic Forum.

World Economic Forum. (2023). Future of jobs report 2023. World Economic Forum. https://www.weforum.org/reports/the-future-of-jobs-report-2023/

World Economic Forum. (2023). The future of jobs report 2023. World Economic Forum.

World Economic Forum. (2025). *The future of jobs report.* World Economic Forum.

Xamrakulova, X., Mirzaeva, Z., Shabbazova, D., Sabirov, A., Rasulova, Z., Ismoilov, B., & Mukhriddin, A. (2026). Project based marine biodiversity education to improve ocean literacy and conservation attitudes among secondary students. *Natural and Engineering Sciences, 11*(1), 211–220. DOI: 10.28978/nesciences.261015

Xiao, S., Roh, T., Park, B. I., AL-Tabbaa, O., & Seo, K. (2026). Unpacking the Role of Digital Dynamic Capabilities in ESG Performance: A Social Exchange Perspective on Organizational Trust and Identification. *Business Strategy and the Environment, 35*(2), 1951–1969. DOI: 10.1002/bse.70273

Xu, J. (2024). AI in ESG for financial institutions: An industrial survey. *arXiv Preprint arXiv:2403.05541*. https://arxiv.org/abs/2403.05541 DOI: 10.2139/ssrn.4949354

Xu, C., & Cho, S. E. (2025). Factors affecting human–AI collaboration performances in financial sector: Sustainable service development perspective. *Sustainability (Basel), 17*(10), 4335. DOI: 10.3390/su17104335

Xu, X., Arshad, M. A., He, Y., Liu, H., Chen, Q., & Yang, J. (2025). From skilled workers to smart talent: AI-driven workforce transformation in the construction industry. *Buildings (Basel, Switzerland), 15*(14), 2552. DOI: 10.3390/buildings15142552

Yakob, M., Sahudra, T. M., & Sukirno, S. (2025). Transformational Leadership of Principals: Driving Excellence in Education Quality. *Al-Ishlah: Jurnal Pendidikan, 17*(1), 1658–1667. DOI: 10.35445/alishlah.v17i1.6887

Yan, M.-R., Yan, H., Chen, Y.-R., Zhang, Y., Yan, X., & Zhao, Y. (2026). Integrated green supply chain system development with digital transformation. *International Journal of Logistics*, *29*(3), 394–415. DOI: 10.1080/13675567.2025.2492217

Yim, I. H. Y., & Su, J. (2024). Artificial intelligence (AI) learning tools in K-12 education: A scoping review. *Journal of Computers in Education*. Advance online publication. DOI: 10.1007/s40692-023-00304-9

Yin, R. K. (2018). *Case study research and applications: Design and methods* (6th ed.). SAGE.

Yu, Y. C. (2026). Leveraging Agentic AI for Enhancing Multiple Assessments on Hands-On Learning. In: May, D., Auer, M.E. (eds) 2025 Yearbook Emerging Technologies in Learning. Learning and Analytics in Intelligent Systems, vol 59. Springer, Cham. https://doi.org/DOI: 10.1007/978-3-032-09058-4_1

Zarghami, S. A. (2025). The role of economic policies in achieving sustainable development goal 7: Insights from OECD and European countries. *Applied Energy*, *377*, 124558. DOI: 10.1016/j.apenergy.2024.124558

Zhang, C., & Yang, J. (2024). Artificial intelligence and corporate ESG performance. *International Review of Economics & Finance*, *96*, 103713. DOI: 10.1016/j.iref.2024.103713

Zhang, J., & Patel, V. L. (2006). Distributed cognition, representation, and affordance. *Pragmatics & Cognition*, *14*(2), 333–341. DOI: 10.1075/pc.14.2.12zha

Zhang, Y., Jiang, H., & Gong, Q. (2024). Dynamics of human-machine task allocation in intelligent production processes: A case study. *Computers & Industrial Engineering*, *194*, 110354. DOI: 10.1016/j.cie.2024.110354

Zheng, Z., & Lee, C. L. (2025). A meta-analysis of ESG factors in the real estate investment trusts sector: Exploring their impacts on REITs performance. *Engineering, Construction and Architectural Management*. https://www.emerald.com/ecam/article/doi/10.1108/ECAM-05-2024-0652/1259586

Zheng, J., Zhang, J. Z., Kamal, M. M., Liang, X., & Alzeiby, E. A. (2025). Unpacking human–AI interaction: Exploring unintended consequences on employee well-being in entrepreneurial firms through an in-depth analysis. *Journal of Business Research*, *196*, 115406. DOI: 10.1016/j.jbusres.2025.115406

Zirar, A., Ali, S. I., & Islam, N. (2023). Worker and workplace artificial intelligence (AI) coexistence: Emerging themes and research agenda. *Technovation*, *124*, 102747. DOI: 10.1016/j.technovation.2023.102747

Zlateva, P., Steshina, L., Petukhov, I., & Velev, D. (2024). A conceptual framework for solving ethical issues in generative artificial intelligence. In *Electronics, communications and networks* (pp. 110–119). IOS Press. DOI: 10.3233/FAIA231182

About the Contributors

Hussain Alagele is Head of Banking Management Economics Department College of Business Economics | Al-Nahrain University, Iraq Professional Profile Professor Dr. Hussain K. Hussain Alagele is a distinguished academic leader and a senior faculty member at the College of Business Economics, Al-Nahrain University. Holding a PhD in Business Administration with a specialized focus on Organizational Behavior, he has established himself as a prominent authority in aligning human dynamics with institutional excellence. Throughout his career, Prof. Alagele has been a catalyst for academic innovation, bridging the gap between foundational management theories and the transformative demands of the modern era. His scholarly contributions are widely recognized for their multidisciplinary approach, integrating social science with technological and environmental paradigms. Areas of Expertise & Research Interests Prof. Alagele's extensive research portfolio focuses on the intersection of leadership, technology, and sustainability: Organizational Dynamics: Advanced Leadership strategies, fostering Innovation, and analyzing Human Behavior within complex systems. Technological Evolution: Harnessing Artificial Intelligence (AI) and leading Digital Transformation to enhance organizational efficiency. Global Sustainability: Strategic implementation of Sustainable Development goals and Clean Energy initiatives within the public and private sectors. Market & Financial Strategy: Expertise in Banking Economics and advanced Marketing frameworks tailored for the creative economy. Contact Information Email: hussain.alagele@gmail.com Location: Baghdad, Iraq | Postal Code: 10011

Nagham Neama is the Dean of the College of Business Economics and a faculty member at Al-Nahrain University in Baghdad, Iraq. She holds a PhD in Business Administration, specializing in Financial Management. A prolific researcher, Dr. Neama has authored numerous publications across diverse academic fields, including Finance, Business Administration, Marketing, and Strategic Leadership. Her scholarly work also explores contemporary areas such as Sustainable Development, Artificial Intelligence, Digital Transformation, and Organizational Leadership.

***

Duggirala Aravind is currently associated with the Department of Aviation, ASET Institute of Science and Technology, Chennai, India. He previously completed his Bachelor's degree in Electrical and Electronics Engineering at MITS University. His research interests include aviation operations, renewable energy technologies in air transport, Artificial Intelligence, Computer Science, Logistics and Business management.

Kasukurthi Aravind is an MBA student in Airlines and Airport Management at ASET College of Science and Technology, India. His interests include innovation, entrepreneurship, global business, and artificial intelligence.

Bitto Benny is an Assistant Professor in the Department of Management at CHRIST College, Pune. He has been actively associated with the Department of Commerce and the Student Welfare Office at CHRIST (Deemed to be University), Bengaluru, where he contributed to organizing several national and international conferences and academic events aimed at fostering holistic student development. He is currently pursuing his Ph.D. in Commerce at CHRIST (Deemed to be University), Bengaluru, and holds an M.Phil. and M.Com. from the same institution. Mr. Bitto Benny serves as a reviewer for Web of Science-indexed and other reputed international journals. His research has been published in Scopus-indexed journals, and he has presented papers at various national and international conferences and seminars. Additionally, he has participated in several workshops and training programs in academic research, enhancing his expertise in research methodologies, tools, and analytical techniques.

Anusha Bijoy is an Assistant Professor in the Department of Commerce at Christ College, Pune. She holds an M.Sc. in Chemistry from CHRIST (Deemed to be University) and a B.Sc. in Chemistry from Union Christian College, Aluva, and completed her B.Ed. from Bangalore University. Her academic interests include applied chemical sciences, green synthesis of nanoparticles, and conducting polymers for biomedical applications. She has completed internships at CHRIST University and B.S. Abdur Rahman Crescent Institute, Chennai, and has published research papers in the Scopus-indexed journals. She is skilled in analytical thinking, time management, and interpersonal communication, and is passionate about continuous learning and teaching.

Suhashini Chaurasia has over twenty-seven years of teaching experience in Computer Science and Information Technology. She is currently serving as Associate Professor and Head of the MCA Department and also acts as the Chief Coordinator for BBA and BCA programs at Tulsiramji Gaikwad-Patil College of Engineering and Technology, Nagpur. Her primary research interests include Artificial Intelligence (AI) and Machine Learning (ML), with a focus on interdisciplinary applications of intelligent systems. Dr. Chaurasia has more than 70 research publications to her credit, including papers in reputed Scopus-indexed, IEEE, and Springer journals and conferences. She has authored two academic books — Linux Operating System and Software Engineering — and contributed multiple book chapters in international edited volumes. She has seven Indian patents published and one granted utility patent for 20 years, along with four copyrights. Her Scopus record includes 18 indexed documents and 23 citations. She is also a Member of the Board of Studies at Rashtrasant Tukadoji Maharaj Nagpur University. In addition to her academic and research contributions, she has organized and participated in numerous Faculty Development Programs (FDPs), Orientation and Refresher courses, workshops, and symposia at both national and international levels.

Arun Antony Chully, CMI, is the Director and Principal of Christ College Pune, affiliated with Savitribai Phule Pune University. He holds a Ph.D. in Management and specializes in Human Resource Management, Organizational Behaviour, and Business Ethics. He has been associated with Christ University Bangalore and Christ University Lavasa Campus, contributing to teaching, academic administration, and student mentoring. His academic interests include values-based education, leadership development, and institutional effectiveness. Fr. Arun's work reflects a commitment to integrating academic excellence with ethical and holistic education in line with the CMI educational philosophy.

Sandeep Gupta received his B.Tech. degree in Electrical and Electronics Engineering from UPTU Lucknow in the year 2006. He has completed his Ph.D. from NIT Allahabad in the area of control and power systems with AI techniques. He is presently working as an Associate Professor at Graphic Era (Deemed to be University), Dehradun (India). He has a total of 15 years of experience. His areas of interest in research are the application of artificial intelligence to power system control design, FACTS devices, renewable energy, power electronics, and stability of power systems with machine learning. He is a member of numerous professional organizations, including IEEE, IE, IRED, IDES, IAENG, IAER, and the Society of Professional Engineers. He has been the author or co-author of 150 papers published in international journals and presented at different national and international conferences. He is currently guiding the research scholars under Machine Learning, Control & Power Systems, Wireless Technology, and Internet of Things.

Piali Haldar earned her MBA from the Institute of Rural Management Anand and completed her PhD at Birla Institute of Technology, Mesra. Her core areas of specialization include rural marketing, rural development, branding strategy, and consumer behaviour. With over 20 years of experience in academia and research, she has published extensively in renowned journals listed in ABDC and Scopus. She has authored one textbook on Marketing and edited three academic books. Dr. Haldar has presented her research at numerous national and international conferences and has contributed more than 50 papers to reputed journals, edited volumes, and conference proceedings.

Ambika Jaiswal is a revered personality dedicated to the noble cause of education. Her profound understanding and experience in the field of Computer Science bears testimony to her profound excellence. As an Assistant Professor, she has been imparting knowledge to post-graduate students for the past 16 years. An exemplary academician, Ms. Jaiswal's involvement in administrative, examination, co-curricular, extension and professional development related activities is remarkable. Her contribution towards extension and dissemination activities and various curricular & co-curricular activities is substantial. She has served on numerous pivotal committees at the Sant Gadge Baba Amravati University, including Examination, Student Development, Perspective Planning, SEC Committee, Student Progression, Software Development Activities, Startups, IIL, Avishkar, NSD, and others, making invaluable contributions. Contribution to corporate life through committees and duties assigned by the authority is delegated by her. Her involvement in institutional governance is also evident through being a member on various committees. Ms. Jaiswal's research, publications, and academic contributions are remarkable. She is doctorate in the field of AI, ML, Mobile Cloud Computing, where her extensive research work has resulted in a multitude of publications in prestigious journals and conferences, significantly advancing the frontiers of knowledge. Her development efforts have also yielded innovative solutions that have garnered widespread recognition within the academic fraternity. Her dedication towards teaching, learning and evaluation related activities is excellent. She has guided numerous projects, dissertations, and seminars, nurturing the academic pursuits of her students with unwavering commitment. Ms. Jaiswal is also affiliated with various esteemed academic bodies, such as IEEE, IETE, and CSI. An exceptionally diligent, dedicated, and committed educator, her prime objective has always been to contribute towards the growth and upliftment of students. With her unwavering passion for academia, a deep-rooted commitment to imparting quality education, a zeal for cutting-edge research, Ms. Jaiswal continues to inspire generations of learners, shaping their minds and guiding them towards a bright future. Her field of research are AI, ML, Cloud computing, MCC, DL.

Dev Mandal currently serves as an Assistant Professor in the Department of Management at Brainware University, Kolkata. Before this, he worked at ICRA Analytics Ltd and Shriram Finance Ltd. He holds an MBA in Finance and a Bachelor of Commerce degree from Vidyasagar University. Additionally, he has successfully cleared the UGC NET and WB SET examinations in Management.

Lovia Pebri Melati is a practitioner and researcher in the field of information technology at Esa Unggul University, Jakarta, Indonesia. Her interests include information systems, digital transformation, data management, and applied computing. She has been actively involved in academic and practical projects related to system development, technology implementation, and digital innovation to support organizational efficiency and problem-solving. Her work reflects strong analytical thinking, adaptability, and a commitment to continuous learning in emerging technologies. Lovia is dedicated to contributing to the advancement of information technology through research, collaboration, and the development of innovative and user-oriented digital solutions in academic and professional environments.

Raghu N has Ten years of experience in Academic and Research. He received the Ph.D. (2020) in Electronics Engineering from Jain University, and B.E. in Electronics and Telecommunications Engineering from VTU University, Karnataka. His research interests were in RF Communication and Image Processing. He has published his research findings in various Scopus indexed Journals and International conferences. He is a member of various professional bodies.

Ravikumar R. N. is currently a Postdoctoral researcher at Universiti Malaysia Perlis, Malaysia. Also, working as an Associate Professor in the Department of Computer Engineering at Marwadi University, Rajkot, Gujarat. He has 14+ years of national and international teaching experience. He completed his PhD at Amity University, Rajasthan, M.E at VMRF Deemed University, B.E at Anna University, Chennai. He is the co-founder of the Research Activities Club at Marwadi University and trains students on research activities, which leads to the various publications. He has published numerous research articles in Scopus, SCI journals, Book chapters, and Conference papers. Also, he holds several patents and authored books. His specialization is ML, DL, Federated Learning, Recommendation Systems, and Optimization Techniques.

Jyoti Rana is a distinguished academician and researcher with a strong background in marketing and commerce. She holds a Ph.D. in AI applied in customer journey studies and has authored over 20 research publications in Scopus and ABDC indexed journals. Dr. Rana has participated in and presented papers at many national and international conferences. Her keen research areas are marketing, retail, artificial intelligence and customer journey.

Shashi Rani is a mathematics educator and academic with a strong commitment to student achievement and innovative teaching. She holds a Bachelor of Arts, a Bachelor of Education in Mathematics, and a Master of Science in Mathematics, has qualified UGC-NET, and is currently pursuing a PhD in Mathematics. She also has professional experience as an Assistant Professor of Mathematics at DAV PG College, Karnal. Known for her hardworking nature, punctuality, honesty, and positive approach toward students, she aims to contribute meaningfully to education and inspire the next generation through mathematics.

Shivansu Sachan s currently pursuing a Ph.D. in Management. He holds a Master's degree from Integral University, Lucknow, and a Bachelor's degree from IHM, Lucknow. He has six years of academic and professional experience with reputed organizations and institutions. He has consistently enhanced his skills and knowledge through various courses, training programs, seminars, and conferences, and has also delivered several lectures in the hospitality sector. He is presently working as an Assistant Professor at Chhatrapati Shahu Ji Maharaj University, Kanpur.

Neeraj Saxena is a Professor at MIT Art, Design and Technology University at Pune and has a total relevant work experience of 29 years, out of which 26 years have been in academia and three years in the industry. He has a PhD in Finance and MBA in Finance. He is a distinguished Academician and a passionate researcher who has made a significant contribution to finance education and research. He combines the rigor of academic theory with the insights gained by operating in the industry, giving him the ability to leverage his expertise and deliver value as a mentor, teacher, and thought leader in the field of finance and management education.

Shruti Saxena is a member of the faculty at Pune Institute of Business Management, Pune, India. She has over 22 years of total experience, including 14 years in academia and eight years in the industry. She has a PhD in Finance and MBA in Finance. As a dedicated academician and a successful researcher; she incorporates a rich mix of theory and industry expertise in her teaching. She has experience and perspective, which assists her in guiding students and contributing significantly to the areas of finance through research, teaching, and educational research-based industry knowledge.

Binastya Anggara Sekti has been a lecturer at the Faculty of Computer Science, Esa Unggul University, Jakarta, since 2016. He is actively involved in the Artificial Intelligence and Information Security Study Group. He holds a Bachelor's degree in Informatics Engineering from the Bandung Institute of Technology and a Master's degree in Information Systems Management from Trisakti University, Jakarta. Prior to entering academia, he accumulated over 25 years of professional experience as an IT practitioner in various companies across Jakarta. His work focused on developing data centers for internet service providers and delivering IT solutions for the manufacturing and oil & gas sectors. His research interests include artificial intelligence, cybersecurity, and the development of IT infrastructure.

Anand Shukla completed his Ph.D. in mathematics with AI techniques from NIT Allahabad. He has 13 years of experience and is currently working at JSPM University, Pune, Maharashtra. His areas of interest in research are the application of artificial intelligence with machine learning. He is a member of numerous professional organizations. He has been the author or co-author of 40 papers published in international journals and presented at different national and international conferences.

Vibhuti Tyagi is Professor and Head of the Management Department at the Raj Kumar Goel Institute of Technology, Ghaziabad. She has done her graduation from Kumaun University & her Doctorate in the area of Business Administration from Dr B R Ambedkar University,Agra.She has done Executive Program in HR Analytics(EPHRA) from IIM Lucknow. She is a supervisor to many Ph.D. scholars in the area of Human Resource and has 24 years of academic and administrative experience. Her area of expertise is Human resource and Organisation behaviour. She is an Accredited management teacher(Human Resource) and has held many administrative positions at the institute as well as at the University level. She is a member of many professional bodies such as AIMA, GMA, TERA, AIMS etc. She has authored 3 books one on Professional Communication and Organisation Behaviour and others in the area of Human Resource Management (Which is available on online portals) . She is a Chief Editor of the Journal SAARANSH, an International RKG Journal and is a member of the Editorial Board of many journals of national and international fame. To her credit she has more that 20 papers in Scopus, Sci, ABDC INDEX and Peer reviewed journals.

Amit Verma is an Assistant Professor in the department of Commerce, Kalicharan PG College Lucknow, Uttar Pradesh, India. He had done LLB, MBA,

Ph.D. in Commerce & qualified UGC NET Two Times. He was also awarded with Honorary Ph.D. in Management. Recently, he worked as ICSSR Project Director for Short-term Empirical Research Project (Collaborative) entitled- Digital Transformation of Health Services- A Comparative Study of Bhopal and Lucknow. He was also invited as Resource Person and Keynote Speaker in various National Seminars sponsored by ICSSR. He has been nominated as Academic Member of Communication Institute of Greece, Athens, Greece. He was also invited by the Saint Augustine University of Tanzania (SAUT) in Mwanza, Tanzania, East Africa as a Chief speaker in Media Management Seminar. He served in various capacities in different reputed Colleges and a Private University of Delhi NCR, Uttar Pradesh & Uttarakhand and provided in-depth academic knowledge in various subjects. He has extensive hands-on experience in conceptualizing strategies, building and knitting confidence level, measuring and evaluating efficiency of performance of young learners. He participated in various development programs, workshops, conferences, seminars and FDP'S. His strong point does not stop at creating an interest for the concept and communicating the required knowledge, counselling (personal & professional), planning a specific career, shifting attitude towards solving problems, nurturing basic values which added worth to the workplace. He has strong belief in self-motivation, an urge for excellence and the feeling of independence which helped in ensuring updated knowledge and a structured reorientation of the subject matter. He is very much inspired by Swami Vivekananda and his philosophy and he willingly follows the Swami Vivekananda philosophy of life. He is Secretary of Commerce and Management Association, India. He is life member of Lucknow Management Association, Lucknow and President of Swatantrata Sangram Senani Shrikrishna Verma Charitable trust, Lucknow. He is also member of Editorial Board in different International and National Journals such as International Journal of Multi-disciplinary Research and Technology, KAVYA Publication, ACME, KVIM Journal of Management & many others. He is the author of Research Papers in peer-reviewed journals, including in ABDC, SSCI, and SCOPUS-indexed journals. He has also reviewed a large number of research papers. His publications encompass edited volumes that bridge the gap between academics and industry. He wrote Books on the subjects Essentials of Management, Organisational Behaviour and Research Methodology. He also edited books Entrepreneurship Amidst Pandemic COVID19, Emerging Business Practices and Trends during COVID-19, Innovative Business Practices in the Present Digital Era and Future of Marketing: Trends and Changes, The Vision of Viksit Bharat: Holistic Growth and Development of All Sectors, Catalysts of Change Interdisciplinary Research on India's Growth Story etc.

Index

A

B

C

D

E

F

G

H

I

L

M

P

R

S

T

W

www.ingramcontent.com/pod-product-compliance
Lightning Source LLC
LaVergne TN
LVHW060004031026
849161LV00025B/1365